Winter and Summer Dances, Fig. b (See Plate 39)

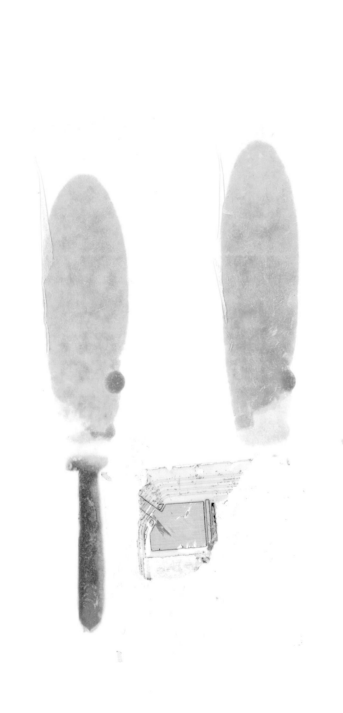

ZUÑI KATCINAS

PISCHEL YEARBOOKS
A DIVISION OF HERFF JONES
P.O. BOX 36, MARCELINE, MISSOURI   64658   816—376-3523

ZUÑI KATCINAS

AN ANALYTICAL STUDY
By RUTH L. BUNZEL

FORTY-SEVENTH
ANNUAL REPORT OF THE

BUREAU OF
AMERICAN ETHNOLOGY

TO THE SECRETARY OF THE
SMITHSONIAN INSTITUTION

1929-1930

With a new Publisher's Preface and with 36 full page full color plates, reproductions from the original art in the Smithsonian Archives published here in color for the first time.

Nationwide Exclusive Distributor
to the Book Trade and Museums
MacRae's Indian Book Distributors
Box 2632, Santa Rosa, CA 95405

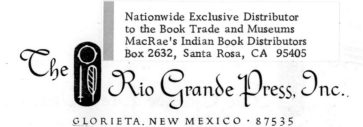

The Rio Grande Press, Inc.

GLORIETA, NEW MEXICO · 87535

The Rio Grande Press, Inc.,
Glorieta, N.M. 87535

Zuni Katcinas: An Analytical Study
by Ruth L. Bunzel
47th Annual Report of the Bureau of American Ethnology
Reprinted by permission of the
Smithsonian Institution
Washington, D.C.

First edition from which this edition was reproduced
was supplied by the
GALLUP PUBLIC LIBRARY
Octavia Fellin, Librarian
Gallup, N.M. 87301

Library of Congress Cataloging in Publication Data

Bunzel, Ruth Leah, 1898-
  Zuni katcinas.

  (A Rio Grande classic)
  First issued in 1932 as part of the 47th annual
report of the Bureau of American Ethnology.
    1. Zuñi Indians--Religion and mythology.
2. Katcinas. I. Title.
E99.Z9B86 1973   970.3   72-13917
ISBN 0-87380-099-0

A RIO GRANDE CLASSIC
First published in 1932

First printing 1973

The Rio Grande Press, Inc.
GLORIETA, NEW MEXICO · 87535

A Note on the Color Plates

Many of the art plates that were printed in the first edition in black and white are here reproduced for the first time in full color, but presented as individual color plates instead of several figures on each plate. The same figures also appear printed in black and white plates, exactly as they were printed in the first edition. Thus, there is a repetition of art that was unavoidable; it was required by our printing and production techniques. There was no economical way of substituting color plates for black and white plates, per se.

In the first edition, two plates only (46, opposite page 1064, and 50, opposite page 1074) were printed in color. Each of these figures are in this edition printed as full page full color plates, and their new positions are indicated in the *List of Color Plates*. In the same positions, the original plates (each with four figures) are printed in black and white this time, instead of in color. Here, again, an art repetition that seemed to us warranted and desirable.

The Smithsonian Institution found five original color sketches of katcinas that belong with this material, but for some reason were not included in the first edition either in color or black and white. We traveled to Zuñi Pueblo, obtained identification of these katcina figures, and we present them here as five different full page full color plates.

More details, and acknowledgements, are set forth in the Publisher's Preface following these words.

The Publishers

LIST OF COLOR PLATES

Publisher's Preface

Over the years since we founded The Rio Grande Press (in 1962), we have had many requests to reprint at least two of the papers from the 47th Annual Report (1929/1930) of the Bureau of American Ethnology of the Smithsonian Institution. One of these papers was *The Acoma Indians,* by Leslie A. White, and the other was this one-- *Zuñi Katcinas; An Analytical Study,* by Ruth L. Bunzel. The first edition of this penultimate volume of the old series is exceedingly rare and difficult to come by, seldom appearing on the out-of-print book market, and when it does, being priced at $75.00 to $100.00. Yet the papers in it, all dealing with New Mexico Indians, are much needed and used by modern researchers, students, scholars and those involved with the Indians themselves.

Miss Octavia Fellin is the friendly, gracious and knowledgeable librarian of the Gallup Public Library. Time and again through the years, she would urge these titles--at least--upon us. But, knowing the vital part that color, per se, plays in the Indian ethos and mystique, we were reluctant to undertake to reprint the books facsimile, i.e., without color.

In the first edition of the 47th Annual Report, for the years 1929/ 1930, but not published until 1932, the handsome color art collected by Leslie A. White, and the exquisite color sketches of the Zuñi Katcinas, were printed in black and white instead of full color. Since 1932 was the very height of The Great Depression, one must suppose that the cost of color printing was too much for the Bureau's budget, so that unsatisfactory (but acceptable) black and white publication was better than none at all. Hence the printing of color plates in black and white (except for two in *The Zuñi Katcinas*--see *A Note on the Color Plates* ahead of these pages) in both papers, and in fact, throughout the entire volume.

Late last summer, Miss Fellin again urged us to consider these two papers, so we did; to do so, she loaned us her library's nice first edition of the 47th Annual Report (for which we say, many thanks!). We reflected, as we weighed the pros and cons, that 1932 wasn't all that far away in time, so. . .we wrote to the Smithsonian, inquiring if it would be possible for them to locate the original color art, and if so, could we reprint the papers as separate books and this time publish the art in the full color it should have been printed in 40 years ago?

Dr. Clifford Evans, Chairman of the Smithsonian's Department of Anthropology, wrote to us on September 8, 1972, saying, among other things: ". . .your publications are known to us and it would be a contribution if you did publish this material in its original colors. . . the materials. . .(you request). . .are in the anthropological archives. . . we will do everything we can to assist you." Further correspondence passed between us, with Dr. Herman Viola assuming charge of the Smithsonian Anthropological Archives in the meantime. In due course , we received beautiful transparencies of the original art--most of the original color in The *Ácoma Indians* paper, but only a part of the *Zuñi Katcina* sketches. The rest were not in the archives.

Upon studying our graphic arts capacity and the material we thus had to work with, we came to the conclusion that it would not be technically or economically possible to substitute color plates in the exact position of the same plate printed in black and white. We had no choice, really, but to reprint the first edition papers facsimile, and then add the color sketches as (in effect) duplicate illustrations. In this way, neither the sequence of copy nor the pagination of the original layout would be disturbed, but the color plates would be there also. We might mention, in passing that we always try to retain the original folio pagination of papers we extract and publish as individual books from older anthology-type volumes. Throughout the literature and bibliography of the Southwest, countless citations to pages or illustrations would render our edition useless if we changed or altered the pagination, certainly of the text material.

When Drs. Evans and Viola sent us the handsome transparencies of the original color sketches, included were two (illustrating five separate katcina figures) that belonged with the paper but were not included either in color or black and white in the first edition; no one at the Smithsonian now knows why the art was left out in 1932. Nothing in the text indicates whether these illustrations were supposed or not supposed to be included. There was no identification on the original sketches, and accordingly, none was supplied by the Smithsonian.

Our only recourse was to travel to Zuñi, which we did. There, thanks to the good Father Niles Kraft, of the Zuñi Catholic Mission, we met Zuñi historian and artist Mr. Alex Seowtewa. Mr. Seowtewa was quite willing to identify the unidentified figures on the transparencies, which he did promptly and with the ease that indicates a perfect familiarity with the subject.

There's a very good reason he knows all about Zuñi katcinas, but we cannot reveal what it is. Mr. Seowtewa is involved in a painstaking, historic, artistic project of such awesome dimensions that we were completely wonderstruck in what he has done in the many years he has worked midway to completion. What he is doing is sacred to the people of Zuñi. Eventually, the project will be open to non-Indian visitors to Zuñi, but not now. We were ourselves stunned at what we were so graciously permitted to see; what we saw is a sheer artistic marvel. Artist Seowtewa is obviously working under the inspiration of a towering tradition that reaches back into time a thousand years or more; his amazing talent comes down to him naturally from ancestors of countless generations. We took a photograph of Mr. Seowtewa with one of his superb paintings, but unfortunately it was too late in the day and the pictures developed so poorly as to be of no use in this book.

So we present here a one-volume edition of *Zuñi Katcinas* with 36 new color plates; two of these are on the front endpaper, two on the back endpaper, and 32 printed back-to-back will be found every 16 pages throughout the text.

Our search for biographical data on author Ruth L. Bunzel took us from the *World Who's Who in Science* (1968 edition) to her directly; she is alive and well, still part of the great Columbia University anthropology faculty, but as of the winter of 1972, she is working with the art faculty at Bennington College, Bennington, Vermont. We talked with Dr. Bunzel at length; we invited her to send us a foreword or preface, which her busy schedule did not permit her to do much to our regret.

Dr. Bunzel was born in New York City (where she still maintains a permanent residence) on April 18, 1898, the daughter of Jonas and Hattie Bunzel. Her undergraduate work was done at Barnard College, with an A.B. in 1918. She took her Ph.D. at Columbia in 1929. She was a fellow of the Social Science Research Council and the Rockefeller Foundation. She has done professional research in her disciplines in New Mexico, Arizona, Guatemala, Mexico and the Chinese community in New York City. Her memberships in professional organizations and societies are too numerous to mention; she has been heaped with honors by her scientific colleagues around the world. She has written many articles and monographs; she was editor, with Dr. Margaret Mead, of the splendid book *Golden Age of Anthropology* (1960). We are pleased, indeed, to publish an early work of such a distinguished scientist.

We have also used the index from the first edition en toto, i.e., as it was in the first edition, without change. Hence, there is mingled among the entries, index entries for the other papers *(The Acoma Indians, Isleta, N.M., Introduction to Zuñi Ceremonialism, Zuni Origin Myths,* and *Zuñi Ritual Poetry)* in the 47th Annual Report. Here again, our thought was to maintain the pagination integrity of all of the papers (and the index as well) in that volume. We believe the inclusion of the total index will be helpful to users of either the first edition or our edition; we hope so, anyway.

Zuñi Katcinas; An Analytical Study, is the 94th book we have published and the 92nd beautiful Rio Grande Classic. We are pleased that we were able to rescue the beautiful color plates published here for the first time from the obscurity of archival files. We publish this book, and these beautiful color plates, with total respect for the Zuñi people, their traditions, their culture and their delightful way of life. Of all the pueblo Indians, the Zuñi are those that follow the old ways most closely. Perhaps our edition of this book will be of help, where the years have inadvertently brought forgetfulness in the traditional ceremonies.

Robert B. McCoy

La Casa Escuela
Glorieta, New Mexico 87535
February 1973

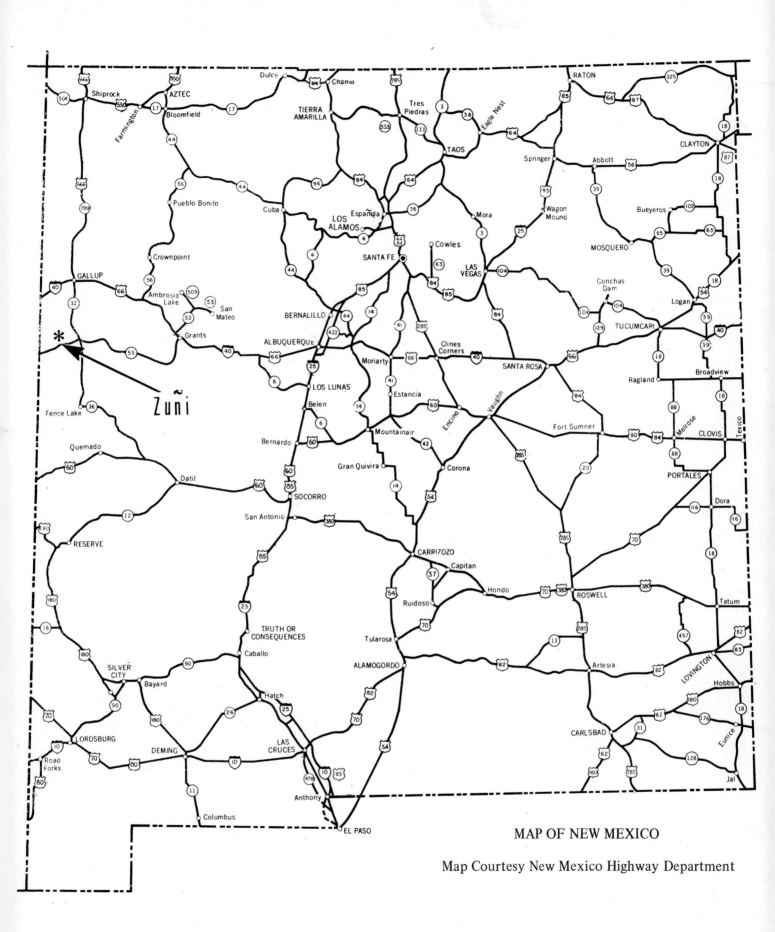

MAP OF NEW MEXICO

Map Courtesy New Mexico Highway Department

FORTY-SEVENTH
ANNUAL REPORT OF THE

BUREAU OF
AMERICAN ETHNOLOGY

TO THE SECRETARY OF THE
SMITHSONIAN INSTITUTION

1929-1930

UNITED STATES
GOVERNMENT PRINTING OFFICE
WASHINGTON : 1932

ZUÑI KATCINAS

AN ANALYTICAL STUDY
By RUTH L. BUNZEL

CONTENTS

ILLUSTRATIONS

PLATES

ZUÑI KATCINAS: AN ANALYTICAL STUDY

By Ruth L. Bunzel

PART I. AN ANALYSIS OF THE KATCINA CULT AT ZUÑI

INTRODUCTION

The Katcina cult is one of the six major cults of Zuñi, and might indeed be called the dominant Zuñi cult. It includes many of the most beautiful and spectacular ceremonies, and the ceremonies which attract the most popular attention. Furthermore, it is the one cult which personally reaches all people, since all males belong to it and are required to participate in its ceremonies. Moreover, at the present time it is an ascendant cult. At a time when the societies are declining in membership, and the priesthoods experience difficulties in filling their ranks, when ceremonies lapse because no one competent to perform them survives, the Katcina Society is extending its activities. More katcina dances are held each year than in Mrs. Stevenson's time, and the dances last longer. It is true that some of the older dances are no longer performed, but on the other hand for each dance that lapses two new ones are introduced. It is the most vital, the most spectacular, and the most pervasive of Zuñi cults; whatever foreign elements it may at one time or another have incorporated, its ideology and form are aboriginal and characteristic, and for the average Zuñi it is the focal point of religious, social, and æsthetic experience.[1]

THE NATURE OF KATCINAS

The Katcina cult is built upon the worship, principally through impersonation, of a group of supernaturals called in Zuñi terminology koko. The myth of their origin is given on page 604.[2] The koko live in a lake, Hatin k̨aiakwi (whispering spring), west of Zuñi, near St. Johns, Ariz. In the bottom of this lake they have a village (Kołuwalawa, katcina village) reached by ladders through the lake. Here they spend their time singing and dancing, and occasionally they come to Zuñi to dance for their "daylight" fathers. They live

---

[1] A brief discussion of the katcina cult and its position in Zuñi life is given on pp. 516 to 525.
[2] Compare the English version by Cushing (Outlines of Zuñi Creation Myths, p. 403 ff.) and Stevenson (Zuñi Indians, pp. 32-34).

on the spiritual essence of food sacrificed to them in the river, and clothe themselves with the feathers of prayer sticks. They turn into ducks when traveling back and forth to Zuñi.

The first katcinas were the children of humans lost through contact with contamination, unwilling sacrifices to atone for sin. By origin and later association they are identified with the dead. Mortals on death join the katcinas at katcina village and become like them.[3]

In addition to being identified with the dead the katcinas are also especially associated with clouds and rain. When they come to dance they come in rain. They are equivalent to the Shiwana of Keresan pueblos.[4]

In ancient times the katcina used to come to Zuñi to dance for their people in order that they might be gay. But always when they left someone "went with them," that is, died, and so they decided not to come any more. But they authorized masked dances and promised "to come and stand before them." [5] So now when a katcina dance is held the katcinas come merely as rain, and no one dies. So the institution of masked dancing, originated according to legend to assuage the loneliness of parents for their lost children, has become a rain-making ceremony.

The power of katcina ceremonies resides in the masks which, whether ancient tribal property or individually owned modern masks, are believed to contain divine substance, by means of which the

---

[3] Exceptions to this are noted.

[4] Cochiti:

"The kachina embody the spirits of the dead but are rarely thought of as special individuals. However, resemblances to recent dead have been pointed out at the time of a kachina dance, though this is so rare that any theory of ancestor worship has been discarded. The kachina of this village are also called shiwanna 'thunderclouds,' and so are closely linked with the rainmaking powers."—Goldfrank, 34.

"At Laguna kachina and thunderclouds are in different categories, nevertheless the former also help along the general welfare."—Goldfrank, 35, footnote.

"The shiwanna are gods who give rain, health, life; in short, everything that makes for the welfare of man. It is mostly in their visits to the pueblo that they bring these benefits."—Dumarest, 174.

"The sinless go at once (from Shipapu) to Wenima and become shiwanna." When Uritsete wants rain she sends prayer sticks to the shiwanna, who climb into a huge bowl filled with water. This rises into the sky and the shiwanna dip out water with their prayer sticks.—Page, 173.

The men all know that the shiwanna are men, since they have all danced in the kachina. But they think that in putting the sacred mask on their head they take on the holy personality. They think the spirits of the shiwanna are within these masks and that thus they visit the pueblos. If it happens to rain during a dance, the shiwanna sometimes gesture as if to say, "I am making the thunder, I am sending down the rain."—Page 175.

Acoma.

The katsina are exactly like the masked dancers in appearance. They used to come to the village and dance for the people and bring them gifts of food and other necessities. After the people began to grow their own food, the katcina came to dance when the fields were dry and thirsty.

After the great fight with the people the katcina refused to come to the village, but gave the people permission to copy their appearance in masks. (White.)

Among the Hopi they are cloud beings and local spirits inhabiting springs. We know almost nothing of the ideology of the katcina cult among the Tewa.

[5] See Komosona's talk, p. 604.

katcina whose representation is worn "makes himself into a person" (ho'i ya·ḳe'a). Masks are treated with the utmost reverence. The awe which Zuñis feel for all sacred and powerful objects is intensified in this case by the fact that masks are representations of the dead, and, indeed, the very substance of death. Therefore the use of masks is surrounded by special taboos. One must never try on a mask when not participating in a ceremony, else one will die. One must never use human hair or the hair of a live horse on a mask, else that person or horse will surely die. If one is incontinent during a katcina ceremony the mask will choke him or stick to his face during the dance.

The katcinas are very intimate and affectionate supernaturals. They like pretty clothes and feathers; they like to sing and dance, and to visit. Above all they like to come to Zuñi to dance.

The folk tales about individual katcinas in the following pages describe them at home in their kitchens, scrambling for their feathers at the solstices, quarreling amiably among themselves, meddling in one another's affairs. They have a village organization similar to that of Zuñi. Pautiwa is "the boss," as Zuñis say. His p̓ekwin, who delivers his messages, is Ḳäklo. His principal administrative duties seem to be to keep his people quiet long enough to give a courteous welcome to visitors, to receive messages from Zuñi, and to decide when to dance there and who shall go. Pautiwa "makes the New Year" at Zuñi. His representative brings in the Ca'lako crook and crooks for other special ceremonies such as the initiation and the dance of the Ḳana·kwe, thus determining the calendar of katcina ceremonies for the year. Whenever the people at Zuñi decide they want one of the regular katcina dances they send prayer sticks to katcina village (kiva chiefs plant prayer sticks four days before a dance) and P̓autiwa decides whom to send.

Hämoḳatsiḳ, the mother of the katcinas, looks after their clothing when they prepare for dances.

In addition to the official visits of the katcinas when invited with prayer sticks, they sometimes pay unexpected visits on missions of good will. They come to plant and harvest for deserted children, to affirm the supernatural power of the pious and despised. P̓autiwa visits in disguise poor and despised maidens, and leaves wealth and blessing behind him. Katcinas in disguise bring proud girls to their senses by the amiable disciplinary methods so characteristically Zuñian.

In reading these folk tales we can not but be struck by their resemblance in feeling tone to tales of medieval tales of saints and angels—such tales as that of the amiable angel who turned off the wine tap left open by the monk who was so pious that he didn't even stop to turn off the tap when summoned for prayer.[6] The particular situations in which katcinas prove helpful and their special techniques differ, of course, from those of saints and angels. Medieval saints do not ordinarily humble proud maids by contriving in spite of impossible tests to sleep with them and so instruct them in the delights of normal human association and the advantages of humility. But in spite of these differences the popular attitudes and feeling for the rôle of supernaturals in commonplace human affairs are curiously similar. Undoubtedly this modern folklore concerning katcinas has been strongly colored by Catholic influences.

But for all their generally amiable and benign character, there is a certain sinister undertone to all katcina ceremonies. It is said more often of the katcinas than of other supernaturals that they are "dangerous." The katcinas inflict the most direct and dramatic punishments for violation of their sanctity. If a priest fails in his duties, he does not get rain during his retreat, he may suffer from general bad luck, he may become sick and may even die if he does nothing to "save his life." But the katcina impersonator who fails in his trust may be choked to death by his mask during the ceremony. There is always a certain feeling of danger in wearing a mask. In putting on a mask the wearer always addresses it in prayer: "Do not cause me any serious trouble." A man wearing a mask or, in katcina dances without mask, one wearing katcina body paint, is untouchable. He is dangerous to others until his paint has been washed off. Zuñis watching katcinas dance shrink from them as they pass through narrow passages, in order not to touch their bodies.

The first katcinas were children sacrificed to the water to atone for sin; afterwards when they came to dance, bringing their blessing of rain and fertility, "they took some one with them"; that is, they exacted a human life from the village.[7] It was only when masks were substituted for the actual presence of the katcinas that this heavy toll was lightened.

There are hints in ritual that ideas of human sacrifice may lie but a little way beneath the surface in the concept of masked impersonation. The great ceremony of the Ca'lako opens with the appointment of a group of impersonators of the gods. For a year they are set apart. They do no work of their own. In the case of the Saiyataca party they even assume the names of the gods whom they are to impersonate. At the end of their term of office they have elaborate ceremonies in which they appear in mask; that is, in the regalia of death. After all-night ceremonies they depart for the home of the dead. "Everyone cries when they go," as a Zuñi informant says. "It is very sad to see them go, because we always think that we shall

---

[6] Saints also are the blessed dead.

[7] Cf. this with the myth of the origin of death, where a child is sacrificed to the first sorcerer in return for the gift of seeds.

never see them again." The final ceremony of the departure of the Ca'lako is especially suggestive of this interpretation. When out of sight of the village the Ca'lako are pursued by young men. When caught they are thrown down and killed, and the mask is treated like the body of a fallen deer—"for good luck in hunting."[8] On returning the impersonators are met outside the village by their aunts and taken at once to their houses to be bathed before they are safe for human contact.

Identification with the god, and the killing of the god, for fecundity, as found in ancient Mexico, seem to be ideas in keeping with Zuñi concepts. But Zuñi temperament would repudiate the bloody sacrifice. It may well be that the particular technique of impersonation, with its atmosphere of the sinister and dangerous, is the symbolic representation of the extirpated fact. Tales of the former existence of human sacrifice in the pueblos continually crop up.

Frazer, quoting Bourke, gives an account of the sacrifice of a youth at the fire festival (tribal initiation) of the Hopi.[9] Mrs. Stevenson refers to the report of human sacrifice at Zia. There are cases of human sacrifices for fertility among the Pawnee and the Sioux. The prevalence of all forms of human sacrifice among the Aztecs is too well known to require comment. Among the Aztecs, however, are found two striking features: The dancing of priests in the flayed skin of the sacrificial victim, and the identification of the sacrificial victim with the god, as, for example, in the sacrifice of Tezcatlipoca. In the battle with the katcinas at Acoma the katcinas are ritualistically slain so that their blood may fertilize the earth. In the prayers of the scalp dance there are frequent allusions to blood as a fertilizing medium, so possibly the whole complex of human sacrifice is not so remote historically or conceptually as might at first appear.

The persistent rumors of an early prevalence of human sacrifice in the pueblos may be without foundation, but the reworking of a cult that once included human sacrifice is quite in accord with pueblo tendency to absorb ritual from all sides and mitigate all its more violent features.

THE POWER AND USE OF MASKS

The Katcina cult at Zuñi revolves about the fetishistic power imputed to the mask. The myth of the origin of masks is to be found on page 604. The word koko is used alike of the being impersonated and the mask wherein resides the power of transformation. The mask is the corporeal substance of the katcina, and in wearing it a man assumes the personality of the god whose representation he bears. The Zuñi expression for this process of transformation is

[8] This is the one part of the Ca'lako ceremony that I was not permitted to see.
[9] Golden Bough, 4: 215.

"to make him (the god) into a living person" (ho'i ya·ḳänakä).[10]
The mask, therefore, is an object whose sacredness is equaled only by
that of the rain-making bundles of the priests.   The mask partakes
of the attributes of the god.   It "makes the house valuable" and pro-
tects its occupants from misfortune.   And it insures to its owner
powerful supernatural connections which will determine his status
after death.

There are two types of masks.   One type is ancient and permanent.
These masks are regarded as the actual masks given by the supernaturals when the institution of masked dancing was organized.
These masks are held as tribal property and are handed down through
the generations.   Each one represents a named and individualized
god, one of the priestly rulers of the village of the katcinas.   Each
mask is held in trust by a self-perpetuating group, which may also be
the trustee of its complex esoteric ritual.   The masks are kept in
sealed jars in houses from which they are never taken except for their
public ceremonies, and the guardianship of the mask descends through
the maternal lineage that occupies the house in which it is kept.
These masks are taken out only with great ceremony by persons
specially authorized to handle them.   They are regarded as very
"dangerous."   Before wearing such a mask a man must sacrifice food
in the river to his ancestors and to his predecessor in office.   After
wearing he must plant prayer sticks (sometimes the planting of
prayer sticks is part of the public ceremony) and observe continence
for four days.   These permanent masks are never made over into the
likenesses of other katcinas.   Under exceptional circumstances they
may be renewed, but the old mask is not destroyed.   This type of
mask is found among the Hopi (in addition to personal masks) and,
so far as I have been able to learn, is the only type found in the
Keresan villages.   Here the guardianship of these masks is intrusted
to a single individual (the katcina chief), who keeps them "in his own
secret place," outside the village.

There exist in Zuñi, in addition to these ancient and permanent
masks, others which are individual property, which a man has made
to serve as his personal fetish so long as he lives, and as his guarantee
of status after death.   These are the masks that are used in group
dances, and which I have therefore designated as the masks of dancing
katcinas, to distinguish them from the priest katcinas.   Every man
of any standing in Zuñi possesses one or more such masks.   A man
will have a mask made as soon as he is able to afford the expense
involved.   Later he will have another of different form made, so that
whatever dance his kiva may present he may always dance in his own
mask.   When he dies the masks are dismantled and buried for his
use at katcina village.   Then whenever dances are held at Zuñi he

---

[10] See prayer of Pautiwa, p. 699.

may return in spirit to visit his people, wearing the mask which he wore in life. If he has no mask he can not be sure of returning, unless he has been intimately connected with some cult group. Priests possess et·o·we, members of the higher orders of medicine societies possess miwe, bow priests possess lacowan łan·a and other regalia. All of these things give protection and security, and are bonds with powerful supernatural forces. A man who possesses none of these and has no ceremonial affiliations outside of the katcina society will be especially eager to possess a mask "to save his life" and "to make him valuable."

The following is a native account of the manufacture and care of masks.

"When a man wants to have a mask made they will make it for him in the winter. If a man is poor he can not have a mask. Everyone would like to have a mask of his own and if a man is poor he will sell his beads to buy sheep for the feast. Long ago when the people had deer meat the men who were good hunters had their masks. A man will not say, 'I want my mask made,' for that is dangerous.[11] So if a man wants to have a mask made he will work very hard in the spring. He will plant a great deal and he will work very hard all summer so as to have good crops. Then after the crops are gathered in he will say to his wife, 'Now I want my mask made.' He will say this to his wife and his people. 'That is why I have worked so hard.' No one will say to him, 'Do not do it; we are poor people and can not afford it.' No one will tell him that. They will all be glad because they want something valuable in the house to pray for.

"When the turn of his kiva comes in the winter dance series he will practice with them. Then while they are practicing he will go to the kiva chief and say to him, 'You will let me know, my father, four days before we are going to dance. I want my father to be made into a person.' Then all the people of his kiva will be very glad. They always want more masks in their kiva. Then the kiva chief will say to him, 'I am very glad. I will let you know. Now you will see if you have all the materials.'

"Then the man gets the materials. Long ago the old masks were made of buckskin, but now they are made of tanned leather. They can get good leather in the store, so they get it there. But before they had stores the people used buffalo hide or buckskin. When my father was a boy they used rawhide with the hair removed and pounded with stones and greased to make it soft. The young man prepares the hide and takes it to the director of the kiva. Then he gets deer sinew to sew it with.

"If a man wants a helmet mask he will ask for it when they are dancing Hilili or something in which they use that kind of mask.

---

[11] Because the katcinas are the jealous dead and must always be treated circumspectly.

If he wants a face mask he will ask when they are going to dance Koḵokci. Now, if he wants a helmet mask the headmen of the kiva will take coarse white sand and spread it on the floor and wet it, and bury the cowhide in it to make it soft. They will leave it there for several hours. Then they will call in the man who wants the mask and they will measure his head. They measure around the top of his head and from the top of his forehead to the tip of his chin. Then they measure the leather. For the distance around they measure with the thumb and middle finger, and for the height of the face they measure fingerwidths. Then the kiva chief measures and cuts the leather. He cuts a rectangular piece to go around the head and a circular piece for the top of the head. Then he holds the pieces of leather against the man's head to see if they are right. Then the leather is put back in the wet sand. While the leather is in the sand he rolls the deer sinew for sewing. He takes long strips of sinew and rolls them against his thigh to make them strong. He rolls enough sinew so as not to have to make more while he is sewing. He leaves the leather in the sand for about an hour and a half. Then he takes out the strip for the face and sews the two ends together down the back. The sewing must be done very tightly and with very fine stitches so that it will not rip later. Then he sews on the top very tight. The top is still just a flat piece of leather. The two head men of the kiva (otaḵämosi and wo'le) take turns in sewing on the mask, for it is hard work. It takes about two days to sew the mask. This is all done at the house of the kiva chief (otaḵämosi) where the men come to practice their songs. While they are making the mask they tell the kiva people not to come in the daytime to work on their own masks, but they continue to come at night to practice.

"When they have finished the sewing they call in the man for whom the mask is being made and they try it on him. They ask him if it hurts him in any place and if it is too long they trim it off around the bottom. The man keeps it on for a little while and it takes the shape of his head because the leather is still soft. After it is perfectly comfortable they take it off and say, 'Now we shall make its shape right.' Then the man goes out. Then they sprinkle water on the sand to make it wet, and put the sand into the mask. They pack it down very hard. Then they rest. They set the mask down on the floor and cover it so that no one will see it and they go out.

"The mask is made during teckwi, between the time when the kiva heads plant prayer sticks for the dance and the day when the dance is to be given. In the kivas where they have only two days teckwi before a dance they start to sew on the mask before they plant their feathers, but it is always finished during teckwi. During this time the man's people are all busy preparing food for the members of the kiva. His wife and his sisters and all his female relatives grind for him.   He brings in much wheat and corn and he kills 8 or 10 sheep for the feast.

"After the mask has been standing for two or three hours the kiva heads go back and empty out the sand.   They take a round stick and work around the inside to give it a good shape.   When they are finished they set it to dry in the sun under the hatchway.   As soon as it is dry they call the man in again.   This is the same day.   They try the mask on him, and now it fits perfectly.   While he has it on they feel his face through the mask and mark the places for the eyes and mouth.   Then they take it off and the man goes out.   Then they take a needle and prick holes where the marks are.   They used to use needles of deer bone, but now they use any kind.   They take a sharp knife and cut little square holes for the mouth and eyes.   Then they call the man again.   He must go out while they cut the eyes, but they tell him to come back soon.   When he comes in they try the mask on him and tell him to look out.   He looks all around and says, 'Now it is right.' While he has it on they mark on the sides the places for the chin straps.   Then he takes it off and goes out.   After he has gone they sew on two straps of buckskin to tie under the chin.   They sew about four sets of shorter strips to the base of the mask to fasten on the collar of spruce or feathers or fur, and little strips on the top and back for the other feathers.

"After they have finished the kiva chief goes to his corn room.   He gets all kinds of seeds, one grain of each kind, six kinds of corn and six kinds of beans and watermelons and squash and pumpkins and piñon and all kinds of wild seeds (ḳäwawole).   He takes them out with him and when they have finished the mask he removes the shells from the corn and the beans and the piñon and the watermelon seeds and takes them into his mouth and chews them.   Then he sits down facing the east holding the mask and says:

Si	ḳesi	tom	ho'	ho''i	ya·ḳäpa.	Hom	t̓o'	tatciliḳän·a.
Now		you	I	a live person	completed.	Me		you father will have

T̓om	ho'	t̓oconanaḳa	ho''i	yaḳäpa	t̓o' yam
	you	I	seeds with	a live person	completed.	You your

tse'makwin	t̓sume	ho'na	yani·ktciana.	Hoło	awan	t̓ewan
spirit	strong	to us	will grant	Whenever	their	day

yo'apa	t̓o'	ḳäcima	ceman	teḳäna.	Si	lenakya
is made	you	rains	calling	shall live.	Now	this much with

t̓om	ho'	ho''i	yaḳäḳä.
you	I	a live person	completed.

"'Now I have given you life.   We shall have one another as father. I have made you with seeds and given you life.   Bless us with your strong spirit, and whenever our day may come call the rains for us as long as you live.   Now it is finished.   I have made you into a person.'

"While he is saying this he spits out the seeds and rubs them with his hands all over the mask, inside and outside. Then he takes the mask and presents it to the six directions, north, west, south, east, up, and down, saying:

Temła	tekwi	u'lohna'ilapona	ton	lukia	yatena	tsume.
Different	directions	who look after the world	you	this	hold	strong.

"After he has done this he takes white clay (hekohakwa) and rubs it all over the mask to make it smooth, and sets the mask in the sun under the hatchway. When it is dry he takes his stone dish with the blue gum paint (hecamu'le) and holding it in his hand says:

Si	hom	helin	tehya	tom	cinanaka	ho'	yam	tca'le	yakäpa.
Now	I	paint	valuable	your	flesh with	I	my	child	complete.

"Then he takes the paint and paints over the mask, using a little piece of rabbit skin as a brush. This paint is very valuable and after the mask is painted with this it is valuable.[12] Now it is finished; it is a person.

"On the day before the dance, when the men are getting ready, the man's female relatives all come to his house to bake and cook all kinds of food. In the morning the assistant director of the kiva (wo'le) goes out to get long sheaves of yucca. In the afternoon about four or five o'clock all the men who are going to dance go to the house of the kiva chief. When they are all in he asks, 'Is everyone here?' Then they say, 'Yes, we are all here.' Then the kiva chief goes to the house of the man for whom the mask has been made and says, 'We are waiting for you. Are you ready?' The man says, 'Yes, I am ready,' and the kiva chief takes him to the house where the mask is. When he comes in the director says, 'Now, my child, take off your clothing and be strong. Be brave.' Then the man takes off all his clothes except the breechcloth. Then they take him into the middle room and the four head men of the kiva (two otakämosi and two wowe) whip him. The kiva chief whips him first. He takes a bunch of long yucca in his hand and says, 'Now, my child, I shall whip you. You have wanted this and you will be strong.' Then he strikes him four times on each arm, four times on the back and four times on each leg. Then the other three men do the same. They whip him very hard. He is naked all over and often he bleeds from the strokes of the yucca and the tears come to his eyes. When he goes out he can hardly walk.

"As soon as they are finished he dresses and puts on his blanket. Then he goes to tell his people to bring food for the people of his kiva. He looks very badly when he comes in, as though he had been badly hurt. Then his wife and his sisters and all his relatives go with food to the house of the kiva chief. They take about eight big bowls of

---

[12] Sacred.

meat and two big tubs of white bread and two baskets of paper bread and baskets of dried peaches or anything else that they have. Then the man who has made the mask takes a roll of paper bread and a little of every kind of food for the people at the Sacred Lake. Then they all eat and the kiva chief takes the food he has saved and goes out to Wide River [13] and feeds it to the people of the sacred lake, telling them that they are sending to them a new person and asking that they always remember him, that is, always send him to dance at Zuñi.

"Next day when they dance the man will wear the new mask. Before putting on the mask he will say:

Si	hom	t̂o'	ta'tcili	tek̄än·a.	Eł	hom	t̂o'
Now	me	you	father having	shall live.	Not	me	you

kwahoła̧k̄ä	at̂sumana	teamek̄äna.	Tenimacte	hoł	hom	pena'kowa
because of something	punishing	do (not) be.	Be sure	wherever	my	word according to

homan	t̂o'	elakwi	homan	t̂o'	t̂ek̄ohanan	cemana	tek̄än·a.
to me	you	stand before	for me	you	life	asking	shall live.

" 'Now we shall live together, having one another as father. Do not be vindictive against me in your life. Be sure to do as I have said. Now you stand before me. Ask for long life for me.'

"Then he puts on the mask. When the dance is over he brings it home. He has the buckskin covers ready, or if he has no buckskin he uses anything to keep the dirt out. Then he just puts it away. That is all.

"When a mask is put away it is wrapped in buckskin or in cloths to keep out the dirt and is hung from the roof or placed in a jar. The dangerous ones are all kept in jars and all the old masks are kept in jars like ettowe. The mask is never placed on the floor.

"The mask is fed at every meal. Someone will go into the mask room with some food and feed it to the mask. She will take off her shoes before going into the room. Generally one of the older women in the household goes in because she will say the best prayer. She sets down her food and says:

Hom	a·tatcu	t̂on	tinan	ła̧k̄iye.	Itona·we'.	Hon	a·wona·ya·tu.
My	fathers	you	sit	firm.	Eat.		Our end reach.

Yam	tatc an	oneał	tacanakwin	hon a·wona·ya·tu.
Your	father	make the road	long	our end reach.

" 'My fathers, you sit here still. Eat. Let us reach the end of our road. Our father, make the road long and let us go on to the end.'

---

[13] West of the village. The usual place for offerings of food for the katcinas. The food is thrown into the river and is thought to be carried by the river to the Sacred Lake.

"Sometimes for good luck they will send in the youngest child in the house and tell her to go in and feed the grandfathers. Then she will take the food and go in and say:

Nanakwe	isa	itona·we'.	Ho'	e''lyotu.	Ta	hom	käwu
Grandfathers	here	eat.	I	young woman become.	And	my	older sister

hom	papa	atsawak	yotu	ta	e''le	yotu.
my	older brother	young men	let become	and	young women	let become

" 'Grandfathers, here, eat. May I become a woman, and may my older brothers and older sisters reach young manhood and young womanhood.'

"If the mask is not properly fed, he will send mice into the corn room to eat all the corn. Sometimes if he is not fed he will eat himself around the edges so that everyone will know that he has been neglected."

At the end of the Ca'lako festival is a ceremony called Ko'a·ne at which all masks are honored. A native account of this ceremony follows.

"On the day before Ko'a·ne[14] every man who has a mask works on feathers for his mask and also for the Koyemci, and he has them all ready for the morning. That day one man from each clan takes the feathers to the Koyemci. If it is a poor clan only one man will go, but as many as wish may go, and each one will bring a gift for the Koyemci with the feathers.

"On the morning of Ko'ane a set of dancers from each kiva dances in all the houses where they have held Ca'lako and when they have finished dancing in the houses they go to the plaza and dance four times in the plaza. The fourth time they come out they have with them rolls of paper bread which has been sent to them by the women of the Ca'lako houses. Then when they have finished dancing they go out to the east with their rolls of paper bread and they carry with them the feathers which they have gotten in the Ca'lako houses. Hemwcikwe and Tcakwena and Wotemła are dancing, but there are others like Ko'kokci who are not dancing.

"After the dancers have finished dancing in the houses and have gone to the plaza every man who has a mask in his house takes his mask and the prayer sticks that he made the day before and wraps them in his blanket. If a man has more than one mask he takes all of them and a prayer stick for each mask. Then each man goes to the house where his kiva has had Ca'lako to get food for his masks. Before they come in the women of the Ca'lako houses set out two bowls of water and two ears of corn. When they have all come in the head of the house calls the men to come and have water sprinkled

---

[14] "The katcinas go away." The concluding ceremony of the Ca'lako festival. See p. 702.

Masks Appearing at Winter Solstice, Fig. b (See Plate 21)

Masks Appearing at Winter Solstice, Fig. a (See Plate 21)

on their heads. The kiva chief comes first. He steps out and puts his mask on the top of his head. He does not pull it down over his face because that would be dangerous, for he is not going to dance. Then one of the older women of the house takes up an ear of corn and all the other women dip water from the bowls with their fingers and sprinkle the head of the man.

"The older people pray and everyone in the house sprinkles both the man and the mask with water. Then they call another man and do the same thing, and after all the men have been sprinkled each man takes paper bread and corn meal for his mask.

"Then they all go out to the east to Where-the-pumpkin-stands. There Pautiwa is sitting down facing the east. The man who keeps the mask has taken it out there. Then those who have been dancing come there from the plaza. Each has his roll of paper bread and corn meal. They come and stand in line a little distance behind Pautiwa. Then the men who have been dancing come running toward the east, sprinkling corn meal before them. When they come to where Pautiwa is standing they take off their masks and set them down. Then the other men who have brought their masks out set them down and make the road for them going toward the east. Then they all plant their prayer sticks. After a little while the men take up their masks and come home. They leave the paper bread out there, buried in the ground. Then the dancers undress there and come home. The Koyemci are still in the plaza, and Pautiwa sits out there in the east waiting for the corn maids.

"They do this every year. Then for four days after Ko'ane there are no dances, for the katcinas have all gone to the east to visit their people there. After the fourth day anyone who has had Ca'lako house may ask to have any dance repeated. Sometimes they keep on dancing this way for a week or ten days. They can keep it up until the pekwin starts to plant for the winter solstice. Then all dancing must stop while they have it'sumawe." [15]

Ko'ane

(Another version)

"Each year after Ca'lako everyone takes his mask out to Red Earth. Each man takes his own mask, and if a man has more than one he takes them all. The old masks are not taken out at this time. Each man carries his masks wrapped in blankets, and he carries prayer sticks. When he gets out to Red Earth there are six big round holes, about 3 feet deep. There is one hole for each kiva. Then each man goes to the hole of his own kiva and puts his mask down facing the east. There may be a thousand masks there, or several thousand,

---

[15] The rites of fertility magic performed during the winter solstice ceremonies.

perhaps. Then he puts down his bundle of prayer sticks and a roll of paper bread. Then the men who have been dancing in the plaza come there quickly and each takes off his mask and holds it in his hand while he prays. Then they deposit prayer sticks and paper bread in the holes. The men who have been dancing come last and the others all wait until they come. Then after they have all prayed each man takes his own mask out and wraps it in his blanket and comes home. Everyone comes home but the wowe, who stay behind and fill up the holes.[16] Then they come home, too, and only Pautiwa and Bitsitsi are left there.''

When a man dies, for four days someone in his family will work on feathers for his mask. He will make four prayer sticks, one blue one for the sun, two black ones for the dead, and one black one with the turn-around feather for the koko. Then on the fourth day after the man has died his son or some man in his family will work on his mask. He will remove all the feathers and scrape off all the paint. Then he will take the mask and the four prayer sticks and bury them at Wide River.

PARAPHERNALIA

The most conspicuous and characteristic objects used in katcina ceremonies are, of course, the masks. These are made of leather, formerly of elkskin or buffalo hide, now of commercial dressed leather, painted with characteristic designs, and fancifully adorned with feathers, hair, fur, yarn, ribbons, and spruce boughs. The mask, in addition to being a sacred object, is a work of art, and like any other work of art conforms to certain rules of style. New katcinas may be invented from time to time and there is nothing in the nature of katcinas that would necessarily limit the new impersonation to traditional forms. There is, in fact, a very noticeable tendency for the newer masks to be both more varied and realistic than the more ancient impersonations. However, once a katcina has been admitted to the roster, he is given a name and, rarely, a personality, and all details of his mask and costume and behavior become definitive. Everything is considered characteristic, the form and decoration of the mask, the kind and arrangement of feathers and other ornaments on the mask, body paint, all details of costume, including even the arrangement of the bead necklaces, the objects he carries in his hands, posture, gait, behavior, and his call. When any of these features is varied beyond very narrow limits we have a new katcina. This does not mean, of course, that changes do not occur in the get-up of any katcina, especially in the katcinas recently introduced. In general variability increases in inverse ratio to the antiquity and sanctity

---

[16] In 1927 and 1928 the writer visited this place the day after the ceremony, and, although the ground was covered with snow, she could find no trace of the six holes, so carefully had they been concealed. Yet she saw all the men of the village go out with their masks and prayer sticks and paper bread.

of the impersonation. The mask is the most stable and the most
sacred part of the equipment. Costume in the case of the older
katcinas, such as Koᵏokci, is also fixed.[17] But in the newer dances,
such as Wilatsukwe and Kumance, the costume is extremely variegated. Doctor Kroeber secured in 1915 a number of drawings of
Zuñi katcinas. When these were shown to different informants 10
years later they were able to identify correctly all but two of the
drawings. Not all of them were important or popular impersonations.

The masks in spite of their variability in details all exhibit a
remarkable uniformity in artistic style. The most notable feature
of the Zuñi, indeed, of all Pueblo and Navaho masks, is the complete
lack of any attempt at realism. The masks are not anthropomorphic,
with a few exceptions, nor are they representations of animals or
even of mythical monsters. The bear katcina (pl. 41, *a*) is a striking
example of the lack of representative intent even in animal impersonations.[18] The mask which inspires the greatest terror is that of
Hainawi (pl. 32, *b*), which is anything but terrible in aspect. Yet my
informant said that as a child she was afraid to look on Hainawi.
He is terrifying because everyone is familiar with his myth. The
designs painted on masks are those used also on ceremonial pottery,
altar boards, sand paintings, etc. They have no specific association
with individual katcinas or with katcinas as a whole. This excessive
formality of expression is a reflection of a very characteristic trait of
Zuñi behavior. It is found in their secular art, their music, prayers,
tales, and in their conversation and the abstract and impersonal
character of their religious beliefs.

The most notable exception to the highly conventional character
of masks is the set of masks of the Koyemci which are characterized
both by realism and individuality. But the Koyemci are exceptional
in many respects.

Most of the masks are of the helmet type (ulin·e, from ule, within
a deep receptacle), approximating in shape an inverted bucket.
These cover the whole head, resting on the shoulders, and the lower
edge is finished with a collar of feathers, fur, cloth, or spruce branches.
All the permanent masks, with the exception of Tcakwena okä and
Hainawi, are of this type. Other masks may be of the type that
covers only the face (coyan·e, face). These are secured by strings
passing over and around the head, under the hair. Some of these are

---

[17] Substitutions have occurred, cotton shirts for buckskin in the case of Saiyataca and other impersonations; the cotton underdress has recently been added to the costume of female katcinas. Cula·witsi, who
used to come naked, now wears a small breechcloth. This innovation was at the request of the boy who
took the part in 1923. It is a case of the exception proving the rule.

[18] Note in contrast, however, Plate 44, *c*, also bear katcina, and Plate 49, *b*, cow katcina: Plate 50, *b*,
buffalo. These are all comparatively recent innovations. They come only in the winter dances, where
greater liberties are taken with traditional patterns of costume and dancing. They would not be included
in the summer dances, which are more conventional and more sacred.

shaped to fit over the chin (Tcakwena okä), others cover only the upper part of the face, the lower part of the face being concealed by the "beard," a fringe of horsehair attached to the lower edge of the mask.

These shapes are the only part of the mask that is permanent. All else is removed, even in the case of ancient masks. The mask is made up anew each time it is worn. The old paint is scraped off and it is freshly painted. The feathers which were removed at the last wearing are renovated and put back or replaced by new feathers. With the exception of the permanent masks, the mask may be made, by the use of suitable paint and feathers, to represent any katcina wearing that particular form of mask. The Tcakwena masks, however, are not changed, possibly because of the difficulty of obliterating the shiny black paint. There may, however, be other reasons. Among the Hopi these are permanent fetishistic masks belonging to a cult group.

The wearer of the mask looks out through two small openings. The eye openings are ordinarily emphasized by painting of some kind. (See, however, Cu'la·witsi and Yamuhakto, pl. 25.) Long narrow triangles, rectangles, or concentric circles are used. Instead of painted eyes, protruding eyes may be placed above the eye openings. These are made of round pieces of buckskin painted and stuffed with cotton or seeds, and fastened with thongs to the mask. They are used by most of the scare katcinas. The Koyemci have raised rings around the eye openings.

The mouth treatment is more varied. On all face masks the mouth is represented by the lower border, which is somehow emphasized, and from which hangs a fringe of horsehair called the beard. On some of the scare katcinas the mouth is painted with zigzag lines to represent the teeth (Tcakwena, pl. 38), with realistic red tongues hanging from them, in some it is surrounded by rings of braided corn husks (Saiyali'a).

On helmet masks the mouth is sometimes just a small round opening. It may be painted with concentric circles like the eyes or with other designs. But more often a protruding snout of some kind is attached by thongs to the mask. It may be straight or curved, carved of wood (Sälimop'iya) or out of the neck of a gourd (Muluk-takä). It may be a hollow tube through which the breath comes whistling (Ḳäna·kwe), or it may be carved in two parts to simulate the jaws of an animal, and operated by strings held by the wearer (Ca'lako).

The nose is sometimes indicated by a vertical painted line.

Ears are generally indicated by projecting pieces of wood or by flexible twigs covered by cloth or hide (Pautiwa, pl. 21). Or they may be made in the form of squash blossoms, carved of wood or made of slender wooden spokes twined with yarn. Frequently only one ear is indicated, or the two ears may be of different forms. Horns of painted wood are common.

The top of the mask is sometimes covered with a fringe of hair or a sheepskin dyed to simulate hair.

All exposed surfaces of the mask are painted with various pigments, all of native manufacture. The following are the most important:

The whole mask is first covered with a coat of white paint. The pigment is kaolin (hek'ohakwa, white clay), soaked in water. It is used also for slipping pottery. It is obtained by trade from Acoma. However, ordinary whitewash is sometimes used.[19] Everyone has white paint. There are no ceremonies connected with its manufacture.

There are three black pigments: hakwin·e, mitcapiwe, and hekwitola. The first of these is a mineral, the other two vegetable products. Hak'win·e is the common black paint, used in the manufacture of prayer sticks. It is only occasionally used on masks. Since prayer stick making is associated chiefly with medicine societies the manufacture and distribution of this pigment belongs to the societies. A sample of the pigment has been identified by Mr. Paul F. Kerr, of the Department of Mineralogy of Columbia University, as pyrolurite, a hydrated oxide of manganese. The ore is mined on the east side of Corn Mountain and brought in in large chunks. Two or four members of a society will go for the black rock in winter, during the solstice ceremonies. Then the chief of the society will invite girls to come in to grind while the men sing for them. When they finish in the evening the society chief gives each man a corn husk full of the pigment, and to the girls also.

Mitcapi·we (burnt corn) is made from carbonized corncobs which are found in ruins of ancient villages. This pigment also is manufactured by medicine societies. "They look for corn in the back rooms of ruins and bring it in big chunks to the society house. There it is ground ceremonially by the society people. They will ask pretty girls to grind for them, about four girls from the society, if there are that many, and four or six girls from outside. The girls wear embroidered white blankets and white moccasins and many strings of shell and turquoise beads and many bracelets. The head man of the society sits in front of them. Two other men of the society break up the corn into smaller pieces and the head man puts in beads of shell and turquoise and coral and abalone shell and mixes it all together and gives it to the girls to grind. It is hard work. Sometimes it takes two days and sometimes three to grind enough. When they are finished grinding the girls dance in the society house. Then the

---

[19] The specimen which I brought was not in a state that could be identified. According to Mr. Kerr, a portion of decomposed rock, noncalcareous and also not phosphate bearing.

head man gives each member a handful of paint. He gives some to each of the girls, too. Then the women members of the society bring in food and they all sit down and eat. After that they go home. This paint is used for painting masks, and sometimes the priests use it on prayer sticks."

Hekwitola is a fungus found in corn. It is sometimes eaten, especially during the solstice when meat and grease are forbidden. When the corn is husked in the fall, if hekwitola is found in any of the ears it is carefully preserved in corn husks. It is mixed with water for painting the body, or mixed with yucca sirup it makes a shiny black pigment which is used for painting masks. The Tcakwena masks are painted with this. Anyone may prepare this paint.

The yellow pigment, hełupstikwa, has been identified as "limonite, a hydrated oxide of iron, sometimes called yellow ochre. This is mixed with carbonate of lime calcite." The preparation is described as follows: "The yellow clay is found at the Sacred Lake, where the pink clay (see below) is found. The wo'le brings it back with him when he returns from the quadrennial pilgrimage. When he is ready to use it he grinds it up. He grinds it himself and prays as he does it. Then he mixes the ground stone with the dried petals of yellow flowers and Paiyatamu medicine which he gets from the society people. The Paiyatamu medicine is made in the winter during the society meetings. The buttercups and other bright flowers are gathered and dried during the summer. Then in the winter the society people invite pretty girls to come and grind. They grind up the flowers with abalone shells. The wo·we have to get this medicine from the society people. It is never made in summer unless they run out of it and need it in a hurry. Then the society people in the kiva that needs it will make it. The medicine is called Paiyatamu an utea owe, Paiyatamu's flower meal. This paint is used for painting the body and masks, and also for prayer sticks. The yellow stone belongs to the head men of the Katcina society. If the society people need yellow paint for their prayer sticks they have to get the stone from the kiva chiefs. They grind it in their society rooms the same as they do the black paint. They get girls to come in and grind for them, and they mix the yellow stone with the petals of yellow flowers." The pulverized pigment is mixed with water.

A yellow pigment is also made from corn pollen, mixed with the boiled juice of yucca. This gives a glossy paint. It is used for painting the designs on the Tcakwena masks.

There are two pink stains for the body. Of these the most important is called katcina's clay (kok'w a·wan heḵätca),[20] identified by Mr. Kerr as kaolinite or a similar hydrated silicate of alumina. "This belongs to the kiva chiefs and wo·we who collect it on their quadrennial pilgrimage to the Sacred Lake. The clay is found on the shores

---

[20] The usual word for pink.

of the lake. It is brought to the village in large chunks. The wo·we store it in their houses and take it to the kiva when needed. When a man uses it he moistens it with his tongue, calling on the rains, and rubs it over his body. This paint is very sacred. It is used by the Koyemci to color their masks, and on the body, and by Koḳokci. Tomtsinapa and Saiyaḻi'a and Hatacuku and Nawico use it also. Hilili and dancers like that would never use the pink clay."

Another pink body stain, which is used by the dancers who do not use the katcina's clay, is made by boiling wheat with small sunflowers.

The red pigment, ahoko, is hematite, the common oxide of iron, mixed with clay. "The stone for the red paint is mined four miles southwest of the village. It is brought in in large blankets and kept that way until needed. It is not ground. When they want to use it they rub it on a flat stone with water until the water becomes red. If they want a light red they mix it with pink clay. They chew up the clay and spit it out into the red liquid until it is the right shade. Ahoko is used on masks. When they use it on the body they mix it with pink clay."

For painting prayer sticks, dyeing moccasins, belts, etc., they use akwaḻi (blue stone[21]), an oxidized ore of copper containing azurite and malachite in a calcite matrix. It is secured by trade from the eastern pueblos, where it abounds. This is ground up with water. For painting masks a prepared pigment of akwaḻi in piñon gum is used. This is obtained from Santo Domingo in exchange for feathers. It used to be made at Zuñi from akwaḻi and piñon gum, but the Santo Domingo paint is considered better. It is used only for masks. It is "very valuable."

A purplish body stain (ḳeḵwin·e) is obtained from the stalks and husks of black corn. The stalks are chewed and the mixture spread over the body. This is used by Muluktaḳä, Hemucikwe, and the blue Sälimop̅iya.

For painting the face under the mask, and for painting the face on other occasions, an iridescent black paint is used. This has been identified by Mr. Kerr as "fine grains of quartz sphalerite and galena, a ground concentrate of zinc ore. The dark brown sphalerite is responsible for the color of the mixture."

The use of native paints and dyes is giving way to commercial dyes and pigments, especially in staining the body and wearing apparel. Masks, so far as I could learn, are always painted with native paints (they are always decorated by the wo·we). However, some of the bright reds and pinks and blues on masks such as Wilatsukwe look like commercial colors.

---

[21] The correct translation is turquoise. The Zuñi classify blues and greens differently from us. They distinguish loḵäna, pale blue and gray; ḻi'ana, turquoise and light green; acena, bright green; and also a dark blue. The classification of turquiose as a primary color may be due to the use of copper ores as pigments.

The designs, for the most part, are very simple. The mask may be all one color or the face may be a different color from the rest and set off from it by a narrow band. The band around the face is either checked or striped of many colors and symbolizes the Milky Way and the rainbow, respectively. A simple ornament, a circle, a triangle, or zigzag lines, or the familiar cloud symbol is sometimes painted on each cheek. When the back of the mask is exposed it is frequently painted with butterflies, dragon flies, frogs, flowers, or corn. The formal character of these decorations has already been pointed out.

The following comments show the type of symbolic associations with mask designs.

"Sometimes the painting on the mask means something; sometimes not.

"The words of the songs always refer to the rain and the clouds and all the beautiful things that grow on the earth, and the painting on the mask means the same as the song. They paint something on the mask to please the earth and something to please the sky, and so on. The painting on Łelacoktipona's face does not look like the Milky Way, but they call it that anyway to please the Milky Way.

"The red paint on the body is for the red-breasted birds and the yellow paint for the yellow-breasted birds and for the flowers and butterflies and all the beautiful things in the world. The white paint is for the sun.

"The spots of paint of different colors on Homatci and Temtemci are rain drops falling down on the earth. The green is for the green grass."

Considerable ingenuity is displayed in the handling of the difficult lower edge. The simplest arrangement is a piece of cloth. The Koyemci wear a ragged piece of native black cloth, which adds considerably to the crudeness and ludicrousness of their aspect. On other masks an embroidered kilt is neatly folded to conceal the wearer's neck and shoulders (Komokätsik, pl. 35, c). Skins of animals may be similarly used, especially those of fox, coyote, rabbit, and mountain lion (Saiyaⱡi'a, pl. 21, b). A padded collar of cloth stuffed with cotton and painted to match the mask is sometimes used (Saiyataca, pl. 25). But by far the most beautiful masks are those finished with great ruffs of glossy feathers or sweet-smelling spruce. The feathers may be the stiff shining feathers of the raven (Sälimop'iya) or the soft feathers of the turkey (Natcimomo, pl. 55, a). But loveliest of all are the ruffs of freshly picked spruce branches. Spruce is the plant most intimately associated with the katcinas. It symbolizes all the green growing things with which the rain clothes the earth. The beauty of the fresh green wreaths is often enhanced by tipping the ends of the twigs with flakes of snowy popcorn.

On a few masks (Hemuci·kwe, pl. 46, a) towering headdresses resembling those of the tablita dances of the eastern Pueblos are worn.

These are made of light frames of wood covered with cloth, or of thin slabs of wood, with terraced edges painted on both sides with clouds, rainbows, and similar cosmic symbols.

Hair is frequently attached to masks, sometimes to simulate human hair (Ca'lako, pl. 27; Saiyali'a, pl. 21, b; Komokätsik, pl. 35, c). Sometimes it is merely an ornamental fringe to frame the face. In such cases it may be dyed bright red (Kwamu·we, copied from the Navaho).

Animal horns are sometimes worn in animal impersonations (Cow Katcina, pl. 49, b; Deer Katcina, pl. 43, a), or the skin of an animal (Bear Katcina, pl. 44, c). The top of the mask is sometimes covered with hair (Bear Katcina, pl. 41, a), sheepskin dyed black, or flowers (Bee Katcina, pl. 43, b).

"They used to use human hair on masks, e. g., Ca'lako mask. But they found that the people whose hair they had cut off would die four days after they had done it, so they do not do it any more. Now they use horsehair. They never cut the hair of a live horse to use it on a mask because the horse might die like a real person. So they only cut the hair off dead horses.

"Sometimes some of the katcinas wear branches of peach trees in their heads, and if any of the fruit drops off the people pick it up and take it home and put it in their storerooms for good luck."

Feathers are the katcinas' most conspicuous ornaments. They are attached in great bunches to the crown of the mask at the back, thrust into the ears or suspended from them. They are bound together to form great ruffs around the neck. As a rule the importance of a katcina can be judged by the variety and quantity of his feathers. A katcina without feathers is an anomaly, and it is always thought necessary to explain why certain katcinas wear no feathers. (See p. 1048.) All use the downy feather from the breast of the eagle. This is preeminently the feather of the katcinas, the breath of the rain. Even those katcinas who wear no other feathers have downy feathers in their ears.[22] Eagle tail feathers, feathers from the breast and tail of the turkey, owl feathers, and the breast feathers of the yellow macaw are all worn by many different katcinas. "They wear macaw feathers because the macaw lives in the south and they want the macaw to bring the rains of the south. They always like to feel the south wind because the south wind brings rain." Other feathers are worn as insignia of rank or position, or refer to some episode in the myth of the katcina. The downy feather dyed red is the badge of society membership, the wing feather of the bluejay is the feather

---

[22] In prayer stick lore the downy feather has very special symbolism. It is the "pekwin's feather" (see p. 660). It is used in all offerings to the sun and moon, and after these offerings the supplicant must abstain from animal food. It is also used by the priests during their retreats when they want immediate rain, and then, also, after offering the prayer sticks, the supplicants must abstain from animal food. A downy feather is tied to the hair of novices and until it is removed on the fourth day they must eat no animal food. The soft feather from the breast or back of the turkey, and the duck feather (turn-around feather) are the distinguishing feathers in prayer sticks for the katcinas.

of the priests. The feather from the shoulder of the eagle belongs to the hunters' society; the red hawk feather to Ciwana·kwe; wing feathers of the eagle, combined with downy feathers and duck feathers, and fastened to small reeds form the "great feather" (lacowan łan·a), the badge of a bow priest, is worn by all warrior impersonations.[23] The way it is worn is prognostic. If the tips of the feathers point backward the katcina comes peaceably, but if the tips point forward his intentions are hostile, for this is the way warriors wear the feather on the warpath.

The following myth is told to account for the feathers of katcinas.

Why the Katcinas Wear Eagle Feathers

Long ago a boy was set up on a cliff by the witches. He was starving to death. For four days he had nothing to eat.

This boy had a friend, a witch boy, who asked him what he knew. He said, "I do not know anything." So then the witch boy said, "I shall rub you all over with a black ant and then nothing can harm you." He did that and then he took a hoop and jumped through it and turned into a chipmunk. He told the boy to do the same and said it was easy and that he could turn himself back into a person whenever he wanted to. So the boy did it. Then they went up a mountain to hunt. The witch boy went ahead and told him to wait for him while he went to look for birds' nests. Then he turned himself back into a person and gave the hoop to the other boy and told him to turn himself back into a person too. Then he turned himself back into a person and the witch boy said, "Now do you want me to teach you how to do it yourself, the way my mother taught me?" The boy said, "No, I am afraid." Then the witch boy went away and told him to wait for him. Then he went away and left him there and the poor boy waited for four days. He had nothing to eat and he cried a great deal. This was at the place Hakwininakwe, where they get black paint for prayer sticks.

The eagle lived a little ways to the nortn and while he was in his nest he thought he heard something crying a little way to the south. Next morning he went out to hunt. About noon he remembered he had heard something crying in the night and he said, "Oh dear, I wanted to go and see who was there to the south. I heard something crying just like a human person. I wonder who it is, because no one ever comes up here." Then the eagle went to the south and flew around four times and finally he saw the boy sitting in the crack in the rocks, fast asleep. The eagle came down and sat down beside him. He was sitting there in his feathers, waiting. He thought the boy would never wake up. Then he took off his feather dress and he

---

[23] The lacowan łana of the bow priests is made in the Ant Society house with special prayers. (Cf. also Hopi hurrunkwa.) "The war chiefs do not have mi·we, but they have the great feather and it is just as sacred."

turned into a human person. He went over to the boy and woke him up. He touched him over the heart and he woke up. "My child, whoever you are, wake up. I am here. You were left alone and I have come." Then the little boy woke up. But he was so miserable that he just opened his eyes a little and shut them again. Then the eagle said, "Please, little boy, wake up. I shall carry you on my back and take you to my home." The little boy opened his eyes when he heard that the man would carry him home. Then the little boy said, "Yes, please. I am hungry and thirsty and I am not strong enough to go home alone. Please take me." Then the eagle took him and tried to make him stand up but he was so weak he fell right down. Then he said, "Now you try to open your eyes and I shall carry you on my back. You hold on to me and I shall take you down." So the eagle left the little boy and went off a little way and put on his feather dress. Then he came back to the little boy and the little boy just grabbed him by the neck. "Now shut your eyes and we shall go down to your home."

The people were living at Ḳäkima, and the boy had been left a little to the east. Then he took him down. It was in the afternoon, when the sun turns over. His people had been looking for him for four days. He was the son of the katcina chief. The eagle knew it. The people had been looking all over for the little boy and his parents cried all the time. They could not find the boy. Just then the people were coming home from looking for the boy. It was the last time they were going to look for him. Just as they were coming home the eagle brought him down to the spring called Sumḵaia to give him a drink. Then he set him down and said, "Now open your eyes." The little boy dropped down, for his heart was weak. They sat down beside the spring and the eagle said, "Now drink. Then you will feel better and you will walk home. Your home is right there, just a little way off." The eagle said, "Please hurry. Some-one may come and find me here. I am afraid someone will come and find out that I brought you down." Then the little boy drank, and while he was drinking the eagle plucked out six of his tail feathers, and he took downy feathers from under his wings and from his shoulders he took the "spoon feathers" (lacoḵone). Then he pulled up some grass that was growing by the spring and tied it around the feathers. Then he said, "Now you have had a drink and now walk home and take these along to your father. Your parents know that you went with that little boy to look for birds' nests. So take these feathers back to your father and he will think what use he can make of them." So the boy said, "All right." Then the eagle said again, "Take these in to your father. Do not tell him that I gave them to you, but tell him that I brought you down. Your father will know what to do with the feathers. You are going now, and I am going home." Then he started and the little boy went home, walking weakly as if he would fall down at each step.

The women were coming to get water at Kyakima spring, and they saw the little boy coming along. They knew that the little boy was lost and when they saw him coming they knew that it was the little boy that everyone had been looking for.

As they came close one of the women set down her jar and ran up to the boy. "Oh, my son, we know that you have been lost. The people have been looking for you and now you have come back. Where have you been?" He said, "Up in the mountains. I am just coming home." Then she said, "What have you there?" and the little boy said, "I have only feathers. Don't touch my feathers!" The woman kept saying, "I would like to feel them." The boy did not want her to touch his feathers, but she did, and then right away she turned into an owl. Then the boy said, "I told you not to touch them. My feathers are wise.[24] I told you not to touch them. Now I shall give you a home where you will live. You will go to the north of this mountain and you will have a spring there." Then she went there and so right below the eagle place is owl spring where the woman was turned into an owl because she touched the eagle feathers.

Then the boy said, "Now if anyone else meets me I will not let them touch my feathers." So he went home. He was very weak, but he walked home. Everyone saw him coming with his feathers sticking out. Then the people said, "There is the little boy who was lost. There he is coming. He looks weak. I wonder where he has been all this time." He could hardly climb up the ladder, he was so weak. So some of the people went in and told his father and mother, and they did not believe it was their boy, he looked so badly. Then they came out and saw the little boy struggling to climb the ladder. Then his father went down and brought him in on his back, and the little boy was holding on to his feathers. When he came in he said, "Mother, put down a basket." She brought a basket and the boy laid his feathers in it. Then he said, "Father, I brought you these feathers. Eagle brought me down. He found me and brought me down and left me at the spring and I walked home. These are eagle feathers." The father took the feathers and breathed in from them and said, "Father of eagles, give me long life and your strong heart. You travel so far and fly so high that your breath is clear and strong. Make my heart clean like yours. I breathe from your feathers, so make me strong like you."[25] Then he thanked the eagle because he had brought the boy back. Then right away he knew what to do with the feathers. He said, "Our fathers, the

---

[24] Have supernatural power.

[25] Because "The eagle flies high where the air is clean. He never goes where there is dirt and sickness and so we always pray to him for good health."

katcinas, will wear these feathers because the eagle is strong and wise and kind. He travels far in all directions and so he will surely bring us the rains. The eagle feathers must always come first."

That is why the katcinas always wear eagle feathers, because the eagle found the little boy and brought him down and sent his feathers with him.

When a mask of the helmet type is worn, the hair, provided it is long, is plaited in two plaits which are wound around the neck under the mask. With face masks which leave the head exposed long hair is required, and if the wearer has cut his hair, as have most of the younger men, he supplements his shorn or scanty locks with a wig or a switch of horsehair, so cleverly arranged as to be almost impossible to detect. The short-haired or Laguna Tcakwena wears a piece of goatskin to which eagle down is stuck, covering the top and back of the head. Usually the hair is left hanging free, ornamented with feathers according to the ceremonial affiliation of the beings impersonated. Rain dancers wear a bunch of macaw and downy eagle feathers on the crown and downy feathers attached to a weighted string hanging down the back. Some warrior impersonations (Hainawi, pl. 32, b; Tcakwena, pls. 38, 39, 40) wear eagle down stuck to the hair with yucca sirup. The red feather that is the badge of society membership may be tied to the forelock (Tcałaci, pl. 48, c) or to a fillet of yucca encircling the head (Towa Tcakwena, pl. 38).

Female impersonations have their hair dressed in either of two fashions. Maidens have their hair bound over square pieces of wood and fastened with yarn. (Kokwe'le, pl. 35, b.) This is said to be the ancient headdress of Zuñi maidens, and is not unlike the whorled headdress still worn by Hopi maidens. Other female impersonations have the hair done up behind in the fashion at present affected by Zuñi women. (Hemok̠ätsik[1], pl. 28, b.) Some few females who wear helmet masks have the hair arranged in two plaits over the ears, the usual headdress of Hopi married women. (Komokätsik, pl. 35, c. Compare Hopi Kutcamana, Fewkes, pl. XLIV.) In one case (Koła·hmana) half of the hair is loosely tied with yarn, the other half is wound over a curved stick. The Zuñis can not explain this peculiar headdress. The curved stick is such a one as Hopi girls use in dressing their hair, and the Hopi, who have the same impersonation under a different name (Tcakwaina Mana), tell the tale that a raiding party arrived in the village while the girl was having her hair dressed. She seized her brother's weapons and went out to fight the enemy, rushing out with her hair half done. The Zuñi impersonation is also an Amazon, though unconnected with the tcakwena set.

Other headdresses are worn by the men, the usual man's headdress (Tcałaci), the special headdress of the Ne'we·kwe (Nepaiyatamu), the buckskin cap of the bow priests (O'wiwi).

When no mask is worn, the hair is dressed precisely as if the mask were to be worn and a fillet of yucca is bound about the brows.

Face and body paint.—The face is always painted before putting on a mask. Usually two lines are drawn across the face with iridescent black paint (tsuhapa) or red paint (ahoko), or the chin and cheeks are marked with smudges of red or black paint.

"When the real katcinas came to dance they did not wear masks, but they always painted their faces this way. Then they stopped coming because whenever they came some one at Itiwana used to die. They told the people to dress the way they did and they told them to make masks so that the young ones would not know them. That is why they always paint their faces under the masks. And they paint their faces so that if they take off their masks during their rest the young ones who are around will know that they are really katcinas."

The whole body is painted, even when full costume is worn. It is doubtful, however, if this is still strictly adhered to. The unexposed portions of the body are painted white, with a thin solution of kaolin, the exposed portions with paints of different colors. The composition and preparation of these pigments are described in another place (p. 859).

If the upper part of the body is nude it is painted red, pink, black, more rarely yellow, purple, white, or varicolored. The shoulders, forearms, and legs are frequently yellow, and double lines of yellow dots run from the waist to the shoulders and down the arms, both front and back. These tend to make the body appear more slender. They symbolize raindrops or rainbows. The loins are always painted white, regardless of whether kilt or breechcloth is worn.[26] This is "for the sun." One informant offered the explanation that the white paint was used to protect the light-colored clothing. When full costume is worn the whole body is said to be painted white. With long-sleeved garments the hands are painted white. The knees are frequently painted red, sometimes spotted with yellow, "for speed." Runners in stick races always have their knees painted red.

Next to the mask, the face and body paint is the most sacred part of a dancer's regalia. No one must touch a man while he has on his body paint. After he has finished dancing, or if he wishes to stay in his own house between the days of the dance, his body must be bathed ceremonially by his wife or his mother before he can go to his wife. Impersonators of all important katcina priests must have their heads and bodies bathed by the women of their father's clans in the house of

---

[26] Except Cu'la·witsi, whose whole body is painted black with spots of red, yellow, blue, and white. The body paint of Cu'la·witsi is especially sacred. Cu'la·witsi's body is painted by five men of the clan of his ceremonial father. The father picks them out, one for each color. He goes to five men of his clan and says, "I have chosen you to look after the black paint," and they will say, "Yes; I shall do it." Cu'la·witsi is very dangerous. If anyone who does not believe in the katcinas tries to paint Cu'la·witsi the paint will not stay on.

their aunts (father's sisters) before going home to their own houses. One of his father's blood sisters meets him as he comes out of the kiva or in the road as he comes from the shrine at which he has undressed and takes him to her house, where as many women as possible of his clan are waiting for him. The man sits on a low stool facing the east, while his father's sister, or the female head of his father's ancestral household, mixes suds of yucca. Then she prays and sprinkles water on his head. The other women also dip up water. Then the father's sister washes the hair thoroughly. After this, if the impersonation was a minor one, the hands are washed, but in the case of all the Ca'lako participants the whole body is bathed. Then the man is given food and returns to his home.[27]

When no mask is worn, the same magical power that resides in the mask is imputed to the body paint. And conversely, if the body is not painted, particular care is taken in the manner of putting on the mask. Before putting it on, he holds it in his hand for a moment and prays: "I am a poor person, and I am putting on this valuable mask. You will be my father, and I shall be your father. Give me good luck in everything."[28]

Costume.—With the exception of Cu'la'witsi, who is impersonated by a small boy, all katcinas wear some covering, and in recent years even Cu'la'witsi has worn a small breechcloth. Most of the "little dancers" wear only a breechcloth. This usually is a piece of dark blue native cloth (Hehe'a, pl. 54, *a*), but embroidered sashes may be worn in this manner (Grease Boy, pl. 44, *b*) or a strip of commercial cotton cloth with colored embroidery or appliqué at the ends (Sälimop'iya, pls. 30, 31).

The characteristic garment of the katcinas is a hand woven and embroidered white cotton kilt. These are woven by the Hopi of hand-spun white cotton. One man at Zuñi weaves kilts and sashes. Sometimes cement sacks, stretched and pounded to simulate the loose weave of the native garment, are substituted. These kilts are embroidered with black yarn along the lower edge and in color at both ends. They may be further ornamented by a broad blue painted or appliqué band. The kilt is fastened on the right side. A breechcloth of commercial cotton is always worn under the kilt.[29]

---

[27] In cases of doubtful paternity, which are fairly frequent at Zuñi, two clans will claim the man as their "child" and he will go both places to be bathed. An adopted child, or a child of a widowed or divorced woman who has remarried, will go first to the house of his "own" (blood) father and then to the ancestral house of his adopted father. But in an unfortunate case of disputed paternity the two clans had quarreled over the possession of the child on the occasion of his society initiation, and when he danced in the Muaiye neither set of aunts came for him. So he had to wait in the kiva until someone took word to his mother. Then his mother's husband's sister came for him. Meanwhile the other women repented and both sent for him. So he had his head washed three times.

[28] So reports my informant. I never happened to see anyone putting on a mask, but I have seen them unmask most unceremoniously. But the mask is never laid down casually. Unless a special place has been prepared to receive it, it is hung on the wall.

[29] Except by the Koyemci. They wear no breechcloth under their black kilts. During their play the kilt may be removed.

With the kilt is worn some kind of belt or sash, usually a narrow red and green woman's belt and a broad sash, either the broad woven sash with embroidered ends or a Hopi wedding belt, a broad braided belt, with long tasseled fringes. All of these articles are made by the Hopi. The Navaho and the Zuñi also make women's belts.

A large white buckskin is worn instead of the woven kilt by katcinas associated with war or hunting. With these any kind of belt may be worn, often an ordinary silver belt.

The upper part of the body is generally left nude and painted, but shirts are worn by some katcinas. These are usually white. Now they are made of cotton, but in ancient times they were of buckskin.

Many of the more important of the katcina priests wear the embroidered white blanket (miha). This is a Hopi wedding blanket, embroidered with cloud, flower, and butterfly designs in red, orange, green, and black. It is woven by the Hopi and is the most valuable Pueblo textile product. A miha in good condition is valued at $75. Saiyataca (pl. 25) and P̓autiwa (pl. 21) show two ways of wearing the miha.

The usual footgear is a high moccasin of soft buckskin, painted blue, with turnback cuffs of red and yellow. With these moccasins are worn heel pieces of porcupine quill embroidery. These heel pieces are sometimes worn on bare feet. Ordinary brown moccasins such as are worn by older men, and by younger men on ceremonial occasions, are sometimes worn by katcinas. Anklets of spruce twigs are worn with bare feet by Koḵokci and others.

Some kind of band is usually worn below the knee. This may be of black or brightly colored yarn, or a narrow woven belt such as men use to bind up their hair. A turtle-shell rattle is worn on the right leg by most of the dancing katcinas, and the rhythm of the dance is marked by stamping with the right foot. Sleigh bells may be worn on one or both legs, either with the rattle or instead of it. The legs are sometimes covered with native knitted hose or leggings of brown or white fringed buckskin.

A striking feature of katcina costume is the fox skin, suspended by its head from the back of the belt. This is worn by practically all of the dancing katcinas and many others. It is considered as a relic of the earliest days of man, for the katcinas were transformed while mankind was still tailed and horned.[30]

Female impersonations wear ordinary woman's costume—the black hand-woven dress fastened on the right shoulder, a long-sleeved and high-necked cotton underdress (recently silk), and one or two blanket robes over the shoulders. The top robe should be a native white cotton blanket, bordered above and below with woven bands of red

---

[30] Fewkes suggests that the fox skins may be a survival of the time when katcinas were animal impersonations effected by donning an animal skin. He connects this with the use of the flayed skin in Aztec ritual.

Masks Appearing at Winter Solstice, Fig. c (See Plate 21)

Masks Appearing at Winter Solstice, Fig. d (See Plate 21)

and blue. In absence of this, a native woven black blanket is substituted. Under this may be worn a brightly colored fringed commercial shawl. No piton·e (a square of brightly colored silk worn by Zuñi women over their shoulders) is worn. The blankets are fastened together in front with yarn, the way girls fasten their blankets when they dance.

Women's high white moccasins sometimes cover the feet and legs, or the feet are left bare and painted yellow, and the legs are covered with footless woolen hose, such as are worn in summer by the older Zuñi women, who ordinarily go barefoot.

All katcinas wear numerous necklaces of white shell, turquoise, and coral, from which hang ear loops (sato·we) of finely worked turquoise of the best grade. The amount of turquoise worn by any impersonator is limited only by his borrowing capacity. The necklaces cover the whole chest, frequently also the whole back. It is not unusual for an impersonator to wear necklaces valued at more than a thousand dollars around his neck.[31] Silver necklaces, blue yarn, abalone shells, and miscellaneous ornaments are also worn about the neck, and many bracelets and strings of shell and turquoise are wound about the wrists. The way of wearing the necklaces is indicative of rank and position. Necklaces front and back indicate a katcina of importance; necklaces doubled over and worn close to the throat are a badge of society membership.

Warrior katcinas wear the bandoleer of the bow priests over the right shoulder. This is made of white buckskin, decorated with fringes under the left arm and ornamented with a zigzag pattern of shells, four for each scalp taken. A little of the hair from each scalp is sewed into the broad fringed portion. The bandoleers of the bow priests hang by the outer doors of their houses. They are never taken into back rooms. They must always be removed before going into the room with the corn, or before drinking, lest the spring from which the water was drawn be contaminated. The bandoleers of the bow priests may be borrowed or imitated. Other less dangerous katcinas wear bandoleers of beadwork, yucca, cedar berries, or broad ribbon bands. Hunting impersonations wear a pouch such as hunters use to carry their animal fetishes and prayer meal. (O'wiwi, pl. 45, d.)

Arm bands of painted buckskin with long fringes and turkey feathers or painted tabs of buckskin attached to long strings are worn. These ornaments represent the sacred butterfly (lahacoma), a love charm which can make people crazy. "Lahacoma is the brightest of all the butterflies. It is yellow with spots of red and white and black.

---

[31] Turquoise is the Zuñi savings bank. After the sale of wool in the spring a man liquidates his debts and invests the balance in turquoise. Extravagant young men buy motor cars, but the thrifty man buys turquoise, which does not suffer depreciation.

It affects everyone, but especially young girls. It makes them follow
the one who has it, whether they want to or not. It is as if they were
crazy. They must go after anyone who has lahacoma. The Koyemci
always use it. Their father is always looking for lahacoma, and when
he finds it he puts it in their drum to make people come out to dances.
It must be true, because everyone always runs after the Koyemci as
soon as they hear their drum. They use it especially against people
who are not interested in anything and who never come out for dances.
They tell lahacoma to call them, and then they have to follow when
they hear the drum. And when once they come they must always
come after that whenever they hear the drum of the Koyemci. Other
dancers use lahacoma on their arm bands or painted on their masks
to make people come out. White missionaries have to come and ask
people to come to Sunday school or church, but we do not have to do
that. We have ways of making people want to come."

During the summer dancers wear branches of spruce thrust into
their belts and armbands, and carry spruce in their hands. All female
impersonations carry spruce. "Even the Tcakwena wears spruce in
summer. It is to make the world green. In summer the rain dancers
always dance in front of the house where the priests are in retreat,[32]
and one of the priests comes out and sprinkles all the dancers with
meal and takes a branch of spruce."

Objects carried.—All the dancing katcinas except a few, Towa
Tcakwena, Hilili, and a few characters in the mixed dance, carry gourd
rattles in the right hand and spruce in the left. The rattles are made
by shaking the seeds out of dry gourds and inserting in their place
small pebbles. The handle is inserted in the side. They are very
different in form and sound from the rattles of the medicine societies,
in which shells are used instead of pebbles. Special kinds of rattles
are carried by various katcina priests. Saiyataca, Hu·tutu, and the
Sälimop̣iya carry rattles of deer scapulae, Ḳäklo carries a stuffed
duck skin hung with little tinkling shells, the Ḳäna·kwe carry rattles
made of turtle shells, similar to those worn on the leg.

Warrior impersonations carry bow and arrow in the left hand, in
addition to spruce, and frequently a bunch of giant yucca instead of
the rattle in the right. Whipping katcinas, like the Sälimop'iya and
Saiyaḷi'a, carry yucca in both hands. As with the wearing of the great
feather, the manner of carrying yucca switches indicates the katcina's
temper and intentions. When he is friendly and comes just to dance
or to show himself in the village he carries his yucca with the points
back and the roots forward. But when he comes to whip, whether in
punishment or exorcism, he carries the tips forward. The whipping is
always done with the tips of the leaves. When whipping the children
at their initiation the yucca switches are bound together to give

---

[32] See p. 514.

them greater firmness and are replaced with fresh as soon as the ends become limp. Katcinas are always instructed not to whip anyone who is carrying corn or water or any woman who is with child. After striking anyone the katcina passes the yucca before the victim's face, saying, "May you be blessed with seeds." Since he gives his blessing while wearing a mask, white people and other outsiders are never struck during these demonstrations.[33]

Several katcinas carry feathered wands or long staves with feathers (Muluktakä, pl. 46, d). P'autiwa and other katcina priests carry bundle of prayer sticks which are planted or otherwise disposed of in the course of their visit, or taken out with them to be planted later. Female impersonations carry branches of spruce or perfect ears of corn. This by no means exhausts the list of objects carried by the katcinas. One of the "little dancers" (Hehe'a) carries a bag of sand and red pepper, another a young spruce tree. Several of the scare katcinas carry great stone knives and the Ca'lako carry stone axes thrust in their belts out of sight. Almost anything which adds character to the impersonation may be brought.

The only katcina sets which have their own drum are the Short-haired or Drum Tcakwena and one of the mixed dances. The drum is made of a bundle of clothing wrapped very tight in a strong buckskin and tied with thongs. It resounds when struck with a drumstick. The Koyemci sometimes bring a wooden drum which they use in the intermissions between dances.

Hilili, whether dancing indoors or out, do not sing for themselves but bring their own choir. These men are dressed like society members and wear masks. They use a pottery drum which they borrow from one of the societies.

During the winter dance series the katcinas dance indoors. Each kiva invites one of the medicine societies to sing for them. The society brings its own drum, which is played by the official drummer of the society, who is also the leader of the singing. They do not sing while the katcinas are dancing, but in the intervals between dances, while the "little dancers" are going around.

Every katcina carries in his belt a small package of seeds which is called his "heart." This package contains corn of all colors, squash, melons, sometimes wild seeds, but not wheat, pumpkins, or cucumbers. Each man gets the seeds from his wife or mother. They form one of the most important parts of his regalia. A dancer will never go out without his seeds. When a priest requests that a dance be repeated, as he sprinkles each dancer in the line with meal, he takes from his belt his package of seeds. Usually he takes only from the

---

[33] In 1926 a Saiyali'a whipped a white school-teacher who was standing too close. He was rebuked by the katcina chief for "having given away his good luck."

first two or three in line. These are kept and planted next spring, and are believed to grow faster than other seeds. The men whose seeds are taken must obtain another package before going out to dance next day. If he should dance without his "heart" he would have no power. It is said that one of the reasons why there is no longer any exchange of dance sets between the Zuñi and Hopi villages is because the Zuñis discovered that the Hopis carried no seeds, and therefore had no power. The Zuñis, however, always carried seeds when they went to dance in Hopi villages, "and so they took all their crops and all their good luck over to the Hopi country, and here we had nothing at all."

Before participating in any masked ritual, in fact, before any participation in ceremony, the head must be washed in yucca suds. Even impersonators of katcina priests, who have been in retreat before their public ceremonies, return to their houses before dressing long enough to have their heads bathed by their wives or mothers. No man ever washes his own hair. In dressing the order is, first the body paint, then the costume, and last of all the mask. There are probably more elaborate rituals of dressing for all the katcina priests. When all the men are ready to go out, as the line of dancers leaves the kiva the chief spits medicine on each one of them. "It is called utea'owe (flower meal) or Paiyatamu medicine. It is made by medicine men in the society houses, and only society people have it. If the kiva chief does not belong to a society he must get this medicine from someone who has it. It is made from the petals of yellow and purple flowers." All the butterflies go to the bright-colored flowers and people like to pick them. Therefore they make this medicine from the bright flowers. They mix it with the paint they use on the masks and body, to make the dancers beautiful. Only the headmen know about this medicine. They take a little of it and as the dancers come out of the kiva to go to the plaza the kiva chief puts the medicine in his mouth and prays: "Now my father sun, you make the day beautiful. You send light and the clouds of all directions to make the world beautiful. You make the days beautiful in all directions. Therefore, we have made this paiyatamu medicine from the bright flowers." So he says and takes the medicine in his mouth and spits a little of it on each of the dancers as they come out.[34]

ORGANIZATION OF THE KATCINA SOCIETY

The Katcina Society (kotikan·e, ko ex koko, katcina + tikan·e, secret society) comprises all the adult males of the community and a few initiated females. The rites of initiation are described elsewhere (p. 975). Girls ordinarily are told the secrets of the katcina cult by

---

[34] This medicine is also a love charm. Mothers use it in the same way on their girls before they go out to watch a dance, "to make them beautiful, so that everyone will like to look at them."

their fathers when they are thought to have reached the age of discretion, at about the age of 12. However, even before this time the secrets of the cult are not as strictly guarded from them as from boys, since they are regarded as less responsible members of the community. Girls may in rare cases be initiated into the Katcina Society and participate in dances. They are sometimes given to the Katcina Society, as they might be given to another society, in sickness. The katcinas cure for "bad dreams" (hallucinations). Frequently girls are whipped in the kiva to cure them of "bad dreams," but initiation is rarely resorted to. Girls may also join, on request, to take the place of an aged female relative, as reported by Stevenson (Life of a Zuñi Child), or they may volunteer to join. Few women avail themselves of this privilege. It is considered "shameless" (kwa ya·tsawilam·e).[35] Mrs. Stevenson is in error in stating that girls take vows of chastity [36] on joining the Katcina Society. There are three female members of the Katcina Society at the present time, and all of them are or have been married. A married woman has recently applied for membership.

The function of the Katcina Society is the presentation of masked dances and rituals, but it also cooperates with the priestly hierarchy in all great ceremonies in which masked personages appear.

The head of the Katcina Society is the katcina chief (komosona, ko + mosona, chief or leader). He is appointed for life by the council of the priests, from the Antelope clan. Usually he trains some young man in his family to succeed him, and on his death or retirement his selection is ratified by the priests. The katcina chief is assisted by the katcina p̣ekwin, similarly appointed from the Badger clan, and two katcina bow priests, members of any clan selected from the bow priesthood. The office of katcina p̣ekwin has been vacant for several years, three incumbents having died in rapid succession. This series of disasters made possible candidates afraid to accept the office and grave concern is felt over the failure to fill this important post. Because of this vacancy the initiation ceremony has not been held since 1919.[37]

Theoretically the power of the katcina chief is very great, but it is hedged and checked by the independent powers of the kivas and the

---

[35] Not because she is a woman, but because she has been forward, in offering to join a ceremony without being invited. To join a society when there is no need, like buying a pew in a fashionable church, is regarded as an undignified grabbing at prestige, and consequently carries no prestige. "Joiners" are looked upon with amused contempt, for having expended so much goods in such a fruitless cause.

[36] Chastity, as a way of life, is looked upon with great disfavor. No one comes in for harsher criticism, in life and literature, than the girl who refuses to marry. This does not apply, needless to say, to ceremonial continence.

[37] This circumstance has given the whole clan a "bad name." The Badger people in general and the Onaawa priesthood in particular are accused of trafficking with whites, and the death of three office holders of the clan is considered a reflection of this pollution. The office was filled during the winter solstice of 1928 and the ceremony commanded for the spring of 1929.

various cult groups (see below).[38]   He officiates at many important
ceremonies and is regarded as a repository of katcina lore.   He has,
of course, powerful supernatural connections.   He is not a priest,
hence not a member of the council (Mrs. Stevenson's "First Body of
the Aciwanni").   However, his advice is sought by the priests in all
important matters, and his word carries great weight.   He is always
referred to by title rather than name and his children have taken his
title as a patronymic.   The present incumbent is a man of great
personal influence.   He is a most rigorous observer of all ancient
practices and exacting in his demands on those who hold office under
him.   He is bitter in his denunciation of those suspected of trafficking
with whites and those who are lax in preserving the secrecy of all
religious rites.   Since the retirement of Tsawela from the office of
bow priest Komosona has been the leader of the conservative ("Catholic") faction.

The katcina p̃ekwin is his subordinate and assistant.   The two
katcina bow priests serve chiefly as messengers of the katcina chief.
They sometimes bring in the line of dancers in the summer rain dances,
although this duty belongs theoretically to the katcina chief and his
p̃ekwin.   As bow priests, they have the office of guarding secret
rituals, punishing intruders, and general policing.

The membership at large of the Katcina Society is composed of six
groups,[39] very unequal in size, each with its own organization.   These
are primarily dancing societies.   At the head of each group is the kiva
chief (otakamos·i, literally dance chief).   He is called kiva chief in
the following pages because the term has become accepted in Hopi
usage, and clearly describes his place in the sacerdotal organization.
There may be in each group one or more assistant kiva chiefs (also
called otaka·mos·i, and two or more wo·we (literally "creature").
The kiva chief is the responsible head.   He sets the dates for
dances of his group,[40] decides what dance is to be given, calls
rehearsals, teaches the participants their songs, superintends the
preparation of the masks, plants prayer sticks before the dance and
observes the usual ritual requirements attendant thereon, and on the
day of the dance stands in the center of the line and leads the singing.
The two wo·we have charge of the paraphernalia of the dance.   They

---

[38] An interesting case of the checks upon authority in Zuñi occurred in connection with the last initiation
ceremony.   For a time there was some doubt as to whether the ceremony could be held, although it had
been ordered by the priests.   The member of the Great Fire Society, whose office it was to make the sand
paintings in the kivas, refused to cooperate.   He had many old scores to settle with the priests—he had
once been persecuted for witchcraft, and was cordially hated.   So, like Achilles, he sulked in his tent until all
the priests came to him and ate humble pie.   Then he deigned to serve.   Until he had been mollified, the
ceremony could not go on, because no one else "knew how"—that is, had the necessary supernatural power.
Others might be able to make the paintings, but they would not know the prayers, so they would not be
potent.

[39] Called up̃a·we, from up̃e, "within," a verbal stem meaning "to be in" in the literal and ceremonial sense of being in retreat.

[40] Except the first dances of the summer and winter series, held on set dates of the Zuñi calendar.

collect and decorate the masks. They paint the masks, the men themselves attach the feathers and other ornaments. The wowe superintend the gathering of other clothing and the spruce boughs that are so prominent a part of the paraphernalia of the katcinas. In addition to the regular wo·we for the dances, each group has at least one special Ca'lako wo'le, and a Sälimop̃iya wo'le. They may, of course, serve in double capacity. This is the theoretical organization, which is much broken down at present. None of the groups has the full quota of officers. Muhewa, for instance, has only one wo'le on whom falls all the exacting tasks connected with the presentation of masked dances and the Ca'lako ritual.

Each of the six divisions of the Katcina Society is associated with a ceremonial building, the kivas.[41] In Zuñi these are square buildings, contained within the house groups. They have no doors on the streets, the entrance being through the hatchway in the roof, the method by which all Zuñi houses were entered until recent years. The kivas may also be entered through doorways leading into adjoining houses. The windows on the street are tiny apertures; they do not contain panes of glass or mica. Usually they are filled with small stones or stuffed with cloth. The kivas have ledges running about the walls, such as used to be common in Zuñi homes.

The fireplace is a boxlike structure with open side, located in the center of the room, directly under the hatchway. There is no flue, and the smoke escapes through the opening above. Zuñi dwelling houses have excellently constructed corner fireplaces with chimneys. The inner ladder rises behind the fireplace. Zuñi kivas do not have the shipapu, the hole in the floor, symbolizing the place of emergence, which is found in ancient and modern kivas in other villages. The location of the kivas is indicated on Kroeber's map of the Zuñi village.[43] Kroeber points out the fact that they are all located on courts or plazas.

The six kivas are named, and the dance groups are named from the building with the addition of the suffix meaning "people." The names of the kivas are derived from fortuitous and trivial associations. The six kivas are associated with the six cardinal points, as follows: He'iwa (he'i, wall, wa, locative suffix) with the north; muhe·wa (muhe-, dung, wa) with the west; tcupa·wa (tcu-, corn kernels, up̃a, kiva group, wa) with the south; ohe·wa (ohe·-, brains, wa) with the east; upt̂sana·wa (up̃a, kiva group; t̂sana, small, wa)

---

[41] The Zuñi word is kiwitsin·e. Kiva is a Hopi word which has become the standardized term in literature of the Southwest for the ceremonial rooms of peculiar construction which are found in all ancient and modern pueblos. Usually they are isolated buildings, circular in form, and either partly or wholly subterranean. The structure, esepcially of the fireplace, is always unmistakable. The multiplicity of kivas in early ruins suggests that in early times they were differently employed. I do not know the etymology of the Zuñi word, but I suspect a Shoshonean derivation. Ki is the stem for house in all Shoshonean dialects, which makes the Hopi etymology perfectly clear. Zuñi contains no stem ki, kiwi, or anything like it. Polysyllabic stems are very rare.

[43] Kroeber, 1918.

with the above; he·ḳapa·wa (he·ḳapan·e, back wall, or place behind
a wall, wa) with below.   There is no fixed order for visiting the various kivas, although the association with the directions would indicate
a fixed ceremonial circuit.   Each masked personage has his own route
through the village.   He'iwa is the chief kiva.   Here is set up the
great solstice altar, and here are held the ceremonies that usher in the
new year 10 days later.   Here also is made the great altar and sand
painting for initiation of little boys.   It is located on t̂sia'awa (t̂sia'a,
to cut or tear, wa) plaza.   Adjoining the kiva but unconnected with
it is the ceremonial house of the town chiefs (called t̂eciwan·i, t̂e,
place, ciwan·i, priest) which is considered to be the actual center of
the world, and is the most sacred place in Zuñi.   The court is entirely
inclosed, except for two narrow passages leading to it, which were built
over until quite recently.   In t̂sia'awa are held all the outdoor dances
of the katcinas.   They visit the other three recognized plazas of the
village, but spend most of their time in t̂sia'awa.   Here the Koyemci
remain at play during their dances.   Here are held other important
outdoor ceremonies, the presentation of Łe'eto·we to the light, the
dance of the Łewe·kwe, and the summer dance of the Ne'we·kwe.
Other ceremonies which involve the setting up of complicated altars or
bowers in which the chiefs of the tribe sit are held in the large plaza
(t̂ehwito łan·a), probably because it is more spacious, although the
fact that the ancient Spanish mission church adjoins the large plaza
may have something to do with it.

Except for esoteric ceremonies, the kivas are rapidly falling into
disuse.   In folk tales which reflect older conditions the kivas were
used for all ceremonies, including those of the medicine societies, and
for all preparations for ceremonies.   They were also the clubhouses
of the men, as they still are among the Hopi.   During the winter
months Hopi men spend most of their time in the kivas, weaving,
gaming, and story-telling.   Even in Mrs. Stevenson's time [44] Zuñi
kivas were used to a much greater extent than at present.   At that
time the winter dances of the Koḳokci were held in the kivas.[45]
Now they are held in the houses of the kiva chiefs.   The chief summer
solstice altar used to be set up in the kiva to which the katcina chief
belonged; now it is set up in his house and the all-night ceremonies
of the return of the katcinas are held there.   The use of the kiva is
coming to be more and more restricted to the strictly esoteric ceremonies of the Katcina Society.   All public ceremonies are held outdoors or in the homes of prominent officials.[46]

---

[44] Zuñi Indians, p. 62.

[45] Zuñi Indians, p. 145.

[46] According to mythology the kivas were built by order of Ḳäklo, when he announced the first coming
of the masked gods, as houses in which to receive the divine children.   In the Zuñi mind they are associated exclusively with the mysteries of the katcina cult.   Nevertheless the winter solstice ceremony of
the war gods is held in he'iwa kiva, a circumstance which reflects historic phenomena at variance with
native dogma.

The various kiva groups are regarded as related as elder and younger brother, as follows: When the elder brother group is dancing the younger brother will be invited, through a gift of corn meal to the kiva chief, to participate, and will furnish the female impersonations. A man who for one reason or another misses the dance of his own group will participate, if possible, in the dance of the brother group.

In addition to the six dance groups there are associated with the Katcina Society a large number of cult groups which control the great calendrical ceremonies of the katcina priests. It has already been pointed out that the Zuñi distinguish two types of masked impersonations, the katcinas, which I have called the dancing katcinas, and the katcina priests. The katcina priests do not come to dance. They never dance outdoors. If they dance at all it is before special groups, and in the kivas to the songs of other choirs. This is not considering dancing in the same sense as the dancing of the Koǩokci or other groups who provide their own music.[47] They come to perform certain priestly functions, to "make the New Year," to reaffirm the gods and bring their blessings, to initiate the children into the mysteries of the katcina cult. They are, indeed, priests wearing masks. They wear ancient masks, permanently associated with a single impersonation, which are tribal and not individual property. The impersonators are chosen either by the council of priests or by special cult groups who are the trustees of their ritual.

A cult group may be defined as any self-perpetuating body whose chief function is the preservation of an esoteric ritual in connection with some sacred object. The cult groups of the katcina cult are, therefore, similar to priests, although they are not called priests by the Zuñi. The group may consist of one man, like the "keeper"[48] of Tcakwena okä, it may consist of three or four men, like the "Ǩäklo people" or the Saiyataca wo·we, or a large group, like the "Pautiwa people." The members of the cult in some cases themselves perform the ritual (Ǩäklo); in other cases they delegate the performance to others. Furthermore, the sacred object which forms the central feature of cult activities may be cared for by another group (the mask of Ǩäklo, which is kept in the house of the katcina pekwin and removed and returned by a group of men of the Corn clan). This intricate type of organization is not confined to masked impersonations.

The masks used in the impersonations of the katcina priests are ancient and permanent. They are "from the first beginning"

---

[47] The exceptions are the Koyemci who mimic in the plaza the dances of other groups and the Sälimopiya and related katcinas who sometimes come in the winter dances. But these are not the "real" sälimopiya, i. e., they do not use the ancient masks.

[48] Tcakwena Oka il·ona, from il·i, literally to be with, in the double sense of possessing and belonging to an object of ritual (it is used also literally for the possession of property: kwanil·i, to have something, to be wealthy). A man also "has" a society, that is, belongs to a society (tikili). The gods are "those who have the roads" (a·wona·wilona). The word is usually translated by Zuñis as "the ones who look after us."

(tcimiḵänapkowa). According to tradition they are the very masks that were made when the katcina cult and the custom of masks were first instituted by order of the masked gods themselves. They may, however, be replaced by order of the priests in exceptional circumstances.[49] Each represents a named and fully individualized katcina. The masks are usually repainted and redecorated each time they are used, but they are never made over into the masks of other individuals.[50] They are not the property of the men who keep them or wear them; they are held in trust like the rain-making fetishes of the priests, and are second only to them in sanctity and power. There are at least 52 such masks, exclusive of the 12 masks belonging to medicine societies and the large group of masks of the Ḵana·-kwe ceremony. The location of each of these is general knowledge. In the back rooms of Zuñi houses are probably many more ancient masks whose ceremonies have lapsed.

The impersonators of these katcina priests are sacred in a way that the participants in rain dances are not. They are chosen by the cult group or the priests, to whom they are responsible. They are, therefore, outside the jurisdiction of the Katcina Society. The exceptions to this are Käklo and the Sälimopiya group who participate in the first whipping of little boys. These beings, whose chief function is the affirmation of the power of the Katcina Society, represent the katcina chief and his associates and are responsible to them. Even when impersonators of katcina priests are not themselves cult members they must plant prayer sticks and observe all the ritual restrictions. Frequently they observe regular retreats. The Koyemci, for example, observe a strict retreat of 14 days, the longest and strictest in Zuñi ritual. Often the impersonators must learn complicated esoteric rituals and long chants, like that of Saiyataca.

The following table shows in outline the activities of these cult groups. It gives the names of the permanent masks, the house where each is kept (the numbers refer to the numbered houses on Kroeber's map of Zuñi village), the membership of the various groups associated with each impersonation, and their principal activities.

---

[49] See p. 931.

[50] Like all categorical statements in regard to Zuñi ritualism, this, too, must be qualified. The classification of the monsters is not clear. Natacku is an ancient and permanent mask. It is permanent, necessarily, by reason of its form, and ancient, because "they wouldn't bury it. No one would want to have another made like it, because it can not be used for anything else." Therefore there must be someone to "look after" Natacku—the germ of a cult. But the other masks that come with him, and share his function of disciplining recalcitrant children, are not, to the best of my knowledge, permanent masks. Nor, so far as I know, is Ahe'a, who has a prominent part in the initiation ceremonies and might well be called a katcina priest.

Name of katcina	House No.	Membership of cult group	Chief ceremonies	Choice of personator	Principal activities
Pautiwa	161 (Pik.)	Mask is kept by family of chief priests, Pi'tcikwe clan. All men who have personated Pautiwa at winter solstice form cult group for perpetuation of ritual. They, too, are Pi'tcikwe clan, or child of Pi'tcikwe. Assisted by members of Sun clan.	1. The New Year	1. Chosen by cult members from Pi'tcikwe clan or child of Pi'tcikwe. If not already a member of cult group, becomes a member by virtue of this participation.	He "makes the New Year." Is present at making of New Year fire; reads omens for the year; leaves at kivas crooks for the appointment of Ca'lako participants. Cult activities involve learning long esoteric chant, and frequent prayer-stick plantings.
			2. Mo'lawia	2. Must be Aiyahokwe clan or child of Aiyahokwe chosen by priests at Itiwana (?).	He brings in the Corn Maids. The impersonator makes monthly prayer-stick offerings. He plants alone, and learns his ritual from "any old man."
			1. Komhalikwi	1. He must be Corn clan. He is chosen by members of Corn clan.	He comes to exercise during period between winter solstice and the New Year. No cult activities. All the women of the Corn clan grind for him.
Saiyalia (4)	414	The four personators form a cult group from the winter solstice until Ca'lako.	11. The New Year	Chosen by priests on sixth day of teckwi. The particular individuals are selected by the dance chief from a kiva designated by the priests. The sanction comes directly from the priests.	They are exorcisers. They come on the last night of teckwi to take away the old year; they whip the children at their initiation; are summoned by the katcina chief to punish any infringement of the rules of the katcina society.
			2. Final whipping of boys, after Ca'lako. 3. First whipping of boys. 4. Rabbit hunt.	The same	So far as known there are no cult activities except prayers. Probably they must observe continence and plant prayer sticks.
			5. Special occasions	Appointed by kopi'laciwan'i by order of komosona.	To punish offenders against the katcina cult and to administer general whipping to avert bad luck as a result of the infringement of rules.

Name of katcina	House No.	Membership of cult group	Chief ceremonies	Choice of personator	Principal activities
Citsuḳä Kwelele	422	Koko Łana order of Big Fire Society.	New Year	Chosen by Big Fire Society (probably by Koko Łana order).	They dance for the New Year during all night ceremonies in He'iwa kiva, and assist at making of New Year fire. Cult activities are concerned with curing. Come with Koko Łana at curing ceremony which initiates into this order. Curing songs connected with this ceremony.
Tcakwena Oḳä	210 (Badger)	Badger clan man or child of Badger from this house.	New Year. Rabbit hunt.	Mask is worn by man who has charge of it.	Visits all houses of village to bless women in pregnancy and childbirth.
Koyemci (10)	87	The masks are kept by the people of the Hekiapawa priesthood. The personators form a temporary cult group, which changes each year.	All rain dances. Ca'lako. First whipping of little boys.	At New Year the priests appoint Father Koyemci from certain clans and certain societies in fixed rotation. He appoints the other nine men. They hold office until after Ca'lako, and ordinarily return to office after four years.	They assist with clowning at all rain dances, have all-night ceremonies in their house at Ca'lako, bring in Ḳäklo, and assists at first and second whipping of boys. Many minor ceremonies. Cult activities: They use special dialect; have many esoteric songs and chants; monthly prayer-stick plantings at distant shrines; 16-day retreat preceding and throughout Ca'lako festivities.
Saiyataca Hututu Yamuhakto (2)	56 (Pik.)	Saiyataca wo'le and his associates hold office for life, and have charge of the perpetuation of the ritual. The personators form a temporary cult group during period of incumbency. The chief wo'le is Nawicti.	Ca'lako	Appointed by priests at New Year, and hold office until the following December. With the exception of Cula'witsi who must be Badger or child of Badger, personators may be chosen from any clan. Cula'witsi is a little boy and is assisted by his ceremonial father.	Great public ceremony for fertility at house which they dedicate at Ca'lako. Cult activities: All personators of the Saiyataca party plant prayer sticks monthly at distant shrines throughout year of office. Observe a 4-day retreat immediately preceding public ceremony. Saiyataca has a long esoteric chant, and furthermore must perform special ceremonies throughout the summer to prevent frosts.

Name	Mask	Ceremony	Personators	Activities
Cu'la·witsi	56 (Pik.). X-163-a (another mask).	First whipping of boys	Selected by head men of 'Uptsanawa kiva. He is a man and may belong to any clan.	See below, Sälimopiya party.
	This mask belongs to the sälimopiya cult. See below.			
Ca'lako: He'ikwe 387 (badger), Muhekwe 538.[2], Teupa'kwe 130, 'Ohekwe 159, 'Upsanakwe 150, Hekiapakwe 108.	The masks are never touched by the people of the houses where they are kept. Each kiva has a Ca'lako wo'le, who takes care of the mask, clothing, etc., and transmits the ritual. The personators form a cult group for the period during which they hold office.	Ca'lako	2 personators chosen by the head men of each kiva the day after the New Year. Since they receive the crooks of the priests at their appointment, their sanction comes directly from the priests.	Each Ca'lako set has a great public ceremony for fertility in a different house on the night of Ca'lako. Cult activities: Monthly prayer stick plantings; 4-day retreat before public ceremony; esoteric chant; the personators work during the summer for the house where their ceremony is held and the house where their mask is kept. There are minor ceremonies at the removal and return of the masks.
Kaklo	House of the katcina pekwin.[3]	Twice, at intervals of 8 days, at quadrennial[4] whipping of little boys.	1 of the 4 men who form the cult group. Not necessarily the eldest.	He visits all the kivas to announce the coming of the katcinas to whip the boys. The cult group meets at frequent intervals to repeat their chant, which is very long and esoteric. They probably observe regular retreats and prayer-stick plantings, but information is lacking.
	The mask is kept in the house of the katcina pekwin and cared for by 2 men of the Corn clan, who act as servants to the personator. The ritual belongs to a group of 4 men, Pi'tcikwe and child of Pi'tcikwe.			

[1] These two masks are not, strictly speaking, koko. They are included in this table because of the important place they occupy in the calendar. At the New Year ceremony they appear with true katcinas, and perform similar functions. This is not the case with the other mask of the Big Fire Society (Koko Łana) which is never brought out publicly, and functions only in curing ceremonies. This is true also of the two Ne'we·kwe koko.

[2] Out of town. Old house 325.

[3] There was no katcina pekwin in 1926 and the mask was still in the house of the man who held this office in 1919, where the ceremony was last performed. The mask will not be transferred when the new pekwin is appointed, but only after the next performance of the ceremony.

[4] The ceremony has not been held since 1919, because so many of the children are away at school and also because there have been changes in the office of katcina pekwin. The office is vacant and there is no successor.

Name of katcina	House No.	Membership of cult group	Chief ceremonies	Choice of personator	Principal activities

Sälimopiya group____
2 Yellow S.____
2 Łelacoktipona_
2 Blue S.____
2 Red S.____
2 Nawico____
2 White S.____
2 Anahoho____
2 Speckled S.____
1 Culawitsi____
2 Black S.____
2 Upo'yona____
	142 (eagle).
	414 (corn).
	252 (badger).
	292 (Pík.).
	×163A.
	161. (Pík. chief priest)
		Each kiva has a special Säli-mopiya wo'le, who looks after mask, clothing, etc., and ritual.	Quadrennial whipping of little boys.	Personators appointed the day Ḳäklo first comes by head men of kivas, as follows:
				He'iwa: Yellow S.
				        Łelacoktipona.
				Muhewa: Blue S.
				Tcupawa: Red S.
				        Nawico.
				Ohewa: White S.
				        Anahoho.
				Upťsanawa: Speckled S.
				        Culawitsi.
				Hekiapawa: Black S.
				        Upoyona.
					They visit the whole village exorcis-ing and finally whip the little boys in the plaza. The personators ob-serve an 8-day retreat from the day following Ḳäklo's coming, until their public appearance. They are the only groups to use kivas for re-treats. The old masks are sup-posed to be used only for this cere-mony. If they are taken out at any other time, the wearer must "count days." When Cula-witsi comes at Ca'łako, he wears a differ-ent mask. The salyatła masks are kept with the Blue Sälimopiya, but they do not belong to Sälimo-piya group. They constitute a separate cult. (See above.)

Kyäna'kwe [5]____	391____	All male members of Corn clan or their children, members of Tcupawa kiva "belong" to this ceremony.	A quadrennial giveaway dance performed in mid-summer following the whipping of little boys.	The members of the cult group dance, by order of the priests, who command the dance by giving a crook to the chief at the winter solstice.	A large public dance probably pret-ceded by retreat. Frequent meet-ings to practice songs and prayers.
42 Ololowiċḳä____	(?)____	There are 3 men who "know" the ritural of this mask and its appurtenances.	Performed at irregular in-tervals, is supplement to last rain dance of sum-mer series.	The chief of the cult (Kalawasa) performs this ritual at request of Pekwin.	A phallic ritual to insure virility and protect against venereal disease. The ceremony involves use of para-phernalia, knowledge of special prayers. Personator must be con-tinent and probably plants prayer sticks.

| 37 | Hainawi (probably also his companions, Homatci, Temtemci, and A'hu'e). | Komosona's house. | Appears irregularly by order of Komosona. | Chosen by Komosona | Used to come to behead boys who revealed secrets of initiation. Now comes to frighten those who tell. Accompanied by Homatci, Temtemci, A'hu'e. Impersonator must recite prayers. Probably must be continent and plant prayer sticks. |

⁵ These are not kokc.

PREPARATION OF DANCES

Each kiva is required to present at least three group dances during the calendar year. These occur during the three months following the winter solstice, during the three months following the summer solstice, and during the five days following the Ca'lako. Each kiva must, furthermore, cooperate in the winter dances of the other five groups, either by presenting a group dance of its own or by sending representatives to dance with another group. They may in addition send "Little Dancers," isolated impersonations, to dance between the rounds of group dances.

The order, but not the dates, of the winter dances is fixed. The kiva chief of the group that is to present the first dance of the season receives a cigarette from p̄ekwin commanding him to appear. The date for this dance used to be fixed at eight days after the New Year, but now it occurs "whenever they are ready." The duty of presenting the first dance of the season falls in succeeding years on the different kivas, as follows: He'iwa, muhe·wa, tcupa·wa, ohe·wa, hekapa·wa, up̄sanawa. The dances of the kivas are supposed to follow one another in the same order. Each kiva sends in messengers to announce their dance, and to present a cigarette to the group that is to follow next in order. Certain kivas, however, are procrastinating. If after the passage of a reasonable length of time the next group gives no signs of preparation for its dance, its place will be taken by some more energetic group. The order and dates of dancing in the summer series are not fixed, except the first dance which must be performed eight days after the solstice by the kiva which presented the first winter dance. Of all the groups, he'kapa·kwe is the most dilatory. In the fall of 1923, for instance, it did not dance at all after Ca'lako, and gave no ko'upt-conan·e (the large winter dances; see below), and so they dropped out of the summer series that year also. The following year they were very tardy in giving their winter dance, and the following summer they had not yet begun to rehearse on August 28, when my informant reported to me the dissatisfaction of the theocracy. "They should all dance during the summer when we need rain, but now it is the end of August, and they have not yet begun to rehearse. Everyone is angry about it because no one wants rain in the fall when we are working on our wheat harvest, and yet that is the time the hekapa·wa people always dance. They say that their chief is a witch, and so no one wants to dance with him. The men would rather dance with other kivas. That is why they can never get ready in time." Muhe·wa also is inclined to be tardy. Their organization is very much broken down; they have only one wo'le, who is also Ca'lako wo'le. He is a very old man and the duties are too much for him. Their dance directors, too, are elderly men, and the younger men are lax in their duties. In 1927 they did not dance

Masks Appearing at the Initiation, Fig. a (See Plate 28)

Masks Appearing at the Initiation, Fig. b (See Plate 28)

the required dance after Ca'lako, although the younger men of the kiva put on a cow dance, as an extra dance the first night. In 1928 they did not appear after Ca'lako until the very last night, when they were represented by one old man accompanied by four little boys about ten years old dancing Hemuci·kwe. On the last day three men danced in the plaza. Tcupa·wa is the most energetic of the kivas. They always dance early in the summer, and both the years that I witnessed Ca'lako they had large groups out dancing Muluktaka from the first night on. They were the only group dancing for the first two nights.

The winter dances are known as ko'uptcona·we (the gods being in sundry places). These dances are held at night, in the houses of the chiefs of the kivas, the various groups visiting all the houses.

The group which receives the cigarette presents the ko'uptconan·e. This group must dance Kok̓'okci or one of its variants. In recent years, however, other traditional dances, such as Tcakwena or Wo·temła (the mixed dance), have been substituted, although this is not considered orthodox. The other groups, notified four days in advance by masked messengers of the forthcoming event, may present any traditional dance, or a novelty, or may merely be represented by isolated dancers or dancers appearing with other groups. Five female impersonators in the group that is presenting the dance carry sacks of seed corn which are presented to the five kivas where the group dance as guests. The seed corn is left on the altars, and later distributed to all present in the room. The officiating group receives in return from the other groups five bundles of prayer sticks which are planted the following day by messengers usually designated by the group presenting the prayer sticks. The men planting the prayer sticks are the only ones to observe continence and therefore on their piety depends the efficacy of the offerings.

The summer dances theoretically must be the same dances as presented by the kivas at their own ko'uptcona·we, and therefore, if orthodoxy ruled would also always be Kok̓okci or its variants. However, both Tcakwenas and Wo·temła are frequently danced in summer. This may be either because they are repeating an unauthorized selection of the winter, or because although the selection in winter was orthodox, the rule that the second half of the year must duplicate the first has been broken.

During the five days after Ca'lako each kiva is required to give a dance which is traditionally the property of that group, as follows:

heiwa, T̓owa Tcakwena.
muhe·wa, He·muci·kwe.
tcupa·wa Muluktakä
ohe·wa Wo·temła
upts'ana·wa Tcahumo'a·we (drum Tcakwena, also called Laguna Tcakwena)
hekäpa·wa Maheṭinaca

This program also is not strictly adhered to. Maheṭinaca is no longer popular because these dancers are unduly familiar with girls and women,[53] and is therefore no longer danced. In 1924 hekapa·kwe did not dance at all, in 1927 they combined with ohe·kwe (they were entertained in the same house), and in 1928 danced a mixed dance using a bundle drum and otherwise different from that of ohe·wa. Omissions from the full program have already been noted. Furthermore, it is customary for kivas entertained in the same house to dance together. Whenever any kiva departs from the rule of performing Koḵ'okci at its ko¹uptconan·e or summer rain dance, it is always one of these traditional kiva dances that is performed, never one of the new or borrowed dances.

Extra dances may be introduced into the calendar at any time the katcinas are "in" by any group of young men who wish to dance. These are usually new or borrowed dances, elaborate to the point of garishness in costume, difficult in music and dance step, and generally "fancy." This type of dance is also frequently performed by assisting groups at ko¹uptconawa. The usual times for interpolating new dances are late winter and early spring, the early fall, between the wheat and corn harvest, before the katcinas are "sent home" in November, and the night of Ca'lako and the five days following. They are organized by the young men with the approval and cooperation of the kiva heads. "When they want to have a new dance like the Cow dance or any other dance they have not had before, they ask the katcina chief if it will be all right to have that dance, and he will decide. No matter what kind of new katcina they make up this way, they join the people at the Sacred Lake, just the way new babies are born here. They pray like the others, and they have just as much power. Still the people are more afraid of the old masks, because they come from long ago."

Group dances, therefore, seem to be of three kinds:

Koḵokci and its variants, Upiḵaiap'ona and Hakcina Cilowa (rare), which should, according to rule, be performed at all the regular dances of the winter and summer series.

Traditional kiva dances, which are performed during the five days following Ca'lako, and may be substituted for Koḵokci at the summer and winter series, or performed by assisting groups in the winter series.

New or borrowed dances, which may be performed by assisting groups at the winter series, or introduced as extra dances during winter or summer.

In dances of the regular series the kiva chief decides about when he would like his men to perform. He sends word to all the men of his kiva to meet at his house for rehearsals. The two wo·we, provided

---

[53] The name is derived from mahe, fæces; tina, to sit.

the kiva has the full quota of officers, carry the message. The usual time for delivering messages of this kind is at the time of the evening meal when the men are almost sure to be at their homes. That evening, after the women and children have retired, the men convene. The kiva chief announces that the time has come for them to dance, and tells them what dance he has chosen, asking, "What do you think of it?" The men reply, "Very well," and the rehearsal proceeds.

The first matter is learning the songs. Certain dances have traditional songs, e. g., the Drum Tcakwena imported from Laguna, and preserving its songs in the Keresan tongue;[54] Ķäna·kwe, whose songs are in a foreign tongue which Mrs. Stevenson believes to be Keresan; Hemuci·kwe, who sing only three short songs which are traditional, but in the Zuñi tongue; and Hilili, with songs in a foreign tongue, possibly Hopi. For other dances new songs are or should be composed each time the dance is performed. Generally new words are set to traditional airs, but sometimes innovations are introduced into the melodic frame. The songs are made by any man with a talent for poetry and music. He need not be a member of the kiva that is giving the dance, but may be invited to do this. The words of the songs are part of the katcina characterization. Towa Tcakwena, for example, always "talks sharply." His songs sometimes are homilies to the young. (See p. 1018.) After Ca'lako he always has one song calling the Koyemci by name, with comments, usually of an uncomplimentary character. They have other songs also in which other members of the community have their pecadillos held up for public ridicule. Men are twitted for the infidelity of their wives, and any error in ritual will be seized upon. For example, "I am Towa Tcakwena, and I go about all over to see the world. I came out from the Village of the Masked Gods and came to ———. Here they were having an initiation. They were putting a child into the Ciwana·kwe Society. There my mothers of the Dogwood clan gave their child a drink. . . ."[55] Mahetinaca has similar songs. "The Raw People are dangerous. They are wise. But even the Raw People are afraid of the Bear girl. When she showed her claws in the plaza, even the Raw People ran away." The allusion is to a girl of the Bear clan who chose the spectacular moment of the Yaya dance to humble her successful rival in love. The jilted maiden lived in a house on the plaza and when she saw her rival dancing in the plaza she and a cousin rushed from the house, dragged the girl from the circle of dancers and beat her up in proper Zuñi fashion. At Zuñi only women indulge in fist fights as a method of settling rivalries in

---

[54] Stevenson, p. 218.

[55] The song is paraphrased. The text was not recorded and not all the words were audible to the writer. The allusion was to two women who knew no better than to give a drink of water to their "child" during his initiation, thus violating his sacredness. He must not touch food or water during the ceremonies.

love. Even the gentle Koꞣokci, although their songs usually are descriptive of rain and growth, may allude mildly to the failings of their friends. The references are usually more veiled. "Our two daylight fathers journeyed to the east to visit the sun and the moon. When they returned their children questioned them, 'What did the Sun say to you?' But they had not seen the sun." This refers to a journey by two of the priests to Washington to lay the grievances before the Commissioner of Indian Affairs. They returned without having seen him, and the people who had been led to expect great things of the journey felt that their messengers had bungled things badly. The following are typical Koꞣokci songs. These were recorded on the phonograph by Mr. Georg Herzog in 1927, and the texts were afterwards recorded by the writer.

I

"Guess, younger brother,
Whose fine tracks go all about here ?
All over my water-filled field
He has walked about."
"Can you not guess,"
Thus he said to his younger brother.
"The child of the rain makers,
The water frog,
Goes about hurrying his fathers, the rain makers."

"Fathers, hurry!
Beautiful ones,
Cloud over your child.
When the water spreads out
Your child will sit in the water
Calling for rain."

Uhu ehe ye·lu
Uhu ehe ye·lu

Rain makers of all directions
Lightning comes beautiful.

Aha ehe
Aha ehe
Uhu ehe ye·lu.
Aha ehe
Aha ehe
Uhu ehe ye·lu.

"The rain makers of the west
Cloud over the heavens."
Thus all the corn plants say to one another.

Aha ehe etc.

II

"Say, younger brother,
Where are you going?
Here you go about greeting us with fair words."
"Hither at the north edge of the world

Smoke Youth
Delights in the songs of the masked gods.
So he says,
Therefore he goes about
Greeting all the rain makers with fair words.''
Thus the Dogwood clan man said to all his children.

''As dusk comes on
Who sings fairly their beautiful songs ?''
Because of their words
My inner room is filled with all kinds of riches.[56]
Uhu ehe
Uhu ehe
Aha ehe
Aha ehe

III

In the west at Flower Mountain
A rain priest sits
His head feathered with cumulus clouds
His words are of clouding over Itiwana.
''Come let us arise now.''
Thus along the shores of the encircling ocean
The rain makers say to one another.

Aha ehe
Aha ehe

In the south at Salt Lake Mountain
A rain priest sits
His head feathered with mist.
His words are of covering Itiwana with **rain.**
''Come let us go.''
Thus in all the springs
The rain makers say to one another.

Aha ehe
Aha ehe

''The beautiful world germinates.
The sun, the yellow dawn germinate.''
Thus the corn plants say to one another.
They are covered with dew.
''The beautiful world germinates.
The sun, the yellow dawn germinate.''
Thus the corn plants say to one another.
They bring forth their young.

Aha ehe
Aha ehe.

''The beautiful world germinates.
The sun, the yellow dawn germinate.''
Thus the corn plants say to one another.
They are shaken by the wind.
Aha ehe
Aha ehe.

---

[56] The singer, a member of the Dogwood clan, made this song for Mr. Herzog (Smoke Youth).

The kiva chief supervises all rehearsals. If the dance is new or unfamiliar the rehearsals may extend over a period of several weeks. The participants meet every night for a while, then for a few nights may not meet, but meet to rehearse again for a number of nights preceding the dance. For traditional dances about four or five rehearsals are held during the week preceding the dance. When the kiva chief decides that the men have sufficiently mastered the songs he definitely sets the date. The dance chiefs and wo·we cut prayer sticks for the katcinas and plant them four days before the dance is to take place. "Only the headmen plant prayer sticks. They do not let all the men plant because some of the foolish young boys might not care what they did. They might sleep with their wives after planting prayer sticks, or otherwise violate their sacredness, and so spoil the dance and bring misfortune on all the men taking part." If the dance belongs to the regular winter series, on the afternoon the prayer sticks are planted two katcinas appear in the village and visit all the houses where the kivas habitually hold their winter dances, to inform the officers of other kivas to prepare for the forthcoming festival. These men then notify their men and the subsidiary dances are prepared in the three following days. The time is short, so the kiva chiefs select well-known dances of their groups, or some dance that the young men of the group have one time presented as an extra dance. Or if they do not wish to make even these hasty preparations those who wish to dance come as isolated dancers. In that case at least one man must be delegated to dance with another group to take to the leading group the bundle of prayer sticks. In the summer the people are apprised of the coming dance when they see the headmen go out to plant their prayer sticks.[57]

Planting prayer sticks out of season always is a sign of some ceremony about to take place. The observers infer what the ceremony is from the ceremonial affiliations of the man and the direction toward which he is headed with his prayer sticks. Two days before the dance the father of the Koyemci is notified by the kiva chief, who takes him a package of meal. He must collect the other Koyemci from farm or sheep camp.

After the prayer sticks are planted the chief work of the wo·we begins. Early the following day he goes around collecting the masks for the dance. "He will take his blanket, and his assistant will go with him to help him. He knows which men of his kiva have masks, and he goes to their houses. He goes to the houses of the men who are going to dance and to others who have masks. If there is any uninitiated person in the house when he comes he will say, 'I have come to get a pumpkin' (mo'le, literally a round object). Then

---

[57] Some kivas plant feathers two days before the dance. My informant did not know which kivas had this custom, but knew the practice varied.

they will know that he has come for a mask. Someone will take a cloth and go into the back room and wrap up the mask and bring it out to him. He will wrap it in his blanket and take it to the kiva. So they go around to all the houses and then they take the masks to the house of the kiva chief. When they have them there they start to paint them. Usually only the two wo·we paint the masks, but sometimes the kiva chief helps. No one else is allowed to paint masks.[58]

"First they take off any feathers or trimmings that are left from the last dance. Then they scrape off all the paint and wash the mask and put it aside for a day to dry. Then they put on a very thin coat of white paint and put it aside to dry again. Then they put on the blue gum paint or the other colored paint. They always do this with prayers. They say, 'Now I am making you into a person. I am making you beautiful with valuable paint so that everyone will have his eyes on you.' They do not pray for the white paint. This is 'cheap paint.'

"After it is dry they rub the mask with balls of yucca fruit to make it shiny. Then they put on the black paint for the eyes. This is the paint that has sirup of yucca fruit to make it shiny. Or if they have bees' honey they use that instead of yucca sirup. They pray with the bees' honey: 'I am using this honey for your flesh. You belong to the south, and you will bring the clouds of the south. And you, bee of the east, you will bring the east wind that comes before the rain. And you, bee of the north, you will be the one to bring the north wind that comes before the rain. And you, bee of the west, you will be the one to bring the rain that comes as soon as day breaks.' They use the honey because the bees come on beautiful days and the children like to catch them. The honey is thick, and they want the rain to come thick and soak the earth. They chew up the honey and spit it out on the masks from their mouths.

"Then they put on the feathers and other trimmings without prayers. The man who is going to wear the mask puts on the feathers, because there are no prayers for the feathers. He furnishes the feathers and clothing."

The men who own masks of suitable shape for the dance that is to be given wear their own masks. The masks have some mark of identification on them. In dances like the mixed dance, where all the masks are different, each man tells the wo'le what character he wishes to impersonate, and, if satisfactory, the wo'le paints the mask accordingly.

"The day before the dance the men go around and borrow the rest of the costume. Each man takes care of his own costume. If he does not know he asks the wo'le what kind of clothing he will need.

---

[58] Many masks observed by the author at various summer and winter dances did not appear to have been freshly painted. Probably they are only repainted when they become very dilapidated.

Finally he goes to his wife or mother and says, 'Bring me some seeds.' Then she gives him two or three kernels of corn of all colors, and all kinds of seeds, and he wraps them in a corn husk.

"When the dancers are getting ready to come in, they first have their hair washed by their wives or sisters. Then they go to the kiva to dress. First they paint the body, then they put on the clothing, then they put on the mask, and last of all they put on their seeds. Before going out of the kiva the man takes the package of seeds he has brought from home and spits on it and says, 'Now you shall be my heart. You shall make me into a Raw Person. You will bring me good luck, for me and for all my people, so that their corn may grow.' Then just as the men are going out of the kiva to dance, the kiva chief goes to the door and takes Paiyatamu medicine into his mouth and spits it out on each man as he goes out of the door."

The winter dance series begins after dark. The men have their hair washed in the afternoon, and go immediately after their evening meal to dress in a house near the one they are using in lieu of a kiva. Often they use an adjoining room. The evening before the kiva chief has taken to the chief of one of the societies a package of corn meal, with the request that his society officiate at their dance. During the afternoon preceding the dance the society chief (or p̄ekwin) sets up the altar of the society in the house of the kiva chief. In the evening the society brings its drum to the house, and a group of singers to furnish music for the katcinas who do not dance to their own songs. At nightfall the headmen of each kiva sacrifice food in the river to the ancients and the katcinas. (They have done this regularly every night since rehearsals began.) For the night dances indoors masks are not required. But if anyone asks that the dance be repeated next day, masks must be worn for the outdoor dancing. Theoretically only the initiated and grown women may see these unmasked dances of the katcinas, but as a matter of fact very young children are permitted to attend.

If the dance belongs to the summer series, on the evening preceding the dance, in the house of the kiva chief, a final rehearsal is held.[59] At about three o'clock in the morning the dancers come out and sing and dance for a short time in each of the four plazas. This is the entrance of the gods into the village. The men wear ordinary clothing and blankets, and are unmasked. No one dare see them at this time lest he die. The high, clear calls of the katcinas, and the loud singing in the still night waken the whole village. After making the rounds of the plazas the dancers retire to the kiva, where they rest for the balance of the night. In the morning they return to their

---

[59] Except the first dance of the season, "koɫuwalawa." They enter the village masked at sundown, dance in all the kivas, and retire to the house of the katcina chief where all night ceremonies are held. Next day they come out at sunrise and dance four times in all the plazas before touching food or drink, unless it rains before that time, in which case they may drink.

homes for breakfast and to have their hair washed. If the hair is to be worn open, after washing it is plaited to make it wavy. Otherwise, if long, it is done up in two plaits which are wound around the neck under the mask.

The hours of the morning are spent in assembling the last odds and ends of clothing. The dancers come out for the first time shortly before noon and dance in all four plazas. They should make the rounds of the plaza four times before retiring for their noonday meal (in the first dance of the season, they actually do), but usually on the last three rounds they dance only in tsia'awa and tehwitołana. On the last round they dance also before the house where the priests are in retreat, and one of the priests comes out and sprinkles each of the dancers with meal, and takes from one of them a branch of spruce. After finishing their morning dancing the men retire to the kiva where food of all kinds is brought by their wives or sisters. Members of the kiva who are not taking part in the dance are privileged to share the meal in the kiva.

The dancers come out again to dance between three and four in the afternoon. This time they dance four times in ts'ia'awa, retiring for short rest periods to the street east of the plaza. The actual visits to the plazas are longer than in the morning. There is a definite sequence of songs and an apportionment of songs between the morning and afternoon sessions, but I was unable to discover the system of sequence. This can not be done until the songs are recorded on the phonograph. The attendance at dances always increases as the afternoon progresses—the morning dances are performed to empty housetops—and the best and newest songs are saved for these hours. There is always a special farewell song for the last appearance of the katcinas in the evening. When muhewa kiva danced Upiɢaiaᵽona in September, 1927, they introduced an innovation in melodic structure and dance step in their farewell song, and each day this song had to be repeated two or three times. (Anyone in the audience may request the repetition of any song, and the dancers must comply.) The dance was performed for eight days "because everyone liked their songs," amid drenching rains and a rotting wheat harvest, and it was undoubtedly this song that was responsible for the popularity. The dance terminated the last day with the appearance of Ololowickä and the grinding ritual.

Theoretically anyone may request the repetition of a dance the following day.[60] Practically this privilege is restricted to priests and society chiefs. " 'Poor people' would be too bashful to ask them to dance again." During the last song the unmasked leader sprinkles meal on the Koyemci. A little later some priest in the audience descends from the housetop to sprinkle meal on the katcinas. He

---

[60] Mrs. Stevenson reports that the summer dances of the Kokokci were never repeated. Katcina dancing is at present an ascendant cult.

repeats a long prayer to the leader of the dancers and to the father of the Koyemci. If he wishes the dance repeated the request is made at this time. Then he sprinkles the line of dancers with meal, taking from some of them their package of seeds, from others twigs or spruce or yucca switches. From the female impersonations he takes their perfect ears of corn. If the dance is to be repeated, the Koyemci Pekwin announces after the dancers have withdrawn from the plaza, "Grandchildren, we shall stay overnight."

The men remove their masks and costumes in the kiva and go to their houses for their evening meal. If the dance is to be repeated they return to the kiva to sleep. Or if they wish to remain at home their wives must bathe their bodies and next morning they must again wash their hair. When the dance is over, next day the wo·we return the masks to their owners, with the formula, "May you have corn, may you have squash, may you be blessed with light" (to' miyatu·. to' mola·tu·. to' tekohanan antiktciatu·). The men return their borrowed clothing and ornaments with a similar blessing.

PATTERNS OF DANCING AND SINGING

Dance patterns, like patterns in mask and costume and music, develop along the line of minor variations on a well-established and fairly restricted form. The principal thing about katcina dances, which is probably of great importance historically, is that they are all line dances, in contrast to unmasked dances which are all circle dances. The form, of course, may be modified by the limitations of the space in which the dance is performed. The line of 90 dancers in the grinding ritual fills more than three sides of the plaza and almost surrounds the central group, but there is no circular movement, and we must view the formation as a group with a line of dancers behind it. The circle dance is the common type throughout North America, and the fact that it is found in the pueblos in their curing and war dances, but never in their katcina dances, is striking.

Except in the large plaza, the line of dancers is always formed against a wall. Where there are female impersonations, they occupy the space nearest to the wall, the male line being nearer to the center of the open space. Certain individual female impersonations, however, such as Koła·hmana, Ahe'a, Komokatsik, dance in the male line, near its head. Tcakwena has a female solo dancer who dances out of line in front. ("Front" is used always to mean the open space away from the wall. Indoors it is nearer the audience. Outdoors, of course, the audience occupies the housetops on all sides.) The leaders of the dance occupy the center places in the male line, the kiva chief being the central figure. He gives the signs for the beginning of songs and holds the song sequence. The female line, which is always shorter than the male, is massed toward the center.

Some dances (Koḳokci) require the presence of a couple, male and female, at the head of the line, who go through certain peculiar motions and have certain esoteric prayers. Only three men know these prayers, and they must be invited to perform for all kivas.

Usually the line forms in definite order before the dancers leave the kiva, and proceeds without change on its round of the plazas. This seems to be the rule for all the traditional dances. Where there is a double line the two lines enter simultaneously. The line is always led by an unmasked leader who "makes their road," scattering prayer meal before the line of dancers. He takes up his place nearest the point of exit. In the dance plaza this is on the eastern side of the plaza, near the southeast exit. In houses, the leader walks the full length of the room, from door to altar, and turns and takes his place opposite the door. The spectators always occupy the side of the room near the door. This is not the "valuable" place. The door of a Zuñi house is always placed at a corner, generally on the long side of the room. The end of the room farthest from the door is occupied by the altar, the side of the room opposite the door is left free for dancing. The space between the dancers and the door is always packed solid with spectators, who courteously part to let the dancers through. As soon as the first dancer reaches his place he starts to dance, each man picking up the step as the line closes up and straightens out. By the time the last dancers reach their place the rhythm of the dance is well established. After the songs are finished the dancers leave the dance place in the same order in which they entered.

Certain dance groups, especially the newer dances, vary this pattern and break their ranks in going from one plaza to another or even between songs. Hilili, for instance, break rank as soon as the song ends, the dancers running around the plaza until they are summoned by their leader for another song. Kumance have special entrance and exit songs, in different rhythm from the dance songs, which they sing on going from one dance place to another. The dance is a progress from the kiva through the streets and back again into the kiva. The procession pauses at certain points on its route to dance. In counting up the day's program of dances the number of times the group comes out of its kiva is counted. The number of pauses on each circuit is irrelevant.

The usual dance step is a vigorous stamping with the right foot (to which is usually attached a turtle-shell rattle or a string of sleigh-bells to mark the rhythm. On alternate beats the heel of the left foot is slightly raised. In some of the more vigorous of the young men's dances (kumance, hilili, etc.) both feet are raised alternately, with a kind of prancing step. This is much more exhausting, and is used for the most part by dancers who have choruses to sing for them.

Kumance, however, employs this step, and the men also must do their own singing.   This is the dance step that is used by all the impersonators of the katcina priests when they dance in their Ca'lako houses, to the music of society choirs.   It is also used by society members during the dances of their winter retreat, when they have a choir of the society to sing for them.   It is used by Łewe·kwe when they dance in their house (with a separate choir) but not when they appear in the plaza, and the whole society sings and dances.   For this they use a slow, easy step, the dance movement being a circular movement of the whole group of dancers.

KoꞰokci dance shoulder to shoulder, with their backs to the audience, making quarter turns to the right between songs.   The female line stands behind the male line, facing them, and turns with them. UpiꞰaiaꝑona face either right or left, turning frequently, the movement flowing continuously from one end of the line to the other.   The turn is always away from the audience.   The Drum Tcakwena use the same step, using with it a characteristic bent posture.   T͡owa Tcakwena uses the same step, emphasizing the turn with characteristic arm movements.   Muluktakä dance facing back, making a full turn between songs.   Wo·temła face sidewise but do not turn.   Hemuci·kwe and Hilili were the only groups which I saw face the audience while they danced (except UpiꞰaiaꝑonÄ in the two grinding songs for OlolowicꞰä). Solo dancers usually use the same step as the dancers in the line. Sometimes, however, they use a more vigorous step and move back and forth in front of the line.   Certain solo dancers have characteristic movements.   Hehe'a and HemokätsiꞰ always dance out of step.

The rhythm of the dance is always a simple two-part rhythm. Where a drum is used the drum rhythm and the dance rhythm coincide.   The rhythms of the songs are more complex, but have not yet been analyzed.   Mr. Herzog has recorded a number of dance songs, but his analysis of the correspondence between drum, dance, and voice rhythms is not yet complete.   As the song nears its close there is usually a ritard which ends in a skipped beat.   The song stops, the dancers stand for an instant with foot poised, and the song finally closes in very rapid time.[61]

The song is divided into a number of named sections, each with its characteristic melodic features, with a system of repeats so complicated that I have not yet been able to fathom it, although it seems clear enough to the singers.   Once they are started on the proper song of sequence by their leader, the balance follows without any confusion.

It might be well to point out the limitations of Zuñi dancing.   The formation of the dance is restricted to straight lines.   There are no

---

[61] The same device, without the final acceleration, is characteristic of grinding songs, but I did not notice it in the dance songs of the medicine societies.   It is a very marked characteristic of Hopi katcina songs.

elaborate dance figures, no interweaving of dancers, no use of grouping as an esthetic feature. It is all dancing in place. The group itself does not have movement. Bodily movements are restricted to movements of the feet and some slight use of gesture with the arms. There is no running or leaping, no high, deep, or wide movements, and no posturing with the body. The dance at Zuñi is not an independent art, and does not use the essential choregraphic technique, which is a dynamic handling of spatial relations. The dance at Zuñi is entirely subsidiary to music and is employed merely to emphasize it.

Yet it would be a great mistake to infer that Zuñi dancing is tedious or lacking in emotional appeal. The precision of movement, the regularity of rhythm, the invariability of the form, combined with beautiful and subtle musical patterns, is intensely moving. The monotony and impersonality and the complete and intense absorption of the participants have a hypnotic effect on the spectator. According to Zuñi ideology, the dance is compulsive magic. The supernaturals are constrained by the use of their corporeal substance, i. e., the mask. They must come with all their attributes, including rain. No one can watch a Zuñi dance for a half hour or more without being moved by the compulsive force that lies behind the esthetic form.

DISTRIBUTION OF KATCINA DANCING

Katcina dances are performed in all the pueblos except Taos, where, up to the present, no trace of the cult has been found. It has developed luxuriantly at Zuñi and among the Hopi. In both places it is the cult which controls the most spectacular rituals, which draws upon the widest base, and makes the greatest popular appeal. Although no single ceremonial occasion among the Hopi commands quite as much attention as the snake dance, the katcina cult has two major ceremonies (Powamû and Niman) and an unlimited number of minor festivities, and its activities hold the center of the stage throughout the winter and spring months. At Zuñi, although the winter solstice ceremonies form the keystone of the ceremonial system, the point of greatest intensity is unquestionably the Ca'lako ceremony, the culminating ceremony of the Katcina Society. Katcina ceremonies are public, spectacular, and popular.

Among the eastern and western Keres, katcina impersonation is a well-developed esoteric cult. Unfortunately masked ceremonies may not now be seen by whites in any of the eastern pueblos, and great reluctance is felt about imparting any information about katcinas. The Keresan cult seems to have the same types of katcinas found farther west: The dancing katcinas, rain and cloud beings, who are controlled through impersonation in dances "to call the rain," and "dangerous" supernaturals impersonated in mask at important ceremonies such as initiations, solstices, etc. Many of the individual impersonations are the same as those found farther west. We may conclude that although less exuberant, the Keresan katcina cult is about the same as that of Zuñi in ideology, technique, and ceremonial patterning.[62] However, it does not overshadow other activities, as is the case at Zuñi.

Unfortunately, our information concerning katcina impersonation in the Tanoan pueblos is fragmentary and very unsatisfactory. The Tewa are secretive in all things and especially secretive concerning katcinas. Doctor Parsons [63] attributes this secrecy to the proximity of Mexicans, who everywhere are barred from katcina ceremonies. Its very existence has been repeatedly denied and long was in doubt. There is no single eye-witness description of any masked ceremony; no comprehensive account of the ideology ritual and organization of the cult; no information upon which to base an opinion of the rôle of the katcina cult in communal or individual life. Whatever the cause may be, such extreme secrecy is incompatible with the full flowering of the cult. From what slight information we have, the cult in all Tanoan villages appears meager and rudimentary. Various theories are offered in explanation of the different patterning of the same material in different villages. It has been suggested that the katcina cult is of western origin and never took deep root in the east; and, conversely, in the east it has been crowded out by church worship while it continued to flourish in the west, where Catholic influence was less strong. Either or both may be true in the absence of any conclusive evidence.

The general type of mask and costume is similar for all villages, and certain special impersonations are found under similar or different names in different pueblos. Wherever this has been observed it has been noted in the following remarks on individual katcinas. However, these facts of special distributions baldly stated do not seem particularly significant. It seems to the present writer significant that something resembling Zuñi Koƙɔ·kci is danced in every pueblo from which we have data, but it also seems quite insignificant that a dance generally called nawic, but at Zuñi called Nahalico (there is another different mask called Nawico), also has a wide distribution. The characteristic face painting of this katcina in connection with a headdress of four turkey wing feathers has been spread all over the region. The dance has no particular character at Zuñi. I have not actually seen it nor read descriptions of it elsewhere, and therefore its distribution must remain one of those quaint facts of wide dissemination of apparently trivial and fortuitous details.

Very little credence should be given to native accounts of provenience of specific features, when these accounts deal with events outside

[62] The katcina cult of Keresan villages has been described for Cochiti by Dumarest (Notes on Cochiti) and Goldfrank (Social and Ceremonial Organization of Cochiti); for Laguna by Parsons, for Acoma and San Felipe by White (mss).

[63] Social Organization and the Tewa, p. 150.

memory of living men. The Zuñis claim to have borrowed one of their Tcakwena dances from Laguna (see p. 1022). However, at Laguna it is claimed that the Tcakwena dance is of Zuñi provenience.[64] The same is true also of other dances: Hilili, which the Hopi claim was recently introduced from Zuñi, and to which the Zuñi, on the other hand, attribute a Hopi origin. Unquestionably there is a great deal of intertribal borrowing of ceremonial details and of whole dances. It seems to go in all directions. I have myself been present when Hopis from various villages and a visitor from San Felipe were comparing ceremonies and swapping katcina songs. The San Felipe man was learning the songs for the katcina corn grinding, a ceremony which interested him greatly. In return he was teaching his Hopi friends the Keresan words of a Shiwana song. Neither spoke the language of the other. The explanations and translations were in English. It is always interesting to catch a bit of culture at the moment of transfer; in this case, the casual way in which sacred information is passed about is instructive. It shows the fluidity of detail under the rigid pattern, which becomes more and more striking the more we learn of variants in pueblo culture.

In general, we may say that most of the group dances which occupy fixed and important places in the Zuñi calendar—Koḱokci, Upiḱaia-p̣ona, Tcakwena, Wotemła, Hemucikwe, Muluktaḵä—are found in other pueblos, while the occasional dances are more local in distribution. We may conclude, therefore, that these fixed dances are more ancient—which might have been guessed in the first place.

The problem is, perhaps, not a historic one at all but rather one of esthetics. There is a style of religious behavior common to the pueblo peoples; all, furthermore, utilize the same religious material, the same paraphernalia, the same techniques for controlling the supernatural. The varied adjustments of the material in conformity to the ritual style is analogous to similar problems in decorative art—the individual reworking and recombining decorative motives within the narrow limits of a tribal style.

Considered from the standpoint of any large problems of the history of human civilization, the pueblos form a small unit, and the slight differences of patterning among them vanish in the face of the great differences between the pueblos and, say, the rest of North America.

The fundamental and striking traits of the katcina cult, common to all pueblos, to the best of our knowledge, are five: The existence of a large group of supernaturals who live in a lake and are identified with clouds and rain, and, surely at Zuñi and Cochiti, and possibly elsewhere, with the dead; the impersonation of these supernaturals by means of masks in a series of spectacular group dances "to call the

---

[64] Parsons: Notes on Ceremonialism at Laguna.

rain," and at a number of secret ceremonies designed to perpetuate the cult, and to serve other special purposes; the initiation of all adult males "to know the katcinas," and the use of whipping by fear inspiring katcinas at the ceremony of initiation; [65] the enormous sanctity of the masks, which can cause death to a negligent wearer, which must always be handled with the greatest reverence, and which must never be seen by Mexicans (in the east by whites); the complete identification with the supernatural through wearing these masks. The rest of the katcina ritual, such as the use of corn meal, prayer sticks, prayer feathers and altars, singing and dancing, retreats before dances, sexual continence, etc., are common to all pueblo ceremonial.

Impersonation of supernaturals is a religious technique world-wide in distribution. The two most common methods of impersonation are by animal heads and pelts, and by masks, but impersonation by means of body paint, elaborate costume and headdress, or the wearing of sacred symbols is by no means uncommon. In the pueblos, where magical power is imputed to impersonation, all techniques are employed. Outside of masking, the most striking impersonation is the symbolic representation of the bear, described on page 531. The use of masks is distributed over the whole world. Masks were used in dramatic representations in medieval Europe and classical Greece. They are used similarly in many parts of Asia, especially in India, Ceylon, Java, China, and Mongolian Asia. In Melanesia [66] and West Africa masks are used to inspire awe in connection with tribal initiations. The uninitiated believe they are being visited by supernaturals, there are long periods of retreat for the novices and the elders before the public appearance of the masked beings, and in many other ways the ideology of the cult in both regions is similar to that of the pueblos. The appearance of the same complex of associated ideas in three widely remote areas is one of the most striking cases of parallelism.

In North America there are several regions where masks are used, among the Iroquois, on the northwest coast, and in the pueblos. Some animal impersonation is found on the Plains. [68] The use of masks was highly developed in middle America since Maya times, and was very conspicuous in Aztec ritual, together with the curious custom, which is probably unique with them, of dancing in the flayed skin of sacrificial victims.

What seems peculiar to the pueblos is the enormous fetishistic power imputed to the mask, which compels the presence of the gods as rain, and which exposes the wearer to dangers from which he must

---

[65] Among the Hopi, although only members of certain clans can belong to the Pawamû Society that "owns" the katcina cult, and participate in the esoteric ceremonies and retreats of Powamû and Minan, all boys are whipped to know the katcinas and can thereafter participate in public katcina dances.

[66] Codrington, The Melanesians.

[68] Parsons: Spanish Elements in Pueblo Katcina Cult (ms.).

Masks Appearing at the Initiation, Fig. c (See Plate 28)

Masks Appearing at the Initiation, Fig. a (See Plate 31)

guard himself ritualistically. Moreover, there seems to be no other place in which the personality of the wearer is so completely absorbed.

It has already been pointed out that impersonation extending over a period of time is found among the ancient Aztecs. The youth chosen as a sacrifice to Tezcatlipoca impersonates the god for 20 days, and during this period lives in honor and is finally sacrificed, and thus united with the god on the last day, and his flesh is eaten in communion by the priests and populace. We have already suggested the possible relation of katcina dancing to human sacrifices (p. 846) and to the fertility cults of ancient Mexico.

Doctor Parsons has made a good case [69] for the influence of the Catholic missionaries on the development of katcina ritual. When one surveys the enormous amount of concrete details that she amasses in proof of her point that katcina dancing is an adaptation of religious dancing of Spain, one must be convinced of the readiness of the pueblos to incorporate Catholic ceremonial into their own ritual. One is struck, too, at the enormous impetus which contact with the Catholics gave to the growth of the cult in those villages where it could develop unhampered by the church. As pointed out by Doctor Parsons, the cult reached its greatest exuberance in villages where Catholic contacts were brief and superficial. But that the larger patterns or the underlying concepts are of European origin seems more doubtful. Communications with the supernatural through impersonation, the use of masks in spectacular ceremonies for rain, fertility, and healing are widely distributed in aboriginal America, and many of the most striking features of the cult flourished in pre-Columbian Mexico. The underlying ideas of the fertilization of the earth are part of the general North American Indian background.

---

[69] Spanish Elements in the Katcina Cult of the Pueblos.

PART II. SOURCE MATERIAL FOR THE STUDY OF ZUÑI KATCINAS

LIST OF KNOWN ZUÑI KATCINAS

Katcina priests:
  Katcinas appearing at the winter solstice.
    *1. Pautiwa.
    *2. Saiyaɫi'a (four).
    *3. Citsuka.
    *4. Kwelele.
  Katcinas appearing after the winter solstice.
    *5. Tcakwena oḵa.
    *6. Natacku.
    *7. Atocle (Suyuki).
       Also Sälimoβiya.
  The Koyemci
    *8. A·wan tatcu.
    *9. A·wan pekwin.
    *10. A·wan pi'ɫaciwani.
    *11. Muyap'ona.
    *12. Ecotsi.
    *13. Naɫaci.
    *14. Itsepaca.
    *15. Posuki.
    *16. Ḵälutsi.
    *17. T͡s'alaci.
  Katcinas appearing at the coming of the gods (Ca'lako).
    *18. Cula·witsi.
    *19. Saiyataca.
    *20. Hu·tutu.
    *21. Yamuhakto (two).
       Also two Sälimoβiya (see below).
    *22. Ca'lako.
  Katcinas appearing at the preliminary initiation of little boys
    *23. Ḵäklo.
    *24. Hemoḵätsi or Ahe'a (not an old mask).
    25–30. Sälimopiya, as follows—
       *Ɫuptsin'ona (yellow; two).
       *Ɫi'an'ona (blue; two).
       *Cilow'ona (red; two).
       *Ḵohan'ona (white; two).
       *Itapanahn'ona (many colored; two).
       *Ciḵän'ona (black; two).
    *26. Ɫelacoktiβona (two).
    *27. Nawico (two).
    *28. Anahoho (two).
    *29. Cula·witsi (one).
    *30. Uβ'o'yona (two).
  Katcinas appearing at the preliminary and final initiation of boys—
    *36. Saiyaɫi'a (four).

Katcina priests—Continued.

    Punitive and exorcising katcinas—

        *37. Hainawi.

        38. Homatci.

        *39. Temtemci.

        *40. A·hute.

           Also Saiyaɫia.

    Other old masks—

        *41. Ḳäna·kwe, a large dance group consisting of several leaders and
            an indefinite number of other dancers.

        *41a. Koɫa·hmana.

        *42. Ololowicka.

Dancing katcinas:

    Traditional dances performed in regular summer and winter series—

        Koḳokci—

           *43. Koḳokci.

           *42. Koḳwe'le.

           *44. Siwuluhsietsa or Komoḳatsik (sometimes with Koḳokci).
              Also sometimes Koɫa·hmana (No. 41, a), Ahe'a (No. 24) Ḳänatcu
              (No. 84), Uꝑo'yona (No. 30).

           *46. Upiḳaiap'ona.
               With him also Koḳwe'le, and other single masks, as above.

           47. Hekcina Cilowa.
               With them also Koḳwe'le, and other single masks.   With the
                 grinding ritual, the following:

              *48. Paiyatamu.

              *49. Oḳen'ona.

              *50. Hehe'a.
                 Also Ololowicka (see above).

         *51. T̂owa Tcakwena.   With them as solo dancers.

           *52. T̂om'inaꝑa.

           *53. T̂cilili.

           *54. We'wap.

           55. Hupomo'otca.

           56. Moḳaiaꝑona.
             Also Tcakwena oḳa.

        *57. Tcahumoawa (drum tcakwena; also called short-haired or
            Laguna tcakwena).   With them as solo dancers:

           *58. Hatacuku (several).

           59. Tsi ḳohan'ona.

Wo'temɫa or mixed dance.   Representatives from among the following:

        *60. Kukuculi (leader of the mixed dance).

        *61. Ḳälawan·i.

        *62. Aince koko (two variants).

        *63. La'saiyaꝑona.

        *64. Tsupianawe.

        *65. Suyuki (not the same as Atocle).

        *66. Ma'loḳätsik (salt woman).

        *67. Ohapa (bee).

        *68. Tecamiḳa (echo).

        *69. Ya'ana.

        *70. Na'le (deer).

        *71. Hetsilulu.

        *72. Icana Ts'an A·tci.

        *73. Wo'latana.

Dancing katcinas—Continued.
    Wo'temła or mixed dance—Continued.
        *74. Mokwala.
        *75. Wahaha.
            Also: Uβo'yona (No. 30), Hainawi (No. 37), Homatci (No. 38),
                Temtemci (No. 39), Ahute (No. 40), Käna·kwe (No. 41),'Ahe'a
                (No. 24), Komokatsik[1] (No. 44), Känatcu (No. 84), Hehe'a
                (No. 50), Waḵaci (No. 91), and many others not identified.
    Group dances regularly performed after Ca'lako:
        *76. Mahetinaca (discontinued about 1915).   With him as solo dancer
            came—
            *77. Ho'wiwi.
        *78. Hemucikwe.   With him as solo dancers come any of the following—
            *78. Nahalic oḵa.
            *79. Ḵänil'ona.
            80.
                Also Mitotaca (No. 114).
        *81. Muluktaḵä.
        Also Tcakwena (Nos. 57–59), Towa Tcakwena (Nos. 51–56), and
            Wotemła (Nos. 60–75).
    Group dances performed in connection with regular winter dances, and
    irregularly, as desired.   Mostly of recent introduction.
        *82. Nahalico.   With them as solo dancer.
        *83. Nahalic a·wan mosona.
        *84. Ḵänatcu.
        *85. Wamuwe.
        *86. Hilili.   With them as solo dancers:
            *87. Ḵäḵäli (eagle) two.   And as singers:
            *88. Tcałaci.
            89. Tenenakwe (about eight or more).
        *90. Pasiḵäβona.
        *91. Waḵäci.
        *92. Mu·kwe, with—
            *93. Mu'kwe oḵä.
        *94. Kwamumu, with—
            *95. Kwamumu oḵä.
        *96. Wilatsukwe, with—
            *97. Wilatsukw oka.
    Sioux or buffalo dance
        *98. La'pila we, and as solo dancers:
            *99. Siwolo (buffalo).
            *100. A'łana.
            *101. Ainanuwa.
        *102. Kumance, and as solo dancers.
            *103. Kumance Penakwe.
            *104. Drummer.
    The "Little dancers," isolated impersonations, usually by little boys, in
    connection with winter dances.   They do not come in dance formation.
    They do not ordinarily wear old masks.
        *105. Itetsona.
        *106. Natcimono.
            Also, Hehe'a (No. 50), Nahalico (No. 82), Sälimoβiya, Lelacok-
                tiβona (No. 26), Uβo·yona (No. 30), Nawico (No. 27),
                Cula·witsi (No. 29) (all colors), Hatacuku (No. 58), etc.

Miscellaneous:
　　*107. Nepaiyatamu (a burlesque of the Ne·we·kwe, in mask).
　　　　Navaho dance (not sacred)—
　　　　　　*108. Yebitcai (solo dancer).
　　　　　　*109. Pakoko with
　　　　　　*110. Pakok oka.
Society masks (not, strictly speaking, koko):
　　*111. Cumaikoli (belonging to Cuma·kwe).
　　*112. Saiyaɫi (belonging to Cuma·kwe).
　　　　Masks of Ne'we·kwe:
　　　　　　*113. A·wan koko ɫana.
　　　　　　*114. Mitotaca.
　　　　Masks of Great Fire Society:
　　　　　　115. A·wan koko ɫana.
　　　　　　　Also Citsuḵä (No. 3) and Kwelele (No. 4).

THE WINTER SOLSTICE [1]

Ƥautiwa

(Plate 21, *a*)

Costume.—On his head he wears feathers from the breast of the macaw (lacowan ɫuptsina). Standing upright behind eight tail feathers of the macaw bound to a little stick with native cotton cord, with the fastenings covered with downy feathers from the breast of the eagle, the whole called lapaƥoan·e. A single feather from the tail of the eagle sticks out behind. The top of the mask is covered with black hair. The face is painted turquoise, with black painting about the eyes, like the Sälimoƥiya. This painting is called lomuloktan·e tunaƥa "cloud oblong eyed." "It is like the fine clouds that appear just before the sun rises." The large ears are made of flexible twigs, covered with black hair. "He has large ears with holes in them so that he can hear everything his people ask for. If anyone has very sharp ears and hears something that is just whispered in the next room we say of him, 'You are a regular Ƥautiwa.'" He has a projecting snout (oton·e); fox-skin collar.

He is fully clothed in white. He wears a white shirt. This is of cotton, but in former days it was of fringed buckskin. He wears a dancer's kilt with a blue band, embroidered sash, red woven belt, fringed buckskin leggings, blue moccasins, black yarn about both legs, fox skin. "He wears two embroidered robes (mihe·we), one on top of the other, because he is bringing good luck and he wants his people to have plenty of fine clothing. He wears many necklaces of shell and turquoise, both back and front, and on his wrists, because he is a valuable dancer."

When he comes at the new year he carries in his right hand a twig with a bluejay feather tied to it (ɫatsiton·e). The twig is from the

---

[1] For description of the winter solstice see p. 534.

shrub puɫi, which is used by the priests for their prayer sticks. In his left hand he carries the six teɫna·we, the crooks of appointment for the six Ca'lako and their houses, and many prayer sticks. Each teɫna·we consists of one long and two short sticks wrapped together in a corn husk, and the six teɫna·we are tied one over the other. He leaves one on the roof of each kiva.

When he comes after Ca'lako to bring in the Corn Maids, he carries in his right hand a long staff with feathers at the base, in the left a gourd of water "to bring rain in summer," many prayer sticks, and a tiny basket filled with white meal.

Pautiwa's mask is kept in the house of the chief priesthood (Dogwood clan), along with the masks of Upo'yona, the black Sälimopiya, and a Ca'lako (K. 161).

Pautiwa is one of the most impressive of Zuñi impersonations. If possible a tall man of stately bearing is chosen for the part. He wears rich and tasteful clothing and a profusion of feathers and ornaments. All his movements are measured and stately. When he enters the plaza in the midst of the hilarious dancing of Citsuka and Kwelele at the winter solstice the whole atmosphere of the ceremony changes.

In mythology Pautiwa is represented at komosona of the village of the katcinas. It is he who always receives and welcomes visitors and hears their requests. He makes up the calendar of katcina ceremonies. No katcina may come to Zuñi unless Pautiwa sends him. Therefore it is Pautiwa who brings to Zuñi crooks (teɫnawe) of appointment for the principal participants in all major ceremonies to be held during the coming year. The teɫnawe for Saiyataca, the Koyemci, Ḳäklo and the Ḳana·kwe, if they are to come, are taken by the Pautiwa to the kiva the evening before the new year, and handed out the following morning; those for the Ca'lako are left on the kiva roofs the following evening.

In folk tales Pautiwa displays the most honored of Zuñi virtues, dignity, kindliness and generosity and also beauty. He has many love affairs with mortal maids, whom he rewards richly, and he is unfailingly generous to his mortal children. In tales it is always to Pautiwa that the Zuñis appeal when in trouble.

Ceremonies.—Pautiwa comes three times during the winter. He comes to "make the New Year," to bring in the Corn Maids after Ca'lako, and he comes during the solstice, four days before the new year. "Pautiwa never dances when he comes. Sometimes he sends his son, Upo'yona, to dance in the mixed dance or during ko-'uptcunawa.

"When he comes during it·iwan·a he is called Komhaɫikwi, 'katcina witch,' because he comes late at night when no one can see him.

"On the morning of the fifth day of it·iwan·a [2] the people of the Corn clan all go to the house next to muhewa kiva. Here the women grind corn of all colors. Each person grinds a little, as fine as wheat flour. They make it into balls, and it must be ground so fine that the balls will not break when they are thrown down. They test it, and when it is fine enough they put the balls in a basket. Then they cook for the people who are coming in the evening.

"In the evening the Corn clan men choose someone for Pautiwa. On this occasion he must be Corn clan or child of Corn. The Corn clan man takes the basket of fine meal and goes to meet the impersonator of Pautiwa at Wide River. In all the kivas the men have built fires and are waiting for Pautiwa. He comes very late, about 2 or 3 o'clock. Only the head men of the kivas wait for him; sometimes only one man will wait for him alone in the kiva. When Pautiwa comes he goes first to tcupawa kiva. He climbs up to the roof quietly and throws a ball of corn meal down into the kiva. Then he goes away quickly and goes to muhewa and does the same. Then he goes to ohewa, uptsanawa and heiwa, and last of all to hekapawa. Then he goes home to Wide River. No one sees him when he comes. [3]

"After he has gone the head men of each kiva take the ball of flour and divide it among all who are there. They all inhale from the meal and say, 'Now he has brought in to us the warm breath of summer, so that we may have good crops.' So they say and breathe the blessing from the corn meal. The Ca'lako wo'le takes his portion of the meal and wraps it in a corn husk and takes it home and puts it aside. Then if they are afraid of early frosts in summer, the Ca'lako personator will use this meal to pray with when he plants his prayers sticks or prays in the morning. The wo'le keeps this meal for the two Ca'lako personators from his kiva. Saiyataca is not chosen from any special kiva, and so no one saves corn meal for him, but his wife must cook sweet corn for him and grind it for him to pray for the warm days."

On the sixth day of the fire taboo the members of the Pautiwa cult, men of the Dogwood clan or children of the clan who have impersonated Pautiwa on previous occasions, meet in a house of the Dogwood clan to select the impersonator for the coming ceremony. They choose one of their own number, or an outsider of suitable clan affiliation and unquestionable character. Dogwood clan and child of Dogwood serve in alternate years. The impersonator is notified that evening by an "old man" (cult head?) of the Dogwood clan, who goes to the appointee's house with corn meal. Long prayers are recited on this occasion. If the man serves for the first time, he must learn his complicated ritual, including long prayers, "from some old man

---

[2] See the calendar of the winter solstice, p. 534.

[3] The impersonator wears ordinary clothing, and is wrapped in a blanket pulled over his head. Because it is dangerous to look at him on this occasion (he is komhalikwi), it was impossible to learn whether or not he is masked, but probably he is not masked.

who knows how." All members of the cult (other less reliable information, all men of Dogwood clan) cut prayer sticks for Pautiwa on the ninth day of the solstice. These he brings to the kiva that evening and plants sometime the following day

Before sunset on the ninth day of the solstice the mask of Pautiwa is taken, with the masks of the Saiyaɫi'a, to he'iwa kiva. The Pautiwa mask is probably called for in the house in which it is kept by a group of men of the Sun clan. However, precise information on this point is lacking. These men are present in the kiva all night to "take care of Pautiwa." Just before sunset pekwin or one of the bow priests (pekwin brought him in 1928, although this is a duty of the bow priests) call for the impersonator at his house and take him to the kiva. He brings with him the teɫnawe to be given the impersonators of the katcina priests the following morning. The impersonator of Pautiwa remains in the kiva all night, but he does not dance. At dawn he is dressed by the men of the Sun clan, and accompanies the other gods when they take the fire out to the east. When they return to the kiva he dances in mask for a short time. His big ceremony is in the afternoon.

"When Pautiwa comes to make the New Year he comes from Sand Hill in the afternoon and goes around the village. He goes around the outside of the village, coming in closer to the houses each time. He walks right into the river, without paying any attention to his valuable clothes. The water may come up to his knees or his waist, but he will not get wet. They say he goes around the houses four times, coming closer each time. When he comes to Sunshine Place on the south side of the village he goes to a certain house where there is a hole in the wall. The man who takes care of this place takes out the slab that covers the front when he sees Pautiwa coming, and Pautiwa puts his face close up against the wall and looks in. Inside are his 'babies' (wihe·tsana), and Pautiwa looks at them to see how the year will be. If the babies have fallen down it means that the people will have bad luck with sickness during the coming year. He also looks for signs of seeds and corn and water. As soon as he leaves the man who takes care of the place replaces the slab and covers it over with plaster. No one sees what is inside but Pautiwa. There are four such places in the village, on the four sides. They are called wihepawa. There are three or four 'images' in each of these holes.

"After he has finished going around the village he goes to he'iwa kiva. Citsuka and Kwelele are dancing on the roof. As soon as they see Pautiwa coming they go inside, and inside the Great Fire Society start their song for Pautiwa. They always sing for Pautiwa. Citsuka married Pautiwa's daughter. They sing 'tecolani telulani Pautiwa.'[4] As they sing this, Pautiwa, who has come up on the roof

---

[4] The song leader of the Great Fire Society, when asked the meaning of this song, quoted the beautiful passage in the firekeeper's prayer (p. 640) describing winter. The song has been recorded by Mr. Georg Herzog.

of the kiva, throws into the hatchway the twig he is carrying in his right hand. Then those below throw up corn meal and shout. He kneels down facing the east and puts down one crook for he'iwa Ca'lako, and prays. He picks up the stick which the people inside have thrown up, and waves it around to take away all the bad luck. Then p̌ekwin comes out with a bowl of corn meal, and Citsuka and Kwelele come with him. They are going with P̌autiwa to the village of the katcinas.[5] P̌autiwa goes down first, then p̌ekwin, then Citsuka, and Kwelele. They go down and go to Uptsanawa kiva [6] and P̌autiwa leaves a crook there. They go to all the kivas, and then go out to Wide River, going home. P̌autiwa has brought the New Year when he brought the crooks.

"When he goes to Wide River he takes off his mask. Here men of the Sun clan are waiting for him. He takes off his mask and comes back.[7] He goes directly to the house of the village chief. Here are gathered all the priests, and men of the Dogwood clan, and all the important men of the village. When P̌autiwa comes in they all greet him and say, 'Have you come? Be seated.' Then he sits down. The village chief makes a cigarette and smokes to all directions and they pray. Then he says, 'Now tell us what happened to you when you went to see your babies.'[8] If anything was wrong P̌autiwa will bow his head and say nothing, and then he will say, 'The babies were lying down wherever I went. That is bad, but let us hope that it may not be true. We must all pray that it may not come true.' Or he will say, 'There was a mark of bow and arrow,' and that means that there will be war. Or if he sees tracks coming toward him, that means good luck; and if he has seen green things growing, he is always glad, and he says, 'Fathers, clean your houses and hope for good crops. They have let me see green things wherever I went. Beautiful things were growing everywhere. I know that we shall have a good year.' If he sees anything nice he is always happy and tells the people. Last year (1925) he told the people that he saw rivers coming toward him, but they were all dry rivers, and, indeed, we had no snow all winter, and the rain came late in summer. So it always comes true.

"After he has told the people this, his aunts (father's sisters) come to get him. They take him to their house, and the Dogwood people are all there. They wash his head, and so his part is over."

Corrections and additions to the above account.—P̌autiwa goes out to Sand Hill about noon. Here he is dressed by certain men of the Sun clan. He approaches the village in mid afternoon. He encircles the village four times in narrowing circles. On the third circuit he plants

---

[5] See Citsuka's myth, p. 925.

[6] See, however, p. 913 for order of visiting the kivas.

[7] Probably he plants the prayer sticks given him by Dogwood men at this time.

[8] The prayer that precedes P̌autiwa's reply is given in text on p. 693.

prayer sticks in permanent excavations on the outskirts of the village, as follows: In a field to the north, near the old well; in a field to the west, near the house of Nastacio; in the bed of the river, south of Sunshine Place. There was probably a planting in a field to the east, but this was not observed. If there was such a planting, it preceded the planting to the north. After leaving the river bed, he goes to look at his "babies." These shrines are visited as follows: Pałtowa (east), Sop'iyahnawa (north), He·kapawa (west), Tek̯älnawa (south). (This was not observed.) He enters the village from the west. As soon as he enters the plaza the dancing stops. If Citsulk̯ä and Kwelele still have things left, they throw them quickly to the people. He marks the hatchway of the kiva with four lines of corn meal. The kivas are visited in the following order: He'iwa, hek̯äpawa, tcupawa, muhewa ohewa, upts'anawa. The balance of the account is substantially correct. (Observed 1928, 1929. R. L. B.)

"When P̓autiwa comes after Ca'lako to bring in the corn maids he is called mola·kwatok̯ä or a·t̓owakwatok̯ä.[9] On this occasion he must be Mustard (aiyohokwe) clan or child of Mustard. He is chosen by the Mustard people, but he wears the same mask. He brings in the Corn Maids on the last day of Ca'lako, after all the katcinas have left to go to the east.[10]

"The kiva chiefs pick out the men to impersonate the Corn Maids during the night or on the morning of ko'ane (the gods depart, see p. 945). There should be four from each kiva. Their ceremonial fathers must help them dress and furnish their clothing. The young men who are to impersonate the Corn Maids wash their hair and braid it so that it will be wavy. Then his father's wife or sister brushes his hair.

"In the afternoon after the katcinas have gone to the east each man who is going to help bring in the Corn Maids goes out with his wife and a young girl to run for the boy. The wife takes a brush with her, and the little girl carries a water gourd, or a few straws from a broom stuck in her belt so as to run fast. Then when the men have all their things ready they go to Where-the-pumpkin-stands. The girls do not go so far, but stay at Red Earth. The man and the woman take the young man to where the P̓autiwa mask is staying.[10] At Red Earth are many girls who are going to run for the boys, and a man from the Mustard clan goes there to start them off. When the girls are all there he will count them to see that there is one girl for each young man. When they are all there he says to them, 'Now, all the katcinas have gone. Now watch me. I am going a little way off to the east and you must watch me. When I give you the signal

<hr>

[9] For description of the ceremony, see Stevenson, p. 277, and Parsons, Journal of American Folk-Lore, 29:392, see also Plate 60 for Bitsitsi.

[10] At Ko'ane every man takes his own mask to Where-the-pumpkin-stands and after depositing sticks brings it back. The P̓autiwa mask, however, is left out in the field until evening.

you will start to run.' Then he lines up the girls facing the east and goes a little way to the east. Then he prays and says, 'Now these corn maids will run. Whoever comes first to Pautiwa will be the first one to come in to Itiwana.' So he says. The girls all watch him and as soon as he throws up the meal they start to run. Whoever leads will stop when she gets right behind Pautiwa and then all the others must stop right where they are. Then they count them off, and each young man will take the place of the girl who has run for him. Then they get ready. The Corn Maids do not wear masks. They paint their faces black and yellow and they wear bright ribbons on their sleeves and shoulders. After they are all dressed Bitsitsi comes and Pautiwa gets up and they bring in the Corn Maids in the evening."

The following myth is told in explanation of the ceremony of the Corn Maids.

The Corn Maids

Long ago, the people were starving. The Corn Maids had run away because the people were careless about corn. So the Corn Maids ran away and went to the village of the masked gods. The people played with corn bread and threw it away, and they threw the corn into the corn rooms any way. They did not pile it up carefully the way we do now. So Yellow Corn Maid went to all the houses in the night and told the Corn Maids to come with her. They said, "All right, we shall go." They did not know where to go. Pautiwa in the village of the katcinas heard it and he said to the Yellow Corn, "I have heard that you have decided to run away and that you do not know where to go. I do not want you to go away. Come with me so that my people will not always be punished. They will learn again. Your home is in the village of the katcinas, so that my people may not starve for all time." He did not want the Corn Maids to go to the Hopi or to some other people. So Pautiwa said, "You will come with me." So all the Corn Maids, Yellow, Blue, Red, White, Speckled, and Black followed him. The Black Corn went behind to make the road dark so that the people would not find them. Therefore, when anyone is very lonesome for some one who has died, they give him the juice of the black corn to drink to make him forget.

Pautiwa took the Corn Maids with him and he laid them down in the middle of the lake. He told them, "Now, my children, you will lie still. When I am tired hiding you, I shall go and rest. Do not talk, I do not want my people inside to know that you are here." Inside, the people were dancing. Pautiwa stayed outside in the middle of the lake and the people came out and asked him whatever they wanted to know and they never noticed that he was hiding the Corn Maids.

Here at Itiwana the people had plenty of corn, but it was not good. There was no meat on it. All the corn piled in the corn rooms looked sick. The people noticed it and began to say, "Why is it that when we put the corn in it looked all right, but now it does not look right, and we are using it up so fast because there is nothing on the ears?" They kept on using up the corn, and when spring came the men planted. The women took out the seeds and the men planted them, but they never came up. It was as if they were dead. Their heart had gone away to the village of the katcinas. One year passed and the next came and the people had nothing. In some houses where they had looked after their corn right they still had corn. Finally the careless people went to work for the other people. They wove and span and ground for them. They worked for those who had corn, and so they had something to eat. Finally those who had no corn gave away everything they had for a basket of corn. So they were punished.

The priests tried to find out what was wrong. They knew that the Corn Maids had gone off and that that was why they had nothing but they wanted to find out what they should do. The town chief spoke thus. Then he sent for the other head men to talk over what they should do. They came and talked about it. Then they sent for Ahayute at Where-the-cotton-hangs. They came in and asked, "Why have you sent for us? We are here." So they said, "Our Corn Maids have been gone for four years, and we want to find out where they have gone to." So they said, "We shall try and find out where they have gone." So they went out and called the Tenatsali [11] boys. These boys are very wise. They came and they said, "We have come. Why have you sent for us?" Then the chief priest said, "We have been starving for four years. We want you to see if you can help us find the Corn Maids. We want you to find where they have gone."

So the Tenatsali boys tried. They went all over, to all the lakes and to the ocean. They looked in all the different directions but they could not find them. Then they called A'nakläkia.[12] He went all over, to the north and to the south and in all the different directions, but he could not find them. Then the Ahayute tried. They sent down a fly in the west, just a little dirty fly like we have in the houses. In the village of the katcinas they knew that the Corn Maids were hiding. All the katcina women were inside cooking by the fire and the katcina children were playing outside. They ran inside and said, "The fly is coming." The katcina women were wise. They knew that the Ahayute had sent the fly to find the Corn Maids so they said to the little katcinas, "Here, take this pumpkin stew and set it down outside so that the fly will go for it and burn her tongue." She

---

[11] Tenatsali is an unidentified plant used by the priests for their prayer sticks. When eaten it enables the user to locate lost property. It is administered by a priest.

[12] Datura (Jimson weed) used by medicine men to detect witchcraft.

is wise, Ahe'a.[13]   Then she took her pot of pumpkin stew and poured
it into a bowl and set it out.   The fly came along and went right for
it because it was sweet.   She burned her tongue.   That is why the
fly has never been able to talk since then and could not tell the
Ahayute where the corn maids were hiding.

The Ahayute had bows and arrows.   They used their arrows
with the points down so that they could go up easily.   They went
up to the sky.   They went all around and did not see anything but
the wind.   So they came down and they went out in all directions, to
the west and to the east and everywhere.   Whenever they went out
the priests did not eat and did not drink and did not go out.
They just sat in their room until midnight waiting for them.   Then
after the third night they came back and said, "Now, our fathers,
now this is the third night.   We have been everywhere and could not
find them.   We have always helped you.   Everything you have asked
we have been able to do.   This is the first time we have failed.   We
are not wise enough.   Someone else must be wise to find them for
you.   We can not find them."   The Ahayute had brought the
people up when they were down under the earth and they had always
been able to help them, but now they knew there was someone wiser
than they who had hidden the Corn Maids.   Then they said, "There is
someone you could try.   Try Ne'we·kwe.   He might be able to find
the corn maids.   We have heard that he is as wise as we are.   We have
always heard that."

So they called a Ne'we·kwe man.   They sent for him and he came
to the ceremonial room of the town chief and he asked them, "Why
have you sent for me?"   They said, "You know that we have been
starving for four years.   We have sent our children to look for the
Corn Maids.   We have sent three times and no one has found them.
Now we want you to work on prayer sticks for your Ne'we·kwe.   We
know him.   He always sits on the Milky Way."   So the Ne'we·kwe
planted prayer sticks for him to come.   Finally he came in the night
after sunset.   He came in and sat down and he asked, "Now I have
come.   I would like to hear why you have sent for me."   Then the
chief priest answered and said, "We have been starving for four
years.   We have tried three times, and none of our children have
been able to find the Corn Maids.   They have not found them at all.
The Corn Maids must be somewhere.   We want them to come back
so that we may have crops again, and so that my children may be
happy."   So he said.   Then Ne'we·kwe answered, "Yes, indeed, I
shall try.   I shall see what I can do.   But now I shall ask you people
if you really want the Corn Maids to come back for four years (he
meant four days, but he was Ne'we·kwe;) you will not drink and you
will not eat and you will sit here and wait for me.   You will not go

---

[13] The grandmother of the katcinas.

home to your wives, but you will wait for me here. I shall go for four years, and perhaps I shall find them." So he said to them, and then they asked one another if they would do all he had said. Then the chief priest said, "Yes, my son, we want the Corn Maids to come back. No matter how tired and hungry and thirsty we may be, we shall sit here and wait for you for four years. We really want the Corn Maids to come." So he said, "I am going now. Make your thoughts clean and make your hearts clean that I may bring the Corn Maids." Then he took ashes from the fireplace and went out.

When he got outside he threw up the ashes and right away there was a milky way in the sky. It came down to him and he jumped on it and sat down. It took him to the south and around to the east. At dawn he came down at his home at Ashes Spring.[14] The priests were in retreat. They thought he would be gone for four years, but he always came home at night. It takes a person twenty days to go to the south ocean, but he was wise and went in one day to the south and came back. He went to the north and the east and the west. He went to the west last, and there he dropped down from the Milky Way. Then he said to the Milky Way, "I have made you to protect my people. You will stay in the sky so that everyone will see you and watch you." That is why the Ne'we·kwe have the Milky Way in their ceremonial room and they sit on it.

He came down in the west and dropped into the Sacred Lake. There Pautiwa was hiding the Corn Maids. He just walked through the lake and never got wet. He came to him and he said, "How are you, my father? Are the Corn Maids here?" Then Pautiwa was glad that he had come. Now he could rest, so he was glad he had come. Then he said to the Corn Maids, "Now we shall go back to Itiwan·a. They want you. They will treat you well because they want you badly. They have nothing to eat. Let us go."

So then Ne'we·kwe went first and the Corn Maids followed him. Then Pautiwa got up and dipped his water gourd into the lake and followed them. "Now I shall go with you and take this sacred water so that when my people plant the corn the rain will always come." So they came here to Itiwana and went into the ceremonial room of the priests, first Ne'we·kwe and then the Corn Maids and Pautiwa. That is why Ne'we·kwe always brings the Corn Maids after Ca'lako and Pautiwa brings in the water in his water gourd so that they may have good luck with the summer rains. We call Ne'we·kwe Bitsitsi when he brings the corn maids, and we call Pautiwa Mo'la·kwatokia and A·'towakwatokia.

---

[14] A spring near Ojo Caliente, sacred to the Ne'we·kwe.

The Return of the Corn Maids

(Variant)

Long ago Bitsitsi was living in the Milky Way. Then the Corn Maids ran away and many people were looking for them. Then the man in the Milky Way saw everything, because he was up in the sky, and he found the Corn Maids and brought them back to Itiwan'a. He saw the Corn Maids and he told the priests that if they would do as he told them he would bring back the corn. Then the chief priest said that they would do whatever he said and he told them, "You must not eat or drink or talk for one night and one day until after dark, and you must not sleep or go out." The chief priest said, "Very well." Then they spread out a blanket for him and he sat down.

After about two hours he went out to the southeast and after he had gone about 5 miles he planted a yellow prayer stick and came back. He stayed there for about three hours and then he went out again to the southeast and about 3 miles beyond where he had planted the yellow prayer stick he planted a blue prayer stick and then he came back again. The people were still sitting there. Then he waited another three hours and went out again and went about 4 miles farther and planted a red prayer stick. Then he came back again and the people were still sitting there. After two or three hours he went out again and went about 2 miles farther off and planted a white prayer stick. Then he came back. The people were still sitting there. He stayed there for two or three hours. The people did not talk or smoke or eat or drink or go out. He said, "Poor people! You must want the Corn Maids to come back." Then he went out again, about 3 or 4 miles beyond where he had put the white stick and here he planted a prayer stick of many colors. He came back again and the people were still sitting there not talking. He stayed about two or three hours and then he went about 4 or 5 miles farther and now he was near the ocean. A little ways from the ocean he planted a black prayer stick.

The Red Corn Maid and the Speckled Corn Maid were sitting on the surface of the ocean and they saw him. Then they went in and told their sisters, "Some one is coming." Then Yellow Corn Maid said, "Very well."

Then the man went back to Itiwana and he stayed there a few hours. The people were still sitting there. They were hungry and thirsty, but they did not eat or drink; and they did not smoke or talk. Then he said "Poor people! This is the last time I am going out. I will surely bring back the Corn Maids." Then he went out and went way off to the ocean. He came there and went right into the ocean. There were many girls there and one of them said, "Let us go in to our sister." So they went in and she spoke to the Yellow Corn Maid, and the Yellow Corn Maid said to him, "How do you

Masks Appearing at the Initiation, Fig. b (See Plate 31)

Masks Appearing at the Initiation, Fig. c (See Plate 31)

do?" and she told him to sit down. Then she said to him, "What do you know? What did you wish to say?" Then he said, "I want you to go with me to Itiwana." They said, "Why?" He said, "The priests want you." Then she told him, "You go out and bring someone who is always happy, who never worries. Then we will go. If you can find anyone who is happy all the time we will go." Then he said, "Very well," and went out.

He went a little ways and saw a cottontail rabbit. He caught him and brought him in and said, "Here he is. This man is always happy; he never worries." Then the girls said, "He is right. This man is happy all the time. We know it. Now you get ready and we shall go with you. Now kill it." Then he killed the cottontail and skinned and put the skin, ears and all, around his neck. Then he took a piece of bone out of his arm and a piece of the ear and fastened them together and made a whistle.

So he took them to the east to all the different pueblos and finally he came to Itiwana with the Corn Maids. And so when they bring in the Corn Maids after Ca'lako they always come in from the southeast.

References.—The mask of Ῥautiwa is illustrated in Stevenson, Zuñi Indians, Plate II.

The winter solstice ceremony described (incompletely) by Stevenson, Zuñi Indians, p. 108. The Molawia ceremony described fully by Parsons, and by Stevenson, Zuñi Indians, p. 277.

There are frequent references to Ῥautiwa in tales collected by Benedict (unpublished manuscript) and Bunzel (text versions, unpublished).

Parallels.—Hopi: Ῥautiwa (Fewkes, Hopi Katcinas, Pl. II). A katcina of avowed Zuñi origin, introduced on first mesa with the Sia (Zuñi) Calako, about 75 years ago. This ceremony of the Sitcumovi clans is a Hopi potpurri of important Zuñi ceremonies.

The significant Hopi parallel is with Ahül (Hopi Katcinas, Pl. VII, also pp. 33–35 and 67; Voth, Bunzel, unpublished notes). Ῥautiwa is functionally related to this katcina who inaugurates the Powamu ceremony, much as Ῥautiwa "makes the New Year." (Powamu celebrates the return of the katcinas after their long absence.) Ahül marks the hatchway of the kiva with lines of meal, to announce the coming of the katcinas, just as Ῥautiwa marks the kivas to announce the coming of Tcakwena oka, the Sälimop'iya, and the various scare katcinas during the four days following. Fewkes identifies Ahül with the Hopi sun god. At Zuñi the impersonation belongs to the Dogwood clan, but Ῥautiwa is dressed and attended by men of the Sun clan, "because," as the chief of this group explained, "he is our child. He belongs to the sun."

Compare also Hopi Ahülani, the Soyal katcina, the first katcina to return at the winter solstice. He is accompanied by two katcina maidens, who distribute seeds to women in the kiva, as the Zuñi katcina maidens do in the dances following the winter solstice.

SAIYAŁI'A

(Plate 21, *b*)

Costume.—The top and back of the mask are covered with coarse white horsehair. He wears a big bunch of eagle tail feathers sticking out behind, and a bunch of owl feathers (muhuku lahatcipon·e). His face is painted blue. He has ball eyes and a large mouth with long, sharp teeth made of folded corn husks. He has a coyote skin wrapped around his neck. Two blue horns.

When he comes at Itiwan·a, his body is painted black with hekwitola (see p. 859), and marked with crescents of red and blue and white, like the painting on Kolo·wisi. The calves are painted the same as the body, and the thighs are white. He wears a native blue kilt as a breechcloth, and a fringe of black hair around his waist, like Cula·witsi. He wears a white tasseled belt and a blue leather belt. Blue leather armbands with butterflies for the summer birds and the green grass. Fox skin. Two turtle-shell rattles, one on each leg, tied with small red belts and black yarn. In the right hand he carries yucca, in the left uptcialan·e, a staff of wood with black goats' hair hanging from a sinew on one side. He also carries telnan·e for good luck for the New Year. This has the following feathers: eagle, chaparral cock, chicken hawk, isiton·e, red hawk, bluejay, ḳewia, łaialuḳo, duck (the "turn-around feather").

At the initiation (first and second whipping), he wears many feathers. He wears a downy eagle feather in the forelock and a downy feather dyed red on each horn. In his hair are many downy feathers which are given to the boys. His body is painted with pink clay from the Sacred Lake. He wears a large white buckskin fastened on the right shoulder. The rest of his costume is the same. In the right hand he carries yucca; in the left, bow and arrow. (Pl. 32, a.) He is dressed like this when the priests send for him when there is something wrong. He is always dressed like this when he is "dangerous," but when he comes for the rabbit hunt for good luck, he is dressed as at It·iwan·a.

There are four masks of Saiyałi'a. They are kept with the masks of the Blue Sälimop̄iya. (K. 414.) They use the same masks at It·iwan·a and the initiation.

"When the Saiyałi'a come at It·iwan·a they are called Puhu'atina·-kwe (the ones who do 'puhu').

"It all starts when p̄ekwin tells the people to keep the fire inside. Then on the fifth day of the fire taboo (maḳe teckwi), P̄autiwa comes in the night (i. e., the sixth night according to Zuñi counting). Then on the fourth day after this, the Saiyałi'a come in in the evening with Citsuḳä and Kwelele. The impersonators are chosen by the priests. They decide which kiva should take away the baḍ luck, and they say, 'Perhaps it will be he'iwa kiva.' Then the katcina bow priest goes to the kiva chief of he'iwa and says, 'Our fathers have picked you out and you will be the one to watch and take the old year away. You will pick out some good men who are never unhappy to take the old year away.' Then he answers, 'It is well. I shall pick out men from my kiva.' The priests pick out the kiva that will take the old

year out the day after Ṗautiwa comes in the night, that is on the
sixth day of the fire taboo.   Then the kiva chief selects the four men
from among the men of his kiva.   He goes to the house of the first
man and the man says to him, 'Be seated.   Why have you come?'
Then he answers, 'Yes, I have come.   I have thought of this house.
I have thought in my mind that our people want us to send out the
old year.'   Then the man answers, 'I can not say no.   I shall be
the one.'   Then the kiva chief goes to the house of another man and
tells him the same thing, and no one can refuse, because the priests
have chosen them.

"Then right away the men's wives begin to grind to take food to
the members of the Great Fire Society, who sing for the New Year.
Then on the fourth night the katcina bow priest helps them to dress.
When evening comes Citsuḵä and Kwelele come in.

(At about this time the Saiyaḷi'a impersonators go to he'iwa kiva.
They are unmasked and wrapped in blankets that conceal their
costume.   The masks have already been taken to the kiva, possibly
by the katcina bow priest.   R. L. B., 1928.)

"Late at night the Saiyaḷi'a put on their masks and come to the
kiva.   They dance for the old year.   After they have danced a
little while, the katcina bow priest goes to their houses and brings in
the baskets of corn that their wives have ground.   He goes to one
house and comes back and then he goes to another house and brings
a basket from each.   Then he pours water into a bowl and puts the
meal in it and mixes it [16] and gives it to the people who are there.
In the kiva are all the priests, the keeper of the sacred fire,[17] the
Great Fire Society (also men of he'iwa kiva and men of the Dogwood
and Sun clans.   R. L. B.)   All these people drink.

"Just before daylight the Sayaḷi'a go to all the kivas saying 'puhu,
puhu, puhu, puhu.'   No one is in the kivas, but they think the old
year is in there and they want to hurry him out.   Then they come
back to he'iwa kiva and wait for dawn.   When they feel the wind
from the east, they make the New Year fire in the kiva.   Blood-pud-
ding-man [18] makes the fire with a fire drill, and Citsuḵä lights his
torch.   Kwelele carries out the ashes and the four Puhu'atina·kwe
carry out the sweepings from the kiva.   They say they are carrying
out the corn.   Then they go out to the east, to take the old year out
and meet the new year.   They go out of the village to the place called
Where-the-pumpkin-stands, and leave the fire there.   Then they all
come back and dance in the kiva.   After they are finished, Citsuḵä
and Kwelele wait for Ṗautiwa, and the Puhu'atina·kwe go off with the

---

[16] This drink is called tcuḵina·we and is considered a great delicacy.   The corn is first boiled, then dried
and roasted and ground into very fine meal.

[17] Tsupal'ilona, "the one who has the blood pudding," see p. 959.

[18] According to more reliable authority, the head of the Great Fire Society makes the fire and lights
Kwelele's torch.   Citsuka does not have a torch.

old year. They take it away. They swing their staves as they go to sweep away what is left of the old year."

The Saiyaḽi'a come also for the initiation of the little boys. For the description of their part in this ceremony, see p. 978.

They are the only ones to come for the final initiation. At this time they are called Temapiḳämaka, "they show them the way." (See p. 998.) They come also as punitive or exorcising katcinas at irregular intervals.

Folklore:

How Sayaḽia Got His Collar

When the Sayaḽi'a first came to Itiwana they did not wear the coyote skins around their necks. They had just plain masks. They were poor and naked. They came to Itiwana and finished their dance. Then before going home they went to Corn Mountain to hunt. They went with Ahayute to Corn Mountain and were hunting. Two of the Känakwe were there too. They also were hunting with Ahayute. Ahayute had been to Itiwana. They had their crooks and were going home.[19] So they asked the Sayaḽi'a to go with them. The Sayaḽi'a were dangerous, but they did not look so terrible before they had the coyote skins on their necks. So the Ahayute said, "There are all kinds of animals where we live, and you can have their skins for your clothing." So the Sayaḽi'a went with them. The Ahayute climbed up Corn Mountain. When they came to their home they began to sing the way the Ḳänakwe do, "Huita! Huita!"[20]

The little coyotes were living on Corn Mountain. They heard it and they came to the Ahayute and said, "Who is making that noise around here? It sounds like a give-away dance." Then Ahayute said, "Don't you hear the katcinas below there? Last night there was a give-away dance at Itiwana and the katcinas came along with us and they are having a give-away dance below here." The Ahayute had a good idea. They had been calling "Huita," because they wanted the little coyotes to jump off the mountain so that the Sayaḽi'a could use their skins on their masks. "How can we go down?" said the four coyotes; "it is far. How can we go down?" "Just look for corncobs and stick one in your anus and the wind will carry you down." So the coyote looked for a corncob. He went home and got one and came back. "I don't know how to stick it in." "Here; I will do it for you." Then he said, "Now, you just stand here and bend over." The coyote was standing at the edge of Corn Mountain and he bent over and the Ahayute stuck the corncob in his anus. They did the same with all four of them, and then

---

[19] At the winter solstice prayer sticks are offered to all deities, and they are believed to come on that day to get their feathers.

[20] The Ḳänakwe and other katcinas who distribute food to the populace call out "Huita," as they throw their things to the people.

MASKS APPEARING AT THE WINTER SOLSTICE

a, Páutiwe; *b*, Saiyali'a; *c*, Citsuḵä; *d*, Kwelele

MASKS APPEARING AFTER THE WINTER SOLSTICE

a, Tcakwena Oḳa; b, Natacku; c, Suyuki or Atocle; d, Atocle Otsi.

they said, "Now, you just go to the edge and jump off and the wind will take you down to where they are having the give-away dance." Then they stood up and went to the edge, and then right over they went, the poor coyotes! There they went down and they burst open. "Oh, oh, oh, oh!" they said, and they died.

There below were the Sayaɫi'a, hunting rabbits. They came there to where the poor coyotes were lying. One came up to them, and he called the others. "Who is it that killed these?" he said. Their fur was so pretty that the Sayaɫi'a said, "Never mind about hunting rabbits. There is not much to eat on them, and their skins are not big enough to wear. Let us skin these." So the four Sayaɫi'a skinned the coyotes. There were just four of them. Then the one who had found them finished first, and he took the skin off and pulled it out and hung it on a tree to dry a little. Then he took it and tried it on his neck and tied it in back. The others looked at him and said, "Oh, how nice you look now! It is much better that way. We will all wear it that way now." Then all of them took their fur and fixed their necks that way. That is how they came to wear the coyotes' skins on their necks. Before that they had come to Itiwana without any fur, but Ahayute gave them these skins. They told the story about the give-away dance, and so they came to wear fur around their necks.

Citsuk̄ä and Kwelele

(Plate 21, c)   (Plate 21, d)

Costume.—"Citsuk̄ä is the white god (koko k̄ohana). He is dressed all in white. His mask is white. His nose is lightning, and over his ears is painted more lightning. On his face is painted hepakin·e (a circular design of different colors, similar to the painting on the masks of Sälimop̄iya) for the differently colored lightning." On his head he wears small feathers from the breast of the macaw and downy feathers of the eagle. At the back lapap̄owa, tail feathers of the macaw and downy eagle feathers. Spruce collar.

"His clothing is all white, white shirt, white embroidered blanket fastened on the right shoulder, white dance kilt with a blue band, embroidered sash, white fringed leggings of buckskin, blue moccasins, black yarn around both legs with bells on the right leg. Yarn and beads on both wrists, and many necklaces around his neck, doubled over the way the society people wear them. He carries yucca in the right hand and a bull roarer.

"Kwelele is called the black god (koko k̄win·e). His mask is all black with white crescents for eyes, and a zigzag stripe for nose. His feathers are the same as those of Citsuk̄ä. His ears are rolled corn husks. Spruce collar.

" The upper part of his body is nude and painted purplish black. He wears a dance kilt, embroidered sash, red woman's belt, fox skin behind. He wears arm bands of blue buckskin with feathers hanging from them. He has spruce twigs in his arm bands and in his belt. Blue moccasins, yarn on both legs, with little bells. In the right hand he carries yucca, in the left a torch of cedar bark and an ancient fire drill. (The torch is left in the fields at dawn, and he carries yucca for the rest of the day.)

"The masks of Citsuḵä and Kwelele are kept with that of Koko Łan·a in the house of the Great Fire Society. Their ceremony belongs to this society. Citsuḵä and Kwelele live at Cipapolima."

Ceremonies.—Citsuḵä and Kwelele come publicly only at itiwan·a, but they bring in Koko Łan·a when he is called in to cure sickness.

When Citsuḵä and Kwelele come at itiwan·a they must be impersonated by members of the Koko Łan·a order of the Great Fire Society. During itiwan·a they meet to select the impersonators. All members of the society contribute food or things like tobacco purchased at the store for Citsuḵä and Kwelele to throw away to the people.

They come in on the ninth day of the fire taboo, in the evening. During the afternoon the masks are taken out to a field to the east of the village, by members of the Great Fire Society, who assist Citsuḵä and Kwelele to dress. Just before sunset they enter the village by the eastern road. They go at once to He'iwa kiva where they dance for a few minutes on the roof. Meanwhile p̃ekwin has assembled the impersonators of P̃autiwa and Saiyali'a. At sunset they enter the kiva. Here brief ceremonies are held. After about 20 minutes they come out again and go to the ceremonial house of the Great Fire Society. Here they remove their masks, and eat the supper that has been brought to the house by female members of the society. In the Great Fire Society house are the members of the Koko Łana order of the society, and the choir that is to sing during the night. Late at night Citsuḵä and Kwelele are summoned to He'iwa kiva by the bow priest. They put on their masks and follow him, accompanied by their choir and the head men of the Great Fire Society. They reach the kiva about midnight. Until day no one must see them except those privileged to be in the kiva. In the kiva are the priests, the chiefs of the Katcina Society, Tsupal'ilona, the impersonators of P̃autiwa and Saiyali'a, members of the P̃autiwa cult, the Sun clan men who "take care of" P̃autiwa, choirs from He'iwa kiva and the Great Fire Society. Anyone entering the kiva during the night must remain in and awake until the ceremonies close at sundown the following day.

During the night the two choirs sing alternately certain named song sequences and Citsuḵä and Kwelele and the Saiyali'a dance. Anyone

who dozes during the night is soundly thrashed by Citsuḳä. At one
point in the ceremonies the head of the Great Fire Society asperges
the audience with water from the medicine bowl on the altar. After
this Kwelele runs out and sits on the roof for a while, and is followed
by Citsuḳä, leaving the Saiyaḷi'a alone dancing in the kiva. Both
return after a short time. During the night p̓ekwin and the chief of
the Great Fire Society both keep watch of the stars, and at the
approach of dawn notify the men of the Sun clan to dress P̓autiwa.
When he is ready, the chief of the Great Fire Society kindles fire with
Kwelele's fire drill and lights Kwelele's torch. There are four songs
for the making of the fire, and as soon as the fire comes the choir stops
and sings the "going away" song. If the fire comes quickly, it is an
omen of good luck. Then the gods, p̓ekwin, komosona, and Tsupal'-
ilona, take the fire out to the east. Kwelele carries his torch, kindled
from the new fire, Tsupal'ilona carries a brand from his fire. There is
contradictory evidence as to who carries the ashes and sweepings.
Citsuḳä leads, carrying an ear of corn. Wherever he stops and lays
down his ear of corn the party stops. Tsupal'ilona lays down his
brand, Kwelele extinguishes his torch. After brief prayers the party
returns to the village. This is the end of the fire taboo. The people
all hasten to take the fire out of their houses, for those who take their
fire out early will have good luck during the coming year. It is not yet
six o'clock and still quite dark. As soon as the singers of the Great
Fire Society return to the kiva from taking the fire out of their own
houses, the gods dance until full daylight (eight o'clock or later). At
this time anyone may enter the kiva, and many men, women, and
children who were denied entrance during the night go to receive the
blessing of the gods.

After eating and resting in their house Citsuḳä and Kwelele return to
the kiva and dance on the roof while the crooks of office are being distributed within. As each impersonator receives his crook, the choir
calls out the name of the god. After all the crooks and the feathers
for the Ḷeweˑkwe dance have been distributed, the choir sings Citsuḳä's
songs, and the two gods dance on the roof, throwing large quantities
of food and other articles to the populace. This continues until
P̓autiwa comes at sunset. (Observed in part 1928, 1929.)

Mythology—A long time ago the people were living at Koḷuwalawa,
katcina village, and the Black katcinas (Koko aˑk̓win·e) were living near
katcina village. One day the chief of the katcinas called out a deer
hunt for four days from that time, and on the same night the chief
of the Black katcinas called a deer hunt for the same time. On the
day of the hunt after the midday meal the Black katcinas went
about a mile away and made a circle, and the katcina village people
made a circle also, and the two circles overlapped and the people
began shooting against each other. Then the katcina village

people got angry and went home. About midnight the black gods took
their images and rounded up some deer and antelope and mountain
lion and jack rabbits and cottontail rabbits and wood rats. Then
the porcupine came and made a corral for the deer and one for the
antelope and one for the mountain lion and one for the jack rabbits
and one for the cottontails. They made five corrals.

The katcinas did not kill any game all year, and there was no
rain.[21] Two girls went down to the corrals where the deer were. The
katcinas were looking for game, but they never found anything.
They ate their buckskin clothes and their moccasins because they
could not get any meat.

Way off in the east at Cipapolima lived Citsuḵä, one of the white
gods. Every evening when he was on his housetop he saw lightning
in the southwest. Then he said,"I had better go down where the
lightning is. There must be rain there."

Next morning he took his seeds of corn of all colors and beans and
watermelons and muskmelons and pumpkins and squash and he
went down to the southwest. Soon night came on. He had a
little dish of sacred meal and some water and some medicine and a
bull roarer. He whirled his bull roarer and sprinkled meal to the
north, west, south, east, up, and down. Then he went on, far into
the southwest. On the fifth day in the afternoon he came to a place
where there had been rain just a few minutes before, and lots of
water was running down. He went on a little farther and came to a
little lake on a hill with water running down from it. Here he planted
his corn and beans and watermelons and muskmelons and squash
seeds, and he built a little house there. He stayed there and ate his
buckskin moccasins and his leggings, and he was as poor as a crow.
He stayed there 14 or 15 days, and then one afternoon he went out to
see the country. He went out and saw a creek and cottonwood trees
by the creek and he saw two girls washing buckskins. They put it
into the water and spread it out and then looked to see if anyone
was near. Then they did it again. Citsuḵä stood there watching
the girls. Soon one of the girls saw him. They asked him, "Do you
know what we are doing?" He said, "Yes." They said, "What?"
He said, "You are washing deerskin." They said, "Yes, but you
must not say anything. Long ago when our people and the people
from the village of the katcinas went hunting deer on the same
day, they both made big circles, and our people got all the deer in
their circle, and the other people did not get any, and they got angry
and went home. Then we rounded up the deer and put them in a
corral. If you do not tell anybody we will take you up to our house
and you can watch the deer." The young man said, "All right."
Then he took the buckskin to help wash it and he saw a little bit of

---

[21] The implication is that the katcinas withhold rain because they are angry.

meat on the buckskin and he pulled it off and ate it. Then one of the girls said, "Poor man, he has not had anything to eat," and she went up to the house about a half mile from the creek and brought some meat, and he ate it. Then they went on washing the buckskin.

In the evening the girls took him back to their house with them. Their father knew he came from a different country. The girls made supper and they ate. After supper the old man asked questions, and asked, "Where have you been?" He said, "I come from Cipapolima. I was living there and we had no rain. And I looked down here and saw lightning, so I came here and I planted some corn and beans and melons and squash. To-day I was looking around and I saw your girls washing a buckskin." The old man said, "All right. If you stay with these girls you will be all right." Then they went to bed.

After breakfast the next morning the old man told the youth to make a pair of moccasins. He gave him a deerskin and he made a pair of moccasins and a pair of leggings. He had nice clothes again now. In the evening he went to the corrals and called out to all the people to come down. Each family got one deer and one mountain sheep and one antelope and one jack rabbit and one cottontail rabbit and one wood rat. Each family got one of each kind of animal and took them home. The second day he did the same. The man stayed there four days and then he went to look after his cornfield. His cornfield was getting along all right and his muskmelons were nearly ripe. He took deer meat with him. He worked all day in his cornfield and in the evening he went home. Every fourth night he gave each family one deer and one mountain sheep and one antelope and one cottontail rabbit and one jack rabbit and one wood rat.

Up at the village of the katcinas was Pautiwa. One day he put on his duck shirt and went swimming in the lake. He went out to the southwest and after he had gone a long way he saw cornfields and he saw a little lake and he swam into the lake. When he got there he took off his duck shirt and went up to the camp house and looked in. He saw the young man eating a dinner of deer meat. The young man heard him and put the deer meat under his knees. Then Pautiwa went in and greeted him. And the young man said, "Sit down." Pautiwa sat down and talked to the young man. "I think you are eating deer meat." "No, I never eat deer meat." "Yes, you look well. You have enough to eat. Perhaps you are married." "No." "Yes, you look well. I think you are married," Pautiwa said, "You tell me. I have a nice daughter and I will bring her to you to-morrow." Then the boy told him, "A long time ago the people from the village of the katcinas went out to hunt deer, and the black dancers went to hunt deer the same day. And they made a large circle and the black gods rounded up all the deer in

their circle. Then the people from the village of the katcinas did
not get any and they went home and the other people drove all the
game into corrals. After a while I saw the lightning here and came
and made a cornfield and the two girls took me to their house to
watch the game." "Is that so?" "Yes. I will show you. To-
morrow night I shall give each family a deer." Then Pautiwa said,
"Well, to-morrow I will bring my daughter and you will stay with
my daughter. She is a nice looking girl, but she's a little thin
because she has not had enough to eat." The boy said, "All right.
I think I have some meat here." Then Pautiwa ate the meat, and
then he went home. After that the boy went home.

Next day he went to his cornfield, and his wife wanted to come with
him, but he said, "No, you stay here." He took along some meat for
his dinner. Soon two ducks came swimming up the lake. Pautiwa
took off his duck shirt and went into the house, and the girl did the
same. The man saw the girl and he brought some deer meat and they
had dinner. Then Pautiwa said, "I must go home. Tonight you
take some deer out and you and my girl come to the village of the
katcinas." Then the young man said, "I will make them all black
crows[22] tonight, and don't you let them eat any corn." Then Pautiwa
went home, and his daughter stayed in the field that night.

In the evening the boy went down to the corral. Everyone came
down and he gave them each one deer. Then he said to the two girls,
"You had better go into the mountain sheep corral." Then he put a
mountain lion in to watch the deer, and then he went to the mountain
sheep corral and put a wolf in with them, and he went to the antelope
and put a yellow coyote in there, and he went to the jack rabbits and
he put a wild cat to watch them, and he went to the cottontails and
put a badger to watch them. Then he went home. Everyone went
home. He killed a deer and skinned it. Late at night the two girls
went to bed. Citsuḵä sat by the fire. He took a handful of corn
pollen and a handful of salt and put it into the fire and covered it
over with ashes. Soon the salt got very hot and popped. Then the
deer started to run out, and the mountain lion ran after them, and
the wolf and the wildcat and the coyote and the badger did the same.
Then all the crows went down to the man's cornfield, and Pautiwa's
daughter was busy all night chasing the crows away, running from
side to side waving her arms and calling out. After a while the crows
flew away and the deer ran all over the country. Then Citsuḵä took
Pautiwa's daughter home to the village of the katcinas.

That is the reason why every year at the end of December Citsuḵä
comes from the east, and next day Pautiwa comes in from the west,
and they go down to the village of the katcinas together.

That is all.

---

[22] The overworked pun on the words koko, crow, and katcina.

VARIANT

Cïtsuḳä came up at Cipapolima. Now in the east there was no rain. The earth was all dry and nothing could grow. So Cïtsuḳä and Kwelele came out and came toward the west. They came to a place called Epati (Moccasin) a little to the east of Corn Mountain. Here a few little green things were growing. They stayed there and went hunting because it was dry in the east. So they stayed and went hunting at Epati. When evening came they sat down facing the west, and way off in the west they saw lightning and black clouds. But at Epati there was no rain. They saw the lightning again, and Citsuḳä said to Kwelele, "Do you see the lightning?" "Yes." "It must be far off. I wonder how long it will take us to go there. Let us try to go there. There must be people living there. Let us go tomorrow." So he said to Kwelele, and he answered "Very well."

Next day they awoke and went to the west. It took them only one day to go to the village of the katcinas, because they were wise. They came to the mountain near the village of the katcinas and they climbed the mountain and sat down on top and looked down into the lake. There was a vapor hanging over the lake. From where they were sitting on the top of the mountain they could see the pretty katcina maidens working at the lake. They were washing a buckskin in the lake. "Oh," they said, "Here we are. I think this must be what we saw making the lightning last night. These must be the people whose lightning we saw last night. Look, they are washing a buckskin. We have had no deer, but see what good luck they have here. They have rain and deer too." So they said as they sat on the top of the mountain. "Now let us go down and go in and see them," they said. So they went down and went toward where the katcina maidens were working. As soon as they saw them coming they said, "Oh dear, now they have caught us. They have seen us washing the buckskin. Let us go right in." They were trying to hide the game from the Ḳäna·kwe. So they picked up the buckskin and ran in. They came in and said, "Oh dear! There are people coming. They are right outside. They saw us washing the buckskin. Now what shall we do?" Then P̓autiwa said, "We shall just tell them that you were washing your clothes, for they are white like the buckskin."

Just as they were talking in came Cïtsuḳä and Kwelele. As they came in everyone was making a noise and one could not hear the other. They came in. Then P̓autiwa said, "My children, be quiet for a moment. Someone has come here." So he said to his people. Then they all stopped dancing and they made the two strangers sit down. Then P̓autiwa asked them, "What place have you come from? We thought that we were all together here, but you were not here." So he said. Then Cïtsuḳä said, "Yes, my father, we have come from the east. Our home is over in the east at Cipapolima.

But over there everything is dry. There is not a drop of rain. There is no lightning and not a mark in the sky. It is dry, and the sky is all clear and shining. There was nothing growing and there were no animals. We are starving. We came out to look around (hunt) and we thought we would go back home, but then we thought that maybe we had better come here. Then we came to a damp place and grassy, and we thought we had better come in and see you before we went back home." He said this so kindly, but even as he spoke he told of the great trouble he had had. Everyone listened to him with sympathy because he spoke so kindly. Then right away the katcina maidens liked him and Pautiwa also liked him, so he said, "I am glad you have come. You have had much trouble to find a damp place. Now you have come to a damp place. You were looking for deer, and now you have come to where the deer are. You shall stay here a few days, and then you shall go out and look around and you shall take the deer and rain back to the east with you." They had not sent out the deer and the rain because they knew of Citsuḳä and they wanted him to come to them.

Then he stayed there for a few days. Right away Pautiwa's daughter loved him and that day he married Pautiwa's daughter. After he was married he went out with Kwelele to hunt around the village of the katcinas. He brought in many deer. He stayed for four days at the village of the katcinas, and then he said to Pautiwa and to his wife, "Now I have stayed here long enough. I can not live here. I must live at Cipapolima because I belong to the society people. I shall only come here once a year. You will meet me at Itiwan·a and I shall come to visit you. The people at Itiwan·a think that you bring the new year, but I am really the one who brings the new year from the east. You will meet me in Itiwan·a, and take me with you to see my wife. That is the only time that I shall see my wife." Pautiwa was very pleased, because he had sent for Citsuḳä to come. That was why he had kept back the rain and the deer and that way finally got him to come. And now his son-in-law promised him that he would come each year to bring the New Year from the east, and Pautiwa promised him that he would meet him each year at Itiwana and bring him to the village of the katcinas to see his wife. So after he had stayed for four days at the Sacred Lake he went back with Kwelele to Cipapolima.

That is why Citsuḳä only comes at the winter solstice. He comes to bring the New Year and then Pautiwa comes to meet him and takes him to see his wife. He stays there for four days. And that is why Citsuḳä's society, the Great Fire Society, always sing and drum for them when they come to make the New Year. And that is why the people always think that the New Year comes from the east. And when babies are born they think of them as coming from the east, too.

When a woman is in labor they say, "The baby is coming. I think it is at Nutria now, or perhaps a little nearer, at Black Rock."

That is the story of how Citsuk̯ä came to find the village of the katcinas. They needed him there and they made him come. And that is how he comes to bring the New Year.

(See also Stevenson "Zuñi Indians," p. 135.)

Tcakwena Oka

(Plate 22, a)

Costume.—The mask is a chin mask, painted black with round yellow eyes and mouth. Her hair is done up behind like a Zuñi woman's.

The drawing shows how she is dressed when she comes to dance with T̄owa Tcakwena. Then she wears an ordinary woman's black dress, with a cotton underdress, and an embroidered white blanket folded and fastened on the right shoulder. White moccasins. Many bead necklaces, back and front, and on both wrists. White downy eagle feather in the hair. She carries a gourd rattle.

But when she comes at the New Year and for the ceremonial rabbit hunt after the initiation "she looks dangerous." She wears the red feather (the badge of society membership) in her hair. Her dress is the ancient Zuñi native garment, black with a dark blue embroidered border. It is fastened on both shoulders and is open down the front. She wears no belt (because of her connection with childbirth?). On her feet she wears sheepskin boots, with strips of rabbit fur wound around her legs. Otherwise her legs are bare. She carries a gourd rattle and rattles as she goes.

This is an old mask. It is kept in a Badger house near the bridge (K. 201). In 1925 they made a new mask for her, which is kept along with the old one in the same house. The following account of the occasion is not without interest.

"This spring (1925) they made a new mask for Tcakwena Ok̯ä because twenty years ago a man died while he was wearing the mask and ever since then we have had much sickness and especially many babies have died.[23]

"Tcakwena Ok̯ä comes at the winter solstice in the evening before P̄autiwa brings in the new year. That day the man who is going to be Tcakwena Ok̯ä gets his things ready. He gets the old Zuñi dress of black native cloth with a blue border and he gets the boots of sheepskin and the rabbit-skin strips to bind around his legs. He gets all his things ready and then he picks out young men to come with him as Sälimop̄iya and he tells them to dress and wait for him on the west side of the village. Then when he has everthing ready he goes

---

[23] From whooping cough during the summer of 1924.

for the mask.   The mask is kept in a jar in a house near the bridge.
On this night the man went to this house to get Tcakwena Oḵä.   He
stood in the room where she is kept and said, 'Now, my mother, our
time has come.   Now we shall go out to meet our people, for our time
has come.   You are the one to bless my people with children.   And
now this year whoever is with child you shall give an easy delivery
and bless her that her baby may grow to maturity.'   He said this as
he stood beside the jar in which the mask was kept.   And they say
that as he put out his hand to take the mask it shook itself from side
to side.   The man saw it but he thought that perhaps he had knocked
the jar with his foot and shaken the mask.   He was not sure, but he
put in his hand and took the mask out.   Then he said to his son who
had come with him to help him dress, 'I think I saw our mother shake
her head, but I am not sure.   I may have knocked the jar and made
it so.'   Then his son said to him, 'Yes, I guess you just touched the
jar.'

"So they went out and went five or six miles to the west to the
place where Tcakwena Oḵä used to live long ago.   When they came
there it was near sundown.   The boy helped his father dress.   He
put on the dress and the boots and tied the red feather in his hair
and last of all he took up the mask and said, 'Now we shall go in to
our people.   They are all there; we shall go to them for they are all
waiting for us to bless them with children.   Now let us go.'   So he
said, and put on the mask.   As he put it on the son tied the strings
that hold it in place.   Then the son said, 'Now I shall start.   I shall
go ahead slowly and wait for you.'   Then Tcakwena Oḵä went four
times around her rock praying and saying that she was going to
Itiwana to bless the women with children.

"By this time the men who were going to be Sälimop̄iya were all
dressed and were waiting for her on the west side of the town.   So she
started from her rock and came along calling out her cry.   When
she got to Wide River she called out again and all the people waiting
for her on the west side of the town heard her coming and went to
Wide River to meet her.[24]

"So she came in.   The man was perfectly well.   He had no cold
and no pain anywhere.   They all came over the bridge and came into
the village and he stopped at every door and said, 'I have come to
bring you good luck and especially to bless you with babies.'   As the
people in the houses heard her coming they all went out.   They took
their rubbish and ashes to the door and just as she came they threw
it out.   They throw out all their bad luck with the ashes and rubbish,
and she brings them good luck in its place.   So she came along Sun-

---

[24] Long ago she used to come before sundown and then all the Sälimop̄iya dressed at Wide River and met
her there.   But now she comes after dark and therefore the Sälimop̄iya do not dress.   They just put on
their masks and wrap themselves in blankets.   They get ready in Heḵäpawa kiva and go out to meet her.

Old Masks Appearing Irregularly, Fig. a (See Plate 33)

Old Masks Appearing Irregularly, Fig. b (See Plate 33)

shine Place [25] and she came to our house. The people in the next house got their ashes ready to throw out and they had the corn meal ready to sprinkle with a prayer as they threw out their ashes. She came to our door and we threw out our ashes and sprinkled meal. So she went on. But she went just a few steps and suddenly she groaned and fell down. I thought that it was all part of her performance and I laughed. But all the Sälimopiya ran up to her and picked her up. She was trembling all over. They were going to bring her into our house, but someone said, 'Don't take her there. There are children in that house. Better bring her in here.' And so they took her into the next house. They brought her in and laid her down, for they thought she was fainting. They rubbed her stomach for they thought perhaps she had a chill. But after about fifteen minutes they saw that she was not getting any better, so someone said, 'Take off her mask.' So the man's son tried to take off the mask, but it was stuck fast to his face. So they pulled it and finally they got it off and his skin came off from his face with it. Then the people saw that he was already dead and they all cried. Then they called in all his people and many people went in there and tried to cure him, but he never came back to life. The Sälimopiya were all in there. They still had their masks with them, but they were afraid to go out and finish up. Way late at night the katcina chief heard that they had not been to all the houses of the village, so he went there and he said, 'Our child is dead, but you must finish up your work, no matter how sorrowful you feel. You must finish, because misfortune will surely come to our people if we do not go through with everything.' So then the dead man's young son put on the mask and went out and went to all the houses of the village. He finished it up. He never thought that the mask was dangerous and might kill him also.

"It was an old mask, and no one thought of burying it with the dead man. It had his flesh on it, for it had stuck to his face when they tried to take it off, but in spite of this they never thought of burying it. But ever since then we have had misfortune. We have had much sickness, dysentery, and tuberculosis, and many bad sicknesses. So after a while the people began to think that perhaps it was on account of this mask, for Tcakwena Okä comes to bless the people with children, and to have itsuma·wa [26] for them. Last spring the bow priest decided that they would have the ceremonial rabbit hunt, although there was to be no initiation. They wanted Tcakwena Okä to come with the rabbit hunt so that all their bad

---

[25] South of the village along the river.

[26] A ceremonial term for planting, applied to certain type of fertility magic practiced at the winter solstice and in connection with the rabbit hunt. Images of clay are placed on an altar and later planted as the seed from which the real object shall grow. For description of the rabbit hunt, see Stevenson, p. 88; Benedict, ms.

luck might be taken away. So they came to the dead man's son and asked him to have a new mask made, for they were afraid they would have misfortune if they used the old one again. So the man had the mask made. The Katcina Pekwin made it for him. And now maybe they will bury the old mask, for it is dangerous."

She comes at it·iwan·a, to bring women good luck in childbirth. This is in the evening, after Pautiwa has gone after "making the New Year."

In the afternoon of the New Year the man of the Badger clan who owns the ritual of Tcakwena Oḵä goes to her shrine, about two miles west of the village, to dress. About the time Pautiwa leaves, the Sälimop̄iya impersonators are also seen going out toward the west. These are appointed by the kiva heads, and most of them are very young boys.

After nightfall (about nine o'clock), Tcakwena Oḵä, accompanied by the Sälimop̄iya, enters the village from the west. She is masked and clothed as described above. The Sälimop̄iya are masked, but fully clothed in ordinary shirts and trousers. They do not wear blankets. They carry yucca switches in both hands. Tcakwena Oḵä leads, walking very fast and shaking her rattle continuously. She is followed by the Sälimop̄iya in line. Some of them leave the line occasionally to strike with their yucca anyone who comes too close. They are followed by a boisterous crowd of boys who try to see how close they can come without being whipped. The katcinas walk close to the houses, winding in and out past every door. As they approach each doorway, the women of the house, who have been waiting up for them, open the door and throw out at them a shovelful of live coals. These have first been waved around in every room of the house, as a rite of purification. After throwing out the coals, all the women of the house stand in the doorway, sprinkling meal on the shoulder of each katcina as he hurries by. On reaching the dance plaza, Tcakwena Oḵä enters the house of the town chief for about ten minutes, while the Sälimop̄iya wait in the plaza, running about and giving their call, and lunging with their switches at any passers-by. The crowd that is following them becomes quite rowdy.[27] Every few minutes women in the houses on the plaza open their doors to throw out more coals. After a few minutes Tcakwena Oḵä comes out and shakes her rattle to call the Sälimop̄iya. The party then leaves the plaza and the village. (Observed January, 1929. R. L. B.)

Mrs. Stevenson reports that this group is accompanied or followed by unmasked personages, whom she calls Łelele. The writer saw no such persons, although various informants assured her that Łelele had, indeed, come. She surmises that this is merely another name

---

[27] This was the only occasion on which the writer was molested on the streets of Zuñi, although she frequently went about at night unaccompanied.

for the Sälimop̄iya on this occasion.   The Sälimop̄iya "and Łelele" return without Tcakwena Oǩä on the four following evenings.   The writer did not see them on this occasion.   If they came, they came very late and did not visit the house east of the village where she was staying.

Following the initiation Tcakwena Oǩä comes for the rabbit hunt with the katcinas.   To this rabbit hunt everyone goes on foot. They hunt in the old way, forming circles and driving the game toward the center.   The blood of the first rabbit killed is rubbed on the legs of Tcakwena Oǩä "so that Zuñi women may have their babies easily, like rabbits."   After the rabbit hunt Tcakwena Oǩä lies in for the increase of livestock and babies.   She lies on a sand bed in one of the kivas, and is tended by women who wish for her blessing in child-birth.   Men who desire her blessing on their flocks and herds bring miniature animals of clay to the house of her lying-in.

Tcakwena Oǩä also comes as solo dancer with the Towa Tcakwena dance set.   "She never had any chance to dance, so P̄autiwa let her come with Towa Tcakwena.   She is their sister, so she comes with them and dances in front and gives the calls for their dance."   She was observed dancing with Towa Tcakwena after Ca'lako in 1928, but not in 1927.   Doctor Parsons reports seeing her with them after Ca'lako in 1925.   On that occasion she was impersonated by a famous ła·hmana.   (Notes on Zuñi, p. I, 213.)

References.—The appearance of Tcakwena Oka at the winter solstice described by Stevenson, Zuñi Indians, page 140; Parsons, Notes on Zuñi, page 169.   The rabbit hunt and the subsequent lying in of Tcakwena oǩa is described in Zuñi Indians, pages 89–94; Parsons, Notes on Zuñi, pages 157, 179.   Also in the unpublished Benedict manuscript.

Her myth is recorded briefly in Cushing, Outlines of Zuñi Creation Myths, page 424; Zuñi Indians, page 36; also text version, p. 599.

Parallels.—Hopi.   Tcakwaina mana (Hopi Katcinas, Pl. IV), "the elder sister of the Tcakwaina," who dances with that set, resembles Tcakwena Oǩä in name and appearance.   It is a war impersonation.   The headdress and paraphernalia of this katcina are those of the Zuñi Koła·hmana, with whom the impersonation is probably related.

There are marked similarities, also, with Hehe'e, a phallic impersonation with Hehe'a (Hopi Katcinas, Pl. XI).   Compare also with Hopi Kokyan wüqti (Hopi Katcinas, Pl. XXIX), spider woman, the grandmother of the war gods.   Compare also with Hahai wüqti, the mother of the Natackas, who comes with them during Powamû.

Laguna.   Compare Shotorok·a, Parsons, Notes on Ceremonialism at Laguna, pages 97–99, Figure 6.

NATACKU

(Plate 22, *b*)

Costume.—The mask comes down over the head and has a huge snout.   It is painted pink with spots of white.   On his head he wears the "great feather" of the bow priests (lacowan łan·a) made of two eagle wing feathers bound to reeds, and surrounded with downy eagle feathers and feathers from the neck of the duck. The base is covered with red flannel. Blue horns, with small feathers hanging from them. Fox skin collar.

The body is painted pink with clay from the sacred lake. Large white buckskin fastened on the right shoulder, embroidered white dance kilt, blue moccasins. Yarn on both legs. Many necklaces. In his right hand he carries spruce, in the left a bow and arrow.

The mask is an old one, but I could not learn in which house it is kept. There seems to be no cult of Natacku. He has not appeared in many years.

"Long ago, Natacku used to come after itiwan·a to frighten the children. This used to be the day after Pautiwa brought the New Year, or the next day. He would go around the village and ask for meat in the houses where there were children. They have not had him come for many years."

ATOCLE OTSI

(Plate 22, d)

Costume.—The mask is painted black with white spots. He has long coarse hair falling over his face. Large ball eyes, a red snout. On his head lacowan łan·a. Around his neck a fox (?) skin collar and a wild-cat (?) skin over his shoulders.

The body is painted red with zigzag marks in white. The thighs are white, the forearms and calves black with white spots. He wears a buckskin kilt, embroidered sash, and red belt. Fox skin behind. Blue moccasins, and blue leather arm bands. In his right hand he carries a large knife, in the left bow and arrow.

(The drawing was secured by Dr. Elsie Clews Parsons, and there is no accompanying information.)

ATOCLE (SUYUKI) [28]

(Plate 22, c)

Costume.—She has long coarse gray hair with eagle down in it. The mask is painted black with white spots. She has protruding eyes "so that she can see better," and a large mouth. On her head she wears lacowan łan·a "because she is strong and dangerous." There is eagle down in her long beard. She wears a fawn skin collar.

She wears a black woman's dress and blanket. Formerly she did not wear the cotton underdress, or the fine white moccasins, but moccasins of rabbit fur. She carries a cane and a rattle of deer

---

[28] Both names are used, apparently without distinction. Both seem to be generic terms for cannibals. In folklore there are an Atocle man and an Atocle woman, and both may, on occasions, be called Suyuk or Suyuki. It is the cannibal woman who figures prominently in mythology. There probably are several distinct, but similar, impersonations.

hoofs in her right hand and a big knife in her left. On her back is a large carrying basket in which to carry away naughty children.

Her call is su-'u-ḵi·'.

"She may come any time they want her. Sometimes she comes with the mixed dance, but she can come at any time. If a woman has a naughty child she will ask the kiva chief to bring in Suyuki. Then she will come and frighten the children. She shakes her cane at them and threatens to carry them off and eat them. She doesn't touch them.

"She used to come sometimes after itiwan·a."

The following is a native account of a visit of Atocle to the peach orchards in summer. During July and August when the peaches are ripe the old people and the children camp at the peach orchards to keep off marauders, and later to pick and dry the peaches. Atocle sometimes comes at this time to beg for fresh meat and peaches.

"So there, after a few days, on Corn Mountain, Atocle built his fire at night. He made his fire on Corn Mountain. Grandmother said to me, 'Hiya! Atocle is about to come down!' So she said to me, but I did not believe it. 'She is lying to me,' I thought. But indeed she was right. He was going to come down. We went to sleep. Next morning again his smoke rose. So indeed it was right. Atocle was about to come down. 'You didn't believe it!' grandmother said to me.

"Just at noon he came down. 'Look over there! He is coming down!' grandmother said to me. The children who were staying with their parents at the peach orchards cried, 'Oh, dear! Atocle is coming down!' they said. Then I ran away to my other mother, my old mother.[29] 'Mother! Atocle came down!' I said. 'All right, go into that rock crevice over there,' she said to me.

"Meanwhile he came to where my grandparents were staying. Atocle: 'Where are the children who live here? They are very disobedient. Therefore I have come down,' he said. 'There aren't any naughty children here,' my grandmother said. 'But this old man—now he has no sense at all!' Thus she said about her husband. She told Atocle. 'Well, what did your old man do?' 'Well, he was going to eat all the tortillas by himself. He hid them.' So the old woman told Atocle. 'I think it's true. Your old man has no sense.' So Atocle said to her. 'No, indeed I have sense!' So grandfather said to Atocle. As he said this to him he sprinkled corn meal on him. He sprinkled corn meal on him, and he gave him peaches and meat. Then, right there, wherever the people were staying, he went about making them come out. He collected lots of food,

---

[29] Mother's elder sister.

6066°—32——60

peaches and meat and bread. When he had lots of food he went to his village of the katcinas. So he went.

"This is what happened. That's all."

Mythology.—When the earth was soft Su'uḵi used to come into the village and go around. Sometimes the women took their babies to the peach orchards and put them to sleep under the trees while they worked. Then if the mother went to the spring or anywhere out of sight Su'uḵi would come. She was always watching. She could smell out the babies and she always waited around the peach orchards near where the mothers left their babies and as soon as the mother left the sleeping baby and went to get a drink of water Su'uḵi came and took the baby and put him in her basket and carried him off. Finally she came home with the baby. Then she put him down and came back and took another one and put him in her basket and took him home too. Then the mothers came back happily after having a drink at the spring, and there the babies were gone! They saw Su'uḵi's tracks. She went barefoot and had long toenails. Then the mothers cried very much, but they were afraid to go after their babies. Then the women who had lost their babies came home and told the people, and they all went out to look for the babies, but they never found them. Finally they came to where the people used to dry their peaches. They knew that Su'uḵi lived there, and they watched for an opportunity to kill her because she had taken their babies.

One day they all made bows and arrows and went out to kill Su'uḵi. They all met together in the kivas and decided that they would not have their babies stolen any more. The women had to go and work in the fields and help their husbands, and they did not want to have their babies taken while they worked. So they all went out. They went into all the caves and all the crevices of the rocks. Finally they came to the place where she lived. She yelled at the people and came out screaming and waving her great knife, with her hair flying. The men were all frightened, but they shot her with their bows and arrows and finally they killed her. Then they buried her and said, "This is where you are going to lie. Now you must behave from now on. We have killed you because you stole our babies. Now we shall call this place Su'ukonakwi." [30]

After they had killed her they made her mask because she was a raw person. Even though she was evil she was a katcina, so they made a mask for her, and they still make feathers for her too, to please her, because they do not want to have any trouble. After they had killed her they thought maybe they had done wrong to kill her because she was a katcina, and so they made feathers for her, and they made a mask for her so that she could come back to Itiwana. The man

---

[30] This is on the road to the south of the village and the people still believe that Su'uḵi lives there. When she comes to dance she always comes from the south.

who had seen her close painted the mask and fixed it the way she had looked. Then in the winter when they were having the mixed dance he came. Early in the morning before sunrise he took his clothes and the mask and went with his relative to the south where they had killed Su'uḵi. The people knew that they had killed her at Su'ukonakwi, but no one knew that he was coming in his mask. When they got there the man who went with the personator helped him dress and fixed him up the way Su'uḵi looked. He put the basket on his back the way she had carried it.

While they were dancing in the west plaza the people standing on the housetops saw her coming. She was tossing her head and running shouting her call. Then the people cried, "There is the woman they went out to kill. She is coming! She has come to life again, and she is angry because the man came after her. She must be very wise." They were terribly frightened, especially the women. They ran away and hid their babies. The men who belonged to the personator's kiva knew that it was he, but the rest of the men did not know. They said, "The one we killed is there. She is coming. Is it all right that she should come, or shall we go and chase her out?" Then the katcina chief went to the kiva that was giving the dance and asked them what they thought. They told him that she was not the real Su'uḵi, but that they had just made the mask. So they let her come in. So she joined in the dance, but while she was there the mothers would not let their children come out to see the dance. She was carrying her basket the way she always had, and the people who had children were very frightened. But some of the people did not care, and they went out to watch her. In the evening they would not let her stay in the kiva, but she went out to the south the way she had come.

The next day they danced the second time. There was one woman who was not afraid of Su'uḵi. Her children were very naughty. She wanted to comb their hair and take out the lice, but they would not let her do it. So she told her children, "There is a woman who eats naughty children. She ate a little child the other day. She is a katcina, and she is coming in. I am going to call her because you are very naughty children." So she went to the katcina chief and told him, "My father, will you please tell this katcina that my children do not behave and will not mind. I know she is not the real Su'uḵi, but just an impersonation, and I think it would be a good idea if he would talk to the children who are naughty and make them behave. He could take them away in his basket and frighten them so that they will behave and mind what they are told." Then the katcina chief said, "That is a good idea, and it will surely be good for some of the boys. She can frighten them so that they will not tell the secrets of the katcina society. I shall tell my people to tell the woman to come and frighten your children." So he went to the kiva, and he told the people what the woman had said.

Then the woman went home and told her children that Su'uḳi had come into the plaza to take them away. She dressed them and took them to the plaza and waited in the plaza with her children. Finally the Su'uḳi personator was told by the katcina chief and all the people that it would be a good idea to frighten the children to make them behave. So she came out and danced in the plaza and there was the woman with her two little children. When the dance was over Su'uḳi looked around all the housetops, and the people waited to see what would happen. Then the Koyemci said to her, "What are you looking for, grandmother?" All she said was, "Su-'yu-ki'." Then the woman said to her children, "She is looking for you because you don't mind me. Here they are," she said to Su'uḳi. Then Su'uḳi said, "Bring those little children here and put them in my basket. They do not mind their mother. I want children to behave, and if I find out that they don't obey their mothers and fathers, then I will eat them up. They have fresh meat on them. Fresh meat for my evening meal!" Then the Koyemci said, "We are going home with grandmother. We are going home to our home in the Sacred Lake with grandmother to eat this fresh meat."

The woman had a strong heart and was not ashamed and she took her two babies and put them in Su'uḳi's basket, and Su'uḳi carried them around the plaza four times. The babies were crying terribly. Then she said, "I am going home now. I shall have fresh meat this evening." So she pretended to carry them off. All the people thought that the children must be frightened to death. Some of them said, "That is a good idea. She will bring them back. She is not really a katcina." The people all thought it was good to frighten the little ones. When she had taken them out of the plaza she changed her mind and brought them back and said, "I am bringing you back to your mother. Now you must always mind your mother and not be naughty. If you do not mind your mother I shall come and get you again. I always hear you. I always hear when the young ones talk back to their mothers, and I will surely come and eat any children that are bad." She said this in the plaza and then she set down her basket and the Koyemci took the children out and took them back to their mother.

That night the children became very sick and on the fourth day they died. Then the people were all talking about it. They said it was not right to allow the katcinas to touch the babies or to carry them around because they are dangerous. They come from the Sacred Lake. They are the dead people, and they are raw. So now when Su'uḳi comes she does not touch the children any more. She comes and shakes her stick at them. She carries a basket on her back and says she will carry the children away and eat them, but she never touches them. A woman whose children are naughty tells the kiva chief that she wants her children punished and then when Su'uḵi comes the children give her meat so that she will not have to eat them. They tell the children to pay her to leave them alone. So we always say to our children when they are naughty, "I am going to send for Su'uḵi to eat you up."

References.—The visit of the monsters is described by Stevenson, Zuñi Indians, page 143; Parsons, Notes on Zuñi, I, 153, 172, 173; Parsons, the Zuñi adoshle and suuke, American Anthropologist 18: 338–347.

Parallels.—Hopi: Natacka (Hopi Katcinas, Pl. IX), (Zuñi Natacku); Natacka Wüqti or Soyok Wüqti (Pl. X), Zuñi Suyuki; Atocle (Pl. XIII), Zuñi Atocle Otsi. They are accompanied by Hahai Wüqti (Pl. VII), (Zuñi Ahe'a).

Fewkes describes their visit as follows: "Later in the day (the sixteenth of Powamu) three groups of Soyoko or monsters, each group consisting of four Natackas, one Natacka mana, one Hahai wüqti, one Hehe'a katcina, and two Hehe'a katcina manas, went to every house of their pueblo, demanding food from the inmates, as they had notified the people they would eight days previously. Hahai wüqti acted as speaker, assuming a falsetto voice, the Natackas emphasized the demands, and Hehea, armed with lassos, tried to rope those who refused. It is customary for the boys to first offer Hahai wüqti a mole or rat on a stick. This is refused, and then a small piece of meat, generally mutton, is held out. The Natacka examines it, and if not large enough hands it back as he did the rat, shaking his hideous head. When the desired quantity of meat is presented, it is given to the Natacka mana, who transfers it to a basket she carries on her back. The girl or woman is then asked for meal, and she offers meal that she has ground from the ear of corn presented by the monsters on their previous visit. This is refused, and more meal is demanded until enough is given to satisfy the monsters, who transfer it to the basket of Natacka mana, after which they retire. (Hopi Katcinas, p. 39.)

Fewkes points out a circumstance noticed by the writer, that Soyok (Suyuku) is a Keresan word, related to shkoya, giant.

In a series of articles Fewkes identifies the Hopi Natacku with masked monsters in Aztec codices. (Fewkes, On Certain Personages who Appear in a Tusayan Ceremony, American Anthropologist, VII, 32–52.)

The Coming of the Gods (Ca'lako)

The coming of the gods (kok'wa·wia) or ca'lako, so called from the most conspicuous participants, is the great annual cycle of ceremonies of the katcina priests. The esoteric ceremonies last throughout the calendar year, starting with the appointment of impersonators at the winter solstice and culminating in a public festival of 14 days' duration in the early part of December, shortly before the winter solstice.

On the ninth day of the winter solstice the priests of the council make the crooks of appointment (tełna·we) for the impersonators of the gods at this ceremony and for the households in which they will be entertained. Those for Cu'la·witsi, the Saiyataca party, and the Koyemci are brought to he'iwa kiva that evening by the impersonator of Pautiwa, and are distributed by p̓ekwin next morning to the men whom the priests have chosen for these offices. Sometime during the preceding week the priests had notified the chosen men of their selection and obtained their consent to serve in these exacting offices. The presentation of the crooks constitutes their formal appointment.

The same afternoon Pautiwa leaves on the roof of each of the six kivas the crook of appointment for the Ca'lako from that kiva. The kiva chief takes the crook and, as soon as convenient, confers with his associates and chooses two impersonators for each Ca'lako, inducting them into office by the presentation of the crook. Although formally appointed by the kiva chief, the Ca'lako appointees, like those of Saiyataca, receive their sanction from the priests, whose crook they hold.

At the same time men (or women) who are willing to undertake the expense of holding the public ceremonies in their houses in order to invoke the blessings of the gods on their households, volunteer to entertain the gods and receive from the priests (or the kiva chief) the longest of the sticks included in the bundle which comprises the tełnan·e. There should be eight such houses, but the expense is so great that not enough men volunteer, and the groups double up as the time for the ceremony approaches. In dearth of volunteers, the obligation of entertaining the gods falls on the priests and kiva chiefs.

The duties of the impersonators commence on the day of their appointment. That evening, after sacrificing in the river to their ancestors, they meet in their ceremonial houses to learn the prayers and other details of their office. These meetings continue throughout the year. In the case of the Saiyataca group and the Koyemci they are held every night, with brief intermissions at the seasons of lambing, sheep shearing, and harvest at the outlying villages. The Ca'lako meet formally only on the four nights following each prayer stick planting, but may meet informally on intervening nights, especially as the time for the public ceremonies approaches. The wo·we, trustees of the cults, are present to instruct. The Saiyataca group meets in the house of the impersonator of Saiyataca, the Koyemci in the house of their "father," the Ca'lako, each in the house of the elder brother. The meetings begin shortly after dark. The early part of the evening is spent in discussion. After the family has retired the prayers and chants are intoned until about one o'clock.

All the impersonators must arise before day, summer and winter, and offer prayer meal to the rising sun in a field to the east of the village. At nightfall they must take a portion of food from the evening meal and offer it with suitable prayers in the river at a point west of the village (Wide River, akwak'äpa).

Each month at the full moon prayer sticks are offered to the katcina priests at distant shrines. The first ten plantings are at springs in the mountains south of Zuñi.

On these days they gather early in the morning in their ceremonial houses to make their prayer sticks. Long prayers are recited at the conclusion of their work. Then after a feast they leave for the shrines which lie to the south at distances of from 4 to 8 miles. The prayer sticks are deposited beside the spring in regular order, and long prayers are offered. The text of this prayer is given on p. 706. The impersonator of Saiyataca recites the prayer, the others joining in, according to the extent of their knowledge. Toward sunset the party approaches the village, marching in regular order across the plains, singing songs of the masked dancers.

Throughout the year each group of impersonators must work for the household which is to entertain them at the great public festival. From midsummer on, every day is spent in labor for their hosts. They do all the work of the fields and build the new home in which the gods are to be received.

On the morning of the tenth planting, which takes place early in October, the impersonators of Saiyataca and Molanhakto receive from the priest the two day counts, cotton strings containing 49 knots. One knot is untied each morning until the day of the great public ceremony. During this period there are plantings at intervals of ten days at rock shrines to the southwest of the village.

The public ceremonies start on the fortieth day,[31] with the arrival of the Koyemci in the evening. They come masked, visiting each of the four plazas to announce the coming of the gods in eight days. They then go into retreat in the house of their father where they remain in seclusion, with the exception of brief appearances in the plaza, until the festival is concluded 15 days later.

Four days after the appearance of the Koyemci, the Saiyataca party comes in in the evening and goes into retreat in the house of the impersonator of Saiyataca. On the same night the Ca'lako impersonators go into retreat in their respective houses.

On the eighth day there is another planting of prayer sticks with elaborate ceremonies at which the gods are summoned from the village of the masked gods.

After they are clothed and masked they approach the village. The giant Ca'lako gods wait on the south bank of the river, but the katcina priests—Cula·witsi, Saiyataca, Hututu, two Yamuhakto, and two Salimopïa—enter the village in mid afternoon. After planting prayer sticks in six excavations in the streets of the village, they repair to the house where they are to be entertained for the night. This is always a new or at least a renovated house, and the visit of the katcinas is a blessing—a dedication. Prayer sticks are planted inside the threshold (formerly under the outside ladder) and in a

---

[31] That is, if the ceremony is not postponed. However, almost without exception, a postponement of ten days is necessary.

decorated box suspended from the center of the ceiling. The walls of the house are marked with corn meal. In an excavation in the center of the floor seeds of all kinds are deposited. Similar rites are performed later in the evening by the six Ca'lako and the Koyemci in the houses where they are to be entertained.

After the blessing of the house, the gods are seated by the p̄ekwin, their masks raised. Reed cigarettes are brought and each katcina smokes with the person seated opposite him, exchanging with him the customary terms of relationship. Then the host (in the Saiyataca house, the village chief serves as host) questions the gods concerning the circumstance of their coming. In the long recital that follows he reviews all the events leading up to the present moment, and invokes upon the house all the blessings of the gods, especially the blessing of fecundity. Two of these chants are recorded in text below.

This litany, chanted in unison by the four leaders (Cula·witsi is not required to learn it), takes about six hours to perform. It is chanted in loud tones and very slowly, in monotone except for the last syllable of each line which is higher in pitch, heavily accented and prolonged. The text of this is printed on p. 710.

The chants of the Ca'lako, which omit the recital of the 29 springs visited by the gods on their way to Zuñi, and curtail other portions, take from one to two hours to perform. The text of one of the shorter ones is printed on p. 762.

All are finished at about 11 o'clock at night, when an elaborate feast is served in all the houses. After this all the masked personages dance until day in the houses of their hosts.

At the first sign of approaching dawn Saiyataca ascends to the roof of the house where he has spent the night, and facing the east, unties the last knot in his counting string while he intones another prayer. Returning to the house, he repeats the prayer. He then thanks the members of the society choir who furnished the music during the night. The dancing continues until sunrise when the heads of all impersonators are washed by the women of the houses where they were entertained, as a symbol of their permanent association with these houses. They receive gifts of food, and sometimes of clothing, from their hosts, but these gifts are in no measure a compensation for their services.

At about noon, after planting prayer sticks and performing magical ceremonies in a field on the south of the river, the Ca'lako gods and the Saiyataca group depart for their home in the west. This closes their year, and the impersonators of the Saiyataca group and the Ca'lako are now free after the exacting period of service.

The Koyemci, however, are not yet free. Throughout the year their duties have been heavier. They hold nightly meetings, participate in the monthly plantings of the other impersonators. Furthermore, at all of the dances of the summer series (six in all, lasting from one to eight days) they must come out and "play," observing all the usual taboos from the evening preceding the dance until the final departure. They may appear also in winter, and if they do must observe the same restrictions. If any extra dances are inserted into the calendar in the summer and fall, as frequently happens, the Koyemci are required to attend.

For five nights following the departure of the Ca'lako gods, dancers from each of the six kivas are supposed to visit all the houses which have entertained the gods. Some of them dance in the plaza during the day. Throughout this period the Koyemci remain in strict retreat in the house where they were entertained. At night they dance in their house; during the day they "play" in the plaza and attend any dancers who appear there. These are days of great festivity.

On the fifth evening they eat early and sparingly, and from this time on food and drink are taboo until the following night. Speech also is forbidden them, nor may they appear unmasked. After they enter upon this period the character of their dancing changes, becoming more solemn. They do not indulge in their usual obscenity. On the following morning they come out early and are taken to be "washed" in the house of the village chief. Here the women give them gifts of food. On coming out, they are taken by men of their fathers' clans to the houses of their fathers' sister. Here they receive valuable gifts from all members of the fathers' clan. Each personator will receive as many as thirty slaughtered sheep, as many baskets of corn or wheat flour, bread, melons, and miscellaneous gifts of clothing, frequently of great value. The gifts are brought to the plaza where they remain until night. Meanwhile, the Koyemci attend upon the various dancers until later at night.

At nightfall the last of the dancers, the Molawia, (see p. 913) have departed. Then the Koyemci in pairs visit every house in the village to invoke upon it the blessings of the gods. At each house they receive gifts of food from the female inhabitants. Returning to the plaza, they take their prayer sticks out to plant. They return to the house of their father late at night, and removing their masks for the first time all day give them to their father to return to the house where they are kept. When he comes back, he thanks his children for their year of work and sets them free. Then for the first time since the preceding evening they drink, and after eating and bathing, return to their homes. Their retreat, 15 days, is the longest in Zuñi ritual.

The culmination of the Ca'lako ceremony is fully described—that is, as fully as any one person can describe any elaborate Pueblo ceremony—by Stevenson (Zuñi Indians, pp. 227–277), and by Parsons (Notes on Zuñi I). The writer observed different portions of the ceremony on two successive years and has little to add in the way of ritual to these excellent accounts. Her more important observations concerned the economic and social aspects of the ceremony.   A native account, in text, of preparations will be published elsewhere.

An abridged version of the Ca'lako is performed at the village of Sitcumovi on the first mesa, and is a recent importation from Zuñi. It came in about 70 years ago when a great famine caused numerous migrations throughout the pueblo region.   The ceremony is described by Fewkes in Hopi Katcinas.

Koyemci

(Plates 23 and 24)

There are 10 Koyemci, differing slightly in appearance and conduct. All wear knobbed masks of cotton cloth, stained with the same pink clay that is used on their bodies.   The knobs of the masks are filled with cotton wool and seeds, and (Parsons, Notes on Zuñi) dust from the footprints of townspeople.   Wrapped around the base of the mask is a piece of native black cloth.   Under this they wear concealed their packets of seeds.

The Koyemci carry the seeds of various native crops, as follows:

A·wan tatcu, native squash.	Nałaci, black corn.
Pekwin, yellow corn.	Itsepaca, speckled corn.
Pi'łanciwan·i, blue corn.	Posuki, sweet corn.
Muyaƀona, white corn.	Ḳalutsi, water gourds.
Ecotsi, red corn.	Ts'ałaci, cipitako.[32]

When the Koyemci come to play for the katcina dances they wear only a kilt of black cotton cloth.   They do not wear under this the otherwise indispensable breechcloth.   Instead they have tied about the penis a cotton cord.   This makes erection of the penis impossible, and symbolizes the sexual impotence of the Koyemci.   The Koyemci on occasions remove their kilts and stand naked before the people. "It is all right for the Koyemci to take off their covering, because they are just like children."

When the Koyemci come to announce the opening of the Ca'lako festival they are clothed in the usual ceremonial costume of white shirt, trousers, and native moccasins.   Hanging from the right shoulder they wear pouches made from the whole skins of fawns.

When dancing in the Ca'lako houses, they wear brown moccasins, and carry their fawn skin bags, as shown in the drawings.   In their own house the mask and moccasins are laid aside.   The masks are kept in a basket on the altar, and when not in use, the moccasins and pouch of each Koyemci are hung on a peg above his official seat.

---

[32] "The corn that is all puffed out with the kernels broken open.   These symbolize the person who is always happy and laughing.   A mother who wants her baby to be happy and to laugh all the time will eat this kind of corn.   The youngest of the Koyemci brings it so that the people may always be happy."

THE KOYEMCI

a, A·wan tatcu; b, A·wan pekwin·e; c, A·wan p̣i'łaciwan·i; d, Muyaɓona; e, Ecotsi.

THE KOYEMCI

a, Nahaci; *b*, Itsepaca; *c*, Posuki; *d*, Ḳälutsi; *e*, Tsahaci.

Old Masks Appearing Irregularly, Fig. c (See Plate 33)

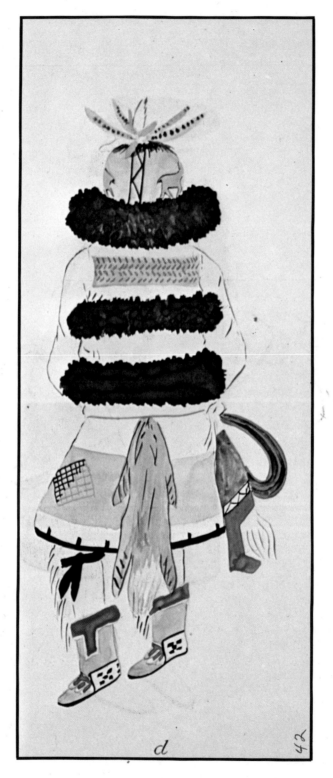

Old Masks Appearing Irregularly, Fig. d (See Plate 33)

One informant contributes the following comments on the Koyemci:

"The father of the Koyemci is chosen by the priests on the last night of it·iwan·a, the night when the Puhu'atinakwe go around. He is chosen by the priests, and therefore he can not refuse to serve. He is always a member of some society, and after he has been chosen he consults the headmen of his society.[33] He chooses the men he wants to go in with him. If possible he will take the same ones as served with him the last time. They always pick for Koyemci the children of important clans, so that they may be well paid by their fathers' clans for their year's work.

"The Koyemci are the most dangerous of all the katcinas. If anyone touches a Koyemci while he has his paint on he will surely go crazy. They carry the sacred butterfly, lahacoma, in their drum to make people follow them. That is why they are so dangerous. Anyone who follows lahacoma will go crazy.

"The Koyemci are different from all other dancers. They do not go home with their paint on. In the evening when they finish dancing if no one has asked them to dance again their wo'le takes sand to their father's house, and they all go there to wash off their paint before they go home to their wives. But if they are to dance again the next day they do not wash their bodies that night, because they must stay in their father's house that night, and may not go home to their wives. They may not go home until they have finished their dance. Other dancers may go home for their supper, but not the Koyemci. When they go around the village to collect food to give away in their dances, their wo'le goes to their houses for them, for they must not go to their own houses, even with their masks on.

"The Koyemci never go out without their full number. Sometimes if one of them can not dance they will have to get someone else to take his place. There must always be ten of them when they go out. The last rain dance started late in the day because one of the Koyemci was sick and they had a hard time finding someone to take his place.

"One must never refuse anything to the Koyemci, because they are dangerous. Last year around Ca'lako my mother received a present of a box of apples. She was wondering whether she should give it to our 'child' when he was washed. She was thinking it would be nice if she would keep that box of apples. While she was whitewashing the house she fell off the ladder and bruised her leg. Then she knew that she must give that box of apples to the Koyemci. She was hurt because she had withheld it from them even in her thoughts. The Koyemci are dangerous."

---

[33] This, apparently, is the traditional method of selection, which seems to have undergone considerable change. (See p. 949.)

Cushing (Zuñi Origin Myths), gives the following description of the appearance and conduct of the 10 Koyemci:

"In time there were born to these twain 12 children. Nay, neither man children nor woman children, they! For look now! The first was a woman in fullness of contour, but a man in stature and brawn. From the mingling of too much seed in one kind, comes the twofold one kind ła'hmon, being man and woman combined. . . . Yet not all ill was this first child, because she was born of love, ere her parents were changed; thus she partook not of their distortions. Not so with her brothers; in semblance of males, yet like boys, the fruit of sex was not in them! For the fruit of mere lust ripens not. For their parents, being changed to hideousness, abode together witlessly and consorted idly or in passion not quickened of favor to the eye or the heart. And lo! like to their father were his later children, but varied as his moods. . . . Thus they were strapping louts, but dun colored and marked with the welts of their father. Silly were they, yet wise as the gods and high priests; for as simpletons and the crazed speak from the things seen of the instant, uttering belike wise words and prophecy, so spake they, and became the attendants and fosterers, yet the sages and interpreters of the ancient dance dramas of the ka'ka.

"Named are they not with the names of men, but with names of mismeaning, for there is pekwina, priest speaker of the sun. Meditative is he, even in the quick of day, after the fashion of his father when shamed, saying little save rarely, and then as irrelevantly as the veriest child or dotard.

"Then there is pi'łan shiwani (bow priest warrior). So cowardly he that he dodges behind ladders, thinking them trees no doubt, and lags after all the others, whenever frightened, even at the fluttering leaf or a crippled spider, and looks in every direction but the straight one whenever danger threatens!

"There is eshotsi (the bat) who can see better in the sunlight than any of them, but would maim himself in a shadow, and will avoid a hole in the ground as a woman would a dark place even were it no bigger than a beetle burrow.

"Also there is muiyapona (wearer of the eyelets of invisibility). He has horns like the catfish and is knobbed like a bludgeon squash. But he never by any chance disappears, even when he hides his head behind a ladder run or turkey quill, yet thinks himself quite out of sight. And he sports with his countenance as though it were as smooth as a damsel's.

"There is potsoki (the pouter) who does little but laugh and look bland, for grin he can not; and his younger brother Nałashi (aged buck) who is the biggest of them all, and what with having grieved and nearly rubbed his eyes out (when his younger brother was captured and carried off by the Ḵyamaḵyakwe or snail ka'ka of the south), looks as ancient as a horned toad; yet he is frisky as a fawn, and giggles like a girl; yea, and bawls as lustily as a small boy playing games.

"The next brother, itseposa (the glum or aggrieved), mourned also for his nearest brother, who was stolen by the ka'ka, too, until his eyes were dry utterly and his chin chapped to protrusion; but nathless he is lively and cheerful and ever as ready indeed as the most complaisant of beings.

"Ḳyalutsi (the suckling) and tsałashi (old youth), the youngest, are the most willfully important of the nine, always advising others and strutting like a young priest at his first dance or like unto the youthful warrior made to aged thinking and self-notioned with early honoring.

"And while the father stands dazed, with his head bowed and his hands clasped before him or like to broken bows hanging by his sides, these children romp and play (as he and his sister did when turned childish), and verily are like to idiots, or to dotards and crones turned young again, inconstant as laughter, startle to new thought by every flitting thing around them; but, in the presence of the ka'ka of old, they are grave, what though so uncouth. And they are the oracles of all olden sayings of deep meanings; wherefore they are called the kayemashi (husbandmen of the ka'ka or sacred dance drama); and they are spoken of, even by the fathers of the people, as the ałashi tsewashi (sages of the ancients). And most precious in the sight of the beings and of men are they!"

The Koyemci used to be selected in rotation from four societies.[34] As in Mrs. Stevenson's time, there are now four groups that serve in turn, designated by their ceremonial affiliations as follows:

He'ikwe, a group of men from He'iwa kiva. They served for the first time in 1920 and again in 1924.

Cowe·kwe,[35] an informal group of men who gamble together. They served in 1925.

Make łana·kwe, a group from Great Fire Society (maḳe łana·kwe). They served in 1926.

Cowe·kwe, another informal group, not the same as above. Served in 1927.

The 10 impersonators form a more or less permanent group. The leader, their "father," receives a crook of appointment from the priests at the New Year, and selects those who will assist him. Ordinarily he will select the same men who served with him at his last turn in office, filling any vacancies caused by death from members of his kiva, society, or some informal group with which he may be associated, always taking into consideration in his appointments clan

---

[34] Stevenson, p. 235; Parsons, Notes on Zuñi, I, 183.

[35] Stevenson lists Cowe·kwe as a doubtful fraternity. She was taken in by a Zuñi jest. They say of the youth who wastes his time gambling that he belongs to Cowe·kwe Society.

affiliation. Any vacancy will usually be filled by a man of similar clan affiliation. The office of Koyemci is a desirable one, because of the rich payments at the end, and there will always be a number of young men who have signified their willingness to serve from whom the leader may choose. The appointments are made as soon as possible after the New Year. Should the group whose turn it is to serve have done anything to cause the disapproval of the priests, it will be passed over in favor of a new group, perhaps one of the groups of no ceremonial status that impersonate Koyemci during the winter dances.

The Koyemci have a very full year. They share all the duties of the other appointees for the Ca'lako—the nightly meetings, the monthly planting of prayer sticks, the work for the house that is to entertain them. Entertaining the Koyemci is the most expensive participation in Zuñi, because in addition to the expense involved in building the house, and the feast on the night when the gods come, the 11 men, the 10 Koyemci and their wo'le are in retreat in the house which entertained them for six days following the ceremony and must be fed throughout that time. So often the crook for entertaining the Koyemci is not taken, and their father is obliged to entertain them in his house. In that case the labor of housebuilding does not begin until the fall. However, throughout the spring and summer the Koyemci go individually to work in the houses of their "aunts," all the women of their fathers' clans, whenever they have special work afoot. In addition to the ceremonies of the Ca'lako the Koyemci must assist at all dances of the katcinas. They attend the dancers in the plazas, and between the rounds of the dance amuse the audience by clowning.

The presence of the Koyemci at the winter dances is not obligatory, but they may appear, if they wish, at any dance after their first prayer-stick planting. If the "real" Koyemci do not wish to appear at any dance, their masks may be borrowed by any other group. There are several more or less permanent groups that "play" at the winter dances, and at extra dances interpolated into the calendar in the summer or fall.[36]

Usually the first public appearance of the Koyemci is after the summer solstice. On the afternoon of the third day following the planting of prayer sticks to the sun, the Koyemci enter the village from the west. They are naked except for their usual kilt of black cloth, and unmasked, with their hair unbound and falling over their faces. Starting on the south side of the village, they pass every house. As they pass, the women of the house douse them with water from the housetops, to induce prompt rain. After visiting every house in the

---

[36] Such a group from he'iwa kiva appeared when Hilili was danced after Ca'lako was over in December, 1927.

village the Koyemci retire to their ceremonial house. On this occasion they are called Tumitcimtci, from the first word of their song. (Observed June, 1926. R. L. B.)

If the quadrennial pilgrimage to the Katcina Village is to take place, the Koyemci leave with other members of the pilgrimage party at dawn the following day. Otherwise they remain in retreat in their house until the third day, when they leave at dawn, some going with the pilgrimage party to Rainbow Spring, the others taking the monthly offering to spring required for their Ca'lako planting. On their return in the late afternoon both groups meet on the plain where they dress and mask. They enter the village with a group of Koḵokci dancers just before sundown. Everyone in the village goes to the southwest edge of town to wait for the return of the gods after their long absence. The high loud calls of the Koḵokci can be heard long before the gods are visible. When the writer observed the ceremony in 1926, the gods entered the village in the midst of the first summer shower after a month of grilling heat, which made the occasion even more joyous than usual. The Koyemci accompany the dancers on their round of the plazas and then retire to their ceremonial house, where the fourth night of their retreat is consumed in dancing. One of the medicine societies has been invited to sing for them. Late at night they visit the Koḵokci in the house where they are similarly in retreat. They do not come out when the Koḵokci make their early morning rounds of the plazas, but come out later in the morning to play.[37]

In general their play might be characterized as childish, in contrast to the more adult and subtle satire of the Newe·kwe. This is in accord with the childish, unformed character attributed to them in mythology. Their sexual character has already been alluded to. Nevertheless they are possessors of the most potent love magic. The game which they have been observed to play most frequently between rounds of dances is the bean bag game, a kind of tag, which their grotesque appearance and uncouth behavior make ludicrous. Occasionally they burlesque dances, but such burlesques as the writer has observed have been crude and unfinished, and lacking in any satirical touch. For their more serious moments when they first come out in the morning, they have the guessing game described by Parsons (Notes on Zuñi, II, 229–237). There are set times at which this is played. Obscene games have been described by Parsons. Also, by a Zuñi informant, a game in which one Koyemci, impersonating a familiar female character in folklore, goes through the motions of intercourse with another (Benedict, ms.). Another popular game is where one Koyemci is trapped on the projecting beams of the kiva and threatened with fire until he throws down his one garment.

---

[37] For accounts of their games see Parsons, Notes on Zuñi.

The Koyemci are the first of the katcinas to "go home" in the fall, and they are the first to return at Ca'lako. They come in eight days before Ca'lako night, in the evening, soon after dark. Again everyone waits for them, and they are sprinkled liberally with meal on their progress through the village. They visit all the plazas to announce the coming of the gods. This announcement is printed in text in the Journal of American Folk-Lore. But before A·wan p̄ekwin makes his announcement, all the others are given a chance to make obscene or ridiculous speeches. Stevenson (p. 952) gives some of these speeches. Parsons quotes her informants, who belonged to the Protestant Mission group, as saying that no such remarks would be made. However, on the two occasions on which I have heard these announcements, many remarks of this character were made. The favorite topic seems to be bestiality. The following is typical: "Now that those who hold our roads, night priests, have come out standing to their sacred place, we have passed you on your roads. Our daylight fathers, our daylight mothers, after so many days, eight days, on the ninth day you will copulate with rams." (At this time of year the rams are put back into the general herds.) Many remarks of this character which I failed to hear were repeated for me the following day by two little boys of 12 who belonged to my household.

After visiting all the plazas the Koyemci retire to their house and are in strict retreat for eight days (nights). On the seventh day they go early in the afternoon to White Rocks to plant their prayer sticks and to dress. When they return to the village in the evening they wear their Koyemci costume, with brown moccasins and their fawn-skin pouches. They have white buckskins over their shoulders. Their masks are pushed up on their foreheads, exposing their faces. They are the last group to enter the village. It is fully dark when they come at about 9 o'clock. Before going to their own house, they visit the houses of the Ca'lako and Saiyataca. They stand before the door, calling the inmates by name in song, and twitting them for stinginess, laziness, domestic infelicity, fondness for American ways. For example, "Our mother ——— gives her children thin coffee and peaches." (There had been no peach crop that year. therefore these had been hoarded. December, 1927.)

When they reach their own house the three leaders, A·wan Tatcu, A·wan P̄ekwin, and Pi'łaciwan·i, are first brought in by the host. They dedicate the house by planting prayer sticks under the door before they enter, by marking the walls with corn meal, and planting prayer sticks in the roof and seeds in the excavation in the floor. Then the others enter and are seated and "given smoke" by ten men, members of the household, friends or relatives. The three leaders then intone a chant which consumes about two hours and is very similar to the chant of the Ca'lako. After this their masks are removed and placed on the altar, and a feast is served. All go out to sacrifice food to their ancestors in the river. After eating they dance for a while in their house, then all but the three leaders mask and go in couples to dance in the other Ca'lako houses. Their visits are occasions of great merriment. (Observed December, 1927, 1928.)

They do not appear for the morning ceremonies of the departure of the Ca'lako, but early in the afternoon they appear in mask and costume and visit again all the Ca'lako houses. They dance and sing on the edge of the housetops. After finishing their song, they descend, exchange bantering words with those within, terminated by the women of the house dousing them with water. Unfortunately, the words were unintelligible to the writer because of the mask. On this occasion they are called Haliliku (mountain sheep), from their dance and the words of their song.

For the following six days they remain in strict retreat in the house which entertained them. They do not leave the house except in mask to fulfill their ceremonial program. If it is necessary for them to leave their ceremonial room, they are accompanied by their wo'le. On the first evening they dance for a short time in their own house. They are in costume but not masked. On the second, fourth, and sixth nights of kot'ina (the katcinas stay), the Koyemci, after their house has been visited by all the dance sets that are out, go, accompanied by their society choir, to sing and dance in all the Ca'lako houses. These are most solemn occasions. The society members, in full regalia, sing, the koyemci dance in slow rhythm in a circle. There are special songs for this ceremony, very different in character from the dancing songs of the societies. After one song has been sung, long prayers are exchanged between the society chief and the host. Sometimes society members play a guessing game with someone in the house, or perform feats of jugglery. After another song the group withdraws, and all present sprinkle the Koyemci with meal. If any of the dancing katcinas have been dancing in the house at the time of the entrance of the Koyemci, they withdraw, and resume their dance after the others have gone. But usually this rite closes the ceremonies for the evening.

On the intervening nights the Koyemci dance in their own house between the performances of visiting dance sets. Here they are unmasked. Their dance step is rapid and energetic, and they dance with the most intense concentration, which is especially moving since most of the men are past middle age, and clearly show the strain of physical exertion.

On the third and fifth mornings of kotina, the Koyemci appear in the plaza with their society choir. They use the same song and dance as on their evening rounds. On these days they play their familiar guessing game, giving away a considerable amount of property to the persons called from the housetops to participate. On other days they appear in the plaza for a few hours in the afternoon, fully clothed and wrapped in blankets (ordinarily the weather at this season is inclement and intensely cold).

On the final (sixth) night, the Koyemci eat their evening meal at sundown (about 5.30 o'clock). The people of the house bring in 10 bowls of meat stew, 10 baskets of paper bread, and 10 tubs of wheat bread and set them down before the impersonators. The father of the Koyemci slowly dips his roll of paper bread into his stew. After he has taken four mouthfuls, he lays down his uneaten roll of bread. This is the sign for the others who have been eating rapidly, to stop. The balance of the food is removed by the wives or sisters of the Koyemci who have come for this purpose, and taken to their houses. From now on until they are freed sometime the following night they may touch neither food nor drink. Large numbers of people go to the Koyemci house to watch this curious evening meal.

On this night the full quota of dances is performed. The dance sets all visit the Koyemci house early in the evening. By 10 o'clock all have been there. Shortly after the Koyemci mask and visit the Ca'lako houses, as described above, for the last time. This is a very solemn occasion. The Koyemci do not now indulge in any clowning or joking. On leaving each house all present sprinkle them liberally with meal. This sprinkling of meal is by no means perfunctory on this occasion, and the murmured prayers are most earnestly spoken. The rite shows the great reverence in which the Koyemci are held. (Observed December, 1927, 1928.)

Early the following morning, the society choir takes the Koyemci to the plaza and sends them home, bidding them farewell in a special farewell song which runs as follows: "Our fathers, Molanhaktu, now you are about to go to your village of the masked gods. From there surely you will not fail to send us your waters."

The balance of their day is admirably described in the following native account. (All the events recorded, except those in the house of the priests and the father's house have been observed in 1927 and 1928. For the ceremonies not observed, the full texts of the prayers were recorded from another informant. These are given on p. 777.)

"Eight days before Ca'lako the Koyemci go into retreat in the house of their father and after Ca'lako they stay in for six days more. So they are in for 14 days. The day that Pautiwa brings in the Corn Maids is the last day they are in. On that day their aunts (i. e., father's sisters) bring them presents because during the whole year they have been praying for the people of Itiwana.

"On the last day in the morning they come out of their father's house. Each brings sacks and buckskins and wagon cloths, and they take them to the plaza. Here they dance. Then pekwin comes

out and takes them into the ceremonial room of the priests.   In that
room are the wives of all the priests and the women of all the houses
where they keep the sacred bundles of the priests.   Each woman
brings with her 10 loaves of bread and 10 rolls of paper bread.   All
the head priests are met in their ceremonial room.   Then the Koyemci
come in and their father talks to the priests and the women and says,
'All year we have been praying for you and now we have finished our
year.   We have worked hard for our people that their crops may grow.
We will never forget, our fathers, that you have picked us out for
this.'   In his prayer he tells them that they have all been praying
for their people and that now they have finished their year.   Then
all in the room breathe in.   Then the village chief prays also and says
that he is very thankful that all year they have worked and prayed
for the people.[39]

After they have finished their prayers, the women spread out sand
on the floor.   They take the father of the Koyemci first.   He comes
forward to the women of the sacred houses.   Then he removes his
breechcloth and stands there entirely naked and the women wash
him all over because the Koyemci are the most valuable of all the gods.
Their paint is valuable, and therefore, they must be washed in the
sacred room of the priests.   All the others watch him and do just
as he does.   They all remove their breechcloths and stand there
naked while the women wash them.   They do not try to cover themselves, but stand there naked in front of all these women.   After
they have all been bathed the p̃ekwin takes them out to the plaza.
As they are going out the women all stand in line and as each goes by
each woman gives each of them one loaf of bread and one roll of paper
bread, because she has touched their bodies.

Then they come out into the plaza.   There their fathers' brothers
are waiting for them.   They get them and take them to their houses.[40]
They take them to their houses; each goes to the house of his
father's sister.   All their father's clan are met in their father's ancestral house.   Long ago the men used to bring deer meat and the
women bread.   Now they bring whatever they have and presents
from the store—meal and flour, meat, whole sheep, bolts of cloth,
blankets, and new clothing.   All the women are sitting around the
wall, and each has her presents on the floor in front of her.   The
Koyemci sits facing the east.   His real aunts mix yucca seeds and
sprinkle his head with water.   He does not unmask.   Each man
brings a prayer stick for him to pray for their long life and for the
rain and the crops.   His father's brother bundles up the feathers and
hands them to the Koyemci, and they both hold them and present
them to the six directions.   The man gives them to him with a

[39] For these prayers see p. 777.

[40] "Someone always meets the katcinas when they are through dancing.   For the others it is their
fathers' sisters, but the Koyemci are different.   It is always their fathers' brothers who meet them."

prayer. Then the Koyemci tells them that all year he has been praying for his aunts, for their long life and for their crops and for all good
things for them. Then they all say, 'Thank you,' and his father's
brother gives him the prayer sticks. Everyone sprinkles corn meal
on his head. Then they all bring him their presents. There will be
really valuable presents like blankets and clothing from his real aunts.
All the men bring whole sheep, and the women grind and bake. Then
he takes as much as he can carry on his back, and the other people
take the rest and they carry it all up to the plaza. The women follow
him with the flour and bread on their heads, and the men take the
meat and store things in a wagon. Each Koyemci's things are piled
up by his place in the plaza. All the Koyemci come like that from
the houses of their aunts.[41]

In the evening after all the dancing is over, after P̂autiwa has
brought in the corn maids and they have finished their dancing in the
kiva and gone out, then the Koyemci's people will come and take
their presents away. They will take all his things to his own home,
to his wife's house if he is married, otherwise to his mother's house.
Then, after everything has been taken away from the plaza, father
Koyemci divides the village into sections and assigns each section to
one of the Koyemci, telling him to go to certain houses and thank the
people for their presents and wish them good luck. So they start out
from the plaza. Everyone else has gone home to his wife. The
Ca'lako people are in only three days, and they have gone home long
ago. These poor men want to go home too, for it is way late at night,
but they are still working for the people. So they go around to all
the houses and stand outside and say, 'Mothers!' They say it so
that those inside can hear them. Then they answer. Then he says
again, 'May you have long life.' (T̂on teк̂ohanan yaniktciatu!) 'I
am praying for you.' ('To'na ho' teк̂ohanan ceme'a!') Then they
say, 'Thank you.' Then they give to him again. They have
already given in the morning, and now they give to him again. The
woman of the house takes a basket of broken paper bread for the
people of the village of the katcinas [42] and some fresh paper
bread for the Koyemci. Then she goes out and sprinkles corn meal
and gives the bread to him. He puts the whole paper bread into his
blanket on his back, and the broken paper bread he puts into his fawn-
skin bag for the ancients. So they go around to all the houses.
Every house in the village is visited this way that night. Sometimes his brother or someone in his wife's family will go around with
him and help him carry his things, and take them home for him when
he has too much to carry.

"After every house in the village has been visited they come back
to the plaza. There is a big fire burning there. Then their father

---

[41] Observed in houses of the Badger clan December, 1927, and 1928. R. L. B. See p. 777 for prayers.
[42] To be sacrificed in the river.

takes them to his house. All his people are there, and his wife has been cooking and baking for them. They come in and go right in to their ceremonial room, because they still have their masks on. When they have all come in each one takes off his mask and prays, 'Now, my father, now I am finished with you. We have finished our work of looking after our people's welfare. May I be fortunate as you have always been. When you were a person long ago you had no misfortune. Now give me long life and a strong body like you used to have when you were a person. Do not draw me back with you, but give me a strong heart.' Thus they all say and set down their masks. Then their father comes and he wraps up the masks in a ceremonial blanket. He says, 'Now, my children, wait for me until I come back.' The poor men have had nothing to eat or drink since the evening before when they had their supper, and now it is midnight already. They have been in retreat for 14 days. They look tired and sick. They have had their masks on all day and their hair is covered with corn meal. Their father takes up the masks and goes out. He goes to the west side of the village to the house where they keep the masks. He gives them to the woman who takes care of them and prays for the people in that house, and they pray for him and thank him. Then he leaves the masks and comes home. He has been gone nearly an hour.

"When he comes back there is a jar of fresh water in the room and a new gourd. He dips out some of the water with the gourd and says, 'Now, my children, rest.' Then he takes a little sip of the water and holds the gourd for the next one and he drinks a little. They all drink a little bit and then when they have each had a sip they get up and go over to the jar and really drink. Until each one has had a sip of the water they are all sacred. Then their father tells them again that he is glad that they have finished their year, and he tells them that they should always be kind to everyone and never hurt anyone. 'Even if you have finished your year you must be kind to everyone now so that when our time comes again we may not have a bad name. Our time will come again in four years.' Then their father sprinkles them all again, and after he has sprinkled them with water they are free. Then the women bring in the food and they eat, and that is the end of it."

The Koyemci occupy so important a place in the life and thought of the people that no paper about the pueblos fails to mention them. The more important accounts of their mythological character have been quoted above. Doctor Parsons's various papers on Zuñi contain many allusions to their practices and to the awe with which they are regarded by the people.

The whole question of the interrelation of the various masked and unmasked clown groups of the different pueblos is too involved to be treated here and must be deferred to some later publication. In this case the idea of masking seems distinctly secondary and the Koyemci are probably more nearly related to clowning societies on the Plains and other parts of North America than to the masked rain beings of the pueblos. Doctor Parsons has pointed out that they are perhaps caricatures of the Spanish padres, nor should their possible relation to the masked devils of Mexican and European carnival dancing be overlooked.

Cula·witsi

(Plate 25, a)

Costume.—On his head, feathers fastened to a short stick; from front to back these are: Turkey, hawk, bluejay, onoɬiko, humming bird, duck. Two thick cotton cords hang over his face on the left side. The mouth and eyes are small holes.

The mask and body are painted black all over with ƙeƙwina and hekwitola and then spotted with yellow (heɬuptsikwa), blue (akwaɬi), red (icilowa yäɬtokä, made from the juice of a plant, mixed with red corn), and white (he'ƙohakwa).

"When he comes at Ca'lako he should be all naked. That is the way he used to come, but now he wears a small breechcloth of black cloth, painted like the body. He wears a fawn-skin bag over his shoulder. This is filled with seeds. On his back he carries a bundle of birds and rabbits which his father kills for him. He gives these to the house where he stays. In his right hand he carries a torch of cedar bark, in his left yamuwe, two sticks of black wood, measured from the inside of the elbow to the tip of the middle finger, with feathers at both ends.

"When he comes for the initiation he wears a belt of blue leather with a long fringe of goat's hair hanging from it. In the right hand he carries a torch, in the left yamuwe. But when he whips the children and goes around the village to take away the bad luck he puts away his yamuwe and carries yucca in the right hand and a torch in the left."

There are really two distinct Cula·witsis. There are two ancient masks. The one that is used at Ca'lako is kept with those of Saiyataca, Hututu, and Yamuhakto in house 56. At that time the impersonator is a little boy, from 10 to 14 years of age. He is selected indirectly by the priests, and must be Badger clan or child of Badger.

The mask that is used for the initiation is kept with the mask of the many colored Sälimopiya in house X163. This house, also is Dogwood. The impersonator on this occasion is an older man. He is picked out by the head men of uptsanawa kiva, and must belong to that kiva and the Badger clan.

Cula·witsi is frequently referred to by the Zuñis as the fire god, but in their own language he is usually called Pekwin ts'ana (little pekwin).

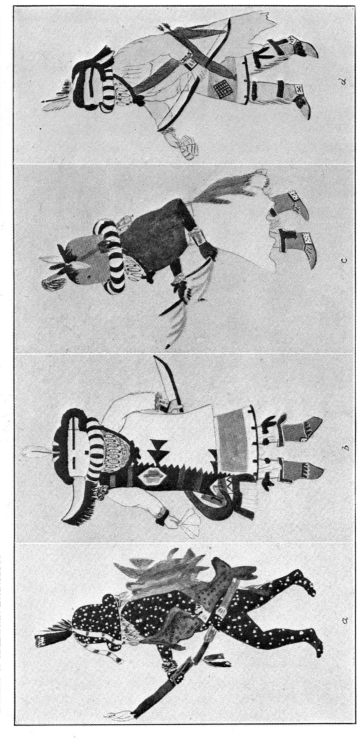

THE SAIYATACA GROUP

a, Cula·witsi; *b*, Saiyataca; *c*, Yamuhakto; *d*, Hu·tutu.

THE CA'LAKO HOUSE

There is some association between fire, the office of p̄ekwin, and the Badger clan. P̄ekwin, in addition to being a sort of "talking chief," is also an officiating priest in charge of the altar. (Possibly he also takes care of the fire?) The katcina P̄ekwin must be Badger clan.[43] Fire making is always the prerogative of the Badger clan. Anyone who builds fires easily and quickly is dubbed tonaci·kwe (Badger person).

On the day preceding the winter solstice the priests select a man of the Badger clan to tend the fire that is kept burning in he'iwa kiva throughout the ten days of the solstice observances. This man is called tsupal'ilona (the one who keeps the blood pudding), and the sacred fire is his "pudding." He in turn selects the impersonator of Cula·witsi from among the young boys of his family. Cula·witsi must be Badger clan one year and child of Badger the next, so tsupal'ilona selects either his sister's son (Badger) or his own son (child of Badger). In selecting a man for the office of tsupal'ilona, the priests must consider whether the man has in his family a boy of suitable age, intelligence, and character for the rôle of Cula·witsi. The office of tsupal'-ilona is hard to fill for other reasons. He must spend most of his time during the ten days of the solstice alone in the kiva, where it is cold and cheerless, although he is permitted to return to his home to eat and sleep. For ten days he must abstain from all animal food, and, of course, observe continence. The priests are sometimes compelled to appoint a man who has no suitable candidate for Cula·witsi, and in that case the man himself must serve in this capacity.

A woman whose son had served as Cula·witsi gives the following description of his appointment: "Late at night the bow priest came. We were frightened and asked him what he wanted, and he told us that they wanted to put our boy in to be Cula·witsi. At first I did not want it and I cried. He was so young. He was only ten years old and had only just been initiated. But I was proud, too, that the priests had picked him out. So we said it would be all right. No one would have thought of picking Jack (another son) to be Cula·witsi, because he has no sense. He might talk back to his parents or get into a fight with another boy, and that would never do for Cula·witsi. But everyone knew that Bob was a quiet, sensible boy and would not make any trouble, even if he was so young.

"So right away his grandfather started working on moccasins for him to wear to the kiva when he went to get his teɫnan·e. We could not buy him new clothes at the store because we are ciwanni in this house and we can not trade for 10 days during it·iwan·a. So he wore his father's blanket when he went to the kiva.

"Pete had put him into the Katcina Society, and so he should have come in with him as his 'father,' but Pete had been Ca'lako and had

---

[43] Among the Hopi the corresponding office, that of fire-maker for the katcina chief, must be filled by a man of the Badger clan in villages where that clan exists, otherwise by one of the related clans.

just finished his year, and it would not have been right to ask him to do all this work for another year and so Pete's kiva father took his place, and brought Bob in.

"Bob is a sensible boy and knew what to do. When they took him to the kiva he was not a bit bashful in front of all those priests and head men. He spoke right out and greeted them [44] and called them father. They were all surprised to hear him talk so nicely, because he was so little. So they answered him and made him sit down. This year Cula·witsi was much older (he was 14) but still he did not know that he should greet the priests. He just stood there and said nothing until his 'father' told him what to do."

Little Cula·witsi is not required to attend the nightly meetings of the katcinas, and he need not learn the long prayers. However, he attends with his "father" the formal meetings of the Saiyataca party with the wo·we on the four nights following the monthly offerings of prayer sticks. The members of the group convene immediately after their evening meal, but the formal recital of the chants does not begin until about 11 o'clock. By this time poor little Cula·witsi is nodding on his stool, but his "father" sees that he does not sleep, although as the night advances, he can barely keep his eyes open. The meetings break up about 2 o'clock, and a very sleepy little boy goes to school that morning.

Cula·witsi offers prayer sticks with the rest of the Saiyataca party. His father helps him to make them, but he himself plants them. His father goes with him to the spring. The springs are from 4 to 8 miles distant. The party leaves about 11 o'clock in the morning and returns before sunset. Cula·witsi and his father lead the group, as they do at Ca'lako. It is frequently very difficult to have boys excused from school for this religious duty.

After kohaito, the plantings are made every ten days for forty days, and then again on the forty-fourth day. On this day the planting is made in the evening. After they have planted their prayer sticks, Cula·witsi kindles fire by friction. This is a difficult job, which requires both skill and strength. As soon as the kindling of cedar bark ignites, Cula·witsi lights his torch, which his father has made for him earlier in the day. He has also gathered great piles of dry brush to be burned as signal fires. In 1928 there were six such fires, two at White Rocks, two at Grease Hill (about halfway in) and two on the Salt Lake Road, just beyond the last houses. The light, dry material flares up quickly, burns brilliantly for a short time, and dies

---

[44] Literally, "he called them by terms of relationship." The person entering a room always speaks first. On entering the chamber of the priests, or any other formal gathering, the proper greeting is: "My fathers, how have you lived this while" (hom a·tatcu, ko'na ton tewanan a·teaiye?) to which the answer is "Happily. Be seated." (ķetsanici. i·tinaķä.) A priest on entering such an assembly or the house of a layman would say, "My fathers, my children . . ." or "My fathers, my mothers, my children . . ." "even if there were only one person there." Second person plural is always used in formal or polite address.

Masks Appearing with Grinding Ritual, Fig. a (See Plate 37)

Masks Appearing with Grinding Ritual, Fig. b (See Plate 37)

down quickly.   As the katcinas stride back and forth before the fires, giving their calls, they are silhouetted against a background of yellow flame.   The party enters the village about 11 o'clock and goes into retreat in the house of Saiyataca.   Cula·witsi remains in retreat with them for the four following days, again encountering opposition from the school authorities.

On the day that the katcinas come in publicly, Cula·witsi is the first to come.   The party leaves White Rocks, where they have dressed, at about 2 o'clock, the hour depending on how long it takes Cula·witsi to kindle his fire.   All the gods enter a house south of the village.   After a short time Cula·witsi and his father come out and cross the river and visit the six permanent excavations in the village streets, which p̃ekwin has uncovered as soon as the party was seen leaving White Rocks.   Into each of these excavations Cula·witsi sprinkles meal.   He recrosses the river and again enters the house on the south bank.   Shortly afterwards all the katcinas emerge. Cula·witsi and his father again are in the lead.   His father goes ahead, carrying his basket of prayer sticks, and handing them to him as required and instructing him in regard to planting them.   After he plants in each excavation he goes on to the next without waiting for the rest of the party to complete their rites.   He reaches his house about the time the others leave the second excavation.   Here he is met at the foot of the ladder by the head of the house.   He plants inside the threshold, and then enters through the roof.   He marks the walls of the house with his torch, thus extinguishing it.   He then places prayer sticks in the box hanging from the ceiling, and seeds on the floor.   Then he is met by p̃ekwin, who leads him to his seat, seats him, and raises his mask until it rests on his forehead, exposing the face.   Thus he sits waiting for the rest of the party.

He does not join the others in the intonation of the long chant which follows the ceremonial smoking.   However, later in the night he joins in the dancing, dancing with the others with brief rests, until daylight, at about 8 o'clock.[45]

The part which Cula·witsi plays in the initiation of boys is deferred to the complete description of that ceremony.

---

[45] When the ceremony was witnessed in 1928 at the height of an influenza epidemic Cula·witsi was the only one of the impersonators who was shown any consideration, although at least two others of the party were seriously ill with influenza on the night of their ceremony.   Nevertheless they danced throughout the night.   "They have to dance all night.   If they sit down for more than maybe one or two songs to rest, the wo·we come to them and make them get up to dance."   Cula·wᴵtsi, however, after dancing for a short time early in the evening, was permitted to rest for the rest of the night, sitting huddled in his corner, wrapped in a blue bedquilt.   However, he seemed none the worse next day for his experience.   Nor, for that matter, did a young man suffering from pulmonary tuberculosis, aggravated by influenza, who collapsed early in the evening, and was seen later, dancing as vigorously as ever.

SAIYATACA

(Plate 25, *b*)

Costume.—On his head he wears the downy feather and a bluejay feather "because he is a priest," and also the feathers of the summer birds. The feathers are actually fastened to a prayer stick. He has one long horn (whence his name, "long horn"), on the right side,[46] "because he brings long life to all his people." His eyes are long, too. But on the right side his eye is small. That is for the witch people, so that they may not live long, but on the left side his eye is long for the people of one heart, "so that they may have long life." Black goat's hair hangs from the horn, and over the forehead. White cotton threads hang down behind. The mask is made of elk skin. The face is painted turquoise. The collar is made of elk skin stuffed with wool.

Long ago he used to wear a buckskin shirt, but now he wears a shirt of white cotton cloth cut very full. Over this he wears an embroidered white blanket folded double and fastened on the right shoulder. He wears a white cotton dance kilt, with a band of blue, embroidered sash, red woman's belt, fringed white buckskin leggings, blue dancing moccasins. He wears a fawn-skin quiver over the right shoulder.[47] He has black yarn about both legs, and many valuable necklaces of shell and turquoise about his neck, back, and front, and on both wrists, "because he is very valuable." In the right hand he carries a rattle of deer scapulæ, in the left a bow and arrow and many prayer sticks.

This is an old mask. It is kept with others of the Saiyataca party, in a Dogwood clan house on the south side of the plaza. The people of this house are suspected of witchcraft. (K. 56–57.)

The impersonator of Saiyataca holds a position of great power and responsibility in the pueblo. Throughout the period of his incumbency he has the rank and prestige of one of the major priests. He is referred to by title (Saiyataca mosona), rather than by name, the Zuñi way of showing respect. His counsel is sought in all matters of ceremonial importance. He lives, also, under the same restraints as a priest. He must not mix himself up in worldly affairs, he must not quarrel, he must not leave the village for more than a day or two at a time, not even to stay at his sheep camp;[48] he must engage in no

---

[46] The horn should be blue.

[47] Not shown in the picture. But see Hututu.

[48] During six months that I lived in the household of the impersonator of Saiyataca he was almost never away from his house, except when he was working for the house which was to entertain him, or absent on some ceremonial visit. Most of the time he sat alone by the fire, engrossed in thought. Although he has a well-founded reputation for laziness, he worked diligently all year for "his mother," to the great amusement of his wife's family. During the period of his office, he laid aside hat and shoes in favor of a silk headband and native moccasins.

unseemly conduct.   Above all "his heart must be good."   He must be kind and gentle with all his people.

The other impersonators, both the other members of the Saiyataca party and the 12 Ca'lako impersonators, share these responsibilities and restrictions, but to a lesser degree.   They also are expected to observe the proprieties.   Adultery, which usually is regarded lightly, is a grave offense among those appointed to impersonate the gods. However, hardly a year passes that one or another of the appointees does not have to be publicly rebuked for this.[49]

When an offense of this kind is discovered, it rests with the impersonator of Saiyataca whether the offender shall be put out or publicly rebuked.   He does not himself execute his judgment, for that would desecrate his sanctity.   Hu·tutu, his bow priest, will do this for him. The rebuke is administered at the next monthly prayer stick planting, during the visit to the spring, in the presence of the other impersonators.

Saiyataca has responsibility also for the calendar.   He must make observations of the moon and notify the father of the Koyemci and the other impersonators two days before the date for the planting of prayer sticks.   He must decide whether the first planting and kohaito shall be at the first quarter or at the full moon.   All other plantings must be at the full moon.   And he must use his discretion about the inevitable requests for postponement.   In this matter he takes counsel with p̄ekwin, so that the dates for Cal'ako may not conflict with those for the winter solstice, but the final decision rests with Saiyataca.

The impersonators of the Saiyataca party are generally chosen by the priests while the societies are holding their winter retreat.   The priests will decide on a suitable man for the rôle of Saiyataca, and then fill the other offices (Hututu and the two Yamuhaktu; Cula·witsi is differently chosen) from the membership of his society, "so as to get men who are good friends and who will work well together."   If their service is satisfactory they will be returned to office, provided they are willing to serve, after four years.   The rotation of societies in the appointment of the Koyemci, as observed by Stevenson, probably arose in this manner.   This rotation has never become so fixed in the case of the Saiyataca group.   If, however, the group proves unsatisfactory for one reason or another, it will be passed over in favor of a new group.

---

[49] In 1927 one of the Ca'lako impersonators was accused of having had improper relations with the wife of a kiva mate.   This added the sin of incest to the wrong of adultery.   Kiva mates are brothers, therefore, according to Zuñi social rules, he was lying with his own sister.   The offense was discovered after kohaito, and at this late date it would have been difficult to get a substitute.   Therefore Saiyataca mosona decided not to remove the man from office.   Hututu, accordingly, administered a scathing rebuke at the next planting of prayer sticks.   "But if it had been the wife of a 'valuable' man, they would surely have put him out."   In 1928 the katcina chief was compelled to rebuke publicly the impersonator of Saiyataca for deserting his wife and quarreling with his mother-in-law.

It is very difficult to get a man to serve as Saiyataca more than twice. By that time he has had all the honor to be had from the office, and is reluctant to assume the responsibilities. The office is costly as well as arduous. Should he refuse, one of the other men who served with him will be asked to serve, should there be one among them of sufficient wealth and intelligence, and of unquestioned character. The priests will try to find a man who has served in one of the lesser rôles, because he will already be familiar with the prayers and chants. Frequently consideration will be given to the wishes of the people who have taken the crook of entertainment. I know one case in which a man who took the Ca'lako crook for the second time asked that the same man be appointed as Ca'lako as had come into his house on the previous occasion. This young man was not even a member of the kiva whose crook his host had taken, but he was nevertheless appointed. In 1928 the people in the Ciwana·kwe society house took the Saiyataca crook, and the Saiyataca party was chosen from the Ciwana·kwe Society. I did not hear specifically that the women requested the appointment, but the general impression seemed to be that the choice had been made in deference to their wishes.

Saiyataca is an impersonation of the greatest dignity and solemnity. The impersonator is generally a man of middle age or older, who is deeply impressed with the weight and importance of his office. He is, therefore, inclined to be heavy. Everything in the impersonation tends to this impression. Saiyataca's gait is ponderous; he walks with exaggerated long strides, very slowly, always standing with one foot poised in the air before bringing it down heavily. At each step he shakes his rattle of deer scapulae with a terrific clatter. His "talk" is declaimed in a loud voice, very slowly, and with marked emphasis, and is of incredible length. His evening chant takes about seven hours to perform. He talks publicly on other occasions also. He has three speeches in the morning, a chant on the housetop at dawn, which is afterwards repeated in the house, a long prayer to the society choir, thanking them for their service, and a farewell speech to his hosts. All are declaimed in the same weighty manner. Altogether, Saiyataca is a very pompous gentleman.

An informant offers the following comments on the impersonation:

"The people think a great deal of Saiyataca. They think of him making the New Year along with Pautiwa. He is the leader. The priests choose him at Itiwan·a from any clan, so long as his heart is good. There is a special wo'le for Saiyataca who holds office for life and teaches the impersonators all the things they must do and all the prayers.

"The Saiyataca people meet every night from itiwan·a until Ca'lako to practice their prayers. Their wo'le teaches them. Then when they have finished their year they go to the house of the wo'le, the day after they go out, and he takes their words back again. He sits holding Saiyataca's hands as he speaks his long talk and the morning talk and the other talks, and at the end the wo'le inhales from his hands, but Saiyataca does not inhale and so the words go out from him.

"Saiyataca plants prayer sticks at the different springs each month with the rest of the Ca'lako people. He is the leader of the party.

"The priests who look after the world pick him out to make the days warm. Each year they pick out some one to look after making the days warm. He is always someone who has a good heart and prays regularly. Each morning before the sun rises he goes out and goes around all the fields and says, 'Now you will go on and produce for my people. They need you. Please hurry and make my people happier.' So he prays during the summer for his people in all the fields. Each morning he prays to the sun and says, 'Our father, sun, let your rays make the days warm so that the crops may grow quickly, and send us your rains, too.' So he prays every morning and every evening, and especially early in the summer and early in the fall when the people fear that the frosts may spoil their crops. When he thinks it is going to be frosty, he goes to his wo'le and says to him, 'Father, I have come to ask you what I should do for the cold days. I am afraid of these cold days. Is there anything I can do for it?' The wo'le is glad to see him, and to see that he is mindful of his duties. He teaches him all the things he must do. The wo'le answers him and says, 'Get baked sweet corn which has been ground to fine meal and take it to the fields in the morning before the sun comes up. Go early and wait for the sun to come up, and then place the sweet corn in your mouth and blow it through your lips to the sun, praying for warmth that the frost may not kill our corn.'

"So that is the way he comes to make the days warm. The people think a great deal of Saiyataca. They think of him making the New Year along with Pautiwa.

"Four days before the Ca'lako come the Saiyataca people go out to White Rocks, and in the evening Cula·witsi lights his fires on Grease Hill. Then they come in and go in to Saiyataca's house. They stay in for days and during that time their wowe stay with them and teach them all the things that they must know. They make prayer sticks and get their masks and clothing ready.

"Then the day the Ca'lako come in they take their masks out to White Rocks, and dress out there. They come in in the afternoon and go out to the house where they are going to stay for the night. When he comes in to his father's house he prays as follows:[50]

"'I have been praying for my people that they may have much rain and good crops and that they may be fortunate with their babies and that they may have no misfortunes and no sickness. I have been

---

[50] His two chief prayers are given in text on pp. 710, 756. Nevertheless, the following picturesque paraphrase is presented as given.

praying that my people may have no sickness to make them unhappy. I want them all to be happy, and to wait for me when my time comes.' So he says, and then he prays again:

"'I am here that my people may have good luck in everything. I am here to throw out the people with double hearts. I have come that my people may have good luck and be happy. I have been planting feathers in all the springs that they may be happy and that they may have plenty of seeds in their back rooms, that their houses may be so full that they have no place to walk in their back rooms. And if anyone tries to injure my people I want them to watch for whoever is doing this, so that he may stand up in the daylight and the daylight people may know who is trying to injure them. I want my people to reach old age and to come to the ends of their roads, and not to be cut off while they are still young. I want my mothers to have many children, so that each may have one on her back and one in her arms, and one walking behind while she is with child. I want my people to have large families.'

"So he prays, and his kindness makes the people cry. It is so beautiful. They love him so much that the tears run down their cheeks when he prays for his people.[51] And especially when he leaves in the morning, all the people in the house cry because he is their child and they do not know when they will see him again.

"He tells them his own story, and says, 'When I was young I was so poor that I thought I never would grow up at all, and now they have chosen me to be the father of my people. When I was young I was so poor and no one thought anything of me, but now I pray for my people in Itiwan·a, so that they may have good fortune. My fathers, the priests, have thought of me in their prayers, and they have chosen me to come here. I thought I would never come to Itiwan·a, but here I have come. I bring my counting string and will untie the knots for you. I have been chosen by my fathers to pray for my people. Besides, I am the one who will make the days warm for the crops, so that they may grow. I can not tell you how this happened, but some day you will hear of it.' So he says, and finishes."

There is no myth about Saiyataca. He is frequently mentioned in folk tales, along with Pautiwa, as chief or priest of the masked gods, who receives messengers from Zuñi and hears their requests. Stevenson (p. 32) refers to him as town chief (K̂akwemos·i) of the village of the katcinas, but in prayers he is always called "Saiyataca, bow priest."

---

[51] As a matter of fact, the two years the writer observed the ceremonies in the Saiyataca house no one was present during the intonation of the chant except the priests and members of the household, who came and went freely. This is not due to exclusion of the populace, but to indifference. Most of the people are bored by the long prayers. They sleep early in the evening and come to the houses about midnight or later for the feasting and dancing. Then the houses are jammed. But for the ceremonies of departure in the morning, the house was crowded and the people deeply moved.

References.—The ceremonies of the Ca'lako are described by Stevenson, page 227. On page 247 she describes the ceremonies in the Saiyataca house. These are not esoteric ceremonies, but are open to anyone who may wish to attend. Also Parsons, Notes on Zuñi I, p. 183.

Parallels.—Hopi: "Caiastacana," Fewkes, Plate II. He figures in the Hopi version of the Ca'lako, which is performed in Sichumovi. He does not appear in any other Hopi village. The Sichumovi ceremony is recognized as having been recently imported from Zuñi. There is no Hopi equivalent of any antiquity.

HU·TUTU

(Plate 25, d)

He is Saiyataca's deputy. His mask is the same as Saiyataca's, except that he has no horn, and both sides are alike. He is dressed the same as Saiyataca, except that he wears a buckskin fastened on his shoulder instead of the embroidered blanket.

His mask is kept with that of Saiyataca in House 56.

Hututu is slightly less ponderous in manner than Saiyataca. His gait is different; he tramps rapidly instead of slowly. His call is deep. He is named from his call.

Parallels.—"Hututu," Fewkes, Hopi Katcinas, Plate III. A recent importation in Sichumovi.

YAMUHAKTO

(Plate 25, c)

Costume.—On his head small macaw feathers and downy eagle feathers. Across the top of his head is a stick of cottonwood (yamun·e), from which he is named, with a tassel of yarn of all colors at each end. The top of the mask is covered with black hair. The collar is of buckskin stuffed with wool or hair. The whole mask is painted blue.

The upper part of his body is painted red with ahoko, mixed with clay from the sacred lake. The shoulders, arms, and legs, and dots down the body and the arms are of yellow paint (hełuptsikwa). He wears a skirt of white buckskin, a tasseled white belt, fox skin. His things are painted white. He wears blue moccasins, and many necklaces, back and front and on both wrists. He carries deer antlers in both hands.

It is an old mask, kept with that of Saiyataca (K. 56). The cottonwood stick is also ancient, and is always put away with the mask.

"Yamuhakto comes only once, at Ca'lako. Sometimes he comes in the mixed dance, but then they never use the old mask, and they call him Hopi Yamuhakto. He comes to bring all kinds of things for the people, so that they may get property easily. He prays for the trees so that they may have wood for their house and for firewood. He stands beside Saiyataca when he prays and helps him, and they mention the trees and all the things he is bringing to the people.

"Pautiwa brings in all kinds of good things for the people and the Ca'lako bring all kinds of seeds, and they mention all these things in their prayers and songs. Long ago the priests had their minds on all these things. They had Pautiwa bring all kinds of good things, and they had Ca'lako bring in all kinds of seeds for the people, and then they thought, 'Now who will be the one to come with them. There is no one to look after the trees so that the world will be beautiful and so that we may have wood for our houses and firewood. There is no one to pray for them.' So they thought, 'Now who will be the one to do this?' They thought of all the katcinas. Now there was one katcina who had nothing. The katcina chief and his pekwin were in the ceremonial room of the priests, and so they sent for this one. Finally he came. When he had come in he asked, 'My fathers, why have you sent for me? I am here and I should like to know.' So they said, 'Everyone is bringing in all kinds of seeds. We want nothing to be forgotten. That is why we have sent for you. Is it all right that you should be the one to pray for all the trees and for all kinds of wood for all the world?' So he said, 'Yes, indeed, I shall be the one. I thought I was very poor. I thought I should never be chosen for anything. But now you have thought of me to be the one to be the father of the wood and I shall be the one to pray for it.' 'Now we shall give you a name. You shall be called Yamuhaktu (carrying wood). You are a tree and under your body the deer lie down to rest at your feet. And when you come to Itiwana you shall carry deer antlers in your hands. When you come to Itiwana there will be Saiyataca praying for all good fortune for his people, and when he has finished you will follow after him.' So, he comes. He just stands beside Saiyataca while he prays and helps him, and they mention all his trees and all the good things he is bringing too."

Two Sälimopiya (see p. 988) accompany the Saiyataca party at Ca'lako. These are yellow and blue one year, red and white the next, and the third, many colored and black.

The impersonators are chosen by the katcina chief the day before Saiyataca comes in to go into retreat. They go out with the Saiyataca party that night, and when the group comes in, lighting their signal fires, it is the Sälimopiya who make the most noise. Their call is loud and high.

They remain in retreat for four days in the ceremonial house of the Saiyataca party. On the final day they come in with them and spend the early part of the night in the Saiyataca house. They do not plant prayer sticks in the streets, or in the house. Later, when the dancing starts, they leave to dance in all the Ca'lako houses. Like the Ca'lako, they strike with their yucca any one whom they see asleep.

On the following morning they accompany the Saiyataca group to the field south of the village where the concluding ceremonies are held. While the Ca'lako run, they run back and forth along the river. If one of the Ca'lako should fall, they cross the river and whip all present, "to take away the bad luck," that is, to avert the misfortune that will result from this mishap. They do not whip the offender, although the disaster is laid to his incontinence.[52] This is the most important part of their duties.

After the ceremonies are concluded the impersonators plant prayer sticks and observe continence for four days longer.

The Sälimop̄iya are among the most brilliant of all Zuñi impersonations. Young men with beautiful bodies are always chosen for these rôles. Their only clothing is the loin cloth, although they always come in winter. They are continually in motion. All their movements are quick and darting. They never walk, but always run, uttering their high, loud call. They have certain characteristic quick movements of the head, with its huge ruff of raven feathers. They make sudden sallies among the spectators, striking out with their yucca switches. They are "dangerous," but they give good luck. The whole impersonation is one of exuberant youth and abounding vitality. Much emphasis is laid on their personal beauty. "Little boys do not mind being whipped by the Sälimop̄iya, they are such pretty dancers."

Considerable dissatisfaction was expressed with the choices for Sälimop̄iya for the Ca'lako ceremony in 1928. One was thought too thin for the part, and neither of them gave their calls loudly enough nor acted with sufficient energy to satisfy the spectators.

CA'LAKO

(Plate 27)

Costume.—The Ca'lako are giants, fully 10 feet tall. The mask is set on the top of a long pole which the impersonator carries in his hands. The garments are distended by hoops of flexible willow, bound together by thongs. The impersonator looks out through an opening in the blankets. When Ca'lako "sits down" in his house during the night ceremonies, the pole is stuck into the clay floor, and the hoop skirt collapses.

On his head he wears small feathers from the yellow macaw and downy feathers. Across the top of the head is a tall crest of tail feathers of the eagle, and standing up behind lapap̄oawan·e, tail feathers of the macaw bound to little sticks, and covered with downy eagle feathers. He wears a red feather hanging from each horn. The face is painted turquoise. He has large ball eyes and a long snout. This is carved of wood of two pieces which are operated by strings held by the impersonator. They open and shut with a terrific clatter. He is the only katcina with a mouth like this. They say that the

---

[52] For a discussion of flagellation, see p. 506.

person who carries Ca'lako must never look up, because if he looks up he will surely die. Therefore, no one except the wo'le knows how it is put together.

Ca'lako has long hair hanging down behind, with downy feathers in it. He has a collar of raven feathers, and below that are two fox skins. These are his arms. Around the shoulders is a dance kilt and below that two embroidered white blankets.

The Ca'lako impersonators wear warriors' caps of white buckskin decorated around the forehead with red ribbon and silver buttons. They wear shirts of native black cloth, trimmed with ribbons of many colors on the shoulders and sleeves. They wear a native breechcloth of black wool, fastened with an embroidered sash. The legs and thighs are bare. Their knees are painted red, their calves yellow. They wear high moccasins of red buckskin, cut like the blue dance moccasins. They carry stone axes in their belts, "because they are warriors." When they carry Ca'lako only their legs are visible. They have yarn about their legs with little sleighbells on each leg.

They have their faces painted with tsuhapa.

There are two impersonators for each Ca'lako. The elder brother brings Ca'lako in in the evening, and the younger brother walks ahead carrying the basket of prayer sticks. When they go out the following morning, the younger brother carries Ca'lako and the elder brother walks ahead.

There are six Ca'lako masks, one belonging to each kiva. They are kept in six different houses, along with the different things Ca'lako uses—the pole and the body, etc. These houses are: He'iwa (K. 387); muhe·wa (K. 538, out of town; old house 325); tcupa·wa (K. 130); ohe·wa (K. 159); upts'anawa (K. 150 ĩeciwan·i); hekapa·wa (K. 108).

"Before Ca'lako the Ca'lako wo'le goes to the house where the mask is kept and looks it over, and if there is anything wrong with it he mends it. If there is anything wrong with Ca'lako, if the strings are broken or if anything is torn, something terrible will happen in the house of the people who keep it. Last year the buckskin of the mask that is kept in our house was torn, and the wo'le said that it meant that some misfortune would come either to our house or to his. And right after Ca'lako, our aunt who had helped us cook for Ca'lako died, and we knew that this was what he meant."

One day during the summer the men of the kiva work for the house that keeps their mask. They offer their services through the kiva chief, and the head of the household sets them to whatever work should be done.

On the third day after the Koyemci come in before Ca'lako, the Ca'lako masks are taken out. On that day feasts are prepared in the six houses where these masks are kept. Early in the morning women who "belong to this ceremony," and the wives of all the men who "belong" to it, bring gifts of food to the house for the mask. Every one who has ever witnessed the ceremony of the taking out of the mask and sprinkled meal on it at this time must return for the ceremony every year, or at least send an offering to the mask, on pain of meeting with disaster. He will fall off a ladder or cut himself with a knife (the two usual punishments for failure in ceremonial observation; falling into the fire and being kicked by a horse are others). The women remain in the house all day to grind and cook.

After dark the back room is swept and a fire is lighted in the hearth. Embroidered blankets and other valuable articles are hung on the walls, and a white buckskin is spread on the floor on the side of the room away from the door (usually the west end). Then the people wait for the men who will come for the mask. Or if the men of the household are priests, they will bring out the mask before the wo'le comes. The Ca'lako masks are "dangerous." No one but a priest and the Ca'lako wo'le would dare touch them.[53] The head of the priesthood removes his shoes and enters the inner room where the mask is kept hanging on the wall. He sprinkles corn meal and takes up the mask. His associates take the body and other paraphernalia, and they bring them into the outer room. He prays, presents the mask to the six directions, and finally sets it down on a cross of corn meal on the buckskin. The body is laid beside it, and the whole covered with another buckskin, to protect it from the eyes of the uninitiated. Only Ca'lako's long snout sticks out from under its white coverings. Then all members of the household and visitors who "belong" to Ca'lako are admitted. They remove their shoes before entering the room. Each one prays and offers corn meal, even the smallest children being taken to receive the blessing of the god.[54]

Late at night when Cu'la·witsi lights his signal fires on Grease Hill, the two impersonators of Ca'lako and two wo·we come for their mask. Long prayers are recited by the chief wo'le and the head of the household. Then food is brought by the women to the visitors. After they have eaten, they get their mask out of the inner room and bundle it in blankets. The two wo·we carry the mask and the body, and the Ca'lako carry large bowls of stew and baskets of bread given them by the house (because they have worked for the house during the year). All this they take to the house of the elder brother Ca'lako where the two impersonators and their wo·we go into retreat that night. After

---

[53] When the people who keep the muhe·kwe Ca'lako moved out of town they sent for the wo'le of muhewa to transport the mask.

[54] When the writer witnessed this ceremony in the house of he'iwa Ca'lako she was taken in to see Ca'lako at this point. She was injudicious enough to offer a pinch of corn meal on the altar. When the report of this got around to the katcina chief he was very indignant. "For," as my informant explained, "one doesn't give corn meal away for nothing. One always asks for something in one's thoughts, and the people are afraid you will take all their good luck with you when you go, because of your corn meal."

they leave all the women are given bowls of stew and baskets of bread to take home.[55]

When the Ca'lako leave the village after their final ceremony they disrobe at White Rocks. The wo·we bring the mask and other paraphernalia back to the village under cover of blankets. They take the mask and the body to the house where it is kept. Here Ca'lako is "made to sit down" again, and sprinkled with meal by all present, before he is finally returned to the inner room where sacred paraphernalia are kept. The mask is completely undressed before it is put away. The wo'le takes the clothing and feathers to his house. He puts the feathers away carefully for another year. These are never used by any other katcina, although the clothing may be loaned. Whatever clothing has been borrowed, he returns with his blessing. The rest he puts away carefully.

The Ca'lako impersonators are chosen by the chief men of the kiva as soon as possible after the New Year. Generally young men are chosen for these offices. Like the Saiyataca impersonators, they must be trustworthy and "of good heart." Throughout the year they meet frequently to rehearse their prayers. They meet with their wo·we the four nights following the monthly prayer stick plantings, and informally as often as possible. They plant at the same times and with the Saiyataca group. Each group cuts its prayer sticks in its own ceremonial house (the house of the "elder brother") and the various groups start out separately but meet on the way to the spring. Their wo'le helps them make their prayer sticks, but does not go with them to the spring.

The Ca'lako are in retreat for four days before their public ceremonies. They go in the night Saiyataca "calls out." On the third day they go early in the afternoon to White Rocks to plant prayer sticks and to dress. There are elaborate ceremonies here that symbolize the visit to the village of the katcinas to get the gods. On the west slope of the hill is an inclosure known as "Ca'lako house." Within it are six boxlike shrines, full of prayer sticks. These are called Ca'lako's seats. They are the places "where Ca'lako sit down when they are getting ready to come." It is probably here that the masks are set after they are assembled, while the impersonators smoke with the wo·we and tell them that they have come for their "father."

The Ca'lako leave White Rocks about the time that Saiyataca reaches his house after planting prayer sticks in various parts of the village. They arise suddenly over the crest of the hill, and come rapidly down to Hepatina. Here they run back and forth on the

---

[55] This minor ceremony is described in full because it is so characteristic of the vast amount of secret household ritual that revolves about the handling of every sacred object. Every old mask is taken out with just such ceremony and with just as complicated economic exchanges.

field and at about sunset proceed to the level field along the south bank of the river where the masks are set up, while the impersonators go to their house to eat and put the finishing touches to their costume.

As soon as it is quite dark the six Ca'lako cross the river quietly and then suddenly rise out of the river bed, each surrounded by a group of singers from his kiva, all singing antiphonal songs. This is the most impressive moment in the Ca'lako ceremonies. The songs are magnificient, and the sudden appearance of the six giant figures in the moonlight is superb. As soon as they reach the village the groups separate, each going to its own house. Here the mask is set down before the door, surrounded by its group of singers who continue their song, while the impersonators enter and bless the house. The rite of the blessing of the house is beautifully described in the prayer of the Ca'lako (p. 762). The mask is afterwards brought in and set down by the altar, while the impersonators are seated and smoke with their hosts and repeat their long invocation.

During the night the two impersonators dance, sometimes "naked," without mask, and sometimes one of them dances with the effigy. It fills the room, from floor to ceiling, and its crest of eagle feathers brushes the beams. Dancing in the house they resemble nothing so much as animated gargoyles with their huge heads and tiny legs and their clattering beaks. They bend over and clap their beaks in the face of anyone who dozes in the house. In one house where I watched two Ca'lako dancing, they both pursued the visiting Koyemci, clapping their beaks at him, and finally chasing him out through the window. When dancing "naked" the impersonators carry yucca switches which they use on anyone whom they see dozing.

The ceremonies of the following morning have been described by Stevenson (Zuñi Indians, p. 256) and Parsons (Notes on Zuñi, I, 199), and I have nothing to add to these accounts.[56]

A Zuñi informant offers the following comments on the Ca'lako impersonation: "All the priests wanted Ca'lako to come, because he and Saiyataca are the most important ones to bring good luck for the people. At the New Year Pautiwa brings in the crooks for them to come. He brings one crook to each kiva. Then the wo·we take them. During the preceding night the priests have chosen the impersonators for Saiyataca and his companions, but after Pautiwa has been here and gone, the wo·we select the men for Ca'lako, two from each kiva, and they decide who shall have Ca'lako houses. The Ca'lako crook con-

---

[56] For the running of the Ca'lako and the final episode in their departure, compare the following account of the running of the Shiwanna at Cochiti. (Dumarest, p. 186.) "Each Shiwanna runs four times. If the other runners do not catch them they go away to Wenima. Then the principales summon them back in half an hour for another race. They run again. The principales name the runners at large from the pueblo. When the Shiwanna lose, they declare they will give much hiani. If they are not caught they will give nothing. Men make such efforts to win that I have seen them die suddenly from running."

tains one long stick and two short ones.[57]   The long one and one short
one are for the house which will entertain Ca'lako.   The other short
one is for the man to take away the bad luck from the village.[58] . . . .
After they are through with dancing to take away the bad luck, this
part of the crook is planted.   The long crook and one short stick are
left.   The wo'le takes these to the man who will entertain the Ca'lako.
This man plants prayer sticks each month in his field on the same day
as the Ca'lako impersonators plant at the springs.

"After kohaito, he takes the short stick from the long one and plants
it.   He still has the long one.   Right after Ca'lako there are five days
of dancing.   On the last day the Koyemci come and take the crook,
and all the people in the house stand in the middle of the room while
the Koyemci goes around the walls with the crook, taking away all the
bad luck.   He does this in every room in the house and then takes
the crook to the plaza.   He plants it later with his own prayer sticks.

"After Pautiwa brings in the crooks, the Ca'lako people begin to
learn their prayers from the wo'le.   They pray for all the people and
for all good things.   When Ca'lako comes in in the evening the owner
of the house has a cigarette ready, which he gives him to smoke.
Then he says, 'How have you prayed for us?   If you tell us that,
we shall be very glad to know it.'   Then he starts to pray:

"'I have come from the sacred lake and I have come by all the
springs.'   (Then he names all the springs where the Zuñi people
stopped when they came up.)   'I have come to see my people.   For
many years I have heard of my people living here at Itiwan·a and for
long I have wanted to come.   I want them to be happy, and I have
been praying for them; and especially I want the women to be fortunate with their babies.   I bring my people all kinds of seeds, all
the different kinds of corn and all different kinds of fruit and wild
green things.   I have been praying for my people to have long life;
and whoever has an evil heart should stand up in the daylight.   I have
been praying that my people may have all different kinds of seeds
and that their rooms may be full of corn of all colors and beans of all
colors and pumpkins and water gourds, and that they may have
plenty of fresh water, so that they may look well and be healthy
because of the pumpkins and the beans and the corn.   I want to see
them healthy.

"'As I was coming by Rainbow Spring, there was a frog with red
legs ready to come with me.   I did not want anyone to miss me, so I
brought him with me.   Then I came to Pocowa and there was a little
duck ready to come with me, so I brought him along too, because I
did not want anyone to stay behind.   All the springs I passed, and

---

[57] This is incorrect.   There are three short sticks.   The third is given to the impersonator of Ca'lako, who plants it with his first monthly offering.

[58] A rite of exorcism held after the New Year.   Each kiva sends in one masked god to go about the village.   They do not all come the same day.

everywhere some one was ready to come with me. I did not want anyone to stay back, so they have all come with me here. They will bring my people long life, and so I did not want any one of them to stay behind. We have all come. We are all here, bringing you good fortune. I want you to be happy. I wish you to be well and to have strong hearts. I have brought you seeds to plant with your crops next spring. I want your houses to be full of seeds and I have prayed that you may be fortunate with your babies, and that no one in this house may drop down. Yes, I have worked hard and prayed for all my people. I do not want any of the roots to rot. I do not want anyone to sicken and die, but I want everyone to stand up firmly on his feet all year. This is how I have prayed for you.

" 'I was poor when I was a little boy, but my fathers, the priests, have thought of me. Someone wise has picked me out. It was in their minds to pick me out and here I am. I was poor, but they have thought of me in their prayers and wanted me to come. So I have come up that you may all be happy tonight.'

"So he finishes, and they set down meat for him to eat. Then they take some of the meat in paper bread, and they go out with the wo'le to Wide River and feed it to the people of the Sacred Lake.

"When Ca'lako comes he brings in all different kinds of seeds, wild things, and peaches and pumpkins and beans and corn. Then when spring comes, the man who has had Ca'lako house plants these seeds in his fields."

THE INITIATION

This rite, through which all boys pass between the ages of 5 and 9 (the age may be delayed now, due to the irregular celebration of the ceremony) is called i·'pu'anaḵä—initiation, the same word that is used for initiation of adults into esoteric societies. It is not an initiation in our sense of admitting the novice into esoteric mysteries. The children learn nothing of the mysteries of the cult at this time and are not yet entitled to participate in its rituals. This final admission is deferred to a later date, when youth is believed to have reached years of understanding (10 to 14, depending on the boy's natural discretion). However, it partakes of the essence of Zuñi initiation, which is the formation of a bond between the individual and powerful supernatural forces. Initiations into special cults are always "to save one's life," from witches, from one's victim in war, from supernatural pursuit. In the case of children, they are initiated also "to save them; to make them valuable."[59] Before this they have no ceremonial status. If they should die they could not enter Kołuwala·wa.[60] The rite, therefore, is similar in purpose to the Christian baptism,

---

[59] A·tehyaḵäna, the word has a double meaning.

[60] There is some confusion in regard to this point, but the most orthodox opinion seems to be that only the initiated may enter the dance house of the gods. There seems to be a modern softening of this doctrine.

which tentatively admits the child to the congregation of the elect until, having reached the age of understanding, he establishes his relations with the supernatural by voluntarily partaking of communion, just as the Zuñi child must, after reaching years of discretion, complete his initiation by being inducted into the mysteries of the cult.[61]

The enormous importance of the rite of flagellation in this ceremony establishes it as primarily a ritual of exorcism and purification.[62]

The preliminary initiation of boys into the katcina cult should be held quadrennially in the spring of the year. It has not been held, however, since 1919, due to the absence of boys in school and changes in the hierarchy. The ceremony was commanded by the priests for the spring of 1929. Unfortunately the writer has never witnessed this important ceremony, so the following pages must be considered merely as notes to fuller accounts. The ceremony is described by Stevenson, Fifth and Twenty-third Annual Reports of the Bureau of American Ethnology, and best of all in the unpublished Benedict manuscript.

When the ceremony is to be held the head of the Ḵäklo cult receives from the priests at Itiwana a teḻnan·e, his order to serve. He notifies other members of the cult group and immediately they start nightly meetings to rehearse their "talk," review the various rituals, and otherwise prepare for their ceremony. The ceremony is timed so that the final public rites fall on the day of the full moon of the third month following the solstice.[63] The retreat, therefore, begins when the moon is six days old. On this night the Ḵäklo people get their mask and go after midnight to dress at White Rocks. See below (p. 981), for accounts of the ceremony on this night.

Ḵäklo leaves Sand Hill (near White Rocks) at sunrise and comes rapidly to the village, borne by the Koyemci. He visits the six kivas and departs at sunrise the following day. In each of the kivas he recites his Tcimiḵänapka penan·e (talk of the first beginning). The recital in each kiva consumes over three hours. Ḵäklo speaks very

---

[61] The writer, however, fails to find any validity in Mrs. Stevenson's distinction of "involuntary" and "voluntary" initiations. The second initiation is no more voluntary than the first. The Zuñis certainly do not use any such terms, nor have they any such feeling concerning them.

[62] The use of flagellation is discussed in another place, p. 506.

[63] I am indebted to Doctor Parsons for pointing out the striking coincidence in time with Easter. Easter in western Christian churches falls on the first Sunday following the first full moon after the vernal equinox; in other words, shortly after the third full moon after the winter solstice. In certain villages of Mexico it is customary for men to whip their little boys in the church on Sabata Gloria (Holy Saturday) "to make them grow." The importance of rites of flagellation in the Good Friday observances of the Penitentes need scarcely be pointed out. It is also interesting to note in this connection that the spring months from Easter until Corpus Christi in all Catholic countries are the usual time for administering first communion to children from the ages of 6 to 9.

Masks Appearing with Grinding Ritual, Fig. c (See Plate
37)

Masks Appearing with Grinding Ritual, Fig. d (See Plate 37).

rapidly and without pause. His "talk" is the longest of any of the katcinas and the most esoteric.[64]

In the kivas are all the officials of the kotikän·e. As soon as Ḳäklo leaves each kiva, the officials there assembled appoint the impersonators of the two Sälimopiya and the other gods who come with them and who are considered as belonging to the Sälimopiya party. They plant prayer sticks the day following their appointment and for eight days observe strict retreat.

Meanwhile the Koyemci go around to all the houses to learn the names of children who are to be whipped. Each Koyemci takes a certain number of houses and remembers the names for these houses, but Tsitsikä must remember them all.

The parents of boys to be initiated notify the boy's ceremonial father—the husband, son, or brother of the woman who first touched him at birth. If he has no father, or if his rightful father, for one reason or another, does not wish to serve, another man is selected. Any boy over 5 who has not already been initiated will be initiated at this ceremony.

Meanwhile in the houses of the boys' aunts (fathers' sisters) the women of their fathers' clan grind for the food that must be given to the ceremonial father. The full account of gift exchanges in connection with this ceremony must be reserved for another place.

On their visits to the boys' houses the Koyemci appoint those who are to cook the dishes of beans of various colors for the gods. To be so selected is a very great honor. On the final day the Koyemci take these bowls of bean stew to the kiva.[65]

On the eighth night the Ḳäklo people again go to White Rocks and enter the village at daybreak. He visits all the kivas again, reciting in each an abbreviated version of his chant. He leaves the village when he hears the approach of the other katcinas. The following gods in mask and costume come into the village from the west in the evening:

> Kolowisi and Tsitsikä.
> Two Muluktakä.

---

[64] The text recorded by Mrs. Stevenson, Zuñi Indians, pp. 43–88, is not the complete "talk." A member of the Ḳäklo cult explained that it was a recital of the order of episodes occurring in "talk" but not the talk itself. The other explanation is that it is the talk used by Ḳäklo on his second visit, eight days later. On this occasion he stays in the village only from sunrise until sunset, and recites in each kiva an abbreviated version of his earlier talk. But the text as recorded would scarcely fill the two hours allotted to each kiva. Furthermore, the style of the text, so different from the imaginative poetic style of other rituals, lends weight to the theory that it is a mnemonic device. Unfortunately I did not have an opportunity to record the text in full. My connections with the Ḳäklo priesthood were formed too late in my visit to get this text. The songs of the Koyemci as recorded by Mrs. Stevenson are substantially correct. This is one of the most important of Zuñi songs. It is a great favorite. Everyone knows it and sings it on all occasions, especially for children. Presumably it is intelligible to the Zuñi but no one can explain it, even those who would gladly do so.

[65] The initiates must eat no meat for four days following their initiation. I did not ascertain whether this restriction falls on the impersonators. If so it would explain why beans are required. On the other hand, compare the importance of beans in the Hopi festival Powamû at which children are initiated.

The Koyemci.

Ahe'a.

Twelve Sälimopiya (two each of the six colors).

Two Łelacoktiƀona.

Two Nawico.

Two Anahoho.

Cula·witsi.

Two Uƀo'yona.

Four Saiyaɫi'a.

They go into Heḵäpa·wa kiva for the night. There are probably night ceremonies of some sort.

The first event of the following day is the dancing of Haciatinakwe (see below) at sunrise. Early in the morning Ahe'a and the two Muluktakä, carrying young spruce trees, dance with Kolowisi in Heḵäpa·wa plaza.

Meanwhile the members of the Great Fire Society have been setting up their altars and meal paintings in He'iwa and Ohewa kivas.[66]

At about noon the Sälimopiya come out as related in the following native account:

"In Heiwa kiva are two yellow Sälimobiya with two Łelacoktipona. Then one of the yellow Sälimobiya and one Łelacoktipona come out and go around to show the people that they are ready to go in and drink to become frenzied.[67] One Sälimobiya and one Łelacoktipona remain in Heiwa kiva all the time. When the people see them come out they are careful not to let the children go out. Finally they go into Heiwa kiva and drink from the "spring." Then they go out again and go around and go into Muhewa kiva. Here they walk up and down the room four times. The blue Sälimobiya and four Sayaɫia stay in this kiva. When the yellow Sälimobiya comes in one blue Sälimobiya goes out and shows the people that he is ready to drink. Then he drinks in Heiwa kiva and comes out and goes around the village and goes into Tcupawa kiva. He walks up and down the room four times. Here are the red Sälimobiya and two Nawico. Then one red Sälimobiya and one Nawico come out and the others remain in the kiva. Then they do the same. After the red Sälimobiya has drunk he goes to Ohewa and here are the white Sälimobiya and Anahoho. One of each come out and go to Heiwa and the white Sälimobiya drinks [68] and they come down and go to Uptsanawa kiva. Here are the speckled Sälimobiya and Cula·witsi. There is only one Cula·witsi. Then one Sälimobiya comes out and goes to Heiwa kiva and drinks and goes to Hĕkiapawa, where the black Salimobiya and Upo'yona stay.

[66] In 1919 there was great difficulty because the Great Fire Society man who "knows how" to make these paintings refused to do them until the head of the Onawa priesthood (a personal enemy whom he wished to humble) came and begged him to do it. His vanity thus assuaged, he consented. He has since died, and there is great concern felt as to who will succeed him. He had a reputation, and indeed bragged about being "stingy" with esoteric knowledge.

[67] This is in the morning.

[68] Anahoho does not drink, but stands on the roof of the kiva while the white Sälimobiya goes in.

Then one black Sälimobiya and one Upo'yona come out and drink. Then they go to Muhewa kiva, and they know that every one has drunk. Then the second pairs that had stayed in all this time start to come out and go around, beginning with the ones in Heiwa kiva. After they have all drunk they all come out and go in pairs around the village to take the bad luck away.

"Then the people all come out. The man of the house makes the road for the katcinas and then runs away. One of the Sälimopiya runs after him and whips him to take away the bad luck.[69] Before they go out the wo'le tells them, 'Now, my children, you will go around and look at the village. You will look carefully, and if anyone is not carrying his mother (i. e., an ear of corn) you will not spare him. Be strong and whip him hard. These are the only ones you will whip. But be careful. Look carefully and do not whip anyone who is carrying corn, and do not whip anyone who is carrying water, and do not whip any woman who is with child.' [70] After everyone has drunk, and after they have gone around whipping for a little while, then the Sayaɫi'a comes out. Then they all go around the village. At about 3 o'clock in the afternoon they are called,[71] and all the katcinas go into Hekiapawa kiva. Here the yucca is ready for them, great bunches of it, and at one end it is tied round and round into a great ball. As soon as one bunch becomes soft they go back to the kiva for another bunch.

"Then they all come out and go to the dance plaza. The pekwin comes first, and then one yellow Sälimopiya, then one blue, one red, one white, one black, one speckled, then one Ɫelacoktipona, one Nawico, one Upo'yona, two Anahoho and Culawitsi. The others are still in Hekiapawa. The katcina chief and the katcina pekwin look after the children in the plaza and see that their fathers do not put too many blankets on them. Then they divide the children into two groups, and when the katcinas are all in line in the plaza, the fathers carry in their children, and the Koyemci count them. Then the first one, the yellow Sälimobiya, whips them four times and then they go on to the next one. They go down the whole line, six Sälimobiya, one Ɫelacoktipona, one Nawico, two Anahoho, one Culawitsi. When they have been whipped by Culawitsi they go up the ladder to Heiwa kiva. The boy looks at the pictures on the wall,[72] and he takes the feather from one of them.

---

[69] Anahoho mounts to the housetop. Here someone from the house brings him a basket or a pottery jar. He waves this around and throws it down into the yard where the Salimobiya are waiting. At Acoma at one point of the initiation ceremonies, immediately before the whipping, the cacique destroys a pottery bowl filled with ashes mixed with water. (White ms.)

[70] During Powamu the Hopi whipping katcinas who go about the village whip to remove sickness and "bad luck" but especially for barrenness. (Cf. Roman Lupercalia.)

[71] Nawico do not go around, but stand on the north side of the church watching the shadow. When the shadow of the church is 3 feet wide, they call the dancers.

[72] There is great confusion as to whether these paintings are on the wall or on the floor. I believe they are mask paintings on the floor.

"The boys always want to be whipped first, so as to get the feather of an important katcina like Ƥautiwa, or one of the nice-looking katcinas. There is one katcina for each boy that is whipped, and if there are many boys they have to draw all the funny katcinas like Ho'wiwi. Tsitsikya keeps track of the children and their names and sees that everything is right.[73] The boys just go down into the kiva and get their feathers and come back to the plaza.

"After the first group of boys have all been whipped, the ƥekwin takes the katcinas back to Hekiapawa kiva, and the second set comes out. They whip the second group of boys and after they are finished the ƥekwin takes them back. Then the Sayałia come out, four of them. They come to the plaza and all the little boys are there. Then one little boy kneels down in front of his father, with two women, one on each side, holding his blankets. The Sayałia stand in pairs facing each other, with the boy in the center. They are very terrible looking and jump around all the time shaking their rattles, and the little boys are terribly frightened. They are not afraid of the Sälimobiya because they are pretty katcinas who come to dance in the winter time with society songs, but the Sayałia are always dangerous. After each whipping the katcina chief and the katcina ƥekwin remove one blanket. If the father tries to shield the little boy by putting his own leg over the child's back, they will surely kill the father. The Koyemci stand beside them and count the strokes. The little boys cry terribly. They always whip first the boys who have beans cooking in their houses, first the boy who has the yellow beans, then the boy who has the blue beans, and so on.

"After the whipping, the boys are taken to the kiva to have feathers tied in their hair, and later to Hekapawa where Kolowisi vomits for them water and seeds."

For four nights the novices fast from animal food. On the fourth morning the ceremonial father removes the boy's hair feather, the symbol of his novitiate, and takes him to his house where his head is bathed. He is given meat to eat.[74] Again there are exchanges of gifts.

Ḳ̂ÄKLO

(Plate 28, a)

Costume.—"On the head, hawk feathers bound to a reed with a fringe of goat's hair. Over each ear a squash blossom. These used to be made of dyed rabbit fur wound over four little sunflower stalks. Now they use red yarn. He wears two squash blossoms so that the people may have many squashes and melons. Other katcinas wear only one. Around the face is painted the rainbow and the milky way. The lines under the eyes and mouth are rain drops.

---

[73] It was estimated by Zuñis that there would be 149 children to be whipped in 1929. So the Koyemci said.
[74] Compare similar ceremony in society initiations.

CA'LAKO

MASKS APPEARING AT THE INITIATION

a, Ḳäklo; b, Hemoḳätsik[i]; c, Łe'lacokti@ona.

"He wears a white shirt, formerly made of buckskin, but now made of cotton. Over this he wears an embroidered blanket folded and fastened on the right shoulder with tassels of yarn of all colors. Embroidered kilt with blue band, embroidered Hopi sash, red woman's belt. White buckskin leggings, fringed in front. Blue moccasins. Yarn on both legs, with little bells on right. Beads and yarn around the neck and on right wrist. Beads and bow bracelet on left wrist. The whole body is painted white, except a strip from the chest to the navel.

"In his right hand he carries a duck called neton·e (sticking out in front). He holds it in his hand while he tells his story in the kivas, and if anyone falls asleep during the narration he hits him on the head with the duck's bill. When K̓äklo is to come, the K̓äklo priest looks for a wild duck. When he finds one in some lake he kills it and removes the skin without cutting. When the skin is dry it is stuffed with cotton and seeds. This is what K̓äklo brings."

Ceremonies.—"K̓äklo comes only for the initiation of young boys, but at that time he comes twice. He comes first when the moon is six days old. Then the K̓äklo priesthood [75] comes together in the house of the oldest member. Here they get all their things ready.[76] Then during the night they go to the house of the Katcina P̓ekwin. He keeps the K̓äklo mask in his house, but he himself will not touch it. During the night two men of the Corn clan come.[77] The women of the house of the Katcina P̓ekwin have been cooking, and when the Corn clan men come they set out meat and paper bread and they eat. After they have eaten they bring out the mask. They spread an embroidered blanket in the valuable place. Then the katcina p̓ekwin takes the men into his back room. They take up the mask and say, 'Now, our father, we have come here for you. Your days have been made when you will come in. Do not bring us any trouble, but bring us long life for all your children. You will come and tell the story of how we came up here. You will bring us all long life. Do not bring trouble or danger.' So they say. Then they take the mask out and bring it to where they have spread out the blanket. They make a cross of corn meal on the blanket and set the mask on it and cover it with a buckskin. Then they sit down and wait for the K̓äklo priests, the two men of the Corn clan, and all the people in the house.

"At about midnight the K̓äklo priests come in, first the man who is going to impersonate K̓äklo and then the others behind him. The

---

[75] There are at present four members in this priesthood. The chief priest died in 1924. The men meet at frequent intervals to practice their "talk." They take turns in impersonating K̓äklo so that even if the older members die there will always be someone who knows the "talk." During the months following their appointment until their ceremony they meet, like the Saiyataca impersonators, every night.

[76] The day before their leader has notified the father of the Koyemci of the approaching ceremony.

[77] The men of the Corn clan are the same men who look after the K̓äna·kwe masks, "because corn is the most important of all things." Note, however, the striking similarity of masks. Also K̓äklo first visits tcupawa kiva, the kiva associated with the K̓äna·kwe.

people in the house have seats ready for them. They say a short
prayer and then they sit down. Then the man who is going to be
Ḳäklo says, 'Now you, our people, are waiting here in this room for
us. We have come for our father. Every night we have looked to
the west and now the moon is about to grow up. We have come to
our father, where he is sitting very still. Now his time has come. We
have come here where you are waiting for us.' Then everyone says,
'Yes, indeed.' Then they eat. After they have eaten they take a
roll of paper bread and pray for the people of the house who have
taken care of the mask. After they have prayed the man who is
going to impersonate Ḳäklo takes up the mask. Then the others
follow him and they go out. They take the paper bread with them
and before they go to their house they go to Wide River and sacrifice
the food to their dead predecessors.[78]

"Then they go to the house of the head of the cult. They get everything ready. Before they went for the mask they had practiced, so
now when they come in they rest. When it begins to get light they
go out to White Rocks. They take their mask and clothing with
them and when they get there the one who is going to be Ḳäklo
dresses. Soon afterwards the Koyemci come there, but they go to a
separate place not far off and dress. The man who is going to be
Ḳäklo dresses and the others help him. When he is ready his people
say to him, 'Now you are ready. Here is your nĕtone.' The
Koyemci are already dressed and are lying down on the hillside hiding
themselves. When Ḳäklo receives his duck he starts to shake it and
the little bells on its neck begin to jingle. Then he begins to say,
'Ḳäklo, Ḳäklo, Ḳäklo,' very fast.

"He keeps on for a long time and then he says, 'Grandfathers!'
(a·nanai!). Then the Koyemci jump up and say, 'What is it,
grandchild? Have you come? We did not see you.' They pretend that they have just come from the Sacred Lake and have come
up from the spring. So they come to him and he says, 'Grandfathers, sing for me.' Then they start their song. He calls them
again and says, 'Carry me on your back and let us go to Itiwana.'
Then one of the Koyemci comes to him and offers to carry him, but he
will not get on his back. He strikes him with his duck. He picks
out the smallest one to carry him, and finally they start. They sing
as they go. In their song the Koyemci always call him Iwaiyuhuna.
This is his name. Ḳäklo is only his call. They take turns carrying
him in. Whenever they change they spread out a blanket and put
him down. Each time they set him down he gives his call and says,
'Grandfathers, carry me on your backs!' When they come near
the village they set him down for the last time at the mission school.
He will not let them carry him over the bridge. He strikes each one

---

[78] A prayer recited by the Ḳäklo chief at some time during this night is printed in text on p. 690.

in turn as they come to take him. Then they say, 'I think our grand-child is afraid of this thing.' The river is full of snow and ice, for it is winter, but they walk right in, and the mud and slush come up to their waists. Ḳäklo has on all his fine, valuable clothing, but they drop him right into the river. They handle him very roughly and he treats them just the same. When they come out of the river on the north side they are all wet. The people are all on the housetops to watch them come in, for Ḳäklo comes only once in four years.

"When they come in they take him to tcupawa kiva. When they get to the foot of the ladder they make him sit down. He makes a lot of trouble there, for he wants the smallest and weakest of the Koyemci to carry him up the ladder. Then the smallest one carries him up and the others help him. They stand below him and support him so that he will not fall. When they get to the top he sits down in the hatchway and the Koyemci sing for him. They sing, 'Now, our grandson Ḳäklo, you will take one, two, three, four, five, six, seven, eight steps to go down and to go to the place prepared for you. You will sit down there.' Then Ḳäklo goes down and sits at the foot of the ladder in the kiva. Then they sing again, a different song. 'Now you will use your own feet to go to the decorated place.' As they sing they run backward. After they repeat this four times he goes to the decorated place. In the kiva are the heads of tcupawa kiva and all the tcupawa people, the Ḳäklo priesthood, and the Säli-mop̌iya wo'le. Ḳäklo sits down in the corner and the rest of the priesthood sit beside him. Then he starts his prayer. He starts just as the sun comes up. It takes about two or three hours. The wives and sisters of the Ḳäklo priests have all been grinding corn for his drink. When the women bring the meal the wo'le takes it and transfers it to another basket and fills the women's basket with all kinds of rubbish to tease them. As Ḳäklo comes to the end of his prayer he says, 'And in eight days I shall come again.' Then he finishes and goes right out and goes to muhewa kiva. The rest of the Ḳäklo priesthood have already left and gone to another kiva. As soon as Ḳäklo goes out the head men of tcupawa kiva select the men to personate the katcinas at the initiation. They select two to be Sälimop̌iya and two to be Nawico. Ḳäklo goes to all the kivas in the following order, tcupawa, muhewa, ohewa, uptsanawa, heiwa, hekiapawa, and when he has been to all the kivas he goes to Wide River. Here the other Ḳäklo priests meet him and help him undress. Then they take the mask and the clothing back to the house of the head priest.

"On the eighth day in the morning Ḳäklo comes again and gives his talk again in each of the six kivas. This time, however, he does not give his whole talk because he must finish in hekiapawa kiva before Kolowisi comes in. He comes to hekiapawa at about sunset and a little after dark he hears Kolowisi blowing on the great shell. Then he stops at once and gets right up and goes out and goes to Wide River. Then the other Ḳäklo priests meet him there and help him undress and they go back to the house of the head priest.

"Early the next morning just as the sun comes up Ḳäklo comes in gain froma Pumpkin Place [80] with one Ḳäna·kwe and all different kinds of katcinas. They are not dressed in full costume, but they wear masks and are just wrapped in blankets. Ḳäklo comes ahead and makes the road for them. They go around the village to bring good luck for the children who are to be initiated. Long ago each man carried an ear of corn with him and when they had gone around the village he went to the house of his father's clansmen. Here everyone sprinkled his head with water. Then they took him into the back room and he undressed there and went home. Now all the men do not carry corn, so they just go around the village and then Ḳäklo takes them all to Wide River and they undress there. This is called haciatinakwe.

"When Ḳäklo goes out to Wide River the other men of the Ḳäklo priesthood are waiting for him there. The katcina p̄ekwin and the two men of the Corn clan also go there. They take the Ḳäklo personator to the house of the katcina p̄ekwin. All the relatives of the katcina p̄ekwin are there and all the women of the Corn clan. He comes in and there are many women there. They set out a bowl of water and then they all sprinkle his head. His father uses an ear of corn, but the women just dip the water with their hands. Then they all eat. While he is eating the two men of the Corn clan take the mask to the back room where it is kept. Then after the Ḳäklo impersonator has eaten he gets up and says, 'Now, my people, be happy.' Then he leaves and goes home. That is all."

Mythology.—Ḳäklo's myth has been recorded by Cushing in his Outlines of Zuñi Creation Myths,[81] and an abstract of his version is given herewith. None of my informants knew of the existence of this myth. In folklore Ḳäklo is the kopekwin of katcina village, and one of the rulers of the katcinas.

Ḳäklo, elder brother of Siwulu'siwa and wisest of the seven sons of Ḳowimas, first sent out by his father to search for the middle, wandered to the north. His face became white from the frozen vapor of his breath; he was blinded by the light and his face became streaked with tears, and his mouth splayed with calling. So he died and was transformed. He cried aloud and duck heard him and offered to guide him. He hung tinkling shells on duck's neck to guide him. But Ḳäklo could not follow her into the lake that lay across their path. Rainbow-worm hearing the song of the sacred shells calls to

---

[80] East of the village.
[81] Thirteenth Ann. Rept. Bur. Amer. Ethn., pp. 406 et seq.

Ḵäklo, offering to bear him.   Ḵäklo offers him a prayer stick with
lacowaʻwe of duck feathers.   When he offers the prayer stick to rainbow, who bends down to receive it, the rainbow reflexion becomes fixed
on Ḵäklo's forehead.   So by bending and straightening, rainbow carries
Ḵäklo to the south and sets him down on the northern shore of the
sacred lake.   As he rests here, after all his misfortunes, he hears from
the conversation of the Koyemci all the evils that have befallen his
people and is further saddened.

Duck therefore goes to koluwalawa and is conducted within by
a Sälimopiya.   Ṗautiwa questions him and he reports the sad plight
of Ḵäklo.   Ṗautiwa orders duck to entice the Koyemci to the lake,
and, when their father recognized Ḵäklo's shells, to bid him make a
raft and assist Ḵäklo to reach koluwalawa.

Duck does as Ṗautiwa bids him.   The Koyemci meet their brother,
and, singing a dirge-like song, bear him to the lake.   The Koyemci
may not enter koluwalaʻwa (they are not dead), but Ḵäklo, conducted by Sälimopiya, enters, scattering meal before him.   As he
enters Culaʻwitsi lights his torch, and so Ḵäklo regains his sight.   He
is welcomed by all the priests of the masked gods.   Ṗautiwa decrees
that since Ḵäklo was a good listener and wise, he should be the
keeper of the myths of the koko, and their speaker.   There he learns
all the customs and rituals of the koko.

The Sälimopiya conduct him out.   Hearing the tinkle of his shells,
the Koyemci come to meet him in the sunrise.   He commands them
to carry him to his people so that they can bring them the messages
with which he has been intrusted, and instruct them in the rites of
the katcinas.

So, singing, they bring him to the village of the people.   Here he is
recognized and welcomed with honor.   Ḵäklo brings the people news
of their lost children, and recites for them in all the six assembly
houses the whole of his Tcimḵänapkä penaʻwe.   Ḵäklo gives his
words (by spirits into the mouth) to four of his listeners who hereafter constitute his cult.

As he and the Koyemci leave, the Sälimopiya, fast runners of the
koko, bring in the two Anahoho, Ḵäklo's younger brothers, also sent
out ahead of Siwuluʻsiwa as messengers.   They had sought Ḵäklo
in the deserted villages, and finding him not they smote their faces
with their sooty hands.

As soon as they arrived, they began to visit the housetops, throwing down from each baskets and jars, which the Sälimopiya destroyed
as offerings to the dead and the katcinas.

6066°—32——63

HE·'MOKA̧TSIK[1]

(Usually called Ahe'a from her call)

(Plate 28, b)

Costume.—On her head she wears a wig of white goat's hair. The mask is a regular face mask with the long chin and nose fastened on. The face is painted all white with red spots like Komoḵätsik[1].

"She is not so well dressed as the picture would indicate. She has no nice pitone, and no nice white moccasins, but only the short moccasins of buckskin. Long ago she did not wear the cotton underdress. She used to wear the embroidered Zuñi dress (black with blue embroidery), but now she wears a Hopi dress."

She carries spruce in both hands to make the world green.

Ceremonies.—She comes for the initiation. She comes in in the evening with Kolowisi and goes into hekiapawa kiva with Kolowisi and the black Sälimopiya. In the morning she dances in the west plaza and suckles Kolowisi.

"She may come in with any dance, because she comes to bring long life, because no one wants to die young. She is always funny when she comes. She always says, "Ahe'a," and sighs. Sometimes when she is dancing with Hilili she gets the songs mixed and dances out of step. Then the Hilili get angry and strike her and knock her down. But she never gets angry when her children knock her down, and if anyone gets angry easily we always tell them 'Ahea never gets angry the way you do.' Everyone likes to see her come."

Myth.—Hemoḵätsik[1] is the great-great-grandmother of the katcinas. Over in the sacred lake the younger ones call her "older sister." [82] She is the great-grandmother of the little ones like Hehe'a and Nawico. She is the only one there who grows old. All the others are young. But here at Itiwana the people used to die when they were young, so they sent in one very old katcina that the people of Itiwana might live to old age. That is why she comes.

Long ago they were having an initiation at Itiwana and over in the Sacred Lake the Sälimobiya and Kolowisi and the two Mulaktakia were ready to come. When Kolowisi was dressed with his fur and feathers, then Hemoḵätsik said, "I am not going to let my child go alone." Hemoḵätsik cooks and bakes for Pautiwa and Saiyataca and Ca'lako and all the head men there. They never let her come to Itiwana, and so she just stays there and cooks for them. She is very poor looking, she has no pretty dress and her hair is all tangled, and so they never want her to come. Still she wants to come. So this time

---

[82] ikiłaci, older sister. I was informed this is correct Zuñi usage, but Kroeber does not record the term. Ikina is the man's term for younger sister. Ikiłaci is, therefore, "old little sister," and is a semihumorous term similar in feeling tone to a diminutive.

Ķäklo said, "No, you must not go. You can not go there. You
are too old. And all our young ones look so pretty. You will dis-
grace them. We do not want you to go with all the pretty young
ones." But she did not want her child to go without her. She is
the nurse of Kolowisi, and so she wanted to go with him. So they
sent her into the back room where Pautiwa and Saiyataca were sitting. They left her there to stay at home. Then the Koyemci and
the Sälimobiya took Kolowisi out of the lake and the two Muluktakia
came along with the tree. They told Kolowisi not to cry out lest
she should hear him and want to come along. So they came out
quietly. But as they left there was a great deal of confusion and
they all asked one another, "Have you forgotten anything?" "Have
you got your rattle?" "Have you got your seeds?" "Are you
ready?" After they had gone it was very quiet so Hemoķätsiki
asked, "Are my children still here?" and she looked around. Then
Pautiwa and Saiyataca told her, "Yes, they are still here. They are
not going to have the initiation after all. They thought that you
were going to follow them and so they postponed it."

Then they sat with her for a while, and after a while they became
tired. Then they went out to practice their prayers. Saiyataca
went out to pray and Pautiwa went into the other room where the
people were all dancing. Then she got up and went out. She looked
for Kolowisi and could not find him, so she knew that they had gone.
Then she said, "I am going anyway. I don't care how poor and old
I am, I am going. They have treated me badly, my grandchildren,
but I shall not be angry with them. I am going after them."

Then Pautiwa came back to his room again and she was gone. He
said, "Our great-great-grandmother has gone after the grandchildren.
Please go after her and bring her back. Do not let her go there. We
do not want her to show herself at the initiation." Pautiwa said
that to the young dancers like the little Hehe'a and the little Nawico
and the people in the mixed dance.

So they went after her. She had only gone a little way when they
caught up with her, and they tried to bring her back. But she ran
away and went along holding her knees. Then the young ones got
tired and said, "Oh, let her go!" So they came back and told Pautiwa, "She went. We tried to catch her, but she ran away and would
not come. So she has gone." Then Pautiwa said, "Well, all right.
I have changed my mind. She will go there and give my people
long life, so that they may grow old as she is. I do not want my people to die young. She shall go and wait on her great-grandchildren
so that they may grow to be old."

As she went along she was saying, "Oh dear, oh dear! Ahe'a, ahe'a!
I am the one to bring long life to my people. I shall cause them all
to grow old. They shall live to take care of their great-grandchildren

as I am doing now. I shall make them all grow old." So she walked along wiping her face and holding her knees. She was a very, very old woman, but she was acting as though she were young.

So she came by the Place-of-the-winds [83] in the evening. All of the Sälimop̄iya and Kolowisi and the others were waiting at Hepatina [84] and there she caught up with them. Then the Sälimop̄iya said, "Why have you come? We left you at home." Then right away she exposed her breast and Kolowisi came and sucked at her breast. When the Sälimop̄iya saw that they did not say anything more, because Kolowisi always wanted to nurse from Hemok̄ätsik̄ [1]. Then the Sälimop̄iya said, "All right," for they knew that if Kolowisi nursed from her he would have a great deal of water to throw up with the seeds for the boys. So they came in and went into hekiapawa kiva late in the evening. When Kolowisi went into hekiapawa, Hemokyatsi went in with him and lay down beside him as if she were his mother. The black Sälimop̄iya went into hekiapawa with Kolowisi.

The Muluktakia do not bring in the tree at night, but they leave it at Where-the-pumpkin-stands and in the morning they bring it in for Kolowisi. Then they dance, holding the tree, and Hemok̄ätsik̄ [1] comes out and dances, holding the green branches of spruce in her hands. Then she comes to Kolowisi, where they have set him up with his head sticking through the wall of hekiapawa kiva, and she suckles him, and he sticks out his tongue and licks her breast. As she dances early in the morning she tells the people that she is praying for them to be happy and to have long life that they may grow to be old like herself; and she tells them that she will be their great-grandmother.

That is the way she comes. Her children still treat her badly the way they did long ago, but here everyone likes to see her.

Sälimop̄iya

(Plates 30, 31)

Costume.—On the head lap̄ap̄owa, made of parrot feathers bound to a stick of sagebrush, with iridescent duck feathers and feathers of the sandhill crane. "They use sagebrush because sagebrush is hard to get through and they want Sälimop̄iya to look dangerous." The painting on the side of the face is hepakine. Collar of crow feathers to frighten the children, because the crows bring bad luck.

The blue Sälimop̄iya (łian'ona) has his mask painted with blue gum paint, his body with the juice of black cornstalks (k̄ekwi), thighs white. He has big eyes and a long snout.

---

[83] Pinawa, a ruin about a mile and a half west of Zuñi, on the south side of the river.
[84] A shrine in a field a short distance southwest of Zuñi.

MASKS APPEARING AT THE INITIATION

a, Na'wico; b, Anahoho; c, Upo'yona.

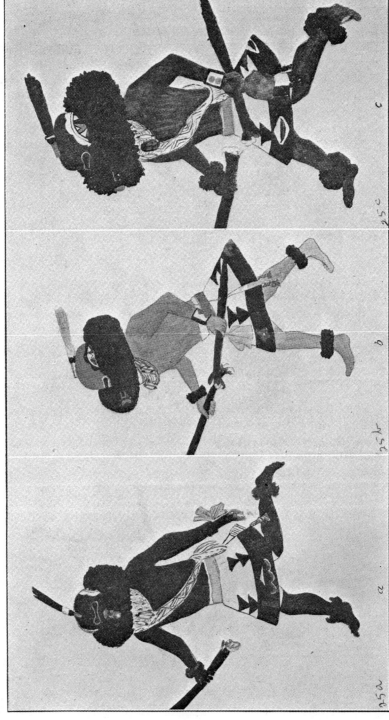

MASKS APPEARING AT THE INITIATION: THE SÄLIMOᴮIYA

a, Łuptsin'ona (yellow); *b*, Łian'ona (blue); *c*, Cilow'ona (red).

Dancing Katcinas: Winter Dances, Fig. a (See Plate 46)
    (This figure and the three following were printed in color in
the first edition, but in black and white from the color plate,
in this edition)

Dancing Katcinas: Winter Dances, Fig. b (See Plate 46)

He wears a special kind of kilt called the Sälimop̄iya kilt. It is embroidered like the ceremonial blanket with butterflies and flowers. Blue leather belt. Bare feet with spruce anklets (tsileakwin).

He carries yucca in both hands. The bunch in the right hand he carries with the points forward and uses it to whip people. That in the left hand he does not use, and carries it with the points back. His seeds (blue corn for the blue Sälimop̄iya) are tied in a corn husk to the bunch of yucca in the left hand.

There are 12 permanent Sälimop̄iya masks, two of each color. They are kept in six different houses as follows:

Yellow (ɫuptsinona), K. house No. 142 E, heiwa (also ɫelacoktipona).
Blue (ɫi'anona), K. house No. 414 Cn, muhewa (sayaɫia).
White (ḵohanona), K. house No. 292 P, ohewa (anahoho).
Red (ciloona), K. house No. 252 Ba, tcupawa (nawico).
Black (cikanona), K. house No. 161 P, hekiapawa (up̄o'yona).
Speckled (itaponaona), K. house No. ×163 a, uptsanawa (culawitsi).

Ceremonies.—The permanent masks are taken out only for the initiation, once in four years. When the Sälimop̄iya come in the winter they take any masks and paint them like Sälimop̄iya. Sometimes if a man does not want to have a mask made up, he will borrow the permanent mask from the man who keeps it. Then he must count days and plant prayer sticks and pay the keeper of the mask.

There is a special wo'le for the Sälimop̄iya when they come for the initiation. He takes care of the masks, paints them, and puts new feathers on them, and takes care of the clothing. He teaches the impersonators what they must do.

The real Sälimop̄iya come only once in four years. But sometimes they make up Sälimop̄iyas to come with the winter rain dance series. They come at the winter solstice with Tcakwena oḵä. When there is to be an initiation they do not come in the winter. (Not correct. They came in 1929.) Two Sälimop̄iya come with the Saiyataca at Ca'lako. (See p. 968.)

The Sälimop̄iya never come with the mixed dance or with the rain dancers. They never come in summer. They always make the people unhappy and their breath brings the wind, therefore they never come in summer.

The Sälimop̄iya impersonators are selected in each kiva the day Ḵäklo comes for the first time. There are two yellow Sälimop̄iya and two Ɫelacoktipona from Heiwa kiva, two blue Sälimop̄iya (and four Sayaɫia?) from Muhewa, two white Sälimop̄iya and two Anahoho from Ohewa, two red Sälimobiya and two Nawico from Tcupawa, two black Sälimop̄iya and two Up̄o'yona from Hĕkiapawa, and two many colored Sälimop̄iya and Culawitsi from Uptsanawa. The next morning all the people selected for the Sälimop̄iya party work on prayer sticks. When they have finished they go out to Wimayawe ohokinima. They go there to get firewood and to get a strong heart. They come there running and they swallow little round stones so that their hearts may be strong when they whip the boys. They practice running. Then they chop firewood, which they carry home. When they come in they cover their faces with their blankets so as not to see anyone. From this time on until the initiation they are not supposed to see a woman. When they come back to the village each group goes to its own kiva.[85] They bring in firewood to build fires in the kivas, for now they will stay in there. In the evening their wives bring their evening meal, but they do not go in and the men do not even look at them. The wo'le comes out and takes the food and brings it in. They stay in the kiva for seven nights, and on the eighth day Ḵäklo comes again. During this time the Sälimop̄iya impersonators practice going down the ladder head first, for this is hard to do. On the fourth night the Sayaɫia impersonators go in at muhewa kiva.

For further details, and for description of the rôle of the Sälimop̄iya in the Ca'lako, see p. 968.

Ɫe'lacoktipona (Wooden Ears)

(Plate 28, c)

Costume.—The face is painted blue. Across the eyes a stripe of alternating black and white blocks. This is the milky way (upiaɫan·e kucoktapa, milky way striped mark). The ears are painted red and yellow for all the beautiful things that grow on the earth. He wears a downy feather in each ear so that he may hear well. Just as the downy feather moves in the slightest wind, so he can hear the smallest sound. On his head parrot feathers with downy feathers, and three cotton cords hanging down the back of his head. Long mouth painted red; spruce collar.

His body is painted red with yellow marks. The forearms are yellow and the legs below the knee. The knees are red with yellow spots. The thighs white. "The red paint is for the red-breasted birds. The yellow arms and legs are for the yellow birds of summer and for the beautiful things that grow in the earth. The yellow spots on the shoulders and arms and knees are drops of rain falling. The white paint on the thighs is for the sun."

He wears a Sälimop̄iya kilt with a blue leather belt. Yarn on both legs and on the right wrist. Leather wristlet on left wrist. Beads and yarn around the neck. On the heels bands of porcupine quill work (weɫiakwine: fur footwear). In both hands he carries bunches of willow switches with bells hanging from them. His seeds are in his whip.

---

[85] This is the only cult group that uses a kiva for its retreat.

There are two masks. They are kept with the yellow Sälimopiya. He comes once in four years to initiate the boys. He comes with the yellow Sälimopiya and goes into Heiwa kiva. They do not take out the permanent mask at other times, but they make up a mask like it. Sometimes he comes at koyuptconawa to dance with Hehe'a and the other little dancers. He never comes with the mixed dance.

Na'wico

(Plate 29, a)

Costume.—On the head downy feathers and yellow parrot feathers, and two eagle tail feathers and one feather of the chaparral cock. "On his ears are squash blossoms with hair hanging down, so that there may be plenty of melons and squashes. His eyes are painted with little lines running out in all directions for the clouds of all directions. His nose is a zigzag line for the lightning." Spruce collar.

"The body paint is pink dancer's clay mixed with red clay. The arms and legs are painted with corn pollen for the corn. They think the corn is happy if they use corn pollen. He wears a skirt like the Sälimopiya with butterflies embroidered on it. The knees are painted red, the lower legs pink. He has beads and black yarn around his neck and yarn around his legs. No rattles or bells. He carries in both hands bunches of willow sticks tied together with little bells. His seeds are in his willow sticks. He wears a leather belt.

"When he comes with Sälimopiya for the initiation he belongs to Tcupawa kiva. His mask is kept with the red Sälimopiya in Badger house (K. 252).

"He comes to look after the time. In the afternoon while the other katcinas are going around he stands near the church dancing. The two of them stand together, marking time and skaking their bells, and looking at the shadow all the time. He lets the other katcinas know when it is time to whip the children. He is dangerous when he whips, but everyone likes to go and watch him while he is watching the shadow, because he is a pretty dancer.

"He always goes down the ladder head first like the Sälimopiya."

Mythology.—When the priests decided to initiate their children they set the date that would be best for the initiation. Then they called the katcina chief, because that is something that the katcina chief must decide. So they called him into their ceremonial room. He came in and said, "My fathers, why have you called me? I have come." Then they said, "Now we have our prayer sticks ready. We have made our crooks for the initiation of our boys and everything is ready, and we want to know what time the children should be whipped. Should it be in the morning or the evening or at midday?" He sat down and thought, "Is there anyone to look after the shadows for us?" [86] We all think a great deal of the church, so someone should watch the shadow of the church, and when the shadow is straight, then that will be the right time for the whipping of the children.   I will watch there this afternoon and pick out someone to watch the shadow," so he said.   "I will watch this afternoon and see what time is best and let you know."   Then he said, "I am going now.   I will look at the shadow and then I will come again."

It was about noon when he went out.   He went to the church.   He started on the south side and went around to the north, and he said, "This will be a good place."   So he waited there.   Just about 3 o'clock, when the sun turns over a lot, he looked at the shadow and said, "This will be a good time."   The shadow was about 3 feet wide. So he went back to the ceremonial room of the priests.   He went in and said, "How are you this while?"   They answered, "Happily."

Then he said, "I have been at our church.   The shadow is about three steps from the wall, and this will be good for the whipping time. Now whom shall we have to whip our children?   They must be the daylight people, and who will be a good one to look after the shadow?" They tried the Sälimopiya, but they were not good for it, and Łelacoktipona was not good and they knew Upo'yona would have to sit in the swing.   So then they came to Nawico and they all said "Now there is one who has nothing to do.   He will be a good one to watch the shadow.   He will come for that.   Everyone who comes for this ceremony has something to do but he has nothing to do, so we will have him watch the shadow.   All the others will go around to exorcise, and look after the village, but he will stay and watch the shadow."

So they called him.   The katcina chief thought of him in a prayer and said, "You are the one we need.   Now our people in the Sacred Lake, we need you.   Now we have thought of you in this room, and we wish you to come over here.   We need you."   Nawico heard it right away and he said to Pautiwa, "Did you hear?   Our fathers over in Itiwana called for me.   Shall I go now or shall I wait?   What do you wish me to do?"   Pautiwa answered him and said, "Go right away.   If they asked for you to come right away they must need you.   Go right away.   And take this along with you and tell the people, 'I have not come only to watch the shadow, but I will pray for the sweet corn too.'   You will take them the sweet corn, because you are the sweet corn, and you will carry the sweet corn seeds." Pautiwa did not want his people to think that one of the katcinas came empty-handed.   They had said that Nawico had nothing to do and Pautiwa wanted them to know that he looked after the sweet corn. Therefore he told him to take the sweet corn seeds.

---

[86] " We always used to look at the sun from the hatchway to see what time to have our meals.   We have marked on the floor the place for the morning meal and the place for the evening meal."

So he came. He tied his sweet corn in corn husks in his willow sticks and he came. He passed Wide River. He passed the rat plaza and came to the ceremonial room of the priests. The people saw him coming. Then the katcina chief got up and sprinkled corn meal for him to come in, and he made him sit down. As he sat down he said, "Is there anything you want me to do? I have come." Then the katcina chief said, "My fathers have asked me to come and I have come here. They asked me what time would be best to initiate our boys when the spring comes. These, our fathers, have already settled how many people should come from the sacred lake, and they have settled all things except what time shall be best for the whipping time. They have sent for me for I am the one to decide this, and I have decided that the church shall decide for us, because it is the center of our village. When the shadow of the church shall be three steps wide it will be time for the children to be whipped. And we have been thinking about the different katcinas and we have picked you out to do this, and that is why we have sent for you. What do you think of it?" So he said, "Yes, indeed. I always do what you, our fathers, think is best. We never say no. So I shall be the one who will look after this for you. My fathers, you thought I had nothing to bring with me, but I have the sweet corn seeds, and I have the little beans (nocihwe)." So he took them out of his bundle of sticks and said, "These are my seeds. I have something that belongs to me. And I shall watch the shadow for you. I shall let you know when it is time." So the priests said, "It is well. Thank you, my child. That is what we need you for. Now be happy, for the time will come when you will come here."

So they said, and that is how Nawico got into the initiation ceremony. He comes to watch the shadow, and he tells when it is time for the whipping of the children. When the time comes for the whipping he stands with his younger brother near the church, dancing and marking time and shaking his bells, and looking at the shadow all the time. That is how he comes.

ANAHOHO

(Plate 29, *b*)

Costume.—Two sashes sewed together and worn as a breechclout instead of the regular kilt. The sticks he carries have turkey feathers and other feathers of little birds attached to them. The second feather is chaparral cock (pohihi); 3, hawk (tsilelika); 4, blue jay (maiha); 5, swallow (?) (anilawa); 6, humming bird (tanya).

The body is painted with white paint (hekcina ḳohana). Spruce anklets.

Two masks are kept with white Sälimop̄iya in Pi'chikwe clan house (K. 292).

(Ana is an exclamation of distress.   The name means "take away bad luck.")

Ceremonies.—"Two of them come at the preliminary initiation of boys.   They come with the white Sälimop̄iya.   The masks are kept in Parrot clan house and they belong to ohewa kiva.   The personator may be from any kiva, but is always selected by the dance director of ohewa kiva.

"When all the Sälimop̄iya go into the kiva to drink from the 'spring' in order to get frenzied, Anahoho do not go in.   They stay in ohewa kiva.   Then when the Sälimop̄iya have drunk they come out and then Anahoho come out and stand on the top of their kiva.   Then the Sälimop̄iya come after them.   They do not like them and they knock them down.   Anahoho do not carry yucca, but little sticks (yamu lacowapa) and they do not hit anyone with their sticks. They are just to take away the bad luck.   (That is during the general rites of exorcism.   But later they are given yucca and whip the little boys who are to be initiated.)

"They wear crow feathers because the crow always comes when everything is quiet and no one is looking for a fight and they bring bad luck.   Then the crow comes and flies around the village four times, saying, 'Kâ kâ' and the people say, 'What does that mean?' Then he says, 'I came to tell you the Navaho are coming to kill the people,' or something bad like that.   That is why they wear crow feathers.   The katcinas were with us in this world when we first came up.   Once when they were having a dance Anahoho came with their collars of crow feathers and the people all said, 'Something is going to happen.'   These people came like crows to warn the people of bad luck.   And in the evening the Navaho came and they began to fight.   Many Navaho were killed, but none of the Zuñis. Then the elder brother Anahoho dipped his right hand in the blood of the Navaho and put it on his face and the younger one used his left hand.   That is how you can tell them apart.   And, therefore, they always wear crow feathers, and that is why they are the ones to take away the bad luck.   The painting on the side of the mask is like Sälimop̄iya because they always come with them."

Anahoho has special secret prayers for "taking away the bad luck." The only person who knows these is an albino woman with no ceremonial connection.

CULA·WITSI

Cula·witsi's appearance and his part in the Ca'lako ceremony are described on p 958.

"When Cula·witsi comes in the initiation the man's ceremonial father will always be in the kiva with him and will help him.   If he is dead his brother or some other relative will take his place and bring Culaꞏwitsi in. His father's clan will look after the paint. Five people from his father's clan will paint him. There will be one for each color; black, blue, red, yellow, and white. The ceremonial father will go to the five men of his clan and say, 'I have chosen you to look after the black paint,' and they will all say, 'Yes, I shall do it.' Culaꞏwitsi is very dangerous. If anyone does not believe in the katcinas the color will not stay on if he tries to paint Culaꞏwitsi. It is always very hard to spot him all over.

"At the initiation Culaꞏwitsi comes in with the speckled Sälimop̃iya. After the Sälimop̃iya are through whipping the boys, they all go into hek̠äpawa kiva and the Sayaꞏa come out. Then when the Sayaꞏa are finished they go to hek̠äpawa and those that are in there come out and each group goes to its own kiva. Then the p̃ekwin and the komosona tell them, "Now you are going home, but first of all you will take away the bad luck from all of your houses. You will go to all the houses and you will not neglect any of them. And if you go to any house and there is nothing put out with which to take away the bad luck, then you will throw down their chimney, no matter how important the house may be." He means that the people of each house must put out a new bowl or a nice basket or something. The women all make bowls and jars before the initiation and no matter how nice the bowl is, they will always put it up on the house-top to take away the bad luck from the house.

"Now when Culaꞏwitsi goes into uptsanawa kiva he and his father make fire by rubbing two sticks together and ignite cedar bark. They work with the fire until it is burning nicely and then they come out. His father comes first. He wears a white shirt and white trousers and a buckskin over his shoulders. He wears brown leggings and moccasins, and lots of beads and a nice belt. Formerly he used to wear an embroidered sash, but now he wears a silver belt. He has a yucca band around his head and a downy feather in his hair and his face is painted under the eyes with tsuhapa. He carries a bowl of sacred meal and a mi'le. He comes first and Culaꞏwitsi follows, and the speckled Sälimop̃iya. They go to heiwa kiva. They stand in the street at the foot of the ladder and the Sälimop̃iya gives his call and one yellow Sälimop̃iya comes out with Ꞁelacoktipona. They go next to muhewa. They go all around and they go last to hekiapawa.

"Then all of them go all around the village. Each woman has put a bowl or a nice basket on the roof. The Sälimop̃iya and Culaꞏwitsi and his father and all the other katcinas (one of each kind) stand in the street while Anahoho goes up on the roof. He stands over the bowl that has been set out and prays thus: 'Now you have been laid out here for me to take you, no matter how valuable you are. You are the one to take away the bad luck from this house where these people are living. And if anyone in this house has a wrong heart (i. e., if anyone is sick) you will die instead of him and take away the bad luck.' Then he throws it down, and if it is a bowl it breaks, but if it is a basket, the father of Cula·witsi and one of the Sälimopiya step on it and break it and then Cula·witsi burns it with his torch.

"When the people first decided to have an initiation they wondered who would be the one to look after the sun and the fire and they thought of everyone and finally they thought of Cula·witsi and that is why he comes in at that time."

There are two Cula·witsi masks. The one used at Ca'lako is always worn by a boy. It is kept with the Saiyataca masks in House No. 56–7 upstairs. The one used at initiation is worn by a man and is kept with the speckled Sälimopiya in ×163a (upstairs).

UPO'YONA (COTTON HEAD)

(Plate 29, c)

Costume.—On the head downy feathers and yellow parrot feathers; three cotton strings hanging down. His eyes are like Sälimopiya. The ears are painted with hakwina, the black paint used for painting prayer sticks.

The body is painted with pink clay (kok an hekätco). The forearms are yellow, also the legs. The knees are red, so that he may be a good runner. The runners in stick races always have their knees painted red. He has black yarn and little bells (musilili) around both legs. He carries willow sticks in both hands when he comes at the initiation and to dance for society songs. Blue leather belt, white kilt, beads on back and front like Pautiwa and the valuable dancers.

His mask is kept with that of Pautiwa in the Pi'chikwe house, i. e., teciwan·i (K. 161). When he comes for the initiation they use the old mask. The personator is selected by He'iwa wo'le from among the members of He'iwa kiva. When he comes at other times they make up a mask like the old one and anyone can wear it.

He comes with the Sälimopiya for the initiation of boys. He comes in before them and goes to the kiva where Kolowisi is to come in. The initiation ceremony started when the first people came here. The rain priests begged the katcinas to come to initiate their children. They took the yellow corn for the yellow Sälimopiya and the blue corn for the blue Sälimopiya and the white corn for the white Sälimopiya and the red corn for the red Sälimopiya and the black corn for the black Sälimopiya and the speckled corn for the speckled Sälimopiya. They prayed to the sacred lake people to send these katcinas to initiate their boys. So in the sacred lake they sent these katcinas here in the night, the ones the rain priests had prayed for. When they came in the people made them try their calls. The yellow Sälimopiya tried first. His call was very loud to frighten the people.

So then they tried the blue Sälimop̄iya and his call was just the same. All the Sälimop̄iya were the same. So then they tried the sweet corn, Łelacoktipona, and his call was a little one. Then they said, "Is there anyone here who can sit in the swing?" (The swing was made of a piece of wood hung on a red woman's belt, with valuable beads for the katcina to sit on.) They wanted to try them all and see if they could find anyone with a good voice to give all the calls. "We must have someone who will sit in the swing before the other katcinas come in, and when they come to the roof they will give their calls and he will answer. One of them may have a big voice and one may have a little voice, but the one who sits in the swing must answer them all the way they call. Who will be the best to do this? Who has the best voice to make all these calls and tell the people to come in? I wonder if there is anyone at the sacred lake to do this for us." So the rain priest said, and the yellow Sälimop̄iya said, "We know who will be good for it. You tell P̄autiwa to send you his young son, Up̄o'yona. He will be good for that, because when the mixed dance comes he can make the calls of all the dancers." "All right, we shall send for him." So they asked for him in a prayer. They sat down and prayed that they might have the son of P̄autiwa for his sweet voice to make the calls. Right away the same night he came. The Sälimop̄iya were still in the rain priests' ceremonial room with the rain priests. Then Up̄o'yona came. He came in and sat down. The sun priest made him sit down. He presented him to each direction and made him sit down. Then he said, "Now why have you sent for me? I should like to hear." Then the chief priest answered and said, "We are going to have an initiation to initiate our boys and all those of our children who have been chosen to whip the boys are in this room. Now we want them to call out and whoever has a sweet voice should answer them just the way they call out. But none of them has a voice that he can make sound like the others. Then we thought of you and we have sent for you to see if you can do it." So he said, "I shall try." Then the yellow Sälimop̄iya gave his call and right away Up̄o'yona called out just the way the yellow Sälimop̄iya had done. And when they had finished the blue Sälimop̄iya gave his call, and Up̄o'yona called out right after him, just the way he had called. And so on. All the others gave their calls one by one, and he answered them all in their own voices. Then the rain priests were very much pleased and they said, "Isn't that nice! Now you shall sit on the swing and wait for these others when they come in. When they come up on the kiva, and before they come in they will call out. And you will be sitting in the kiva and when they call out you will answer them just as you have done now. And your name will be Up̄o'yona Imp̄iyona. You will be Imp̄iyona sitting in the swing." So that is the way he happened to come in for the initiation.

He is just like an echo, and when he comes for the initiation he does just the way it is in the story. When he comes in the winter time or with the rain dance we call him just Upo'yona, but when he comes for the initiation he is called Upo'yona Impiyona.

FINAL INITIATION

After an interval perhaps of several years the boys are whipped a second time and on this occasion the secrets of the katcina cult are finally revealed to them. In early days this ceremony was held at regular intervals and all boys who had already undergone the preliminary whipping and were of age and discretion sufficient to be trusted with this knowledge went through the second ceremony. The usual age was 10 to 12 years. Nowadays the absence of the boys at school has often made it necessary to postpone this part of the ceremony until they return, at the age of 18 or 19.

On this occasion the whipping is administered by the Sayali'a.

"The Sayali'a come for the second whipping of the boys. They are the ones to put them into the kivas, because they are strong. Whoever has been Puhuatinakwe at the winter solstice prays all during the summer and says, 'Now when my time comes to initiate these boys, give me a strong heart to whip them hard so that they may never tell the secrets of the katcina cult.' All summer he prays to be strong. The priests do not want them to be afraid of hurting the boys, but they want them to really hurt them so that they will be really terrified and afraid to tell.

"Formerly they used to have the second whipping of the boys during the four days between the first coming of Sayataca and Ca'lako, but now they do it right after Ca'lako, while the general dancing is going on. When Ca'lako time comes they remember that they must initiate the boys, then after the Ca'lako have gone the katcina chief and his war priest let the people know. They confer with the heads of the kivas and see what time is most convenient. Then they let the Sayali'a personators know. The katcina chief tells the head one, who is called the oldest brother, 'You will come this afternoon. You had better tell your younger brothers to hurry.' Then he tells his younger brothers and they hurry and get their clothing together and go to heiwa kiva to get ready. Then the ceremonial fathers [87] of the boys take them to one of the Ca'lako houses. When all the children are there the katcina bow priest takes aside one of the older boys and asks him his name. Then he goes to Heiwa kiva and tells the name to the Sayali'a and says to them, 'This boy is a little older than the others. So when you go there you will tell your grandfather that you are looking for this boy. Then they will believe that over in the sacred lake the katcinas know even the little boys' names.' So they

---

[87] The same man who officiated at the child's first whipping.

make note of the little boy's name.   Then the katcina war priest goes to the ceremonial house of the Koyemci and asks, 'Who of you wants to come to the whipping of the boys?'   Then two of them go and help the Sayaɫi'a.   When they are dressed and ready to go they say to the Koyemci, 'Now we shall go to where the children are.   Then you will call out the name of the little boy we are looking for.   You will ask, "Where is our little friend?   His name is ———," you will say, "My grandsons are looking for ———," so as to frighten them all.'

"Then they start coming to where the little boys are.   They come looking all around saying, 'Where is little ———?   My grandsons are looking for him.'   Then the little boy who is called cries.   He wants to join the Katcina Society, but he knows that it is going to hurt.   The children can hardly bear it, they are so frightened.   Then the Koyemci come to the door and say, 'Are all our little friends here?'   The town chief will be there and the katcina chief and his p̌ekwin, and all the important men.   Then they will say, 'Yes, they are here.   Come in.'   Then the four Sayaɫi'a come in and the Koyemci wait outside.   They stand in the middle of the room giving their calls and frightening the little ones.   Finally one of them is taken up and he kneels down holding his father's knees.   He has nothing over him but one buckskin.   While he is being whipped all the others cry.   Their noses bleed and they are terribly frightened.   They whip them all in turn, and after they have whipped all the children, then the katcina chief tells the story of what they did long ago when a little boy told the secrets of the initiation.   This is a dangerous thing.   The katcina chief warns them not to tell.

"All the little boys sit around and listen to the katcina chief when he tells the story of what they did long ago.   When he has finished the story he says, 'And now you will be the ones who will wear the masks.   This is the way we call the rains.   Now our friends will show you.'   Then they pick out four youngsters and make them stand in a row in front of the Sayaɫi'a and the Sayaɫi'a take off their masks and put them on the heads of the little boys.   Then the little boys are terribly frightened.   They tell them, 'Do not be afraid,' and they say to them, 'If you are going to dance, this is the way you will wear it.   And now that you have a mask you may whip us.'   Then the Sayaɫi'a holds out his hand and the boy strikes him once on each arm and once on each leg.   They get four strokes from each child.   Then all the children in turn put on the mask and each whips the Sayaɫi'a.

"When they are finished the children kneel down again.   The Sayaɫi'a have a great many feathers.   They count beforehand how many children there are, and there is one feather for each.   The Sayaɫi'a bring them along with them.   They tie them in their hair and they hang down behind, great bunches of them.   Then they take off the feathers and they tie one feather in the hair of each little boy.

"After they have given the boys their feathers the Sayaɫi'a go out. They are very angry because they have been whipped by the children, and if they see anyone on the streets they will surely knock him down and beat him. After they have gone around a little while they go back to Wide River. In their houses the women have been cooking. They make paper bread and cook meat and make all kinds of good things. They want to feed the children because they have been hurt. Then their sisters and women relatives bring four bowls of food from each house to the house where the little boys have been whipped. This is for the children and their fathers and the priests and the people of the house. When they bring in the food the fathers tell the children, 'Take home whatever you like to your mothers.' Then the little boys take whatever they like and wrap it up and take it home to their mothers.

"Sometimes they call the Sayaɫi'a Tenapiǩäniǩä (they show them how) when they come for the second whipping of the little boys."

The costume of Saiyaɫi'a at the initiation and as a punitive katcina is shown in Plate 32, a. For his rôle in the winter solstice, see p. 919 and Plate 21, b.

The text of the warning of the katcina chief to the novices, which recounts the origin of the katcina cult and the danger of betrayal of its secrets, is given on p. 604.

The Saiyaɫi'a may also be summoned by the komosona when he is apprised of any serious breach of the rules of the Katcina Society. During the summer of 1924 a young man sold a mask to one of the traders. The mask was seen in the store by an old Zuñi who works about the place. He recognized it and reported it to the katcina chief who decided to have the Saiyaɫi'a come with the next of the summer dances. Accordingly, in August, when Koǩokci was being danced, the Saiyaɫi'a came in the night. Word had gotten around, however, and the young man ran away and took refuge in the United States Government agency at Blackrock. The Saiyaɫia, however, went around the village, visiting all the kivas, and whipping anyone whom they met, "to take away the bad luck." "If they had found the young man they would surely have killed him," my informant said.

The following summer there was some talk of having the Saiyaɫi'a come because people had been "getting careless." One young man had worn a bluejay feather in his hair while dancing Koǩokci, thus showing that he was a priest, and men had been decorating their masks in their houses instead of in the kiva.   However, nothing came of it.

A single Saiyali'a always comes with the Ḵäna·kwe dance.   He was one of the three gods whom the Ḵäna·kwe captured during their war with the katcinas.

A single Saiyali'a was observed in the big plaza about noon of the day that Ololowicka came in September, 1927.   He did not go in any place and did not dance.   He made the round of the plazas, standing for a few minutes in each.   No explanation was given of his presence except that Ololowicka was coming in the afternoon.   It seemed quite out of his usual character, as an exorcising and punitive katcina.

References.—Saiyali'a's part in the initiation ceremony and the rabbit hunt is described by Stevenson (pp. 89, 99).   Also in the Benedict unpublished manuscript. Parsons, Notes on Zuñi (pp. 155–157, 177–180).   Stevenson, Religious Life of a Zuñi Child.

Parallels.—Hopi: Tunwup katcina (Fewkes, Hopi katcinas, Pl. VII, p. 69). Many details of mask and costume resemble Saiyali'a, the blue horns, large mouth, with long beard, goggle eyes, crest of eagle feathers, fox skin collar, kilt of dyed hair, and body paint.   Tunwup flogs the children at their initiation into the katcina cult in connection with the Powamu ceremony (at the long form, held quadrennially).   Fewkes describes the rite as follows: "In the Hano celebration an altar is made in the kiva at that time by the chiefs, Anote and Satele, both of whom place their official badges upon a rectangle of meal drawn on the kiva floor. Into this rectangle the children are led by their foster parents and flogged in the presence of the inhabitants of the pueblo.   The two floggers, Tunwup, stand one on each side of the figure of meal, holding their whips of yucca.   As they dance they strike the boys or girls before them as hard as they can, after which they pass the whips to a priest standing by.   After each flogging the yucca whips are waved in the air, which is called the purification.   After the children have been flogged many adults, both men and women, present their bared bodies, legs, and arms to the blows of the yucca whips." [95]   (See also Voth, Oraibi Powamu, and Bunzel, unpublished Hopi manuscript.)

Sia: Saiahlia (Stevenson, The Sia, p. 117).   The honaaite (chief of the Querranna) prepares a meal painting for the occasion, covering it for the time being with a blanket.   Upon the arrival of the katsuna the father and child and, if the child be a member of a cult society, the theurgist of the society proceed to the ceremonial house of the Querranna. . . .   The saiahlia (two of the katsuna) stamp about in the middle of the room for a time, then the honaaite leads the child before the meal painting, which is, however, still covered with a blanket, and says to the katsuna, "A youth (or maiden) has come to know you."   The katsuna each carry a bunch of Spanish bayonet (giant yucca) in either hand, and the child receives two strokes across the back from each of the katsuna, unless he be an official member of a cult society; in this case he is exempt from the chastisement.   A boy is nude excepting the breechcloth, a girl wears her ordinary clothing.   The honaaite, addressing the katsuna, says, "Now it is well for you to raise your masks that the child may see."   One of the saiahlia places his mask over the child's head and the other lays his by the meal painting, the honaaite having removed the blanket.   The personators of the katsuna then say to the child, "Now you know the katsune you will henceforth have only good thoughts

---

[95] The children are first acquainted with the mysteries of the cult later, when they see the Powamu katcinas dancing unmasked in the kiva.

and a good heart; sometime, perhaps, you will be one of us. You must not speak of these things to anyone not initiated." The mask is then taken from the child's head and laid by the side of the other, and the boy answers, "I will not speak of these things to anyone." The katsuna then rubs the meal of the painting upon the child, and those present afterwards gather around the painting and rub the meal upon their bodies for mental and physical purification." [96]

Cochiti: Shruiyana. Two shruiyana accompanying ahaye (hemuci·kwe dance). Described by Dumarest as follows: "The two shruiyana had all the body painted black, the mask also except for green on the forehead and lower jaw. The eyes, balls of buckskin painted black and red, were on the outside of the mask. A wild-cat skin was behind and in front a beard of hair. One feather was on top of the mask (fur on top) and downy feathers under the ears. A belt of skin of some sort. Fringes of red wool. Before the parts a fringe of corn leaves. Behind a fox skin, on the feet the skin of a skunk. In the hands two large pieces of yucca. . . . At noon time the shruiyana angrily dismissed the people (their call is u—— u—— u—— u——) in order that the Shiwanna might not be seen eating." (Dumarest, 180, 181.)

Also tsayanawa (bad men) "who keep women and children from approaching the dancers and who whip with giant yucca any dancer who loses his ornaments, in the belief that the dancer has not strictly observed his 4-day fast." (Identified by the editor with "the tsanowani (angry person) of Laguna, who was said to look like natacka of the Hopi. He is bear katsina. He stands in middle of the line of chakwena and he is their chief." (Dumarest, p. 182–183, and footnote.)

"All the male members of the pueblo join the kachina society. Boys vary in age at the time of their initiation. On the third night of the retreat [97] the war captain asks for all the boys willing to join the kachina. Consent of the fathers is sought. Young children and infants may also be presented to the society. On the fourth night the initiation takes place. Each boy has a ceremonial father, a man already in the society; a heluta or kachina leader and a certain number of cuiyana kachina, associated with the thunder clouds, are present. There may be two or four of them. These kachina are distinguished by the colors of different directions and at least one black and one red are always present. The initiate and his ceremonial father are whipped first by the heluta and then by the other kachinas. At this time the boys are not told the society secrets, but only when they are 18 or 19 and ready to participate in the dance does the war captain ask their fathers to inform them privately." (Goldfrank, p. 113.)

Laguna: Compare drawing of ṭsi'·ts'ŭrnŭrts (Parsons, Notes on Ceremonialism at Laguna, p. 100, fig. 10.)

MISCELLANEOUS PRIEST KATCINAS

Hai'nawi

(Plate 32, b)

Costume.—The mask is a forehead mask (coyan·e), with little downy feathers in the beard. There are little downy feathers in the hair. These are stuck on with the sirup of yucca fruit. He wears the great feather (lacowanɫana) and the buckskin bandoleer (ḵepyatonane) because he is a warrior. The face is painted with blood. "His face used to be white, but when he cut off the heads of children the blood spurted all over his face. They say it is real blood." In his right

---

[96] Cf. the Navaho rite of using the sand from sand paintings for healing.

[97] The author does not specify the season or who is in the retreat.

MASKS APPEARING AT THE INITIATION: THE SÄLIMOBIYA

a, Ḳohan'ona (white); b, Itahpanahnan'ona (many-colored); c, Ciḳän'ona (dark).

PUNITIVE AND EXORCISING KATCINAS

a, Saiyali'a; b, Hai'nawi; c, Temtemci; d, A'hu·te.

c

Dancing Katcinas: Winter Dances, Fig. c (See Plate 46)

d

Dancing Katcinas: Winter Dances, Fig. d (See Plate 46)

hand he carries the big knife (atcian łana) which is painted red up to
the hilt, with red paint taken from the Sacred Lake. In the left
hand he carries a yucca whip. His "heart" is in his whip.

He wears a buckskin shirt (na'le ḵeme), a white tasseled belt
(mo'liponi'kwin·e) with a fox skin (lanikwele). Turtle shell rattle
on right leg. Blue moccasins (ketomawe). He has beads around
his neck (takune) and yarn around the wrists (citonpasikwine).

"This is an old mask. They say it is real blood on the face. Only
a strong man will wear this mask. They keep it at Komosona's
house and it is hardly ever taken out. The head man of a kiva can
wear it, but a young man would not dare, because it is dangerous.
If a young man wants to come as Hai'nawi in the mixed dance he
will paint another mask like this, but he will not wear the real mask.
Everyone is afraid of Hai'nawi. When I was a little girl they brought
him in in a dance and I just couldn't go to see the dance because I
was so afraid of him."

Ceremonies.—"He always comes with Homatci. He carries the big
knife because he is the one who cuts off the heads of children who tell.
The real Hai'nawi only comes if some one tells. Whenever anyone
tells they call him.[98] He doesn't come very often now because the
children behave. But if the people get careless about dance ritual
they will call these dancers in to frighten the people. They are talking
about it now because the people are getting careless. One man went
to the toilet in his dance dress, and some of the men have been working
on masks in their own houses. They shouldn't do these things, and
so they think they will have this dancer come when they are having a
mixed dance."

Myths.—Long ago when the people first came up and while the
earth was still soft some one told the secrets of the dance. Then the
chief priest asked in a prayer that Hainawi should come and punish
the boy who had told about the dance. As soon as the boy heard
that the priest had called for this dancer he ran away and hid. He
got some one—i. e., a witch—to help him, and he went down into the
earth. Then the katcina came. There were four of them. Homatci
and Hainawi are the dangerous ones, and Temtemci and Ahute come
with them and stamp on the ground. They went to all the different
villages, to Itiwana and Hawikuh and Matsaḵä and Ḵäkima and
Hecokta. They looked all over for the boy who had told, but they
did not find him. So they went to the twin heroes and asked them
to help them find the boy. So the twin heroes took them and
showed them where the boy was hiding. When they got there the two
dangerous katcinas jumped, and Hainawi gave his call, "Hai'nawi,"
and shook his knife and stamped so that the earth shook. They

---

[98] See warning of the katcina chief at the initiation of boys, p. 604.

jumped a second time and the earth cracked. They jumped a third time and the crack opened about 12 inches. They jumped a fourth time and the earth cracked way open, and there below was the person sitting as though he were in the bottom of a well, and his eyes were shining. Then the twin heroes said, "Are you here?" "Who are you?" "Come out. Our fathers and grandfathers want you to come out." The boy tried to hide. He would not come out. So they sent the twin heroes to bring him out. The twin heroes went in and talked to him. They told him to tell them the truth about what he had said, and they said the dancers would not cut off his head if he confessed. He begged them, "Please save me and take me home, for you are wise." They said to him, "All right." So he came out with the twin heroes. When they came out the dancers jumped four times, and they were just going to cut off his head when the twins interposed and said, "Don't cut off his head. He has told the truth, and he will not do it again. Don't cut off his head until we get back to Itiwana. Then in front of all the people you can talk to him. If you kill him here it won't do any good because there is no one here to see you." Then they brought him in. The twin heroes came first holding the boy between them and helping him along, and the katcinas followed. So they came to Halonawa. Everyone was waiting in the plaza, and they brought him in and they talked to him in front of all the people. The people did not want them to cut off his head, but the katcinas insisted and said, "We must do it so that our bodies will be saved and so that no one will tell again." So they cut off his head and carried it back to the Sacred Lake. That is why everyone is afraid of Hainawi.

Whenever a child tells about the secrets of the katcinas, then the heads of the Katcina Society, the katcina chief, his p̃ekwin, and the warriors of the Katcina Society and the heads of the kivas, meet together in the house of the katcina chief. When they have come in they ask, "What is it you want that you have called us in?" Then the katcina chief says, "Now, our young ones must be careful not to tell the secrets of the katcinas, how they dress and how they use the mask. I want our children to be careful, and if they tell I want some one to punish them. Who will be the best one to come and punish them? We must pick out from among our fathers who will save the Katcina Society." They thought about Atocle, but Atocle is not fit for this because he talks too much. He makes jokes and is not dignified enough to save the Katcina Society. They thought about different kinds of katcinas and finally they came to Hainawi. Then they said, "What do you think of Hainawi? I think he is really honest, and he won't hold back from doing what he has to do. He is really honest. He is the one to do this." So they went on and thought of others to come with him. Finally they came to Homatci, and they said, "These two will come together and either one of them may cut off the head of anyone who tells. They will carry the great knife. Now we will call them and see whether they think well of it. We can not make plans for them to come without asking them." Then they thought again, "There must always be four to come together. We must have some to make a noise. Two other grandfathers must come with them. Let us pick out two more and have them all come together." Then they thought of Ahute, and they said, "He will be the one who will make a noise and frighten everyone with his voice." Then they came to Temtemci and they thought, "These four will always come together when anyone tells about the katcina cult." So they picked out these four and Muyapone and Posuki (two of the Koyemci) to come with them.

So they asked for them here in a prayer and they came. The headmen were all meeting in the katcina chief's house and they came, Hainawi and Homatci and Ahute and Temtemci and the two Koyemci. They were making fearful calls to frighten the people, and the people said, "What are they coming for?" And they said to their children, "Someone has told about the katcinas and they are coming to cut off his head. Someone has told." They frightened their little children and warned them not to tell about the katcinas. They came into the room where the headmen were meeting, and they asked them to sit down. Then they turned into human persons, and they sat down. Then Hainawi asked, "What was it you wanted to say that you have called for us to come? We are here to listen to what you have to say." Then the katcina chief and the katcina pekwin and the katcina warriors said, "We want our people and especially our young ones to be careful not to tell how you come and how you dress. Some day we may have to change it, and we do not want them to tell about it. The katcina cult must be valuable, and no one must tell how you come and how you dress, and if anyone tells, you are the ones we are going to send for. You are the ones who will come and cut off their heads. You will not only frighten them, but really cut off their heads so that the Katcina Society will always be built up higher, so that it will not collapse." So they said, "All right. You have made us, and we shall do as you wish. Whenever you call us we shall come right away." Then they said, "Let us go." Then they told the Koyemci, "You will save anyone who is not really bad. If any little one who does not know any better tells, one who is not really bad, you will be the ones to save him." So they told the Koyemci. "Now that is all, my children. We shall remember you always, that you are brave and strong, and when we need you we shall call you." Then they got up and said, "It is well. Be happy and have long life." Then they went out and went home to the Sacred Lake.

That is how they happened to be picked out.

HOMATCI

Costume.[1]—Mask yellow with red spots; black arrow point over eyes; long beard with eagle down; large wide mouth; hair unbound. Circle of eagle down on crown; behind crest of hawk (?) feathers. Body painted pink; arms red, spotted with white; war bandoleer; spruce in waist.

TEMTEMCI

(Plate 32, c)

Costume.—"The face is painted blue and is spotted all over. The spots are from the blood of the little boy, because he was with Hai'nawi and Ho'matci when they killed him. His face is marked with the bear's paw. Around the face a fringe of black hair. He has wing feathers of the eagle in his large ears. The black of the head is painted white. On his head lacowanɬana. When he comes to frighten people he wears it with the tips forward the way the war chief wears it when he goes to war. But when he comes to dance he wears it with the tips back. He wears other feathers too. These are dyed red. When they killed the little boy he dipped his feather in the blood. He did not want to spoil his lacowanɬana, so he took downy feathers and dipped them in. Coyote skin collar, because the children are afraid of coyotes.

"His body is spotted with red from the blood of the little boy. He painted his arms and legs over with pink clay so that the people would not be afraid of him. He wears a white kilt and a white-fringed sash. Fox skin. He wears arm bands with lahacoma so that they will like him in spite of the fact that he helped them kill the little boy. He wears a bandoleer of supiatonane. Blue moccasins. Yarn on left leg, turtle-shell rattle on right. Yucca in both hands. He carries it with the points back because he never strikes anyone.

"He has a loud voice. He went with Hai'nawi and Ho'matci when they killed the little boy and gave his call to frighten everyone. His voice still frightens the little children and the grown people too. His call is 'Tem-tem-ci! Tem-tem-ci!'"

Ceremonies.—He may come any time with the mixed dance. (He came in August, 1925. R. L. B.)

A'HU·TE

(Plate 32, d)

Costume.—On the head the "great feather" (lacowanɬana) with the duck's head. He is dangerous but he wants to please, so he wears the duck's head. On the back of the head feathers of the red hawk in a row down the middle of the back. Black hair around them.

---

[1] From a drawing collected by Kroeber.

The mask is painted with blue and red stars "for fine nights." He has large ears sticking out with a flat wing feather of the hawk in each. The side of the face is painted with the bear's claw because he is a warrior. He has protruding eyes, and below them black slits through which the man looks out. Coyote skin collar.

He wears a buckskin shirt, embroidered sash and red woman's belt. Arm bands of blue leather with buckskin fringes representing clouds and lahacoma. He wears the buckskin bandoleer with shells, the insignia of the war chief. Turtle shell rattle on the right leg. Fox skin. Body painted yellow, legs white. Blue moccasins. Yucca in right hand; left, bow and arrow, yucca, and a gourd rattle. Sometimes when he is not angry he carries bow and arrow in left hand and rattle in right, and no yucca at all

He comes in the mixed dance with Temtemci, and the others, Hai′nawi and Ho′matci. He goes up to people and says "Ahu·te" and frightens them. He came with the mixed dance August, 1925. He was always the last katcina to enter and leave the plaza. He walked with a peculiar ponderous gait, out of line, giving his deep call, "A′hu·te."

O′LOLOWICK̯Ä

(Plate 33, d)

Costume.—Mask, painted turquoise, with deer, eagle, turkey wing and macaw feathers on crown. Collar of raven feathers. Two girdles of raven feathers around his chest and waist. White skirt, embroidered kilt, sash, red belt, fox skin, fringed leggings, blue moccasins, yarn (with bells?). Phallus supported in belt.

Ololowick̯ä has a characteristic dance step. He trots up and down before the line of dancers. His call is "Olololololo." The brownish fluid ejected from the phallus in the course of the ceremony is a sirup made from peaches (formerly yucca fruit).

The mask and the phallus are ancient. Kalawasa is head of the cult, and the mask is probably kept in his house. Precise information is lacking.

There is considerable esoteric ritual connected with the impersonation of Ololowick̯ä, the operation of the phallus and the preparation of the fluid. There are magical prayers, of course, for all these incidents. Only three men "know how." The performer in 1927 was severely criticized for clumsiness. Omens are read from the character of the flow. (Parsons, Winter and Summer Dance Series.)

Ceremonies.—"They may dance hekcina cilowa (red paint) in summer or winter. It is the prettiest of all the rain dances. The men paint their bodies red, and they have the prettiest songs. So when they decide to have this dance they practice their songs. Some man who has a good voice will teach the men the songs, and they will

practice. Then they select two men for the katcina maidens. They
select the two best looking young men, slender young men with light
skins. They select the men for Hehe'a and Ololowicḳä, too. Then
they invite the men who are to come and play the flutes for the grinding. There are two societies who use flutes in their ritual, the Little
Fire and the Bedbug Societies, and the headmen of the kiva will
invite one or the other of these two to come and play for them. Then
four men will come and practice with them. The flute players listen
to the songs as the men practice, and afterwards they begin to play
them on their flutes. They all practice together. The men sing
and the ones who are going to grind practice the grinding and the two
Hehe'a sit down in front of them and clap their hands so that they
grind in time.

"Then when they are ready the katcina chief plants prayer sticks.
The women in the houses of the two men who have been selected to
be the katcina maidens are all busy grinding. They grind very fine
meal for the men to take to the plaza. Then on the last day all the
men get their things ready. They get their clothes ready, and they
get their drum. The men who are going to grind bring the two
grinding stones and the buckskins to spread under them and the
fine meal.

"The next day they have the rain dance (hekcina cilowawa). There
will be many women dancing in the line, but the two who are to grind
will not dance with them until the third evening. Then on the third
day they come in the evening, the two katcina maidens, four flute
players, two Hehe'a and Ololowicḳä. They come into the plaza.
Each of the maidens carries an ear of corn in each hand and a basket
of fine meal. The two Hehe'a carry the two grinding stones and the
buckskins. They prepare a place for the girls in the center of the
plaza. They spread out the buckskins and place the two mealing
stones down on them. The Koyemci help them. The plaza is full
of people. Then the four flute players take their places on both sides
of the grinding stones. Then the girls take their places. They are
on the south side of the plaza, and the dancers stand in line around
the plaza, always men and women alternating. Then they sing the
grinding songs and the two katcina maidens grind. When they have
finished one song they pile up the meal in the bowls. Then when all the
meal is piled up in the bowls Ololowicḳä pretends that he wishes to
pass water. Then the Koyemci say, "Hurry up, children, our grandfather wishes to pass water!" Then they take the bowl from one of
the maidens and set it down in front of Ololowicḳä. Ololowicḳä
carries an old long-necked gourd sticking out of his belt. Then he
stands over the bowl and pours some of the liquid into it. Then he
goes to the second bowl and does the same. Then the Koyemci put
their hands into the bowls and mix the contents thoroughly and carry

the two bowls around among the people who are standing in the plaza and on the housetops, and the people take some of the meal from the bowls.

"While they are doing this the katcina maidens have gotten up and they begin to dance like the Corn maids, each maiden holding an ear of corn. After they have danced they stop and pray, 'Now we have been praying for all the women that they may do well in grinding. May you always be fortunate as we have been and may your arms never ache when you grind.' Then they dance again, each maiden holding an ear of corn. Then all the women inhale and say, 'May we always be like you when we grind.' The katcina maidens dance that the women may have good luck in grinding, and Ololowicķä comes to purify the men so that if any of them have venereal disease they may be cured and not give their diseases to the women. That is all."

(Ceremony witnessed by R. L. B., September, 1927. At this time it was performed in connection with Upiķaiaᵽona danced by muhe-kwe. The ritual of Ololowicķä was performed in the evening on the eighth and last day of the dance. See pls. 36, 37.)

Ķäna·kwe Mosona (Ķäna·kwe Chief)

(Plate 33, a)

Costume.—The mask is white. "Around the face are the rainbow and the milky way. The back is painted with a dragon fly to make the corn grow fast. The eyes are like tadpoles (mutuliķä) and there are other tadpoles on the back. His ears hang down because they fought with the people of the Sacred Lake. After the fight they fixed their ears with corn husks, and therefore they wear corn husks in their ears." On the head feathers of the red hawk bound together with duck feathers. Spruce collar.

They wear the old native cotton shirts and embroidered white blankets. Blue moccasins. The legs and the hands are painted white. In the left hand a fawn skin bag full of seeds, in the right a turtle shell rattle (kokolonane). This is different from the turtle shell rattle worn on the leg, which is called by a different name.

He has a protruding snout. The opening is round to make the clouds come quickly when he dances.

The Ķäna·kwe masks are kept in the Corn clan house (K. 391).

Ceremonies.—"The Ķäna·kwe only come for one day every four years, and they go right back home. They never stay in the village overnight, because they do not really belong here. They are not Sacred Lake people, but just dancers. They live in the south."

Sometimes one or two Ķäna·kwe come in the mixed dance. They came with the mixed dance, August, 1925. They did not go into the kiva overnight with the rest of the dancers, but went home to the south, and came again the next day.

"The people think a great deal of the Ḵäna·kwe, because when they come for their dance they always bring presents for the priests to pay for their dance.

There are many myths of the Ḵäna·kwe. The battle with the Ḵäna·kwe is recorded fragmentarily by Cushing (Ouline of Zuñi Creation Myths, p. 424), more fully by Stevenson (Zuñi Indians, p. 36). The text version of the Zuñi Creation legend recorded by the author follows the Stevenson version. (See pp. 597, 599.)

The following tale recorded from an official of the kotiḵan·e shares many features with the legend of Citsuḵä (see p. 925), the events in which are believed to have taken place during the war with the Ḵäna·kwe.

"The Ḵäna·kwe are like human people. They do not live at the sacred lake and are not really katcinas. They came out of the earth the way we did. They came out at a great cave southeast of the sacred lake. When they came out they all shouted together and frightened everyone. Then they came to a place whose name I can not remember and there they stayed. They built their houses of black stones. They saw many deer tracks and thought they would make bows and arrows, and hunt. So they made bows and arrows and hunted They built corrals for the deer, and they lived there for two years."

One day two Ḵäna·kwe were out hunting. They were on the top of a mountain and looking down from the high place they saw two girls washing a deer skin. They saw that the place where they had come out was near there, and they wondered why they had not stopped there where the people were living. Then the two of them went down quickly without any trouble, for they were wise.[2] As they came near, the girls said, "Who are these coming? We do not know them. They look dangerous." They were singing and shaking their rattles as they went along. As they came closer the girls said, "Let us go in. We are ashamed to stay out when anyone comes." So they went right in. They pulled the mat over the hatchway, a flat mat of reeds. Then the two Ḵäna·kwe came there and looked to see where the girls had gone. They were singing and trying to coax them out, but the girls would not come. Then they said, "Huita, huita, huita!" (When the first people came up this is the word that they used for "I give," but they do not use it any more.) But even then no one came out. The people of the sacred lake heard them, but they did not want to have them there and so they did not come out. So then the Ḵäna·kwe went home and told their people what they had done. When they came back and told

---

[2] They had supernatural power.

the people they said, "That is a good call that you made there. We
will always use that for our call whenever we come." That is why
the Ḳäna·kwe always use that as their call. The other katcinas
learned it from them, and so they always call "Huita!" when they
have a give-away dance.

References.—Myths (Stevenson, Zuñi Indians, 36, ff; Cushing, Outline of Zuñi
Creation Myths, p. 124). Ceremony described fully by Stevenson, Zuñi Indians,
pages 217–226, and Notes on Zuñi. Masks illustrated (Stevenson, Pl. XLII,
XLIII, XLV, XLVI, XLVII).

Parallels.—The Ḳäna·kwe, like Tcakwena, belong to the war-fertility complex
that is ritualized in both masked and unmasked ceremonies. See also the discussion of Tcakwena, p. 931.) Their dance is the most important "give away"
and for general hilarity is considered by Zuñis to be surpassed only by the scalp
dance. They are undoubtedly among the most important of Zuñi katcinas.

The most striking conceptual parallel is found at Acoma in the ceremony of
the battle with the katcinas, fully described by White. There the association
of war and fertility is strikingly brought out. The two ceremonies have nothing in common. The killing of the hostile gods to fructify the earth, which is
represented dramatically at Acoma, appears fully in the Zuñi myth. The
Zuñi ritual, however, has become so fully assimilated to the pattern of masked
dancing that its symbolism is unintelligible without the myth.

In this connection it is interesting to note that Stevenson reports that the
Ḳäna·kwe songs are in the Sia tongue.

Koɫahmana

(Plate 33, *c*)

Mask like Koḳokci (blue, not white like Kokwe'le; blue is the male
color). Black beard. Fringe of goatskin over forehead. Characteristic headdress, as in picture, half is done up, half not yet complete.

Woman's dress, calico underdress, dance kilt, fastened on left
shoulder, deerskin quiver containing arrows, white moccasins. In
right hand a rattle of deer scapula, in left bow and arrows. Many
necklaces.

This is probably not an old mask.

Ceremonies.—She always comes with Ḳäna·kwe. Occasionally
with Koḳokci or mixed dance. She is the katcina berdache.

Cushing (Outline of Zuñi Creation Myths) describes her as the first-
born child of Siwulu'siwa and Siwulusietsa, thus again linking sexual
abnormality with incest. She is later captured by the Ḳäna·kwe.
Stevenson (Zuñi Indians, p. 37) gives the origin of Koɫahmana as
dating from the time of the battle. "She (Kuyapalitsa or Chakwena)
succeeded in capturing four of the gods of Koɫuwalawa—including Koḳokci, first born of Siwulu'siwa and Siwuluhsitsa. Koḳokci, the first
born, was so angry and unmanageable that Kuyapalitsa had him
dressed in female attire previous to the dance (of the Ḳäna·kwe),
saying to him, "You will now, perhaps, be less angry."

This seems entirely inconsistent with the emphatically gentle character of Koᵏokci, whose very name means the good or gentle katcina. Stevenson has mistaken the position of Koᵏokci in the mythology. The Koᵏokci are the lost children translated, and are in no way connected with primordial incest.

A Hopi myth of Tckawaina mana explains the peculiar headdress which is the same as that worn by this Hopi impersonation. Tcakwaina mana was a rude, ill-mannered girl who always wanted to do the work of men. She would not do women's work. One day when all the men had gone to their fields her mother was dressing her hair in the fashion of Hopi maidens. As her mother was winding the hair over the hoop used as support, a party of Navaho raiders fell upon the village. Tcakwaina mana jumped up, her hair undone, seized her brothers' bows and arrows, and rushed out. She killed the enemy and took their scalps and thus saved her people. Therefore, the people love her, and therefore, she always comes with her hair half down.

(The name Tcakwaina mana was given at the formal adoption into the Asa clan of Sitcumovi to a white girl who rode horseback, wore knickers, and went among men unescorted, "because she is strong like Tcakwaina." It was a very dubious compliment.)

DANCES OF THE WINTER AND SUMMER SERIES

Ko'ᵏokci (The Good or Beautiful Katcina)

(Plate 35, a)

Costume.—The mask covers only the face and has a long beard. His hair is open. On top yellow parrot feathers, three downy eagle feathers hanging down the back. "These are to make the clouds come."

His body is painted with pink clay from the Sacred Lake. He wears embroidered kilt, white fringed belt, and red woven felt, fox skin. He wears spruce in his belt and carries spruce in his hands. He goes barefoot, with anklets of spruce. On the right leg he has a turtle-shell rattle and behind that a rattle of deer hoofs. The turtles are caught every four years in the Sacred Lake, and their rumbling makes the thunder come.

"Koᵏokci never makes people frightened or angry. He is always happy and gentle, and he dances to make the world green. They call the rains, and no matter how hard it rains they keep on dancing. They come all the time, summer and winter, and in summer they make the pleasant days. That is why they are called Koᵏokci.

"During the war with the Ḵana·kwe they were the only ones who did not fight. They never fight, because they are always kind and gentle."

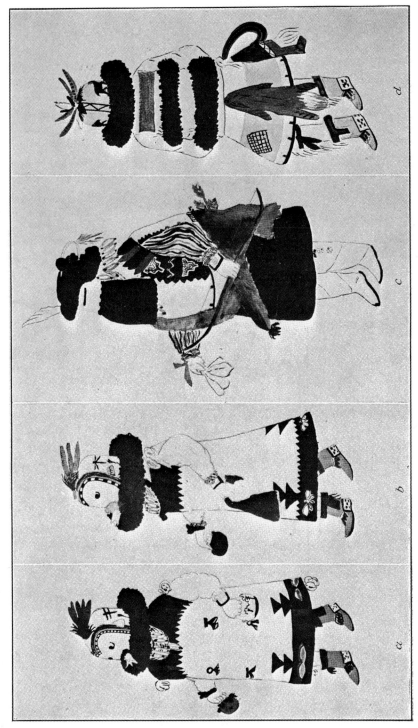

OLD MASKS APPEARING IRREGULARLY

a, Ḵäna·kwe Mosona; *b*, Ḵäna·kwe; *c*, Koḣahmana; *d*, O'lolowickä.

WINTER AND SUMMER DANCES: KOŔOKCI DANCE FORMATION

WINTER AND SUMMER DANCES: KOK̄OKCI

a, Koʼk̄okci; *b*, Kok̄weʼle; *c*, Komok̄ätsiki (Siwuluhsietsa); *d*, Uʼpoʼyona.

WINTER AND SUMMER DANCES: KATCINA CORN GRINDING

Ceremonies.—Koꞣokci must be performed as the opening dance of the summer series, on the return of the katcinas from Koɫuwala·wa. It should also be the opening dance of the winter series, but Upiꞣaia-p'ona is sometimes substituted. Koꞣokci may be danced at any time during the winter or summer series. Mrs. Stevenson calls the summer and winter dance series "the dances of the Koꞣokci."

Myths.—The myth of the origin of katcinas refers specifically to Koꞣokci. (See p. 595.) They are the prototype of katcinas. It is they who are identified particularly with the lost children. This may account for the affection in which they are held and the imputation to them of an unfailingly mild and gentle character.

References.—Koꞣo·kci is such a common Zuñi dance that all literature on the pueblo refers to it repeatedly. It is unnecessary to give a full list of references. The best descriptions are by Stevenson, Zuñi Indians, p. 161, Pl. XXXI; Parsons, Summer and Winter Dance Series at Zuñi. (The writer has observed as many as 56 dancers dancing Koꞣo·kci in summer.)

Parallels.—This is one of the most widely distributed of pueblo dances. Danced by the Hopi under the name "Barefoot Anga Katcina." A San Felipe informant identified the picture as that of their Acuwa. (Bunzel, Journal of American Folk-Lore.) A similar dance without mask danced at San Juan. (Parsons, Social Organization of the Tewa, p. 179. ff., pl. 21.) At Cochiti a similar mask is illustrated under title "Rain-Making Shiwanna" in Dumarest, p. 179.

KOKWE'LACTOꞢI (KATCINA MAIDEN)

(Plate 35, *b*; 37, *c*)

Costume.—The face is white, with a long beard of horsehair. In her hair she wears one downy feather. Over the forehead a fringe of goat's hair. The back hair is wrapped over two pieces of wood and bound with yarn; the hair is wrapped in one direction, the yarn in the other.

Until about ten years ago she wore only the black dress and white Hopi blanket; no underdress and no leggings. The arms and legs were bare and she wore anklets of spruce. Spruce branches in both hands. The hands are painted white, the feet yellow. The female impersonators do not paint under the dress.

She always comes with the rain dance, whether it is Ko'ꞣokci, Upiꞣaiapona or Hekcina Cilowawa.

Mythology.—At the sacred lake they were getting ready for the winter dance series. The Sälimopiya and all the other katcinas who were coming in all had their seeds. Each had a little corn-husk packet, but none of them were really bringing in seeds for the people of Itiwana. So after they had sent in the messenger to announce that they were coming to dance they talked about who should bring in seeds for the people so that they might have seeds to plant in the spring. None of the men like Koꞣokci wanted to be bothered carrying sacks of seeds. They thought they were doing enough in bringing a little package in their belts. So P̂autiwa said to the katcina maidens, "Now you will go in and take the corn for my people, and you will leave corn in every kiva except the one in which you stay." And so they came in and brought seeds for the people to plant in the spring. The men let the women carry in the seeds because the women had blankets under which to hide their bags. They did not want everyone to see that they were bringing in seeds.

That is how they come. Let us say that He'iwa kiva is having the dance. Then the katcina maidens come first to He'iwa kiva. They dance there and when they are finished they go out and go to the next kiva. Here they dance for a little while. There are ten katcina maidens and each one is carrying under her blanket a fawn-skin bag full of seeds. Toward the end of the dance two of the katcina maidens go to the altar where baskets have been set out for them. Then they take their fawn-skin bags and pour the seeds into the baskets. The older sister pours her seeds first, and then the younger sister.

When they are finished dancing the wo'le gets up and takes the seeds and gives a handful to everyone there, even to the little children. And so everyone always comes to the winter dances, and no matter how sleepy the little children are, they always stay up all night to get their seeds, so that their fathers may have many seeds to plant in the spring. And if their fathers are poor, the little boys run out as soon as the seeds have been distributed and go to the next kiva and get seeds there too. And so they get seeds from all five kivas.

They bring in seeds each time they dance in winter. They always bring seeds for the people of the five other kivas, and so each kiva gets seeds five times; that is, each time except at their own dance.

And so it is. Over at the sacred lake are many katcinas and when we have need of anything P̂autiwa picks out someone to do it, and that is the way we do it from that time on.

SI'WULUHSIETSA (KOMOK̲ÄTSIK̲[1])

(Plate 35, c)

(This is her personal name and is esoteric. She is ordinarily referred to as Komok̲ätsik̲ (katcina old woman).

Costume.—"The red mark on the face refers to her myth. She was menstruating when she copulated with her brother and so her face is marked with red. She has a dance kilt wrapped around her neck. She wants to hide her face behind it because she is ashamed. The mask covers the whole head. The hair is of white silk floss. Now she wears regular woman's dress as shown in the picture. In the old days she did not wear the calico blouse under her dress, but her arms were bare. She should not wear the tasseled belt, nor the moccasins. Her feet are bare and she wears anklets of spruce. But now she comes

Winter Dance Group: Sioux Dance, Fig. a (See Plate 50)
(This figure and the three following were printed in color in the first edition, but in black and white from the color plate, in this edition)

Winter Dance Group: Sioux Dance, Fig. b (See Plate 50)

dressed this way. She carries in her hand the mother corn. It is wrapped with spruce branches to make the world green."

She is called incorrectly the mother of the katcinas. She is really the mother of the Koyemci.

Komoḳätsiḳ comes occasionally with Koḳokci, and dances near the head of the line. She also sometimes comes with the mixed dance.

Mythology.—The text version of the myth of Siwuluhsietsa is given on p. 572. Cushing's version of this important myth in Outline of Zuñi Creation Myths, p. 399. Another informant adds the following details:

"She and her brother Siwuhlusiwa were the parents of the Koyemci. They came together and made a spring and then the spring ran. She was menstruating when she went with her brother and that is why the spring ran. It became the Sacred Lake and that is where the mothers of the a·ciwi dropped their babies. The babies turned into animals, but in the night they turned into katcinas. They did not wear masks then, but they dressed just the way they are represented now. The babies grew up right away and turned into dancers. Siwuluhsiwa and Siwuluhsietsa were the only grown-up people. That is why she is called katcina old woman. Siwuluhsiwa is called Great Father Koyemci or katcina husband. There were nine children, and with the father there are ten. The father and the nine made their home on the mountain called Koyemci which is to the north of the lake. Komoḳätsik went into the lake to look after the katcinas.

"In the winter during the period before the winter solstice when the river is full of water they tell the children to take smooth pieces of wood and drop them into the river. They are carried down the river to the Sacred Lake. Katcina old woman lies in the middle of the lake with her mouth open and the sticks just float into her mouth. In her body they turn into 'babies' (wihe·we). They come out one after the other and we tell the children that Komoḳätsik never gets tired having children and never suffers with them. During the winter dance series the katcinas bring in dolls for the children to play with and they tell them they are Komoḳätsik's babies. They call this iṭsumawe."[3]

UṖO'YONA

(Plate 35, *d*)

Dressed like Koḳokci with moccasins. Carries rattle and spruce. (See p. 996 for description of UṖo'yona in initiation ceremonies.) Comes occasionally with Koḳokci.

---

[3] See also description of winter solstice, p. 536.

Upik̄'aiapona (Downy Feathers Hanging) or A'tsamkoK̄ɔ·kci[4]

(Plate 37, a)

Costume.—"He is like Kok̄ɔkci. His face is green for the green world. The mouth is painted all different colors for all different kinds of flowers, white and red and blue and yellow and black, so as to have a fine summer with all different kinds of flowers. He has three downy feathers hanging from the bottom of the mask. He dances for the spring, so that the spring will come quickly with fine days.

"His body is painted black with yellow breast and shoulders for the oriole because he comes early in the spring. The yellow on the arms is for the yellow flowers and the corn pollen. He wears a white dance kilt, white-embroidered sash, red woven belt. Fox skin, blue moccasins. On the right leg a turtle-shell rattle tied on with a small red belt. Gourd rattle in right hand, spruce branches in left. He always carries spruce to make the world green, and in the summer he wears spruce in his belt also. He has his seeds in the front of his belt."

Ceremonies.—Upik̄'aiapona is a variant of Kok̄ɔkci and may be substituted for Kok̄ɔkci on any occasion except the return of the katcinas at the summer solstice. However, since Upik̄aiapona is generally called Kok̄ɔkci one can never be sure just what is meant when it is said, "It must be Kok̄ɔkci."

Parallels.—Hopi anga katcina (Fewkes, Hopi Katcinas, 54, 93, 94, Pl. XXXII).

Pai'yatyamu [5]

(Plate 37, b)

Mask turquoise with black and white border. Turquoise earrings. Parrot and downy eagle feathers in hair, and head band of bright ribbons.

Body painted red with markings of yellow (if he comes with Hekcina cilowa, the body paint is black). Embroidered kilt, fringed sash, red belt, blue moccasins, yarn, necklaces, etc. Carries trumpet decorated with downy feathers.

---

[4] An old name meaning handsome katcina youths.

[5] The name paiyatyamu (Keresan, youth) has three usages in Zuñi. It is the name of the god of flowers, butterflies and music (Zuñi Indians, p. 568; Cushing, Outline of Zuñi Creation Myths, p. 395). Society members offer him prayer sticks at the winter solstice. These sticks are double and are painted blue and yellow, the phallic colors. The word is also applied to the musical orders of the two societies who are flutes, mak̄e, tsana·kwe and pecatsilo·kwe. It is also used by the newe·kwe esoterically to refer to themselves. Magic butterflies and flutes figure in folklore as methods of seduction.

KO'KWE'LACTOKI OKEN'ONA (KATCINA MAIDEN, THE ONE WHO GRINDS)

(Plate 37, c)

Mask white. Black beard. Hair done up in back. Black woman's dress. Bare arms. Miha fastened on right shoulder. White moccasins. Hands painted white. Carries an ear of corn and a sprig of spruce in each hand. Bright yarn around wrist.

Ceremonies.—This impersonation appears in the ritual of Ololowicḳä. For description of the ceremony, including selection of impersonators, see p. 1007. (Parsons, Winter and Summer Dance Series at Zuñi, p. 195.)

Parallels.—The grinding ceremony is similarly performed by the Hopi in connection with anga katcina. (Fewkes, Hopi Katcinas, pp. 93, 94; Pl. XXXII.)

HEHE'A

(Plate 37, d)

Costume.—Blue (should be turquoise) mask with characteristic eyes and nose. Fox skin collar. Single parrot tail feather over right ear. Body painted red. Forearms yellow. Yarn and ribbons on right wrist. Fringed girl's shawl as kilt. Silver belt. Brown moccasins. White fringed leggings tied with yarn.

Ceremonies.—Two Hehe'a appear in the ritual of Ololowicḳä. They carry in the grinding stones and other paraphernalia, arrange it for the katcina maidens, and beat time for the grinding. All their movements are hasty and clumsy. (See also pp. 1007, 1066, 1077, for Hehe'a's appearance in other ceremonies.)

Parallels.—This is another widespread and probably ancient katcina.
Hopi: Hehe'a (Fewkes, Hopi Katcinas, pp. 73, 74; Pl. XI).
Cochiti: "The first personage to appear to the onlookers is the heruta of chief of the shiwanna. The koshare are as indispensable in the secret dances as in everything. Their chief is absorbed by the heruta who says to him in signs (the shiwanna never speak), "Here I have the shiwanna who have come to visit the pueblo and present a dance." "What a liar!" says the koshare. "Where are the dancers?" "Close by here. Ask the people if they want to see them." Then the koshare begs the cacique to ask the people if they want to see the shiwanna, or if the koshare asks himself he spices his questions with pleasantries which are a delight to the people. "This old man asks if you want to see his dancers, the shiwanna. If you want to he bids you say 'Yes!'" The women begin to call out, "Yes, yes." The heruta is always deaf as well as dumb. He says in gestures "I hear nothing at all." The women then start to cry louder, "Yes, yes." The heruta points to his ears and holds up one finger; he had heard only one person. "Yes, yes," begins again. The koshare says, "Call louder. This old man has ticks in his ears; he is deaf." Everybody laughs. Finally the heruta has heard. The koshare says to him, "Come, go get your shiwanna.

6066°—32——65

Show us if you are light-footed in running and bring them to us quickly." The heruta dances where he stands and then disappears round some corner.

Soon he returns with his shiwanna. At their head comes the nalua with his staff of authority in his hand. Behind the nalua comes the heruta. He wears tribal costume, shirt of deerskin, deerskin fringes on the shoulders, and deerskin trouser legs fastened to the belt. He has a black mask in a kind of leathern box the top part of which is covered with woolly buffalo hide. Across the lower part of the leathern ears are two little white eagle feathers. Lightning signs are painted on the face. To the bottom of the mask a rolled-up coyote skin is sewn. (Mask illustrated fig. 22, a, p. 178.) Also Acoma and San Felipe Heruta (White, manuscript).

Jemez. Hymahaie related in character but not appearance (Parsons, Jemez, p. 108; pl. 12, b.)

To'wa Tcakwena (Old Tcakwena)

(Plate 38, a)

Costume.—"He is a society member, therefore he wears the red feather on the right side of the head, and the yucca band. White downy feather on the left side; behind lacowanɬana. His hair is long and hangs down the back, and he has a long black beard too. The mask comes under the chin and is painted black with the shiny paint made from the fruit of the yucca. Large mouth.

The body is painted black with hekwitola. The shoulders and forearms are yellow. On each breast and on the back are designs in yellow (piɬawe, bows). Arm bands of blue buckskin with tabs and fringes of red buckskin. Buckskin kilt, embroidered Hopi sash. Fox skin. Blue moccasins. The legs should be painted black. Turtle shell rattle on right leg. In the right hand yucca, in the left bow and arrow. The leader carries a gourd rattle in the right hand. The dance step is characterized by a peculiar stooping posture.

Ceremonies.—The dance belongs to He'iwa kiva and is always danced during ca'lako and often is substituted for Kokɔkci in the rain dance series.

" Towa tcakwena always has funny songs. He tells the people, and especially the children, what to do. He used to sing like this at the sacred lake and Ƥautiwa heard him and said, ' Now you must go to my people at Itiwana and tell them these songs so that they may know how to live. You will go and sing for them like that.' Ƥautiwa wanted his children to know all these things.

" So Towa Tcakwena came here to dance. First he started and said, 'I am praying for the world to be beautiful for you,' and he said he was bringing the clouds and the rain and that he was a good hunter and wanted his people to have good luck and to live long. He began like this with a nice song, but then he started to sing funny things. He said things like this:

MASKS APPEARING WITH GRINDING RITUAL

a, Upiḵaiap̣ona; b, Paiyatyamu; c, Koḵwe'le; d, Hehe'a.

WINTER AND SUMMER DANCES: ᵀOWA TCAKWENA

a, Tcakwena; *b*, Tomtsinapa; *c*, Tcilili.

" 'Children, you must mind your parents or the earth will crack and the wild man will come out and eat you.

" 'You must not drink water while you are eating or all your teeth will fall out.

" 'Little girls, do not play with the boys or you will menstruate soon and your breasts will get big. And if you have relations with the little boys you will be turned into stones.

" 'When your first teeth fall out in the daytime do not throw them away in the daytime, but wait until evening and then ask your grandmother for new teeth.

" 'Little boys, if your mother is in the sand bed⁶ do not sit on the sand bed or your legs will hurt all the time and you will never be able to hunt.'

"And he said to the old people, 'When you are cooking, wash your pot, when you take it from the fire, so that its lips will not get sore. And take the stone that you set the pot on outdoors so that it won't sweat all the time.'

"He sang all kinds of things like this right out and the people laughed and laughed and they said to one another, 'Yes; that may be true.' He said all kinds of things and all the people laughed. He said:

" 'Little girls, if you play with the little boys you will never grow tall, but you will always be short. And if the little boys go with the girls they will never grow up at all.

" 'I know these things are true,' he said, 'because this is what I have heard from my grandmother, Hemokyatsik, and I always mind what the old people say. And that is why I tell you these things. I want you to mind the old people. This is why I have come and this is why I have the name the unkind Tcakwena or the old, old Tcakwena.'

"That is the way he comes. He always thinks up all kinds of funny things to tell the people. He makes fun of the people, too. If a man is trying to marry a woman who doesn't want him he talks right out about it. He tells them all kinds of things.

" 'If your brother has touched a woman, you must never touch her or you will come to be your brother's enemy.

" 'If a young man sleeps with his brother he must put ashes on his genitals so as not to come to this brother's wife. Boys and girls must not sleep together without ashes.

" 'Girls, you must be careful not to put your feet in your basket. If you do the young man you marry will take you away to his house and you will never be with your mother.'⁷

---

⁶ Lying in after childbirth.

⁷ "It is not good for a girl to live with her husband's people, because if he is living in his mother's house he works for his mother and not for his wife, and if he dies she must go back to her own people empty-handed."

"That is how Towa Tackwena comes. He comes at the end of Ca'lako and sings like this and makes fun of individuals. But he particularly makes fun of the Koyemci. The poor Koyemci have been in retreat for fifteen days and Towa Tcakwena comes and makes fun of them and tells them what their wives are doing and tries to hurt their feelings. They say, 'We have just come from the sacred lake. And what do you think? We saw father Koyemci's wife going over to Pautiwa's house while father Koyemci was here at Itiwana.' Then the Koyemci say, 'Are they really doing things like that at the sacred lake while we are here visiting our friends?' So they make fun of them like that because the Koyemci have not been home for fifteen days."

(When Tcakwena danced after Ca'lako in 1927 and 1928 their songs contained no direct homilies addressed to the children, but had many references to ceremonial breaches of various individuals. See p. 889 for paraphrase of a Tcakwena song.—R. L. B.)

References.—Parsons, Winter and Summer Dance Series, page 187, notes on Zuñi, I, 213. Stevenson, pp. 262, 265.

Parallels.—Tcakwena is danced under this name by the Hopi (tcakwaina). (Fewkes, Hopi Katcinas, 62, 3, Pl. IV.) Laguna: Chakwena (Goldfrank, Cochiti, p. 08); Parsons, Notes on Ceremonialism at Laguna, figure 2. (This is the other Tcakwena.) Cochiti—Chakwena (without mark). San Felipe (Bunzel, Journal of American Folklore, 292). It appears not to be known to the Tewa.

TCILILI

(Plate 38, c)

Costume.—He belongs to the Tcakwena set. Headdress like Laguna Tcakwena. Goatskin and eagle down over his head on crown, tips forward. Red body paint with zigzags of black, forearms and legs black spotted with white. Buckskin armbands with feathers and spruce. Red cotton kilt with snake painted on it, white belt. Fox skin. Bear claws over feet. In right hand rattle (?), left yucca and stone ax. He should wear a bear skin instead of buckskin shirt and around the edge are sewed claws of the bear and other animals that jingle as he walks. He gets his name Tcilili from the jingling of the bear claws.

Ceremonies.—He comes sometimes as solo dancer with Tcakwena.

Mythology.—When the earth was soft he used to come here and step on the children and little animals with his big feet. He would come to where mothers left their babies in the fields and step on the babies. Then they would die and he would eat them up. Then the people were angry and especially the head men. So they went after him and said to him, "You must not come here any more and eat our babies. We don't want you coming around here. Now your name shall be Tcilili. We shall not call you Tcakwena any more, but Tcilili. You shall always walk badly after this, and there shall not be anyone else like you. And we do not want you to

WINTER AND SUMMER DANCES: ʇOWA TCAKWENA

a, We'waꞔ; *b*, A·wan nana.

WINTER AND SUMMER DANCES

a, Laguna Tcakwena; *b*, Hatacuku (with Tcakwena); *c*, Kukuculi (with mixed dance); *d*, Ḳälawari (with mixed dance).

come often any more because you have eaten our babies." That is why he doesn't often come with Towa Tcakwena, but only rarely.

Reference.—Parsons, Notes on Zuñi, 213.

HUPOMO''OTCA (SHORT BEARD)

He belongs to Towa Tcakwena set. He is the friend of Tsitsiko-hane, who comes with short-haired Tcakwena. They are both good hunters.

MOK̭'AIAPONA (BALL EYES)

He has large ball eyes. He sometimes comes with Tcakwena set and dances out of line.

WE'WAP

(Plate 39, *a*)

Costume.—Towa Tcakwena mask. Long hair, eagle down on crown, red feather over left ear. Great feather.

Red body paint, forearms and legs black with white spots. War chief bandoleer. Kilt of bear or wild cat skin, fox skin behind. Bear paws over feet. Carries stone ax in right hand, yucca, points back, in left. Comes rarely with Towa Tcakwe·na set. Arm bands with spruce.

TCAKWENA (SHORT-HAIRED TCAKWENA)

(Plate 40, *a*)

Costume.—He has a chin mask painted black. The eyes represent the new moon with the horns down. The people believe that when the new moon appears with the horns down there will be rain during the month, because mother moon is pouring out water. The top and back of the head is covered with wild goat skin dyed black with eagle down stuck to the hair with gum. On the head lacowanłana with duck's head. He has a large mouth (citsitone, teeth together mouth) with a beard over the chin (huponine) of mixed black and gray horsehair.

The body is painted black with yellow designs. The yellow on the shoulders is for fine days with sunshine and rain and no wind. The rows of yellow spots on arms and chest represent the rainbow. The rainbow stops the rain, but they want the rain to go on, so they do not finish the rainbow, but break it with another design. They call this design piławapana, bow painting.

He wears buckskin kilt because he is a good hunter. Embroidered sash, blue moccasins, fox skin, leather arm bands. He wears the buckskin bandoleer of the war chief. Turtle shell rattle on right leg. Gourd rattle in right hand, bow and arrow in left. Many beads, back and front.

Ceremonies.—Always performed by Upîsanakwe after Ca'lako, and by them or others during summer and winter series.

This dance belongs to uptsanawa kiva. They dance it after Ca'lako and in the summer rain dance series. It is a give-away dance. They always bring lots of bread and other things to give to the people.

The songs are in the Laguna language. This is the dance that went to Laguna. They are the short-haired Tcakwena (tcamoka-wistowe). They are sometimes called drum tcakwena (tcahumoawe).

Two Hatacuku always come with the short-haired Tcakwena. They are Laguna katcinas. Tsitsikohana, a good hunter, sometimes comes with them and dances out of line. He used to bring in a deer and have someone help him skin it.

Folklore.—The people of Zuñi and Laguna have always been good friends, better friends than any of the other Indians. When the people first came here there were dances going on all the time and everyone was happy. They heard that the Laguna people were friendly and warned them when they thought there was going to be war and sent messengers to let them know if anything was wrong and tried to help them in every way. They heard that the Laguna people were kind. Then the Itiwana people heard that the Laguna people wanted to have a dance and that they did not dance like the Itiwana people. So the Itiwana people decided to go there and dance for them. They sent the Tcakwena dance. They practiced their songs here, and when they were ready to go everyone got his clothing ready, the way they do now when they go to the Gallup ceremonial. Some of the women wanted to go, too, and they got ready to go. The men got their masks ready and two men went ahead to tell the Laguna people that the people of Itiwana were coming to dance for them. They told the Laguna people to get a room ready for the dancers to go into. The men who were going to dance bundled up their clothing and walked ahead, and the people who were just going to watch the dance packed their clothing and things on horses and donkeys and went behind. There were many people.

At Laguna everyone was waiting for them. They were baking bread and cooking. They got a room ready for the dancers and the two men who had gone ahead went into the room. The Laguna chief met the dancers as they came to the village and took them to show them their room where they were to go in. The house stood on the west side of the village. It was dark when they got there, so no one saw them come in. The next day they came out and danced in the Laguna village. It was the Towa Tcakwena dance. They danced for two days, and on the third day they were going home again. But the Laguna people, and especially the women, wanted them to dance for four days before they went home. The Laguna men went into the room where they were dressing and made up songs in their own language and had the Zuñi men sing them. The Laguna people liked the Zuñi songs and the Itiwana people liked the Laguna songs, so they exchanged. The Laguna people told them to dance for four days, and so they came out and danced with the Laguna songs. The Laguna songs were all about hunting. The words meant, "Now there is a deer. You are over there. Come to me. I shall put my valuable beads on you. I shall give you all my beads. I shall dress you if you come to me. This is the way we shall live." So they danced with this song and the Laguna people told them, "When you come to your home you will be good hunters. You will always hunt and you will sing the way we have taught you." So they said, "Very well; we shall try it." Then the Laguna people gave them bread and peaches and all the things they had ready to pay them for the dance.

Then they came home and they danced here again for two days after they got back. The people here knew the dancers were coming back and they waited for them. Then when they came they danced here with the Laguna songs, and their dancing was different, too. Then the men got together in the kivas and talked about it, how the Tcakwena dancers came back from Laguna with new songs, and they thought they were nice songs and they liked the Laguna words and the different kind of dancing, too. So after they came back they decided to have two different kinds of Tcakwena—their own old ones and the new ones. So to make them different the ones who had been to Laguna cut off their hair. That is the way we came to have the short-haired Tcakwena. They still sing in the Laguna language, and their dance step is different. They stand up when they dance, but the old Tcakwena dance stooping over. When the men came back from Laguna they brought back with them one of the Laguna katcinas. He is Hatacuku. He is like the Koyemci, but his mask is a little different. There are always two of them, one drums and the other dances. They always speak the Laguna language.

References.—Parsons, Notes on Zuñi, I, 212. Stevenson, p. 265.

HATACUKU

(Plate 40, *b*)

Costume.—The mask is made of cloth painted with clay from the Sacred Lake. He wears turkey feathers in the knobs on his head.

When he comes to drum for Tcakwena he wears only the dark blue kilt fastened on his shoulder, and the string of little bells around his waist. He has no belt and his legs are bare. But when he comes for the winter dances he wears red buckskin moccasins and fringed leggings.

"His mask is not valuable. Anyone can have it. If a young man does not dance with his own kiva or if he has been away while they

are practicing and just comes back the day before they dance and
wants to dance with them, he will have sone one fix him up as Hatacuku
and dance with them.   He will take a piece of buckskin or canvas to
some older man and have him paint it for him.   He measures the
man's face and makes the mask.   He fills the knobs with clay from
the Sacred Lake and paints the mask all over with the same clay.
Then he takes seeds and chews them and rubs them all over the mask
and prays: "Now I have made you into a person hastily.   You will
be as valuable as other people are.   Do not think yourself cheap, but
have a strong soul like the others and bring my people good luck."
He chews seeds and rubs them around the mask, inside and out.
Then the man for whom he has made the mask stands beside him
facing the east.   He holds the mask in his hand and says, "Now you
will never trouble your father who is going to take care of you.   You
will never bring him misfortune or bad luck."   Then he turns it
around four times to take off the bad luck from the man who is going
to keep the mask.   Then the young man takes it out.

"There is no whipping because it is not a real mask.   The young
man must get his mask at another time.   But any man who wants to
join in a dance can wear this.

"He comes with the short-haired Tcakwena and sometimes with the
mixed dance.   Sometimes he just comes with Sälimop̄iya at the winter
dance series.

"He comes from Laguna.   The Tcakwena brought him back when
they went there to dance.   He always talks the Laguna language.
He makes jokes about people."

TOMTSINAPA

(Plate 38, b)

Costume.—The face is painted blue with stripes of black and yellow
around the edge, "to bring the rains to Itiwana."   On the sides of the
head are painted dragon flies "to make the crops grow fast."   He has a
protruding snout with a band of red dyed rabbit fur where it joins
the mask.   On the head yellow parrot feathers with downy feathers
of the eagle.   Standing up at the back of the head a fan of eagle wing
feathers, with black goat's hair where they are fastened.   Spruce
collar.   The body paint is pink clay from the sacred lake.   He wears
arm bands of blue buckskin with tabs of buckskin and turkey feathers.
Embroidered kilt like that worn by Sä'limop̄iya.   Blue leather belt
with silver belt over it.   White tasseled sash, fox skin, blue moccasins.
Yarn on both legs with little bells.   In the left hand a spruce sapling
with yarn of different colors tied around the base, and feathers at the
top (downy feather, hawk, humming bird, oriole).

Ceremonies.—"Tomtsinapa used to come with the mixed dance, but now he comes with the short-haired Tcakwena. There is a long story of how they came to change.

"He always dances out of line and gives the calls for the dancers, for he is a sweet singer. He has a valuable voice. Pautiwa sent him in with the mixed dance and said to him, 'You shall go to Itiwana to bring the people your sweet voice, so that the women may sing sweet songs when they grind the corn, for the corn likes to hear the women sing as they grind. And you will go for the sake of the men also, for they sing for the women as they grind.' And so Tomtsinapa came with the mixed dance to bring the people his sweet voice and to bless them with good crops. He came and danced out of line and gave his call in a loud voice. And when the dancers came to the end of each song Tomtsinapa came to the center and gave his call. The people all liked to hear him and said, 'Oh, hasn't this one a sweet voice!' And every time he gave his call all the people breathed in and prayed, 'May I have a sweet voice like that.' They knew without being told why he had been sent to Itiwana. And he brought his sweet voice to the people."

References.—Parsons, Notes on Zuñi, I, p. 212.

Tsi'ḳohan'o·na

"Sometimes comes with the short-haired Tcakwena and dances out of line. He has a white beard instead of gray and black. He is the best hunter. He carries bow and arrow and a quiver also. He used to bring in a deer and a man who wanted to be a good hunter would help him skin it. His friend is Hupomo'otca who belongs to Towa Tcakwena. They never come in together, but they are friends and always used to hunt together and always killed many deer."

The Mixed Dance

A mixed dance, a line dance in which all participants are differently costumed and masked, may be performed by any kiva during the winter or summer series. After Ca'lako two mixed dances are required. Ohewa regularly dances a mixed dance (Wotemła). Heḳä-pawa has recently substituted the old mixed dance (Towa Wotemła) for the unpopular Maheṫinaca. This latter uses a drum, has different songs, and is otherwise different from the regular mixed dance.

The costumes of the mixed dance are varied and imaginative.[8] Some are "pretty dancers," some terrible or grotesque. They form a motley outfit less attractive to us than the more carefully styled Koḳo·kci. One never knows just what masks will appear with Wɔ·temła. Some are familiar, some are inventions. Ahute, Tem-

---

[8] Photographs of the mixed dance are shown in Stevenson, Plate LXIX.

temci and other "dangerous" katcinas always appear, the others are selected at random according to the preferences of participants and the available masks.

Mixed katcinas are performed in all pueblos. There is probably little correspondence in the individual masks.

KUKUCULI

(Plate 40, c)

Costume.—His face is like Tomtsinapa's. The head is painted black to represent the sky, and the white spots are the stars. On the back of his head is painted a large butterfly. Over each ear he wears a squash blossom. On the head yellow parrot feathers, and at the back standing upright parrot tail feathers with downy feathers and small parrot feathers, spruce collar, the twigs tipped with popcorn to represent stars. He is a sky katcina.

His body paint is red paint mixed with pink clay. The arms and legs are yellow. He wears arm bands of blue buckskin with scallops and fringes of red buckskin. White cotton kilt with blue band, embroidered sash and red woman's belt. Fox skin. Blue moccasins with yarn on both legs. He carries yamuwe in both hands, "because he is the sky." On the yamuwe are turkey feathers and feathers of all the little birds.

He is the leader of the mixed dance. He used to come with Tcakwena, but now he comes with the mixed dance as their solo dancer and gives the calls for them. He comes with the mixed dance that uses the drum.

Myth.—Long ago, Hainawi and Homatci and Temtemci and some other katcina village people used to come in to dance at Itiwana. Then other people came from outside, like Salt woman and Deer katcina and Bear katcina, and Pautiwa always sent them in to dance with the mixed dance. Now the mixed dance had no drum, and some of them wanted to have a buckskin bundle and to dance like Tcakwena.[9]

Now they were getting ready to go to Itiwana and Pautiwa said, "All these outside people have come and joined us. Is everyone here?" Then they thought of all the directions. The bear had come from the east and the white bear had come from the south and the wild goat had come from the north, and there were coyote and deer and all different animals from all the directions. Then Pautiwa asked again, "Is everyone here?" The stars and the clouds from all different directions were there, and the only one that was missing was

---

[9] The buckskin bundle is called teseanane. It is made by bundling different kinds of clothing and cloth of all kinds in a buckskin, wrapping it very tight and tying it with rawhide thongs. The bundle is very hard and resounds when struck.

Winter Dance Group: Sioux Dance, Fig. c (See Plate 50)

Winter Dance Group: Sioux Dance, Fig. d (See Plate 50)

the sky. So they said to Pautiwa, "Our sky mother or sky father
has not come." They did not even know whether the sky was a man
or a woman, because they had never seen him. Then Pautiwa said,
"He must come too, and call out for you. He does not know the
songs because he has not been here, and so he can not sing, but he
shall come and give the calls for you."

So the sky person dropped down. He was black all over and he
was wearing the stars on his head and the stars were shining. He
looked dangerous, and as he came in it got colder. Everyone was
busy getting ready for the dance. They were practicing their songs
and their dancing. Then he came in and Pautiwa said, "Have you
come?" He said, "Yes," and he sat down. Then he said again,
"Why have you sent for me? I should like to hear it now." Then
Pautiwa said, "We have called you down here because everyone has
come here but you. Would you like to join in our dance and go with
us to Itiwana? I want you to decide what you want to do." So he
said. Then sky man answered, "Yes, my father. The people of
Itiwana are offering feathers to the sun and the clouds. I hold them
up, for I am the sky. Therefore it is right that I should come."
Then Pautiwa said, "It is good. Everyone is here now and they all
have their songs. But there is no one to give the calls for their dance.
Therefore you will give the calls for them."

Then they dressed him for the dance. He was black all over so
they painted his body the way he was to look, and they gave him
valuable clothing and feathers for his head. They gave him all the
different things that he wears and then they said, "Now this is the
way you will look." Then Sayataca made him two batons of cat-tail
stalks, and tied feathers to them so that he would go easily. He
walks with short steps.

Then the head men at the katcina village made up a bundle for a
drum, for they had no drum. They laid out two embroidered white
blankets and two buckskins, and between the two blankets they laid
long strings of valuable beads. Then Pautiwa said to the clothing
he was bundling up, "Now I am holding you, valuable clothing. You
shall be valuable to the people. Now all the people will come running
when they hear you. We do not want anyone to stay home, but we
want them all to come out and see this dance. Therefore you are
valuable." He said this to the clothing and then he held the bundle
tight and tied it up. Then Hehe'a was the one to drum for them. He
beat the drum and the sky man started to walk up and down. Then
he came to the middle of the line and he called out "Kukuculi."
Then he called again, "Hu-u-u!" like the Sälimopiya. He tried his
calls and they sounded well. Then they said to him, "That is a good
call that you have given. And that is the way they will call you when
you go to Itiwana. This is the name that you will have."

So he came with them to Itiwana. When they came here the people knew most of the dancers as they came in. But they did not know this one and they said to one another, "His name must be Kukuculi, for that is his call."

So that is why he comes with the mixed dance, because his name is Kukuculi. He comes and gives his call for them. And that is why they have the drum. When Kukuculi came they made the drum. He used to dance with Tcakwena, but he changed and came with the mixed dance and brought the drum with him. The old mixed dance (towa wotemła) has no drum. All the dangerous katcinas like Hainawi and Homatci come with the old mixed dance.

Ḳäławan'i

(Plate 40, d)

Wooden headdress painted with dragon flies, etc. Downy feathers on corners. Very long hair with downy feathers. Mask painted turquoise with bear paws. Ball eyes. Large wooden snout. Spruce collar.

Red body paint, yellow legs and forearms. Two bandoleers of yucca. Embroidered kilt, embroidered sash, red belt, fox skin, yarn on legs, blue moccasins. Right hand deer scapula, left hand bow and arrow and spruce. Arm bands.

Comes with mixed dance.

He lives in springs. His long hair is rain. Once he passed over Zuñi in the air; he was long and shiny like an icicle (a dirigible!).

Aincekoko (Bear Katcina)

(Plate 41, a)

Costume.—The mask is white painted with red and blue and black spots. The top of the head is covered with black hair. He has a big mouth with his red tongue hanging out. He has a hawk feather in each red ear. He wears the red feather in the hair and the yucca band because he is a member of a society. Beads like society people.

The body is painted red, legs white. He wears a blue woven loin cloth and over it a buckskin shirt, embroidered sash, and fox skin. He is dressed like a society member, but wears his dance clothes over the society clothes. He has yucca on the right wrist, a leather wrist band on left. Armbands with lahacoma, yucca in both hands. Blue moccasins. Yucca bands over both shoulders.

Myth.—Long ago there were bears around here, but the society of bears was at Cipapolima. The bears came here from Cipapolima and then the people sent them out in all directions. They said, "Now you, white bear, you will have your home in the south world. That is where you will stay, and when we need you you will come in to cure the people." So they said, and he went to the south. Then they

WINTER AND SUMMER DANCES: THE MIXED DANCE

Aincekoko (Bear); b, La'saiyapa; c, Tsupianawe; d, Suyuki.

WINTER AND SUMMER DANCES: THE MIXED DANCE

a, Malôkätsik̇ı (Salt Woman); *b*, Tecamik̇ä (Echo); *c*, Ya'ana.

said, "Now, father of the bears, black bear, we shall give you a home in the east. That will be your home and when we need you when anyone wants to join (a society?) we shall call you and you will come. You will always come when we call you." So they said, and he went to the east. Then they sent the mountain lion to the north and told him to come whenever they called him. And they sent the wild cat to the west. Then they called Atcialatapa and told him to look after the heaven. They told each animal to look after one of the directions. "And now who will go underneath and look after the earth?" Then they sent badger there. Then they called the stars and said, "You will always come down to the altars because you are the seeds of the heavens." So when the society people put up their altars they always make a meal painting. This represents the sky and they always use grains of white corn for the stars. So they told each one what he was to do when he came into the society.

Then they went out in all directions. The black bear went to the east. He was really a bear and walked around the trees eating piñon nuts. It was at the winter solstice that they sent the animals out. Then he went to sleep because the bears sleep in winter. In February, while the winter dance series was going on, the black bear awoke. The bear wakes up at the first thunderstorm of spring. So he woke up and stretched himself. He looked around. There were no clouds and nothing growing and he was very lonely. Then he thought, "I think it is spring. I do not have to go back again now." The other animals had all gone back to Cipapolima, but this bear had been told to watch the east. Then he thought, "I have heard there are katcinas at katcina village, and if anyone wants to he can go there and join them and go with them whenever they go to dance at Itiwana. I have feathers, too, so I can go there. I think I shall go there."

So he went. He went around to the south so as to meet his brother, the white bear. He came to the south and there was the white bear. He was still asleep. So he thought he would wake him up. But then he thought, "Maybe if I wake you up you will be angry. I suppose you did not hear the rumble of the thunder. When you wake up you will come to the Sacred Lake. So he left him and went on to katcina village. When he reached there he went in. He went in, a big black bear with big feet, and he sniffed at all of them. He smelled of the little Heh'ea and the others. The katcinas were all dancing and singing different kinds of songs. Then he went to the valuable place, where P̃autiwa and Sayataca and all the valuable people stayed. Then P̃autiwa said, "Now, my children, be quiet for a moment. Our father has come here. I want to hear why he has come." So they stopped dancing and everyone took his place. Then he asked, "Why have you come? I know you have come for something, for you have never come here before." "Well," he said, "I have come to join in sometime when you go to Itiwana. I have heard that any animal who wants to come with you can meet you. I have been in the east, but it is lonely there. I was lying down in my cave and I was lonely. Then I heard you over here and I thought I would come here and join you and go with you to Itiwana any time you go. The society members at Itiwana have worked on feathers for me and whoever has feathers can join you here. So I thought I would join you so as to go to Itiwana and be happy with my people." Then Pautiwa said, "We are very glad. We are happy to have you here and to know that you will join us and go to Itiwana." Then he said to him, "You are not just a common person. You are valuable. You are like us who look after the winter solstice." (He meant the valuable people who come at the winter solstice, Pautiwa and Sayataca and Sayałi'a and Citsukia and Kewlele. These are the important people who look after the year.) "Now we shall take you to Itiwana to-morrow. Stay here with us and we shall take you with us to Itiwana."

So when the next day came everyone got ready and all the dancers asked, "Which of us shall go to Itiwana?" He did not fit in with Kokokci or with Muluktakä. So Pautiwa said, "Whenever any of the wild animals want to go to Itiwana they always have to go with the mixed dance. The mixed dance will go with him." So they began to get ready. All the dangerous ones got ready to go with him. Then they began to dress him, "Now take off your fur dress," they told him. So he took off his skin and turned into a person and they began to paint him. They painted his body red with the katcina village clay and began to dress him the way he would look. They put on the red feather because he is a society person. They put on the yucca band and gave him nice beads. He was wearing a blue loin cloth. They said to him, "Don't take off your loin cloth because you are a society member." So he kept on the blue loin cloth and they put the buckskin over it. They gave him arm bands and bunches of yucca. They dressed him and said, "Now you will go like this." While he was getting ready many different new animals came and joined the mixed dance. All the katcinas who do not live at katcina village, like Salt woman, came in and got ready in the morning.

So they took him with them to Itiwana. When the mixed dance comes the people all go out to see who is coming with them, and this time the bear came with them. Then the people said, "Oh, there comes the bear, the society man. He has gone over there too." Then all the men in societies at Itiwana worked on feathers and in the evening when the katcinas finished dancing they took the bear into one of the society rooms. There the medicine chief of the society gave him the big bundle of feathers to take with him to his home in the east when he went back.

That is why the bear comes in the mixed dance. Sometimes he comes dressed like a katcina, but sometimes he comes like a real bear in a bearskin dress. (See p. 1055.)

In the mixed dance the different katcinas come in from all different directions. The first time the new katcinas came to Itiwana they went to the katcina village to get ready, but now they come right from their homes whenever they hear the mixed dance going on. Then in the evening they all go out to Wide River together.

La'saiyapona

(Plate 41, b)

Costume.—On head, downy feathers, feathers of macaw and turkey wing. Band of colored yarn about head. Hair done up in back. Red nose and mouth, blue zigzags on cheeks (like Hehe'a). Spruce collar.

Red body paint. Buckskin kilt, silver belt. Under it a long breechcloth of printed cotton hanging down before and behind. Woolen hose. Red moccasins. Carries arrow in right hand, bow in left. Arm bands, bow bracelet, yarn, necklaces.

Comes in mixed dance with Bear, Tsupianawe, Suyuki.

Tsupianawe (Bananas)

(Plate 41, c)

Costume.—Mask: face turquoise with bear claws, back white with dragon flies. Long wooden snout. Yarn around head. Standing up, a crown of simulated "bananas," in center slender twigs with soft feathers attached.

White shirt, buckskin fastened on right shoulder, embroidered kilt, sash, buckskin leggings, blue moccasins. Yarn around legs. In right hand long leaves of cat-tail or similar aquatic plant, in left, bow and arrow and spruce.

Comes in mixed dance with Bear, etc.

Suyuki

(Plate 41, d)

Costume.—Face mask painted brown, with long black beard, red mouth and tongue. Eagle down in long beard and flowing hair. Cattle horns on a yucca band around head. Lacowanłana.

Coyote or wildcat skin around shoulders. Red body paint, bandoleer, buckskin kilt, fox skin. Blue moccasins. In right hand a stone knife, in left, bow and arrow and stone ax.

Comes in mixed dance with Bear, etc. A Hopi importation.

MALOK̯ÄTSIK̯ (SALT OLD WOMAN)

(Plate 42, *a*)

Costume.—On her head she has piles of raw cotton heaped up the way the salt is heaped up in the Salt Lake. At the back of the head lapap̄oa (a combination of parrot tail feathers, downy feathers, and small parrot feathers). The mask is painted white all over. Around the head strings of beads with a turquoise ear pendant over the forehead. The cheeks are painted with circles of red and blue. A light blue kilt is folded around the neck.

Her hands are painted white. She should not wear the underdress and the moccasins, but just the black dress, the white fringed belt and a white blanket, with bare arms and bare feet, but now she wears the other things.

In her left hand she carries the mother corn (mik̄äpan·e), the flattened ear, such as is left by mothers to take care of their babies when they are away. In the right hand a crook called tatsik̄'ane tsiɫtsik̄ona (crook to make a noise). This used to be given her by P̄autiwa, but now she borrows the crook of one of the rain priests. These crooks are kept with the rain priests' bundles in the sacred houses, and each year at the winter solstice the feathers are renewed. The length of the crook is from the wrist to the inner joint of the elbow. The large feather is eagle; then bluejay; k̄ewia; mocking bird; onaɫik̄ä; humming bird. Hanging from the crook is a lacowan·e of a feather from the leg of the eagle and all the small feathers on the crook. Hanging from the crook are two old abalone shells. She carries the crook to bring the rain.

She comes in the mixed dance. Stevenson, (page 361) describes the appearance of Malok̯aɫsik̯ with Kohakwa ok̯ä (white shell women) and the Sun for an isolated ceremony.

Myth.—Long ago when the people first came here they used to live where the Black Rock Lake now is. When the girls wanted to stay out late with the boys they would tell their mothers they were going to get salt. They would take their sacks and go out and get a little salt and bring it home and then go for more so as to stay out late. And they used to befoul the salt at the edge of the lake and then go out to dig it where it was nice and clean. They treated our Salt Mother as though her body were not sacred. And every day during the winter Salt woman heard the dancing going on at Itiwana, every night and in the daytime too. Then she was lonesome and one night she thought, "I shall go to the south and look for another place to live. I should like to be a little nearer to Katcina Village so that when night comes I can go there to visit whenever I get lonesome. I shall go to the south for I have heard that they come from the south. I shall go there and look around for a place to stay and go to visit the people of Katcina Village.

Now at that time Turquoise man used to stay at a spring a little to the north of the salt lake. In the night she went to Turquoise man and said, "I am going to the south. I do not want my people to treat me the way they do. It hurts my feelings. I am going to run away to the south so that they will have a hard time to find me and will come to me with much labor. Then they will always love me more than anything else. I have made my plans. I am going to the south," she told him. Then Turquoise man said, "May I go with you?" "Yes, you may come with me. Which way had you decided to go?" "To the east," he said. "Let us both run away. They will surely be sorry. Let them come to-morrow for the last time, and then when night comes let us go."

So the next night they got ready, and they started in the morning before daybreak, in the early dawn. Turquoise man came and Salt woman joined him, and they went on together. They passed the narrow place southeast of the lake, the place called "Where the cliffs come together." As she went by she said, "I think I shall leave my feather here." So she took the downy feather from her hair and planted it there, and ever since then this place has been called "Where the downy feather stands" (uhḵahaianim·e). She left the feather there and said, "Now they will find my feather here, and they will never forget my name." So they went on to the south, and wherever they passed the trees died and fell down as though they had been pulled up by the roots. They left an open trail about as wide as the bridge across the river. Then they turned and went a little to the east. Finally they came to where Salt woman now lives. Then Turquoise man asked her, "Now we have passed many places. Now let me know which place you like best." Where they had stopped there was a spring and trees all around. So she thought that would be a good place for her to stay, because there were mountains on all sides. She looked to the west and she saw clouds hanging, and she could feel the wind from Katcina Village. So she thought she would stay there. "This is the place where I shall stay," she said. "I am close to my people at Katcina Village. Now you shall think where you want to stay," she said to Turquoise man. Then he said, "I shall turn and go to the east, that is where I am going." So he turned and went to the east and he came to Santo Domingo (Weɫuwala), and that is where Turquoise man stays now.

Now Salt woman stayed there for four days, and all the time she could hear the dancing going on at Katcina Village. She heard it like whispering in the lake. Then she said to herself, "Now I have stayed here a long time." It was really four years, and she thought it was long enough. "Now to-morrow I shall go and visit my people and see how they are." So next day she started. She went there and when she got there everyone was dancing. She went in. She was white all over and when she came in she brought a draught of cold air. Then Ŧautiwa said, "Now who is coming?" They did not know who it was. It was the first time she had gone there, and they had never seen anyone like that before. So he called his people, "My children, stop dancing for a little while. Someone else has come here." Then everyone stopped dancing. There she was. She was white all over. Then Ŧautiwa and Sayataca asked her, "Where is your home that you have thought of us and come here? We thought all our people were together here, but now you have come." She said, "I am not really your people. I am the salt. I make people well. I am Salt woman. I have been living in the east by my people at Itiwana. I stayed a little to the east of their village, but they treated me badly and so I have gone away to the south. I used to hear you people coming to dance at Itiwana so I have come to visit you here to find out whether I can go to Itiwana with you so that my children there may give me feathers like they give you. I need feathers like yours, and I thought that if I should go to Itiwana with you my people would give me feathers. That is why I have come. I want to go with you so that my people will always remember me and when they are out of salt they will make me a new dress and take it to my lake."

So Ŧautiwa and Sayataca said, "It is well. We are very glad to have you. We always want people to join us in our village here. We shall get you ready to go with us. My people will be ready to go when the fourth day comes," Ŧautiwa said. So she said, "I shall come again in the morning and we shall go. Now, I am going. I have come here gladly," she said, and she went back home. So she went back home, and at Katcina Village they were practicing for the mixed dance.

Now at Itiwana the people went again for salt, and when they got to the lake there was nothing there at all. There was just a salty place. Then the priests and the headmen all went there to see where she had gone. They saw her trail going to the south. They thought they would never have any salt again, for they thought that she had gone all the way to the south ocean. Then they went back and picked up all the little scraps of salt that the girls had thrown away on the road and brought it back, because they were afraid they would never have any salt again.

When the fourth day came she went to Katcina Village and when she got there they dressed her. They laid out a white embroidered blanket for her and a white kilt. Hemoķätsiķ dressed her. They gave her a dress and a blanket and they dressed her. They gave her beads and tied the parrot feathers to her head. Then they said,

"What shall she carry?" Then they said, "You shall carry the crook that the rain priests make from ƙuɫi.[10] This is the way you shall go." So they gave her a crook. So she was ready and she came with them in the mixed dance. They came in in the night and the next morning the mixed dance came out. There she was. No one knew that she was Salt woman. Then they found out that she was Salt woman. She glistened all over just like salt. Then they went to the kiva and asked the katcinas if she was really Salt woman. They said, "Yes, she is really Salt woman. She is living to the south, and she came to Katcina Village and asked to come with us so that you people might work on the feathers for her. That is why she has come with us." Then right away the katcina chief and his p̓ekwin and all the priests worked on feathers for her to take back home. In the evening when they had finished their dance and the katcinas were ready to go home they took her into the ceremonial room of the priests. Then the priests gave her the feathers and said, "Our mother, you have come. You used to be close to us, but you have gone away and now you live in the south. You have gone to the Sacred Lake and have come here with our people. We are glad you have come. We shall always work on feathers for you. Do not hide yourself from us. Always come and we shall always be glad to see you. Now here, you shall have these for your clothing." Then they gave her the bundle of prayer sticks to take back with her when she went to the south.

Then the katcinas went back to Katcina Village and Salt woman went to the south with her feathers, and she made the road for the people to come to her when they needed salt. That is why we have Salt woman come in the mixed dance, and that is why the people always work on feathers when they go to the Salt Lake. They give her feathers to bring the salt. Sometimes, they say, she runs away and there is no salt, but only lots of water. That is how she comes, and she carries the crook of the rain priests to bring rain. She brings the rain as well as the salt.

Oʜᴀᴘᴀ (Bᴇᴇ)

(Plate 43, b)

Costume.—He has flowers all over the top of his head. They are made of corn husks cut up and dyed different colors and sewed together with sinew. The bees are made of cotton or wool shaped and painted and set on thin wires. He wears a bunch of blue feathers sticking out behind. He has honey hidden under the flowers on the top of his head.

Ceremonies.—He comes in the mixed dance, and Hehe'a always comes with him to get the honey from his head. When he comes Hehe'a picks out a man from the crowd of spectators and the Koyemci

---

[10] I have not been able to identify this plant. It is much used for prayer sticks.

call him down from the housetop.   Then Hehe'a helps him to get the
honey.   He carries great branches of cedar and waves them around
to keep the bees from stinging him.   Then he complains that he has
been stung and asks the man to give him food to take home with him
because he has helped him.

"The babies used to be cross when they were teething, and the priests
thought that they ought to have some medicine for the babies, and
they thought that they should have honey to use in the medicine, and
they needed honey also to use in their paints to make them shiny.   So
they thought about the bee and over at Katcina Village they heard
them and P̃autiwa sent the bee here the way he sent the deer because
the people wanted him in a prayer.   That is how he came.   He
has been coming for a long time."

Tecamiḵä (Echo)

(Plate 42b, c)

Costume.—On the head the great feather (lacowan̶la̶na); the mask
is painted black with white spots.   His body is black all over.   He
should not wear the fawn skin.   He wears blue loin cloth.   Coyote
skin around the neck.   He carries a torch to burn the corrals, and
yamuwe, short pieces of wood with pendent feathers.

Ceremonies.—He comes in the mixed dance.

"He is an angry dancer, and the people are afraid of him.   They
called him to come when the earth cracked, and since then he comes
with the mixed dance.   He comes when it is cold, and they say he
brings the cold weather.

"They say he warns the people when misfortune is coming.   Anyone who expects a baby will go to his home and look for omens.   Last
year a man went there and he saw lots of turquoise, but when he
went to pick it up there was none there.   He came back and told the
people, and they said it meant that the people would have lots of
turquoise, and a little later a man came down from Gallup with lots of
turquoise, and the people bought a great deal.

"He doesn't live at Katcina Village, but in a canyon south of
Itiwana."

Myth.—When the people first came here there was no Echo man.
Then there was an earthquake at Where-the-pine-tree-stands.
The people were very much afraid because the rocks were falling.
All the priests went there.   They worked on prayer sticks and made
crooks and took them there and set them down to make the rocks
hold together so that the animals would not come out from underneath.   Yet as time went on the crack got larger.   Then all the priests
met together and said, "What shall we do to make the earth come
together?   We have heard that the Hopi know how to make the

earth come together.   Whom shall we send to tell them to come and help us?   Let us call a fast runner and send him to the Hopi."   So the war chief went out and called in a fast runner.   When he came in he said, "My fathers, what have you to say that you have called me in?   I should like to know."   Then all the men said, "Now, our son, we would like you to go to the Hopi and ask them if they can come to help us.   Tell them your fathers here know them and thought of them here, that they know how to shut up the earth.   Say we have an earthquake here and need their help.   And you will say this, 'You may ask for anything you want and no matter what you ask for, my fathers will be willing to give it to you.'"

Then the priest made for him a downy feather tied to a cotton cord and fastened it in his hair that he might go quickly.   Then the boy left and went to the Hopi and told their chief what the priests had told him.   Then the Hopi chief said, "I shall tell my people and we shall come to-morrow."   So he said.   The boy came back.   He came back quickly because he was wearing the downy feather, and he got back the same night.   The next morning he went to the priests and told them that the Hopi were coming.

So the Hopi man went to the others and he told three of the chiefs to come to his house.   When they came he said, "The Itiwana people have called us.   They have had an earthquake there and they need us to come.   What do you think?   Shall we go?"   Then the three chiefs said, "Yes, we should go, because if we should ever have trouble and need them, then they will come and help us.   It is better for us to go."   Then they all four of them got their buckskins and they said, "Now what shall we take with us?"   Then they said, "You shall go there to the north and ask our grandfather to make us a mat of reeds (łaḵine)."   The Hopi went there and he said, "How do you do, my grandfather," and he replied, "How do you do, grandson." Then the Hopi said, "I have come here to ask you to help us make a mat of reeds for our people in Itiwana.   They have had an earthquake and they have called us to help them and we are going there.   We have four buckskins, and we know that you have a strong body, so we have asked you if you will come and make us a reed mat."   Then he answered, "You shall not carry that.   I shall make it for you and I shall go with you.   It is better so.   The daylight people do not know how to close up the earth.   I shall go with you and show you how to close up the earth.   You are the people to close up the earth here, because this is your country, but over there you can not do it, so I shall go with you and be a great help to the people." So he said.   Then the man said, "Very well.   I shall ask my head ones first.   I must ask them before you can go with me."   So he went back and asked the three chiefs.   He came back without the reed mat and other things.   They asked him, "Why is it they did not let you have the mat?" He said, "Our grandfather is going with us. He is going to carry his mat along. He said we can not help the Itiwana people. He said that only the gods can help them." Then the other three men said, "I think it is all right for him to go with us. But if he goes with us we must not go close to him. He must go behind us and not go first, because if he should go first and drink and if we should drink at the same place we would surely die. He is dangerous. So you go and tell him to be ready, and tell him to start after we have gone." So they said.

So again the man went back, and when he got there the katcina was lying down in his home. When the man came in he said, "Are you lying down?" "Yes." Then he said, "You shall come with us. We shall go first, and you will go behind us. Take your blanket along with you." So the man went home and told them, "Now let us get ready. He will be ready soon." So they rolled up their buckskins and they washed their hair and each one took his buckskin and they walked. They came here.

Here all the priests were waiting for them in their ceremonial room. In the afternoon just as the sun turned over they came. They said, "We are bringing a raw person with us. Will you please have a separate room for him and let him come into a separate room." So they got a place ready for him in another room. The people all went out to see him come in. He came carrying his reed mat, and he went into his room. He went in talking about what the people outside said. In the next room the Hopi and the priests were talking, then they said, "We have sent for you to come because we have had trouble. We have had an earthquake and the crack is getting larger and larger. Perhaps you can help us, and we shall always be glad to return your kindness." The Hopi said "Very well. Now let us go."

All the priests had been working on prayer sticks, so the chief priest went first holding the basket full of prayer sticks and the Hopi chiefs followed him. The other priests followed and way behind came Echo man. Everyone watched them go. They went to the south. When they came to the place where the earth was cracked the chief priest knelt down and set his bundle of feathers in the crack and said, "Now you who have cracked open the earth and are sending the wild animals to come out and destroy us, do not do it. We give you these valuable feathers. Please close this crack and help our people." So he said and set down his feathers. When he put down his feathers he said again, "We give you these." Then the others said, "Shall we stay here or shall we go away?" Then the Hopi said, "Yes, our fathers, we think you had better go away. We do not want you here when we close the crack. Go a little ways off and rest and we shall fix it." So the head priests of Itiwana went back the way they had come. Then Echo man came close and the Hopi men stepped back. They were afraid to stand too close to him, for he was a real raw person, not just a man with a mask. He came and knocked on the rocks in every direction and he laid his reed mat over the crack. Then he stepped on it. The people were afraid he would fall into the crack, but he never did. He stepped on it, and tried it, and the mat never even bent. Then he said, "Now my work is finished," and went away and stayed a little ways off. Then the Hopi men came and spread a buckskin over it, and then they put down another buckskin and there were two of them there. They used their paint that they had brought along with them; it was a paint that they used on their prayer sticks. Again they put down two more buckskins and then felt them in every direction and said, "Now we have done this, our Earth Mother, that you may not open up any more. You must not let the wild animals come out nor the floods to destroy the people of Itiwana. You must not come out and bring them bad luck." So they said.

Then they turned around and came back toward Itiwana. They came to where the priests were met in their ceremonial room. When they came back the chief priest asked the Hopi and said, "Now, my people, you will go to the houses and our people will give you food before you go home. And besides that, what would you like to have? No matter what valuable thing you ask for we will give it to you." So they said to the Hopi because the Hopi men had been so kind. Then they said, "Now, our fathers, we shall just go around to the houses for food to take home with us, and we shall not ask for anything. We may have trouble in our country sometime and we may want you to come and help us. So we won't take anything, and it will be that we shall always help one another." They went around, and they held hands with the Itiwana people, and they breathed on one another's hands. Then again they asked, "What does your grandfather want? What would he like to take home?" Then the Hopi said to him, "Now, you will ask for what you want. You have done the most important thing. You are wise." Then he said, "I do not want anything at all. I am not going back to my home. I am going to stay here. I belong here. I am the one who made the world firm, and if the world comes open again I am the one to close it up. And you, my fathers, you will give me a home where I may live." So he said to the chief priest. Then all the Hopi were sorry and said, "Oh, don't stay here!" They did not want him to stay because he was wise. But he said that he wanted to stay here at Itiwana. So the head priests called the katcina chief and when he came they said to him, "Our father, we have sent for you because this, our grandfather here, came from the west and he wants to stay here, and he has asked us where is a good place for him to have his home." Then the katcina chief said, "To the south, because that is where he made the earth close. That is where he will live. Now we shall take you and show you where your home will be. And hereafter any time when our children, the katcinas, come here you may come with them." So the katcina chief took him to the south and gave him a home, and that is how he happens to live in the south. We call that place Echo House, and when the mixed dance comes, he comes with them. The priests made batons for him because he had nothing pretty to wear or to carry.

When the earth was closed the people were happy, and they called the mixed dance to come and dance for Echo man. They called the sacred lake people to send the mixed dance to please him. When he heard the dancers coming he came carrying his baton. He got here about noon when they were dancing in the west plaza. He could not speak the Zuñi language and all he could say was what people said to him. So whenever anyone spoke to him he repeated what they said. So they called him Echo man. He came from the Hopi, not from here, and he doesn't live at Katcina Village with the other katcinas, but in the south at Echo House.

YA'ANA

(Plate 42, c)

Costume.—On the head yellow parrot feathers. Sticking up at back one tail feather of the eagle. At the left side of the head a downy feather, on the right side a red feather. Black wool over the head.

He wears a dark blue woven kilt as a poncho. Around the neck a band of porcupine quill embroidery, beads, and a strip of red flannel. Red flannel on right wrist. Light blue kilt, red belt, cloth leggings, brown moccasins. Fox skin.

He sometimes comes with Hilili or at any time during the winter dance series. He also comes with the mixed dance.

Myth.—Over at the Sacred Lake Pautiwa said that everyone should stay in and dance because the people at Itiwana were working on prayer sticks for the katcinas. The katcinas at Katcina Village always know when they will get their prayer sticks, just as we know when to expect our pay checks, and on those days no one goes out to hunt because they all want to be at home to get their feathers when the people of Itiwana send them there. But on that day one of the katcinas went out anyway.

Here at Itiwana was a witch boy who had been turned into a Tecamiḵä.[11] Then the katcina chief wanted everyone to work on feathers for him because he did not stay at the Sacred Lake. He was

---

[11] Echo.

Awan Su waa tsi na: Mudhead. Not otherwise identified; not previously published

Sa ya da sha: Longhorn. Not otherwise identified; not previously published

living right here. So everyone made prayer sticks and Tecamikia took them in a bundle to the sacred lake. When he got there he gave his bundle of feathers to P̂autiwa, and P̂autiwa set down the prayer sticks he got from Tecamikia. Then he saw that the boy was a human person and had no mask. He was not a katcina at all, so he took all his feathers to the Sacred Lake.

Then everyone came to get his feathers. They picked them out and said, "This is mine," or "My father made this for me." Each one knew his prayer sticks, and knew that his people at Itiwana had made them for him. So all the people there had their prayer sticks, and they were happy. Then after they had their prayer sticks they prayed for their people in Itiwana. They thanked them and prayed for a strong breast for them in answer to their prayer.

Then Ya'ana came in. He was ugly. He had been out hunting and he came in. He looked around and everyone had prayer sticks. Then he said, "Where is mine?" He went around asking everyone for his prayer stick. Then he came to P̂autiwa and said, "Where is mine?" Then P̂autiwa said, "Everyone has prayer sticks but you." Then he said "Ya'ana!" [12] Then P̂autiwa said, "That is a good name for you. You went out hunting when you should have stayed here to get your prayer sticks, and now no one will give anything to you."

That is why he has the name Ya'ana, and he always says "Ya'ana!" when he comes in to Itiwana to dance. The Koyemci always make fun of him and say to him, "If you don't like it why have you come?"

Natsik̂o (Young Deer)

(Plate 43, a)

Costume.—On the head deer antlers (saiyawe). At the back of the head sticking up tail feathers of the eagle. At the base of the eagle feathers a bunch of owl feathers to bring the rain. He wears strips of red flannel instead of downy feathers, "so that all these things may come easily. He has big ears with red inside. His nose is black and his face green." The back of the mask is painted to look like the skin of a young deer. Spruce collar

He wears a white cotton shirt, but long ago he never wore a shirt at all. He wears an embroidered blanket folded and fastened on the right shoulder, and embroidered kilt, a white-fringed sash, and a red woman's belt. On the legs fringed leggings of white buckskin, with bands of black yarn on both legs. Blue moccasins, fox skin in back. He has no rattle. Necklace of cedar berries with yarn and beads. Beads on both wrists. On the right wrist a band of black

---

[12] An exclamation of distress.

yarn, on the left a wrist band of leather with silver. He carries a crook (telnane), a stick of willow painted white with two tail feathers of the eagle at the end, and a bunch of black goat's hair. Formerly they used frog's spittle (awico) dried.

He comes in the mixed dance.

Myth.—When the people first came here they had no sheep, and they lived on corn and wild seeds and they hunted rabbits and ate fresh rabbit meat and during the winter they caught snowbirds. So during the winter at Ca'lako or during the winter rain dances, or at any time when they were going to have a feast, the men would go out and hunt rabbits and birds. They would brlng in about two rabbits and only two or three birds. They had only a little bit to eat. And if a man were not lucky he would have only three or four little birds. They skinned the birds and boiled or roasted them with ground squash seeds for their feasts. And they cut up the rabbits and roasted or boiled them with corn meal. That is all they had. At that time there were no deer around here, so they had no deer meat. So when their feast days came they cooked their little animals and put their offerings of food in the fire for the people at Katcina Village.

Over at Katcina Village was Säyataca. He spoke to Pautiwa and said, "You are the headman. Now what do you think? Our people in Itiwana are having a hard time to live. They have no delicacies.[13] They do not look well because they always eat only one kind of food. What do you think? Our people ought to have fresh meat. Especially on their feast days they should have something to make them feel better. Now they have only little animals and they last only one meal. What do you think about their having deer?" So he said. "Yes," said Pautiwa. "Everything that they have needed they have always asked for in their prayers. They ask us for everything they need, but they have never asked us for deer. Let us wait and see if they mention deer. They always pray for rabbits and birds, and especially they always ask about all kinds of birds and all the things they live on, but they have never mentioned that they should have deer. We shall listen and see if they ever ask us for deer." He spoke thus. He did not say, "All right, we shall send them deer." He wanted to wait until the people here should ask for it in a prayer. So Sayataca said, "All right. That is up to you. We shall do as you say. We shall wait for them to mention it in their prayers."

Over here the Hunters' Society called out for a rabbit hunt. They told the people all to go to hunt rabbits so that they might have fresh meat for their feast. So they called it out from the top of the house. "I wish now, my people, that you shall go to the south side and wait there. When all of you reach there we shall look around on the south side at the place called Where-the-sack-of-flour-hangs.

---

[13] Yepnawe, any food besides corn.

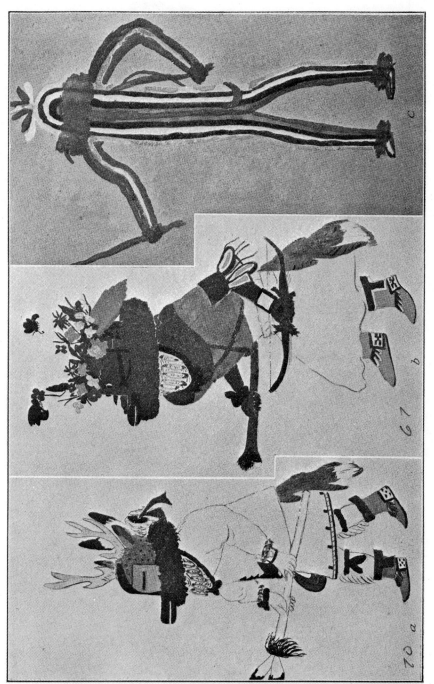

WINTER AND SUMMER DANCES: THE MIXED DANCE

a, Na'le (Deer); *b*, Ohapa (Bee); *c*, Mitsinapa.

WINTER AND SUMMER DANCES: THE MIXED DANCE

a, Hetsululu; b, Ican A·tsan A·tci; c, Aince; d, Wo'latana.

When we all come together there we shall look around and we shall use our warm arms [14] and perhaps some of our people at Katcina Village will wish to lend us their arms. That is all," he said. He never asked for the deer, he just called out for the rabbits. Everyone listened to him.

They were going to plant their feathers (for the dance) on the fifth day. So he called out for four days, and when the fourth day came he called out again in the morning. He said, "Let everyone get ready as soon as possible and go to the place Where-the-sack-of-flour-hangs and see what luck we have. And let everyone take lunch with him to feed our people at the sacred lake." He spoke thus. Then he went to the place Where-the-sack-of-flour-hangs and he got there first and he built a fire there. Finally the people got ready for their hunt and everyone had his paper bread ready and they all went. When they got to Where-the-sack-of-flour-hangs there he was. He had already built a fire, the bow priest of the Hunters' Society. So everyone took his paper bread and put it into the fire and said, "Here, grandfathers, eat. And whoever has had good luck in hunting please lend me your hand and your thoughts." So they said as they put the paper bread into the fire. Then after they had fed our people they ate.

Then the bow priest made the four "holes." He ran in a circle, saying, "Now, my children, you stay right here and do not go outside, and increase here so that my people may kill you." Then the people went in after him and hunted the rabbits inside the circle. He made four circles like this. They call them holes. After they had finished hunting in the four holes he said to them, "Now do as you please and have a good time. Play around everywhere and kill rabbits wherever you see them." So finally they killed lots of rabbits. Some killed as many as eight, and others killed four. Some had more, some less, and they had their meat for their feast.

When they came home they sent the girls out to wait for the boys who had killed the most. Then the girls who had no brothers to hunt for them went out to wait for the boys to give them rabbits when they came home. They ground a great deal of meal, and they cooked dried squash and baked sweet corn bread to pay for the rabbits. As the boys came in carrying their rabbits they gave them to the girls, one or two rabbits and maybe a jack rabbit. Then the girl took the rabbits right in to her mother, and her mother said, "The rabbit is worth a good squash," or "The jack rabbit is worth so much meal." Then the girl put the squash or meal into a bowl and took it over to the boy's house the same evening.

That is the way they had their hunt. They never thought about the deer. Then the headman of the Hunters' Society thought of it,

---

[14] The people of Itiwana are "cooked," while the rabbits, like the katcinas, are raw persons.

because the deer was mentioned in all their songs.   The society was meeting in their ceremonial room to practice their songs, and the men were working on prayer sticks.   That night all the societies were meeting to work on their prayer sticks.   Then the people over in the Sacred Lake made them think about the deer as they practiced their songs.   Their songs said, "Now we are making the road for the rabbits.   Now we are making the road for the deer.   Now we have all the clothing of the deer; here is a deer horn; here is a deer ear; here are the deer's eyes; here is the deer's skin; here is the deer's arm; here is the deer's foot; here is the deer's body and his entrails."   They mentioned all the parts of the deer.   Then they said, "Now here in our house we must think about it very much so that the deer may come close to us."   They knew there were deer in the world, but they were far away to the south.   So the head man of the hunters told his people that they must always think about the deer so that they might come nearer to them.   "Now let the deer come to make our people happier."   So they said in their songs.   They mentioned all the deer's parts so that he might come to them complete with nothing missing.

Over at Katcina Village the people like Pautiwa and Sayataca liked this song.   They were far away, but they heard the song and the way they asked for the deer.   So the next day they all thought about it and they said, "We have heard the Hunters' Society praying for the deer.   What do you think now?   Shall we send them their deer now?"   Again Sayataca asked Pautiwa.   Then Pautiwa said, "Not so fast.   When someone asks for something we must not be in a hurry."   They were getting ready for the mixed dance and Pautiwa said, "Now, my children, practice your songs to go to Itiwana.   And if now while you are practicing any of you feel that you would like to take in the deer, go out and get a young deer to take with you to Itiwana for our people in Itiwana.   Then Hehe'a went out to look for a young deer and he brought it into their house.   When he brought him in Pautiwa made him sit down on the east side of the room and he presented him to every direction.   Then the young deer took off his skin (and turned into a person) and said, "My father, what is it you wanted me for.   I want to know why you have called me in."   So he said to Pautiwa, and Pautiwa answered him, "I have sent for you to go to Itiwana with this dance.   And if you wish you may go with them any time this dance goes there.   You will always be in this dance and we shall dress you the way they dress.   You will do this so that our people at Itiwana may have good luck with your flesh and find deer everywhere, to the east and to the south and to the north and to the west; so that the deer may come in from all the directions and come close to Itiwana so that our people may have deer meat and look better than they look now because of it."   He said this to the young deer.   Then the young deer said, "Yes, I shall do as you wish.   I shall go with them to give our people good luck.   I shall go with the mixed dance."

So they brought in the young deer, and when they were ready to go Coyote said to Hehe'a, "Do not leave me here.   I am a hunter. When your people in Itiwana hunt I give them good luck.   I taught them how to hunt and I should go with you to give them good luck in hunting."   Then Hehe'a said, "I shall ask our father, the chief, first before you come.   You may not go in to Itiwana unless he wishes it."   "Go and ask him.   I will teach the hunters so that they will always know how to treat the deer."   Then Hehe'a went in again and said to Pautiwa, "There is a coyote outside.   Is there any way for him to go to Itiwana to dance with us?   He says he wants to go with us when we bring this young deer in.   He says he wants to go in with us to bring good luck to our Itiwana people. He says he wants to go in to teach the Itiwana people the right way so that they may always have good luck in hunting."   Then Pautiwa said, "Yes, I think it will be all right for him to go with you if he is not bad.   He shall go just as he said, to give the people good luck in hunting."   So they brought him in to Pautiwa.   He was yellowish and he looked funny among all the pretty dancers.   So they presented him to the six directions and made him sit down.   The young deer was afraid of him because he was going to kill the deer when they came to Itiwana.   The Pautiwa said, "Now my child, my young deer, coyote is going along to Itiwana to give our people good luck in hunting.   You must be killed sometime, but you will not really die.   We too used to live in Itiwana, but now we do not live there any more.   Like us you will not really die, but you will come to life again.   So do not be afraid.   Now you are going to Itiwana and coyote is going too, but do not be afraid of him.   He will just pretend to chase you and kill you and you will just pretend to die.   Then whoever in Itiwana wants to be a good hunter will come and get you and carry you into his house and sprinkle your head with water and with corn meal and pray that he may have good luck in hunting. And that is the way they will always do when they hunt deer in the mountains.   Coyote will just pretend to kill you and you will pretend to die and you will lie down in the plaza and this man will come and get you and take you home with him.   That is the way the deer will be killed."   He talked to the young deer like this and the young deer said, "Very well."

Now the people in the mixed dance were practicing their songs and their dance.   They sang their songs and made their motions of the clouds coming up and the rain coming down and all the things growing to make the world beautiful.   They put all this into their songs and made the motions for the words.   After they had learned their songs

Pautiwa said, "Now, to-morrow you will go to Itiwana for the dance." The Pautiwa said to his children, "Now look over your clothing and whoever has extra clothing should bring it and we shall see how we can dress our children." So he said. Then Sayataca laid out an embroidered blanket and beads, and Hemokätsik laid out a belt. Then different katcinas brought the eagle feathers that they use in their dance and an embroidered kilt and leggings and moccasins. So they dressed him. They painted his face blue and painted spots all over his body, and they put on the embroidered blanket and the kilt. They put beads on both wrists and yarn on the right and a silver bow bracelet on the left. All these things belonged to Sayataca. When he was dressed Pautiwa said, "Now it will be well for him to carry a cane. He will not walk upright but he will stoop down and hold the cane with both hands." So he said. So they whittled a stick and painted it white and put the feathers and the frog spittle on it and showed him how to hold it with both hands, stooping down. Then he tried it and turned around and around saying "Hui, hui!" and looking behind to see if anyone were following him.

After they had dressed him and showed him what to do they said, "Now let us dress Coyote." They sent Coyote just the way he was, but they gave him the red feather because he is a hunter and a member of a society. They said, "Now you will wear the red feather because you are in a society." Then they gave him a blue kilt and they painted him brown all over with white spots, and they gave him dance moccasins and a blue leather belt like society members wear. They gave him a cane too. Then they said, "Now let us hear how you will frighten the young deer." Then he said, "Whoooo," to frighten the young deer. Then they practiced. He came after the deer and the deer always ran away and hid himself and Coyote ran after him. "Now this is the way you will go to Itiwana to give our people good luck. I am glad you have come to go there the way I have thought." Sayataca said this.

The next day they started coming over here to dance. Over here the people did not know anything about the deer coming. It was the first time the deer had come in the dance. The people knew that the katcinas were coming the next day so they cooked sweet corn cakes for their feast. Then about four o'clock in the morning they came in and the people heard them come. When daylight came they danced in the west plaza and the people went there to see them. They were surprised. There was a young deer with them dressed like a katcina, and the people said to one another, "There is a little deer and another little animal." They did not know Coyote. The people were all wondering about them. They were very much interested to see the little deer. The women had never seen a deer. Some of the men had seen deer in the mountains, but it was the first time the women had seen deer.

In the afternoon, when the sun turns over (about two o'clock), the dancers went into the kiva to take a rest after their dance and the Koyemci were playing in the plaza. Then Coyote came running after the young deer to show the people how to hunt. He bent down over his cane pretending to smell the deer tracks. Then the Koyemci said "Look at our little grandson! What is he doing? He is smelling another little grandchild. He is going to kill him and eat him up!" Then the Koyemci said, "Our friend (kihe) had better come and look around him and see how Coyote kills the deer. Maybe he won't eat it all up and what is left will spoil." Then the Koyemci said again, "Our friend had better come down and wait until he kills the deer and then he should take the body to his house." Then all the men came down from the housetops. One man was in such a hurry that he rushed down and got there before any of the others and waited around in the plaza. He borrowed a bow and arrow from one of the houses facing the plaza and helped Coyote make a noose. The little deer ran and hid behind the Koyemci, but they ran after him and finally caught him around the neck. Then the little deer fell down and pretended to die. Then the man came up and Coyote told him how to kill the deer. He held his mouth and touched him all over and pretended he was no longer warm. Then he pretended to skin him. Then right away the man took hold of the little deer and put him on his back and carried him to his home to bring good luck to the people.

That is the way they showed them how to kill the deer. And after they had finished their dance the dancers went back in the evening and the little deer went back again too. The man brought him home and laid him down with his head to the east and covered him all over with an embroidered blanket and all the people in the house sprinkled corn meal on him. After a little while he got up and they sprinkled water on his head, dipping up the water with an ear of corn. Then they said, "This is the way we shall get good luck so that the deer may come close for us to have good meat." Then they wrapped up paper bread for him and gave it to him to take home so he might send them good luck. This man had also taken Coyote home with him. After it was dark they came out and went back home to Katcina Village.

When they came to Katcina Village Pautiwa and Sayataca said, "Now, did you do as we told you?" They said, "Yes, and the people were all pleased and were much interested, and we were very happy to have the little deer with us." Then Pautiwa said, "Now, my little child, you have been to Itiwana, and any time the katcinas go there for the mixed dance you may go with them if you wish. And anything like that that our people do not have we shall send to them in this way. And now after this the deer will be close to their village. There are many deer around here in all directions, and now they must all go to Itiwana for our people have called to us for them."

Then one day the deer came here to Where-the-sack-of-flour-hangs, and to Corn Mountain and all around, and when the people went out to get wood they saw the deer close to the village and they killed them easily. That is why in the old days they always had plenty of deer. They asked the Katcina Village people for them and Sayataca sent them to his people. That is all.

HETSULULU [15]

(Plate 44, a)

Costume.—On the head, white feathers of the sand hill crane dyed pink with the pink clay the dancers use on their bodies.

"He is the world. He is marked all over with different colors for the grass and the flowers and all the pretty things in the world. His face is green to make the world green, and on the face are clouds coming up like smoke in three directions. The yellow stripe around the face is for the waters around the world, and the people live at Itiwana, where it is green."

Around his neck is a blue kilt, and another around his loins. In the right hand he carries a stick with a ball of soft red clay at the end, and in his left arm a large ball of the same clay.

He comes in the mixed dance.

Myth.—In the first beginning when the katcinas came here in person to dance for the people there was a p̄ekwin who wanted his people to be happy. He asked the bow priest to call out for the people to be happy. It was after the winter dances were over, it was nearly springtime. There was no dancing and there were no games, and the sun priest said, "I want my people to be happy. I do not want them to be lonely." So he asked the bow priest to call out in the evening that on the fourth day everyone should be ready to play for their father, p̄ekwin. "For our father wants us all to be happy, and especially the young men should be happy. And the young women shall grind and make paper bread and use it to be happy. Our people at Katcina Village will be with us. You shall be happy here and then our father will be happy and our people at Katcina Village will be happy too." When he said that he meant that the katcinas would be happy with them and that they would get the food that they would give to them. But the people in the Sacred Lake heard it and they misunderstood.

The next day over here in Itiwana the people were all busy. The girls all ground a great deal of corn. Over at Katcina Village P̄autiwa said, "Last night the bow priest called out that we must be over there with our people to make their father, p̄ekwin, happy. Now, who shall go? One of our younger children should go to be with

[15] This is his call.

them. I do not want all of them to go, but just one." So he said
to his children. Then he picked out one of the boys and said, "Now
you will be the one to go. You are the strongest of the boys." He
picked out a big, heavy boy. "And now I shall dress you."

For his head he made a long roll of clay and painted it all over
with stripes of different colors and set it on his head and said, "This
is the way you will look when you go to visit my people, and this is
how you will dress to be pretty." He picked out this boy because he
was one of the little boys whose mothers had dropped them and who
had turned into snakes. Therefore he had no children and no brothers
and sisters, but only a father and mother. And when the people at
Itiwana worked on prayer sticks his father never worked on prayer
sticks for him. They never sent feathers for him like the others did.
He never had anything. When all the others got their feathers he was
always left out. He never came here with the other katcinas. He
had no feathers, and so he could not come to be happy with his
people. Pautiwa felt sorry for this boy because he never had anything
pretty and because he never could come to Itiwana. So when they
called out for the people here to be happy Pautiwa thought he would
send this boy. So he dressed him. The poor child! He had only
a poor blue kilt around his neck because he was poor and no one ever
looked after him and sent him pretty things. He did not have anything pretty to wear because he never received any feathers when the
people planted to make the New Year or to make the world green.
That is why he has none of the pretty things that the other katcinas
wear, like beads and embroidered sashes and blue moccasins. He
comes with bare feet. And because he had no pretty things to wear
they painted his body with pretty colors. He did not have any
feathers, so Pautiwa took feathers of the sand hill crane and dipped
them in the sacred pink clay to make them pretty. He gave him a
cat-tail stalk, because he had no yucca, and he gave him beads and a
belt of blue leather.[16] Then he painted his body. First a band of
black made from the clay from springs containing decaying vegetable
matter; next pink from the Sacred Lake clay that all the Katcina
Village people use; next blue made from the same paint they used for
their masks; next red made from sacred lake clay mixed with red
clay. When he was painted Pautiwa put a band of black yarn around
his neck, and he told his people to get clay.

Then Hemokätsik spread out a corn husk and covered it with red
powder and rolled the pink clay in it to make it red. Then she molded
it into a nice shape. Then Pautiwa and the other katcinas looked at
him. "Now that is the way you will go. This is the first time you
will go to Itiwana," they told him. "You have never been to a dance

---

[16] The drawing is incorrect. He should wear a belt of blue leather instead of the silver belt.

there and this is the first time you are going. When you come to
Pinawa [17] you will stay there while you wait for them to begin.
When they begin to play there will be two sides throwing things at
each other. When you come close you will call out 'Hetsululu,' and
you will throw your clay, and if you hit one of the players with your
clay he will go to the other side. You will always say, 'Hetsululu'
when you throw your clay. Now you will go to Itiwana. There was
no way for you to go before, but now you can go this way. It is a
good plan for you to go like this."

Over here the people were making great quantities of paper bread.
The third day came and they all crumbled it in willow baskets. On
the fourth day in the morning the bow priest called out for them to get
ready. So in the morning the girls made a paste of the crumbled
paper bread and rolled it into balls (helikwi motsa), and had them
ready for their brothers to use to play. Then after they had eaten
their morning meal they began. The people were living at Halonawa
then. They started at Halonawa, close to the sand hill. They all
went there calling to one another to hurry. Finally they all got there.
Then the war chief came and divided them into two groups, so that
there would be the same number on each side. Then he said, "Now
begin." Then they began to play, throwing the balls of paper-bread
dough. All the people went out there. The girls had more balls
ready, and when the boys ran out they came and got more balls from
their sisters. While they were playing this way throwing things at
one another the little boy came in calling "Hetsululu," as he came.
No one was watching him but he came calling "Hetsululu." Then
the people looked at him and said, "Who is that coming?" Then
they heard him calling and they said, "Is that Hetsululu? It must
be Hetsululu," the people said. "But he has no pretty clothes and
he doesn't look like a katcina at all." They kept saying it must be a
poor katcina who had no feathers to put around his neck, and no fur,
but only a poor blue skirt. So the people said. Then the bow priest
said, "I called out for our people to be with us. I meant that whatever we destroyed in our game to-day would belong to them. That
is what I meant. But now they have come here themselves. I wonder if it means danger?" He said this to p̄ekwin. Then the p̄ekwin
said, "I do not think so. Maybe they just misunderstood and
sent this little boy in to be with us. And so he must always come
when we have this game, and also he shall come with the dancers
whenever he wants to." And so he always comes when they play
that game. He comes and plays with them, calling "Hetsululu."
The name of the game is heḳä-ikocniḳä.

When he came back to his home at Katcina Village P̄autiwa said to
him, "Now, my child, you have been there. Now after this when

---

[17] A ruin about 2 miles west of Zuñi on the south side of the river.

the katcinas go to Itiwana you will always go with the mixed dance. You will be best in there. And you will always go dressed like that, because if you go that way the people will never forget that it is because no one made feathers for you. And maybe now they will make feathers for you." Pautiwa thought that, but the people never did it.

That is why Hetsululu always comes in the mixed dance. They do not play the game any more, they dropped it about twenty years ago, but Hetsululu comes with the mixed dance and throws his little clay balls. And that is why the people are always very careful to plant feathers for their people at Katcina Village.[18]

ICAN A·T͡SAN A·TCI (GREASE BOYS)

(Plate 44, b)

Costume.—Their masks are all black. On the head and in the ears "spoon" feathers from the shoulder of the eagle. Collar of fawn skin.

"Their bodies are black and covered all over with grease and soot. They eat greasy things and rub the grease all over their bodies. They never wash. They just paint white from the navel to the knees for the sun. All they wear are dark blue kilts and embroidered sashes caught between the legs like a breechcloth. They go barefoot. But they have many strings of different kinds of beads around their necks and beads on both wrists like all the valuable katcinas."

Ceremonies.—There are always two of them and they take turns carrying one another on their backs. They come in the mixed dance.

They do not live at Katcina Village but at sand hill south of Zuñi.

Myth.—There are two grease boys who live with their grandmother on the sand hill south of Itiwana. They eat greasy things and rub the grease all over their bodies and in their hair, and they never wash. They are happy boys. They live on the hill and eat rats. They go to the holes and dig them out and kill the mice and bring them to their grandmother, who roasts them in the ashes. They are very poor, but still they have many valuable beads to wear.

Long ago their mother and father went to the Sacred Lake and left the little boys behind and left their grandmother there with them. Once they were sitting out on the rocks in the evening. At that time the people were living at Halonawa and the men were coming home in the evening carrying wood by means of a band around the

---

[18] The game to which this story refers was played ceremonially until about twenty years ago. Each player has six balls of paper-bread dough "a little larger than our heads." They play until all their balls are used up and stop at about five o'clock in the evening. Hetsululu uses little balls of clay, and therefore doesn't use up his material so fast. It is believed, however, that his clay keeps increasing as fast as he uses it up. The bow priest always calls out, "The raw boy is coming to bring us clay from the Sacred Lake. Watch for it and keep it to increase your corn and all your crops. Whoever catches one of his balls should take it to his home and keep it for good luck with his crops." Then everyone goes out. No one stays home, but everyone goes out to watch for the little clay balls. And whoever catches one takes it home and puts it in his corn room to increase his corn and paper bread so that his food will increase as fast as it is used up.

head. As they came along the boys were sitting on the sand hill right above the trail. A man came along with his load of wood and looked up and saw the boys sitting there. Then the boys were ashamed and tried to cover themselves, for they were naked all over. They were very poor. They never were able to go to see the world because they had no clothes to wear. Their grandmother, too, was sorry that they had nothing to wear. So she thought, "We are very poor. Your father and mother never come to see us. They left us here and they never come to talk to us and they never send you poor boys anything to wear." Then she thought that she would send the boys to the Sacred Lake to see if their parents had any clothes for them to wear. She felt very sorry that her grandsons had to run away and hide whenever they saw people coming, because they had nothing with which to cover themselves. So when evening came she made mush and roasted the wood rats that the boys had killed and set it out for them. Then the little boys took hold of the two rats. Their grandmother looked sharply at them and said, "Please give me the heads of the two rats and I shall put them in my bowl. You may have the bodies of the rats, and I shall be satisfied with just the heads." The poor grandmother had only a little stone dish before her with a little water and some dried herbs. Then the boys twisted off the heads of the rats and gave them to their grandmother and she dipped them in the water and sucked at them as she ate her corn mush. Then she thought, "Oh dear, we are so poor! I hate to tell you poor boys that you must not eat everything." She did not want to scold the boys for being greedy because she felt so sorry for them that they were so poor. Then she thought she would tell the boys to go to the Sacred Lake, and she said to them, "I shall tell you boys what to do, and you will get clothes and good things to eat." [19]

After they had finished their evening meal the boys were sitting beside the fire playing with their bows and arrows. Then she said to them, "Now my sons, as we were sitting here I thought I would like you boys to go to the Sacred Lake where all the fathers and uncles and brothers are. You boys go there and go right in and say, 'How do you do, my people.' Then Pautiwa will say, 'Who are these nice boys who have come in here. I do not know them. We have no boys like them here. I wonder if they belong to our people.' Then you tell them that you come from Itiwana and that you live here at the sand hill, and then they will know you. They will know you, but they will pretend not to know you. They will ask you what you have come for. Then the older brother will say, 'We have come because we are so poor over there at sand hill. Our grandmother is so old that she cannot look around for food. And when we hunt we can only kill little wood rats, one each day. We can not live on one

---

[19] Yepnawe, any food besides corn.

wood rat a day.   And besides we have no clothing.   Near where we live there are many people staying and when we go out to hunt we are ashamed to stay out because we have nothing with which to cover ourselves.   We have to run home when people come because we have nothing to wear.   That is why we have come.   We have come for clothing, if there is anything that you can spare us.' . . .[20]

Then Pautiwa listened and Sayataca and everyone listened.   Pautiwa said, "Yes, it is so.   I shall see how we can fix you up."   So Pautiwa said, "Now here is a blue kilt."   He took out two dark blue kilts for them, and Komokätsik went and got two embroidered sashes that were hanging from the deer horn.   Then she took down the two embroidered sashes and laid them down on top of the blue kilts.   Then Pautiwa said, "Now that is enough to cover you."   They did not have any beads, so Pautiwa said, "There are some beads there.   Those will do for them too."   Then each of the katcinas took off a string of beads and laid them down for them.   There was a great pile of beads for them.   Then Pautiwa said to Sayataca, "Now who shall dress them?"   Then Hututu, bow priest chief of Sayataca, got up and he put the beads around their necks and showed them how to wear them, and he put strings of beads around their wrists.   Their necks were bare, so they brought fawn skins to hide their necks.   Then they put on the blue kilts and the embroidered sashes between their legs and he put a leather wrist band on the left wrist of each one.   Then he said, "Now that is the way you will dress.   You will live at the sand hill and you will come out in the evening.   You will hear our songs every time we sing and when we come near you will notice.   We shall always come in early in the morning before the sun is up.   And when you hear the mixed dance coming you will always come and join in and you need not be ashamed.   You will always come in the mixed dance."   They had bare feet and their feet were greasy, so Pautiwa said, "There are no moccasins to fit you.   But it is not right that you should walk all the time without moccasins.   So when the younger brother is tired, the elder brother will carry him, and when he is rested he will take his turn and carry his elder brother.   You will always take turns carrying one another, and that is the way you will change in the dance."

After they had dressed them they told them they should come to Itiwana to dance with the mixed dance when they heard them coming in from Katcina Village.   They told them what to do.   Then again Pautiwa said, "Now what else did you come for?   Do you need anything besides clothing?"   They said, "We need good things to eat." So they laid out large pieces of dried deer meat tied together with yucca cord, and they both carried the meat.   Then they said, "This is all we came for.   Now we are going home."   So they started on

[20] The narrator jumps to where the boys are at Katcina Village.

their way home. After they had gone just a little ways the feet of the younger one began to hurt on account of the hard stones. He said, "Oh brother, my feet hurt. How shall I go?" Then his brother put down his meat and he said, "You carry this meat and I shall carry you on my back." Then the younger one tied the meat to his shoulders and the older one carried his younger brother and they went on this way. A little farther on the older brother said, "Now you have had a little rest and I have carried you. Now please carry me, because I am tired now. Then again the younger one carried his older brother. They went along and so they came to their home in the night. There was their grandmother. When she heard them coming right away she ran out to meet them and there they came with the kilts hanging down and with their bright sashes and both of them carrying dried deer meat. As soon as she saw the deer meat she spread out a robe and laid the deer meat on it and she covered it with another robe. Then she prayed because they had become rich and because the deer meat was so hard to get. She prayed that her grandchildren might get more deer meat and that the deer might come near so that they might always have meat. After she had prayed over the meat she looked at them and examined their clothing and said, "Oh, is that how they dressed you?" She felt of their clothing and fingered the pretty beads. Then they told their grandmother that they had been asked to come to Itiwana when the katcinas were there, and especially with the mixed dance, and told her how they were to go. They had their dresses and whenever they heard the katcinas they were to go too. Then their grandmother said, "Isn't that nice! Now we won't be so lonesome." Then their grandmother baked cakes of corn meal and pounded the dried meat with stones and then they ate. And their grandmother was so polite to them, and was so proud of her grandchildren because they dressed so nicely and had good meat to eat.

So that is how it happened that the Grease Boys who live on sand hill come here to dance, and they come this way because that is the way they dressed them at Katcina Village.

KOKWATAWU OR SUYUKU (ALSO IDENTIFIED AS MU'ATOCLE AND BUFFALO)

(From drawing collected by A. L. Kroeber)

Mask white, spotted with red, fringed with goat hair. Small upright headdress like crown of blue, yellow and red feather in forelock, at back crest of hawk feathers. Long hair and beard. Goggle eyes. Long wooden snout with tongue hanging out. On left shoulder sun disk with red ribbons. Pink body paint. In right arm holding raised knife, left hand bow and arrow.

The rest of the drawing is not clear. Apparently is carrying or being carried by a Hehe'a. He comes in the mixed dance.

Naa we sha. Last of Initiators. Not otherwise identified; not previously published

Sa le mo be ya: Second from Main Color. Not otherwise identified; not previously published

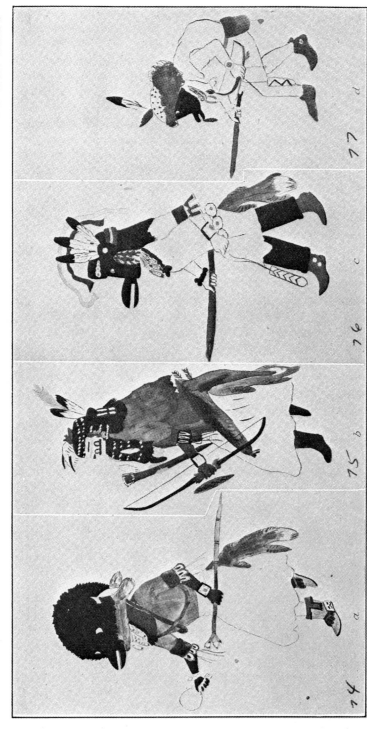

DANCING KATCINAS

a, Mokwala (in mixed dance); *b*, Wahaha (in mixed dance); *c*, Mahefinaca (after Ca'lako); *d*, O'wiwi (with Mahefinaca).

AINCEKOKO (BEAR KATCINA)

(Plate 44, c)

Whole upper part of body covered with bear skin with head still on. Bear paws with feathers over hands. Red feather on head (the bear's feather). Yucca around wrists. Beads like society people.

Dark blue kilt of societies, over that buckskin, embroidered sash and woman's belt. Blue moccasins.

WO'LATANA

(Plate 44, d)

Mask painted brown with spots of black and white. Goat skin over head. Eagle down on head lacowanɬana. Rainbow, cloud and lightning symbols in wood or cloth stretched over frames. In mouth rattlesnake (like Hilili). Skin collar and skin over shoulders.

Red body paint. Double bandoleer of yucca. Buckskin kilt, red belt. Fox skin. Blue moccasins. Arm bands, spruce in belt. On back a carrying basket containing diminutive figure of Hatacuku. In right hand stone knife, in left cane.

Borrowed from Hopi. With the mixed dance.

MOK̃WALA

(Plate 45, a)

Mask painted black. Huge head covered with black goat skin. Blue horns with hanging feathers. Large wooden snout. Coyote skin collar.

Red body paint, yellow shoulders and forearms. Buckskin kilt. Fox skin, blue moccasins. Rattle in right hand, yucca in left. Arm bands, two yarn bandoleers, etc.

Comes in the mixed dance.

WAHAHA

(Plate 45, b)

Face mask with nose, painted white with designs in red and blue. Eagle down in long beard and hair. Hair tied up with belt. Lacowan ɬana on crown, two eagle feathers and peacock feather behind.

Red body paint, one blue and one yellow arm and one blue and one yellow leg (Hopi). Wildcat skin on shoulders, quiver, buckskin kilt, red moccasins and leggings, fox skin. In right hand yucca, in left bow and arrow and spruce, and basket.

He comes in the mixed dance with two girls' masks. They play a game that the Hopis play. He shouts "Wahaha" and then the girls chase him and try to take away his basket. They got this from the Hopis.

"The bear went to the Sacred Lake and they dressed him this way. Before there had been another bear katcina who still sometimes comes with the mixed dance. They didn't have this kind long ago." Compare other Bear katcina, page 1031.

DANCES PERFORMED AFTER CA'LAKO

HEMUCIKWE

(Plate 47, a)

Costume.—He represents the earth and the sky. On his head a high wooden tablet painted with the sun and moon and clouds and stars. The moon is yellow, the background is dark "to represent the dark earth after the rain." The tablet is made of wood and is worn over the top of the head. Two eagle tail feathers and a bunch of owl feathers behind.

The face is green on one side and yellow on the other. The nose is a band of white and a band of black (kucokta). The painting on the side of the face is called "little clouds sticking up" (lakwelanapa).

"When they sweat the clouds come out of the sides of the face. Their bodies are the earth and have springs in them like the earth, and they hold up the sky with the sun and moon and stars.

"They wear spruce all over to make the earth green, on the back of the head, around the neck, and branches in their hands."

The body paint is made of black cornstalks (k̓ekwi). They wear light-blue kilt, arm bands of blue leather, yarn around the neck and legs, bells on left leg, turtle rattle on right, gourd rattle in right hand.

There are only six Hemucikwe masks. They are all different and they are never changed. But they are the personal property of the man who had them made. One belongs to the informant's father, who had it made when he was a young man. His uncle had one, and they were afraid that the mask would be buried with him when he died. So he had it copied so that the number would not decrease.

This dance belongs to Muhewa kiva, who always dance it after Ca'lako. Parsons reports Mitotaca coming with this dance. On first mesa a similar figure (sio humis taamû, Fewkes, Hopi Katcinas, Pl. V) comes with the Sia (Zuñi) Humis.

References.—Hemucikwe is one of the common and conspicuous dances at Zuñi. It is described by Stevenson, Zuñi Indians, page 264, Plate LXXIV; Parsons, Zuñi Ca'lako.

Parallels.—This is one of the widely distributed pueblo dances.

Hopi.—Humis katcina, Fewkes, pages 82 and 83; Plate XXI.

In most villages it is danced at niman katcina, the departure of the katcinas in summer. On first mesa there is a Sia (Zuñi) Humis. (Fewkes, Plate V.)

Laguna.—Hemish, Parsons, Notes on Laguna Ceremonialism 99.

Cochiti.—Ahaye. Illustrated, Dumarest, VI, 1. A summer dance of the ahaye described by Dumarest, page 179 et seq. On this occasion they are accompanied by nahia (leader, the equivalent of the Zuñi bow priest), heluta (Zuñi-Hehe'a), two shruiyana (ferocious katcinas carrying yucca lashes, apparently similar to Zuñi Saiyaḷi'a), and ochasha (sun) katcina.

Jemez.—Hidyasash. (Parsons: Jemez, 110, plate 15, d.)

Nahalic O'kä

(Plate 47, *b*)

Mask like Nahalico. See p. 1065.

Woman's dress, underdress, silk pitone, red belt, white moccasins. Hands white. Carries box, notched stick, and deer scapula.

Used to come to play for Hemucikwe. Has not come for a long time.

Parallels.—In August, 1925, at Hano, first mesa, a female impersonator with a white mask played for Hehe'a. (R. L. B.)

K̓änil'ona (Spring Owner)

(Plate 47, *c*)

On head, downy feather and feathers of summer birds. Mask has round pendent ears and feathers hanging from them. Front of mask painted with forked zigzag down center for nose and zigzags behind ears. Blue frog in back, rest of mask black. Spruce collar.

Wears no clothing, only small dark-blue breechcloth. Upper body to waist, and below knees painted pink, thighs white, no moccasins. Spruce anklets. Carries nothing. Yarn on right wrist, bow bracelet on left. Yarn and beads around neck.

References.—Stevenson, Plate III.

Ma'heti'naca

(Plate 45, *c*)

Costume.—On the left side of the head three tail feathers of the eagle, between the tips of the feathers colored ribbons. These used to be of red flannel. The eagle feathers are fastened to a round disk of turkey feathers (tonalacpone). Red dyed downy feathers. "These are for the red sunset clouds. There are sometimes two, sometimes three ribbons. They represent long life. Around the head a band of rabbit or coyote skin trimmed with a row of beads or buttons for long life." He has protruding eyes, and long hair hanging down behind.

His body is painted white all over for the white clouds. He wears a buckskin skirt, arm bands of buckskin with red fringes for the clouds of evening. Fox skin behind. Red moccasins. Sometimes he wears trousers. He wears a turtle shell rattle on the right leg. He carries a bull roarer in the left hand and yucca in the right.

Ceremonies.—"They come in a large group, all alike. They are nasty dancers. They come in early in the morning and look around for the people who have gone outside to ease themselves. If they find men or women sitting down under their blankets they whip them. So no one likes Mahetinaca.

"They come for the winter rain dance series (koyuptconawa). Only Hekạ̈pawa kiva dances Mahetinaca. They used to give it after Ca'lako, but no one likes this dance so they stopped giving it then, and hekiapawa always dance Wotemła now instead."

The mahetinaca are not married. Their song tells why they have never married. They are jealous of the other katcinas who have wives. There is a story about this."

Myth.—When Mahetinaca came here to dance long ago at the first beginning, one of them did not want to come in with the others. He wanted to bring in a deer to please the people, so he said to his brothers, "I am going this way. I am going to look around." He meant he was going to hunt, for that is the way we say. So he went toward the mountains to the place called Where-the-cotton-hangs (Uhanap̄ana). He went there and he found a spring, and he saw the tracks of some one. He said, "This spring is used by some people. I shall look around and see if anyone is living here. I would like to see them before I go to the dance." So he said. He had gone there to hunt but now he had forgotten all about hunting because he had seen people's tracks. He looked around but he could not find anyone. Finally, to the north of the spring he found a little house. It was evening and there he was still at the spring. Just before dark he saw a light to the north and he said, "Yes, that is where the people come from whose tracks I saw at the spring. I think these must be the people who always get their water there. I will go to the house and if there are no people there to give me my evening meal I will go back to my home." So he thought, and he went toward where he saw the light.

He came in and there were the bat girls. They were all worried about their husband. Their husband was a Ḳäkima boy. There were about eight bat girls and one butterfly girl, and they had one husband between them. They were all married to this Ḳäkima boy. He was the son of the chief priest and he was a handsome youth. He had a nice father, but he did not know any better than to marry these girls. One day when the Ḳäkima boy was out hunting he came to the spring and while he was kneeling down to drink the bat girls came and sat down on the rocks watching him. Then the eldest one said to her younger sisters, "Take that little piece of stone and throw it down. Then he will look up and see us and talk to us." Then the next bat girl took up a pebble and dropped it down where he was drinking. Then he looked up and said, "Who is that?" There all the girls were sitting on the rocks. They were pretty girls.

So he looked at them and said, "You girls come down here. Why did you throw dirt where I was drinking?" They said, "No, we didn't throw anything." Then they came down and played with him, and they were pretty girls. After they had been there a little while they said to him, "You have stayed a long time. Now let us go to our house. You can eat with us and then you can go back home after you have eaten." The boy said, "All right. I am hungry." So they put on their bat dresses and turned into bats again. The eldest sister said, "I shall carry him." Their house was high up. The eldest sister said, "I shall carry you because it is high to our house." He said, "I shall fall off." Then she said, "No. Hold on tight and do not open your eyes. If you open your eyes you will surely fall off." So he shut his eyes and got on her back. So they went up, the eldest sister carrying the Ḵäkima boy on her back and the younger ones following them. They came to their house. They had a great big room. They flew around the room four times and then they went down. Then the boy opened his eyes. He was in a great big room of rocks. It was really a big cave. They told him to sit down and they went into the house and brought out dried meat. The bat girls had already eaten, so they did not eat with him. Then when he had finished he said, "I think I had better go home. It is getting dark now and I think I had better go." The girls said, "No, you had better stay. It is dark and you won't be able to find your way. You had better stay here and our minds will be yours." They meant that they would marry him. He said, "All right," and he was glad because they were pretty girls.

He stayed there for four days. For four days they did not go out but just stayed there in the house with the boy. On the fifth day they told him, "We must go out and look around. We will go down to the spring and get some food for ourselves. We do not eat like you. We must go and hunt our food." So they went and he went out. He was on top of a high place and there was no way to get down. Then he sat there looking over toward Ḵäkima. He saw smoke rising from the village and he thought, "Oh, dear! If only I could get back to my mother!"

As he was sitting there a butterfly girl came. She flew around four times and looked at him. He was a handsome boy. Then she thought, "This is where the bat girls live. I think I shall go down and ask him if they are home." Then she came down and sat down beside him. "What are you doing here? How did you come up?" she asked him. The boy said, "The bat girls brought me up here. I have been here for four days now. They have gone off to look for their food and they told me to come out and look around. I am waiting here for them." Then the butterfly girl said, "I don't think they will come back for a long time. They have forgotten you are waiting here. Now you come to my house with me. I shall always take you with me when I go down and not leave you alone the way they do. So get on my back and let us go.'' He looked at her. She had turned into a person and she was even prettier than the bat girls. So he said, "All right. Take me there now.'' Then she put on her butterfly dress again and he sat down. Then he got on her back and away they went to the east to Butterfly house. She was carrying the boy up-side-down with his head hanging down so that the bat girls would not know which way they had gone.

The butterfly girl had two brothers and her mother and father at Butterfly house. She left the boy outside and went into the house to ask her parents and her brothers if it were all right to bring the boy in. They all said, "Yes; it is all right. I think you want to marry him and it is all right to bring him in.'' So she went out and told the boy to come in. Then they went in. It was noon when they came. Then her mother set out a basket full of corn pollen and a basket of dried deer meat. The butterflies ate the corn pollen and the boy ate the dried meat. After they had eaten they said, "Now we shall go hunting and you must stay here and watch our son. The bat girls may come after him. We know he has been married and they may come after him. So you must stay with him and never leave him. We are going hunting.'' So they told the girl, and then her parents went out to hunt for corn pollen. They went away and the boy and the butterfly girl stayed there.

When the bat girls came home the boy was not there. They looked around and they were very angry. They looked everywhere. They looked Where-the-cotton-hangs and where we have our dried peaches, and up on Corn Mountain. All over the mountain they looked. The boy stayed four days at Butterfly house with the butterfly girl. When the four days were over their mother and father thought, "Now this is the fourth day. Maybe they will come and look for him to-day.'' They were afraid the girls would find him because it was the fourth day. "We are afraid they will come to-day, so you had better go down and see your grandmother and tell her to help you any way she can.'' So her parents told the butterfly girl. So she went down to tell Spider woman. She came in and said, "Grandmother, will you please come up to my home. We need you,'' she said. "Very well, I shall be up there soon.'' So the girl turned and went back home. Finally Spider woman came. She sat down. "What is it that you have wanted me for?'' she asked. Then the butterfly girl said, "I need help. So my mother and father told me to go down and ask you if you could help me any way. We have brought this my husband from Where-the-cotton-hangs. We have taken him from the bat girls and I am afraid they may come to look for him because this is the fourth day. So that is why I went down to ask you to help me." So Spider woman said, "You should have told me this while I was home. I will help you. I will go down and see what I can do for you." So she went down home and she brought up four spider webs. She said, "Everyone must stay home to-day because to-day I am sure they are coming." They went into the house and Spider woman went out and closed the door and she put webs over the holes where they went in and out so that no one could find the holes. She put on four webs and then she went down.

Soon the bat girls came over the west side of Corn Mountain. As they were looking around they met Hawk. Hawk said, "What are you looking for. I saw you here two days ago. I think I know what you are looking for." "Yes, we are looking for our husband." Then Hawk girl asked, "Who is he? "He is a Ķäkima boy." Then Hawk girl laughed and said, "I saw Butterfly girl carrying him. While I was sitting here I saw her carrying him home." "Where does she live?" "She lives at Butterfly house." Then the bat girls went there. They went around and around. Finally they found a little crack where the entrance was. Then they said, "This is where she is staying. They tried to hide the door but we shall get in." So the eldest sister tried to go in. At that time the bats had hands like people but when she tried to get into the door the web caught on her fingers and her hands got webbed like a duck's feet. She could not fly because she had the web all over her. Then the next sister tried and the same thing happened to her. They all tried and they all got the web all over them. They all fell down and could not fly because they were all tangled in the web. They got through three webs this way and came to the last one. The place was getting thin and there were more bats coming. So the butterfly girl's mother told her to take ashes and black corn and put it over the web. Then the bat girls got all dirty and sticky when they tried to break through the web. Then they were tired and lay down there. After a while they felt a little better. Then the eldest sister said, "Sisters, do you feel a little stronger now?" They said, "Yes, we feel stronger now." Then she said, "Well then, let us try and fly." They tried and saw that they were strong enough to fly. Their wings and arms still hurt from their struggles with the spider web. They flew around a little and then they said, "Now this is what we are going to do because you stole our husband. We are going to bring bedbugs to you." Then they flew around and shook their wings over the hole in the web and the bedbugs fell out into the house. So they gave the bedbugs to the butterfly girl because she had stolen their husband. They used to be pretty girls, but now they were dirty and gray and their wings had the spider web all over them, and they had funny faces and they cried because they had been hurt by the ashes and the soot and the spider web.

After they got home they sat down in the room and cried.   They were dirty and ugly.   They were not pretty any more because Butter-fly girl had done this to them.   They were sitting there worrying about it when Mahetinaca came.   Then he wanted to marry these girls, but they did not want him.   They had been married to the handsome Ḵä-kima youth and they were unhappy.   Then he danced for them.   He stayed there a little while to see if they would cheer up.   Then he asked them, "Why are you sad?   What are you worrying about?   I know you are worrying about something."   They would not tell him what worried them.   He tried to play with the girls.   He showed them his dance, and he swung his bull roarer for them.   Then the youngest one said, "Let me do it."   They thought they would give him what the butterfly girl had given them.   They thought if they played with him and touched him he would get dirty and ugly and then they would get rid of the dirt and ashes and give them to him, and then they would be pretty again.   They did not want to marry him because he had a funny mouth and they had been married to the handsome Ḵäkima boy.   Then they went over to him and touched his clothing and asked him about everything he had on.   They came close to him and put their hands all over him.   He tried to play with them, but they did not want him.   Finally, when he was ready to go they said to him, "Come again."   He said, "No, I will never come again.   You do not like me."   Then they said, "All right.   Now we will do this to you."   And they shook their wings and he got dirty and black.   Then he looked and saw he was dirty and said, "Hummmmm."   Then they said to him, "Now that is the way you will always be.   You will be dirty and ugly and you will look sharply at people and say 'hummmmm.'"   And that is the way he is.   When this Mahetinaca was turned into an ugly dirty person all his people became that kind too.   And that is why their noses are black and shiny, and that is why they always go after the people when they go outside and look sharply at them and say "Hummmmm."

That is all, and that is why we do not like Mahetinaca.   Just the way the bat girls gave the dirty things to the butterflies, so they made Mahetinaca ugly so that all the people dislike him.   Even though Mahetinaca are katcinas no one likes to see them, and none of the young men will dance Mahetinaca.   They make nasty songs about the people here.   They say they are singing about people in the sacred lake but everyone knows that it is about the Itiwana people.   And so no one likes to see them.   Not all the people know the story, but they all know there is something wrong with Mahetinaca.

O'WIWI

(Plate 45, d)

Costume.—He wears a chin mask, always painted black. He has ball eyes and a big mouth, and his red tongue hangs out, because he was a mean dancer when he was young. His short black hair is all tangled up. On his head he wears the perforated buckskin cap of the war chiefs. On the top of the head one tail feather of the eagle and the downy red feather to show that he is a society member.

"He wears old clothing and over his shoulder he has a buckskin full of precious things, turquoise and different kinds of beads. His moccasins are on the wrong feet because he is old and can not see very well. He wears beads around his neck and on his right wrist a bracelet of shells like the war chief wears. Over his shoulder he carries a buckskin bag containing little animal fetishes such as the members of the Hunters' Society have. In the right hand a single piece of yucca, in the left a half-finished bow and an arrow, and a large bull-roarer (nununawe).

"He is dressed like this when he comes to teach the people how to hunt, but when he comes at other times he does not have the red feather and the buckskin bag with the animal fetishes."

Formerly only the old men who were too old to dance would come as O'wiwi, but now the young men come this way sometimes.

Ceremonies.—"He is the grandfather of the Mahetinaca. He sometimes comes with Mahetinaca when they come in the winter at Ko'uptconawa, and sometimes he comes to sing for Hilili.

"He is a very old man, the grandfather of the Mahetinaca. When the Mahetinaca come in to Itiwana to dance they do not want to bring their grandfather with them because he is old and poor and they are ashamed of him. But after they have left he follows them and when everyone is watching the dance he comes in, and they are ashamed not to treat him right in front of all the people.

"So after they have left he gets his things ready. He takes a buckskin and wraps in it all kinds of valuable things, turquoise and shell and beads, so that everyone will like him in spite of his old clothes. He gets dressed in a hurry and because he can't see well he puts the right moccasin on the left foot. He carries yucca so that people won't think he is too old to fight and to protect himself as he goes along. He carries a large bull-roarer to make a noise so that the people will know him. Then he takes a buckskin bag with animal fetishes in it. When he was young he was a good hunter and he belongs to the Hunters' Society. Therefore he carries the bag with the animal fetishes and wears the red feather of society members. He is anxious to show all his valuable possessions and show the people that he is a great person.

"So when he has everything together he comes, talking to himself as he comes along. While his grandchildren are dancing in the west plaza he comes to Wide River, and when they are nearly finished dancing in rat plaza [21] he comes in. Then all the people say, 'Oh, there is their grandfather.' O'wiwi is a little ashamed to show himself. His grandchildren are very angry that he has come, but they can not say anything. He does not join in their line, but dances up and down in front of them, making motions to interpret their songs. He makes motions of the clouds and the rain and everything that is mentioned in the songs. When they are finished his children go away and he stays behind. He goes around looking at the people out of the corner of his eyes. After everyone has gone he sits down in the plaza and takes corn meal out of his belt and makes a line. Then he takes the wildcat and the lion and the white bear and the coyote out of his bag and he sets them down on the line facing the south and he prays. As he prays he turns them to each direction. Then he takes his bow and arrow and asks his animals which way to go. Then he goes around the plaza to each direction. He pretends he is looking for the tracks of the deer. He is a great leader of the hunters and he is teaching the people what to do. He makes itsumawa for the hunters. After he has done this, going in every direction looking for tracks, then he pretends he has caught a deer and pretends to lay it down and take the skin off to show the people how. He takes the blood and makes a mark on the nose of his animals, so that they can smell the blood. Long ago he used to make a little fire in the plaza and get meat from one of the houses to burn in the fire to feed to the Sacred Lake people. Then he told the people, 'This is the way you must do, and I will get the meat and eat it. And so I will give you good luck.' They do not do this any more because the people do not hunt any more, but long ago they used to think a great deal of O'wiwi because he brought good luck to the hunters.

"Long ago he used to carry the k̨aettone of the rain priests on his back. He wore poor clothing and poor moccasins and everyone thought he was poor, but he had valuable things on his back. He wanted to marry a girl, but no one wanted him because he looked poor. But there was one girl who lived alone with her old grandmother. They were very poor and hardly had enough to eat, and so this girl married this man. And that night when he took off his poor clothing he had many valuable things in his blanket and in a few months he made them rich. The people all thought that he was poor. No one likes him. They say when he comes that he has come to carry off a poor girl and make her rich."

---

[21] The traditional circuit of the plazas is first west plaza, rat plaza, t̄sia'a plaza, big plaza. The circuit is still made but dancing is usually confined to t̄sia'a plaza with one turn each day in big plaza.

a. Nahalico

b. Nahalic a wan mosona

c. Käna.tcu

d. Wam'uwe

DANCING KATCINAS: WINTER DANCES

Muluktaḵä

(Plate 47, d)

Costume.—On the head, parrot feathers; at the right side of the head two tail feathers of the eagle and one parrot tail feather. The face is painted blue. He has a long curved snout (otontsikon·e); short black hair around the face (utcialane). The top and back of the mask are painted black with lahacoma on the back. "The spruce collar has popcorn at the tips of the branches because Muluktaḵä plants the sweet corn to make the people's skin strong so that it won't crack in the cold weather."

The body paint is the juice from the stalks of black corn (ḵekwi). This is for the black earth when it is wet from rain. He wears buckskin arm bands with tabs of painted buckskin and turkey feathers (asipowopok lacowapa; arm bands feathers having). Dance kilt, blue moccasins, fox skin, turtle shell rattle on right leg, bells on left. Gourd rattle in right hand, in left long staff with feathers (teɫna lacowapa; staff feathers having). Hanging from the end of the staff is a downy feather. The first feather is tail feather of the eagle for the clouds, next hawk feather for the rain, then feathers of all the little birds, because all the little birds sing after the rain. Therefore they always come last.

This dance belongs to tcupawa kiva. They dance it the day after Ca'lako. They also dance it sometimes in the winter or summer rain dance series. Two Muluktaḵä carrying trees come with Kolowisi at the first whipping of boys. (See p. 977.)

References.—Described by Stevenson, p. 265.
Parallels.—"Duck" (waiyush) dance of all Keresan pueblos. Parsons, Notes on Laguna Ceremonialism, 100.

SUPPLEMENTARY AND EXTRA DANCES

Nahalico (Crazy Grandchild)

(Plate 46, a)

Mask has turkey wing feathers tipped with downy feathers, bunch of parrot and downy feathers, face white painted with floral designs in blue and yellow, head covered with goat skin. Spruce collar.

Red body paint, yellow forearms, dance kilt embroidered sash tied with design on two sides, woman's belt, red moccasins, woolen hose covered with colored yarn, arm bands, bandoleer of cedar berries.

He dresses this way when he comes in large group to dance. Society chorus sings for him.

6066°—32——68

Nahalico a·wa Mosona 83

(Plate 46, b)

Mask has turkey (?) feathers upright in back, on crown parrot and eagle. Face turquoise with designs in red, yellow and black and white; back, yellow with dragon flies, carved in back, gourd stem for mouth. Spruce collar.

Red body paint, yellow forearms. Red buckskin over left shoulder dance kilt, brown moccasins with leggings and garters, red belt, arm bands.

Right hand yucca ring, left flute of Payatyamu.

Ḵänatcu 84

(Plate 46, c)

Mask turquoise, red ears, long sharp snout, top of head covered with goat skin, eagle tail feathers and parrot feathers horizontally placed, parrot and downy feathers. Spruce collar.

Embroidered kilt, fringed belt, woman's belt, blue moccasins, red body paint, legs and forearms yellow. Arm bands, yarn; carries spruce and rattle, bandoleer.

He is a gentle dancer. Sometimes comes with koḵɔkci, sometimes a set come to dance in winter. Carries rattle and spruce.

Wamuwe 85

(Plate 46, d)

Costume.—"He has clouds on his cheeks and rain under his eyes." Twisted colored yarn about his head. Spruce collar. Light blue kilt, white tasseled belt, and red woman's belt. Fox skin. Fringed leggings, blue moccasins. Eagle tail feather back of head. Rattle, spruce.

"He is a Hehe'a. He comes in the winter in a large group. Muhewa kiva used to dance it in summer also. It is always a give-away dance. They dance with the bundle drum, and that is how they got their name."

Parallels.—Danced by Tewa of Hano in August of 1925, while Hopi katcinas were forbidden.

Tciɫtci 53

(From a drawing collected by A. L. Kroeber)

Mask.—Back and top black, face pink, with nose and eyes like Hehe'a, red spot on cheeks. Yarn around head, at back lapap̣oawe. Spruce collar.

Appears to be wearing fringed buckskin shirt. Many necklaces.

Haw we we: Not otherwise identified; not previously published

Se wal uu amm bah ya na que: Buffalo Dance. Not otherwise identified; not previously published

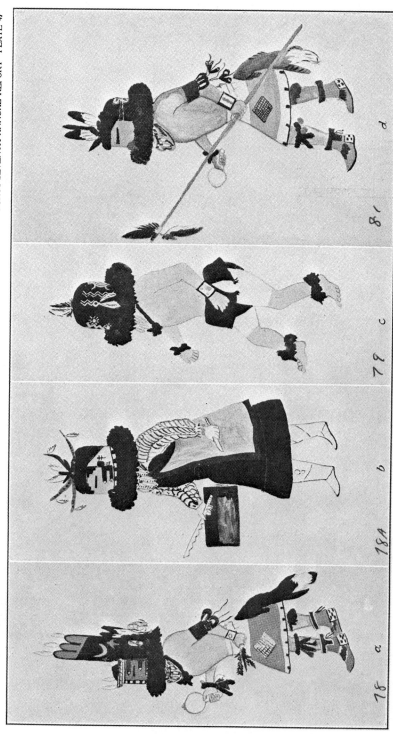

DANCES PERFORMED AFTER CA'LAKO

a, Hemucikwe; *b*, Nahalic Okä (with Hemucikwe); *c*, Ḳänil'ona (with Hemucikwe); *d*, Muluktakä.

WINTER DANCES: HILILI

a, K̯äk̯äli (Eagle); *b*, Hilili; *c*, Tcałaci.

K̰äK̰äli (Eagle)

(Plate 48, a)

Costume.—The mask is painted blue with black designs. Around the head yucca band. On his head a large bunch of parrot feathers and downy feathers of the eagle. Spruce collar.

The body is painted black with blue and yellow. The left shoulder and chest is yellow, the right blue. The right hand is yellow, the left blue. The right leg is blue, the left yellow. White kilt with band of blue, embroidered sash, blue moccasins. On his arms he has wings made by sewing feathers to a strip of corn husk. On his back he wears a shield of buckskin painted blue and bordered with a fringe of red hair. At the top are two upright tail feathers of the eagle attached to a disk of turkey feathers, and four red hawk feathers. At the bottom four more red hawk feathers and a fan of tail feathers of the eagle. The eagle is the chief of the birds, and so he wears the shield on his back. It has the same significance as the lacowanłane of the war chief. He carries little bells in both hands.

He comes with Hilili.

Folklore.—Long ago Hilili came here for the first time. They came for the first time about forty years ago when my mother was a girl. When they first came the people thought they were dangerous because they carried snakes, so all the head priests came together and asked whether it was dangerous to have Hilili dance. The katcina chief and his p̄ekwin were there. The priests had called them in to ask if it was right to have Hilili. Then they sent for a Hopi man married to a Zuñi woman to have him tell them about the dance. They were all in the priests' ceremonial room. The people were all afraid because they were carrying snakes. They were not rattlesnakes, but they were real snakes and the people had no medicine to cure the bites of these other snakes.

The people were all met together, and the Hopi man came in and asked, "My fathers, why have you sent for me? I am not fit to come into this sacred house. But you have sent for me and I have come. What is it that you want of me?" Then the chief priest said, "Our people have come here from the west. They have brought with them a valuable dance. Now our people want to do this dance, but we are afraid of one thing—they carry snakes. That is why our fathers have all come together, and that is why we have sent for you to come here. Is it dangerous to have them?" So he said. The Hopi man was wise. He knew all about Zuñi ways and he said, "Now, my fathers, I thought you people had things for the snakes. We have all worked on our feathers, all who belong to societies. We have made feathers for the snakes and planted them in the winter time," he said. "I do not know why you are afraid of the snakes. They are bringing with them an eagle dance so that the people may have many eagles. There are no eagles here. You have good places for the eagles to build their nests, but you have no one to dance for the eagles. These people will bring the eagles. They are good climbers. They can climb the high mountains, and so they can get the eagles. They will bring the eagles. And now, my fathers, you will decide whether you want it. If you think it will be dangerous to have them dance with the snakes, I shall leave it to you to do as you think best. I do not have to tell you what is right and what is wrong. You will know what is best."

When he had spoken thus the katcina chief said to the priests, "Now, my fathers, I think we had better have this dance so that we may have plenty of feathers for our people at the Sacred Lake. Now, if we have this dance for the eagles the eagles will come from the high mountains and stay close to Itiwana if we pray for them in a dance." The katcina chief wanted to have the feathers because they are valuable. They are our life. The katcina chief is the head of the dance and whatever he says is all right. The priests have nothing to say; not even the chief priest can raise any objection after the katcina chief has spoken. He wanted this eagle dance because he wanted his children, the katcinas, to have many feathers and to be pretty. So the priests said, "It is good. You have said that you want this dance. It is all right." The rain people had nothing to say. They left it to the katcina chief. Then he told his assistant, "Now you shall go to the men of he'iwa kiva who want to have this Hilili dance, and you shall tell them to go ahead with it and practice for it. It is all right." So now the men of he'iwa kiva were pleased and went ahead with their dance. They had the young men dance, and the older men of the kiva sang for them.

The katcina chief did not want people without masks to come out to sing for the katcinas. The Hopi chorus always dressed like human people but the katcina chief here did not want that. So they decided who should sing for them and how they should dress. They made the Tenenakwe (singers) come out to sing for them. All the older men who were too heavy to dance Hilili came as Tenenakwe. The Tenenakwe do not have to be society members but they dress just like members of societies. They wear a little chin mask with the back of the head exposed, and they do their hair in a queue in back. They wear just the dark blue kilt like the society members, and the red feather in the hair. Then after they had their songs ready they got their clothing together. The Hopis would not tell them what the different parts of the clothing meant, so they made new ornaments for the side of the head and represented different things on them— the sun and the moon and the stars. All were different. They made the songs in the Zuñi language but there were not many words, only meaningless syllables.

So when the time came after they had fixed up the ornaments for the head and the feathers, and when they had everything ready, they began to dance. They brought in with them the two Eagle katcinas. Their arms were covered with eagle feathers and they had feathers on their heads and wore downy feathers all over. They came in and everyone liked them. First the Tenenakwe came in, and then Hilili came in, and last of all the two eagles. They looked so pretty that everyone liked them right away. The kiva chief was leading the dance and he danced in the middle. Then he went around to the four corners of the plaza and came to where the singers were standing. He stood among them and the one who was beating the drum watched his head and when he nodded he started to beat the drum and then they all began to sing. The kiva chief began to dance right there among the singers. Then the Hilili dancers began. They lined up on the north side of the plaza and began to dance. Then they danced and when they went in to rest the singers stayed there in the plaza. Then the dancers came out again and danced.

Then in the evening when they were through dancing the katcina war chief took the Eagle katcinas. They still had their paper bread from their dinner in the kiva. So when they were through dancing they took their paper bread and the katcina war chief took them to Corn Mountain. He had corn meal with him, and he said, "Now, my fathers, you have come here from the west. You have come here to call the eagles from where they are staying. Call the eagles from the west and from the south and from all the different directions so that the Itiwana people may have feathers for their dancers." So he said and sprinkled corn meal on them and made the road for them to go to Corn Mountain to build their nests there. Then the men took off their masks at Corn Mountain and said to their masks, "Now, our father has told you to stay here and to call the eagles to build their nests in this place. You are the ones to make the eagles come here. Now we shall leave you here on this mountain." So they said and then they dressed there and brought back their masks and clothing to Itiwana.

So that is why there are always eagle nests on Corn Mountain and all the people from the different villages come here to Itiwana to get eagle feathers. The Hopis brought their eagle dance here and since then we have had many eagles. But the Hopis have given away their dance and so they now have bad luck with eagles in their own country. And that is why whenever Hilili comes the eagles always go out early before the other katcinas leave, and go with their lunch to Corn Mountain to call the eagles. They do not always go to Corn Mountain, but sometimes they go other places to other mountains. But they go out every night. If they dance more than one day they go out each evening and come back the next day and dance.

HILILI K̄OHANA

(Plate 48, b)

Costume.—On this one the face is painted white, but it may be red or yellow or blue or black. There is a snake painted over each eye; that on the right is blue, that on the left yellow. The eyes are square with bands of three colors, black and white and blue. On the head lacowanłana with duck's head. Over the right ear is a round disk painted with a sun symbol, with feather attached. It is called timsaiane. The original Hopi Hilili from which this dance was taken did not have this ornament but the Zuñis added it to make him look valuable. Standing up over the left ear different kinds of feathers, tail feather of the eagle, bluebird, and red hawk. Around the neck is a snake, the head in front and the tail standing up in back. He has a big mouth and long black beard. He has a wildcat skin around his neck and over his shoulders.

Body is painted red with Sacred Lake clay mixed with ahoka. Arms and legs yellow. He wears white kilt with band of blue, embroidered Hopi sash and woman's belt. Fox skin, blue moccasins. Yucca in both hands, around both legs, and on right wrist. Bow bracelet on left wrist. Arm bands with two rows of red buckskin tabs for the clouds. They are very anxious to bring rain, so they wear two sets. Little bells on right leg and on belt.

Hilili came from the Hopi about forty years ago. The current version of the importation is given above. The Hopi, on the other hand, report that the dance was imported from Zuñi. This holds for all Hopi villages.

It is danced in winter at koʻuptconawa. Everyone likes Hilili, so all the kivas dance it. It was performed as an extra dance December 13–16, 1927.

TCAŁACI (TCAKWENA OLD MAN)

(Plate 48, c)

Costume.—His mask is like Tcakwena, black with eyes like Tcakwena. He has white hair (lohaiyaye) and white beard.

"He is dressed just like a society member. Red feather, yucca band around his head, yucca on right wrist, dark blue skirt, silver belt, brown moccasins, black knitted stockings, and little red belts around the legs. He carries two eagle wing feathers in his right hand, like society people. He wears his beads doubled over on his chest like society people. He does not always wear the blanket.

"Long ago one of these masks belonged to Hek̄äpawa kiva, and he used to come in with the Tcakwena dance. Then he did not dress like this. He did not wear the red feather and the yucca and the other insignia of society members, but he wore lacowanłana like the other Tcakwena dancers.

"Now he only comes to sing for Hilili. He is too old to dance but he has a sweet voice, so he sings in the chorus for Hilili. Hilili always have a chorus to sing for them, and Tcalaci is their leader. There used to be only one Tcalaci, but now there may be many of them in the chorus. Anyone who is a good singer may be Tcalaci. All the young men will be Hilili, but the older men who are too old to dance Hilili but who are head men and want to take part will be Tcalaci and sing.

"Tcalaci is so old that he crawls on his knees. Last year when they danced Hilili none of the societies who generally sing for them would sing, and so they had only a group of Tcalaci. It was hard work for the Hilili dancers, because they had to drive them in like sheep. They would not come in, and they fell down all the time and had to be picked up. But when they were all in and began to sing they were sweet singers."

TENENAKWE (SINGERS)

These are the singers for Hilili.

Blue chin mask with black band over lip, black spots on cheeks and chin. Hair tied up behind with red belt. Yucca band, red feathers in forelock, long turquoise strings in ears. Body nude, except for blue breechcloth of societies; bare feet. Beads worn like society members. Chest, back, arms, and legs smeared with whitewash.

(When Hilili danced outdoors in the daytime in December, 1927, the singers were masked but fully clothed in garish and variegated attire. Some of the masks were white chin masks with elaborate decorations in pink and blue, like Wilatsukwe or Kumache, whose masks were probably used.)

PASIKÄPA (OPEN SLEEVES)

(Plate 49, a)

Mask pink with designs in black on cheek, long eye slits, eagle-tail feathers behind, on top downy feathers, hawk feathers, and paper flowers. Blue or black or colored shirt (probably velveteen) with open sleeves, colored ribbons on shoulders. Dance kilt, embroidered sash, red belt, red moccasins, woolen hose with red garters. In right hand, rattle, left bow, ornamented with spruce and colored streamers.

Dances in winter, at ko'uptconaķä.

WAĶÄCI KOKO (COW KATCINA)

(Plate 49, b)

Costume.—He wears a regular mask with the top and back covered with the skin from a cow's head. The horns are either real horns or made of wood. The ears are of rawhide painted red inside. On the head he wears a bunch of red and yellow parrot feathers and downy feathers. Two eagle-tail feathers standing up behind, with a bunch of owl feathers, and a small disk of turkey feathers. Bright-colored ribbon hanging down in back. Spruce collar.

The body is painted with pink clay and yellow paint. The left arm is green, the right yellow. (This is the characteristic Hopi katcina body paint.) The face is spotted all over to represent a cow. The legs are painted white.

He wears a buckskin skirt, embroidered sash, fox skin. Woman's belt over right shoulder, like a bandoleer. He wears arm bands of yarn embroidery with buckskin fringes to represent rain. In the right hand a gourd rattle, in the left a staff topped with eagle feathers fastened to the staff with a disk of turkey feathers, black hair and streamers of blue cloth. Blue moccasins. Turtle-shell rattle on right leg, black yarn on left.

"This is a large dance with a great many people, like a mixed dance. It is danced in the winter by Ohewa kiva. They were the first kiva to dance it, and no one else ever does it. (It was danced as an extra dance by young men from Muhewa on the night of Ca'lako, 1927.)

"This dance was introduced from the Hopi in 1908. At that time Hopi men came to Ca'lako and danced the cow dance for the Zuñis. Ever since that time we have had more cows. (Danced by the Hopi at present.—R. L. B.)

"This is a regular kiva dance in which the head men take part, not like the Navaho dance.

"He represents the cow, but he brings corn too. He has blue seeds."

MUKWE (HOPI)

(Plate 49, c)

Mask.—Face mask with beard, face turquoise blue with ornament of red and white and checkerboard border. On head paper flowers and bunch of eagle and parrot feathers, ribbon streamers.

Body painted red with right shoulder and left forearm blue, and left shoulder and right forearm yellow. Legs yellow. (Powamu painting among the Hopi.)

Dance kilt, embroidered sash, red belt, fox skin, beaded bandoleer, red moccasins, woolen hose fastened with yarn.

Right hand gourd rattle, left hand crooked prayer stick (carried by Powamu).

Parallels.—This is probably the Zuñi masked interpretation of the Hopi Powamu Katcina, who dances unmasked as the culminating ceremony of the Powamu festival.

WINTER DANCES

a, Pasiḳiᵽa; *b*, Waḳáci (Cow); *c*, Mukikwe (Hopi); *d*, Mukikwokä.

MUKW'OKA (HOPI WOMAN)

(Plate 49, *d*)

Koḳɔkci mask and headdress.

Calico underdress, black dress, white blanket with red border fastened on right shoulder. Dress decorated with colored ribbons, white moccasins.

In right hand, basket ornamented with feathers, in left corn. Hands white.

KWAMUMU

(Plate 51, *a*)

Costume.—On the head a bunch of yellow parrot feathers and downy feathers. Sticking up from the center one tail feather of the eagle dyed black and tipped with tiny parrot feathers. The face is painted blue. On the back of the head is painted corn. Red hair around the face. On the left side a representation of a squash with downy feathers hanging from it. He wears arm bands with feathers and buckskin fringes, white kilt, white tasseled belt, fox skin, brown moccasins with fringes, turtle shell rattle on the right leg, gourd rattle in right hand. Across the breast a band of bright satin ribbon studded with disks of silver or precious beads.

KWAMUMU OḴÄ

(Plate 51, *b*)

Chin mask painted brownish yellow with red streak on cheeks, protruding red mouth. Hair drawn back and done up behind with white yarn, no bangs (like Navaho woman). Navaho woman's velveteen blouse, full flounced calico skirt, red woven belt. Many necklaces and bracelets, white moccasins. Right hand spruce, in left some unidentified object.

This dance was borrowed from the Hopi.

WILATSUKWE (APACHE)

(Plate 51, *c*)

Mask: Chin mask with projecting nose, hair flowing with downy feathers down back, headband of colored yarn, over right ear, band of eagle feathers, and in center a sun symbol in yellow; on left, eagle wing feathers and ornament of turkey feathers or horsehair, necklaces of turquoise and bear claws.

No body paint, buckskin kilt, under it a long breechcloth of colored calico, red moccasins and woolen hose. In right hand long arrow, in left bow and other arrows. Yarn on wrist and bow bracelet arm bands.

"They got this dance from the Apache the way they got the Sioux dance. They copied the dress from a picture. The songs are in the Zuñi language, but they are very hard to sing because they shout with a strong voice like the Apache."

It is danced in winter. (See Parsons, Winter and Summer Dance Series, page 177.)

WILATSUKW'OK͜Ä

(Plate 51, d)

Chin mask painted white with designs on cheeks in red and blue. Hair loose. Headband of colored yarn with three upright downy feathers on right, ornament of red feathers on left, horsehair, colored calico skirt and over that sleeveless shirt of fringed buckskin ornamented with shells and porcupine quill embroidery. Full skirt of calico, white woman's moccasins, in back hand two eagle tail feathers with fringe of horsehair.

Comes with Wilatsukwe.

LA'PILAWE

(Plate 50, a)

He wears a headdress of eagle feathers around the head and hanging down the back or fastened to yarn headband. Buckskin shirt with sleeves and embroidered with beads, fringed leggings of white or brown buckskin, Navaho blanket or buckskin kilt folded around the loins. No sash, only a red woven belt. Fox skin. He carries bow and arrows. Carries stone knife in right hand and in left a battle-ax or lance.

A number of them come in the Sioux dance, to dance.

"This dance used to belong to the Sioux. The people here, especially the society people, need the fur of the buffalo for their ceremonies. They used to use bear skin to cover their arms when they had their curing ceremonies in the winter, but for a long time they have not been able to kill any bears around here on account of the white people, and so they use buffalo skin instead.

"So about ten years ago the katcina chief and the other headmen met to talk about it. They thought they would like to have a buffalo dance come here. They thought that if the buffalo came here all the fur-bearing animals like the bear would come near to Itiwana, so that the society people could use their fur in their ceremonies. We had heard that there was a Sioux man living at Gallup, so one man went up to Gallup to get this man to give him their songs for the buffalo. The man went there and got the songs and made Zuñi words for it. Then the Sioux man drew a picture of how the buffalo looked in the dance, and he brought it back here and they made this dance. They

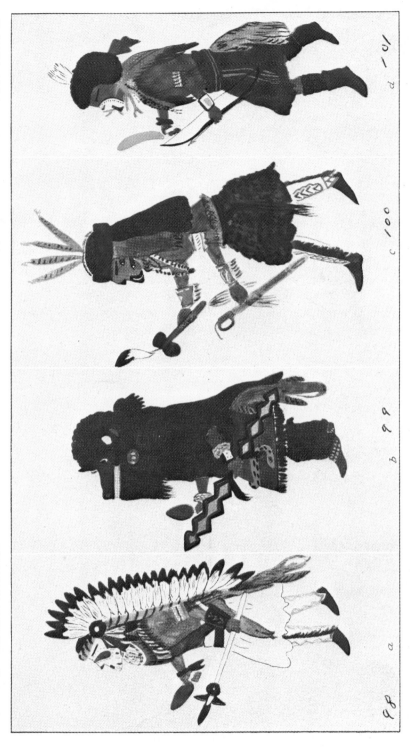

a. La'pi'la'we (feather string)   b. Buffalo   c. A'lana (big stone)   d. Ainanuwa

WINTER DANCE GROUP: SIOUX DANCE

had the dance in the winter. One buffalo comes, and one warrior comes and chases him and kills him, and the others dance. When they kill the buffalo in the dance, whoever comes to him first will take him to his society room and all the members of his society will sprinkle the buffalo with water that they may have good luck."

SIWOLO (BUFFALO)

(Plate 50, b)

Costume.—The mask is a regular chin mask like Tcakwena wears with the buffalo head put on over it. He has red ears and black and white horns. Over his head and shoulders he wears a buffalo hide. His arms are painted red. His kilt is of brown buckskin with a rattlesnake painted on it. The bottom of the kilt is fringed with nails and other pieces of metal that jangle as he dances. Fur leggings with more metal ornaments on the upper edges. Red moccasins trimmed with blue. Fox skin. In his right hand a rattle, in the left a lightning stick and a bunch of black hair. He wears beads on both wrists for he is valuable.

He comes with the Sioux dance.

AŁANA

(Plate 50, c)

He wears a chin mask with a large nose.   The painting on the face is feathers, for he is a warrior.   The face is painted red with the blood of the buffalo.   Over his head he wears twisted strands of beads.

He wears a wildcat skin around his loins, brown moccasins, and fringed leggings.   He wears arm bands of different colors and wide cuffs painted with arrow points.   Around his neck he wears strings of buffalo claws, two strands, in addition to beads.   In the right hand a tomahawk (Ca'lako's ax); in the left a sword in a leather sheath.

He comes with the Sioux dance.   He brings in the buffalo and kills him in his dance.

AINANUWA (OR MEPU)

(Plate 50, d)

Chin masks painted brown, with designs in white, blue, and black on nose and chin, with prominent nose.   Goatskin over head, feather over right ear.   Deer antlers around neck.   Fringed buckskin shirt. Navaho blanket around loins; red belt; fox skin; brown moccasins, with woolen hose.   In right hand a stone knife; in left a bow and arrow.

Comes with Sioux dance and "takes care" of buffalo.

KUMANCE—P̈EYENA·KWE (THE SPEAKING PERSONS)

(Plate 52)

Mask has prominent nose design on cheek, war bonnet, wears beaded waistcoat instead of buckskin shirt, and small Navaho blanket as kilt, fastened with red belt. Bow with long arrow in one hand, in the right a stone war club (not pictured).

He is a solo dancer and dances out of line vigorously. Carries on conversation with drummer between songs, finally threatens him with club.

Drummer wears chin mask with prominent nose, yarn headband, usual man's headdress, arrangement of feathers over right ear. Sleeved buckskin shirt, trousers, red belt, beaded Plains moccasins, brown buckskin leggings fastened with belt with two eagle feathers thrust in each. Carries wooden drum on pole, which he rests on ground. Two eagle feathers in left hand.

KUMANCE

(Plate 53, b)

Mask; chin mask painted white with line of red across eyes and triangular design on chin. Short war bonnet with beaded headband. Hair in yarn-wound plaits over shoulders.

Sleeveless fringed buckskin shirt, fringed shawl, woman's kilt, silver belt, fox skin, brown moccasins with fringed white buckskin leggings tied with yarn. Fringed arm bands, yarn on right wrist, bow bracelet on left. No body paint. In right hand rattle, in left bow decorated with feathers.

This dance is very popular but exceedingly arduous. It was danced as an extra dance the night of Ca'lako, 1928. The songs are not in the Zuñi style, and are probably of Plains origin.

KYEŁŁIKWE

(Note on drawing collected by A. L. Kroeber)

Chin mask painted white, red band over eyes and triangular design on cheeks. Colored yarn around head and above a crown of bear claws. Over right ear a bunch of downy feathers upright with circular ornament of turkey feathers, ribbon streamers over right ear, another bunch of turkey feathers and more streamers. Behind, two eagle tail feathers and bunch of owl feathers. Hair tied up behind with red belt. Shirt of colored velveteen adorned with silver buttons and many colored streamers.

Rest of figure not shown.

WINTER DANCES

a, Kwamumu; *b*, Kwamumu oḵä; *c*, Wilatsukwe (Apache); *d*, Wilatsukw'oḵä.

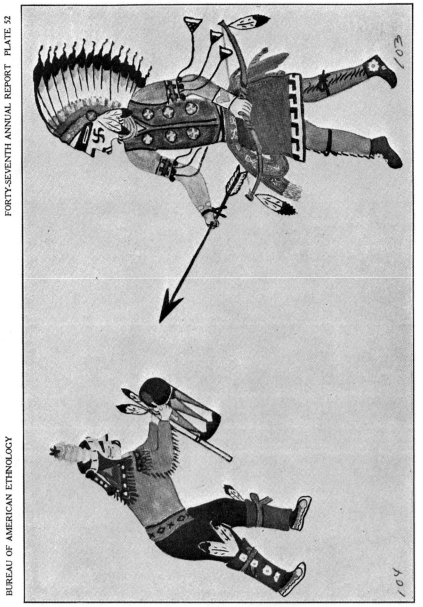

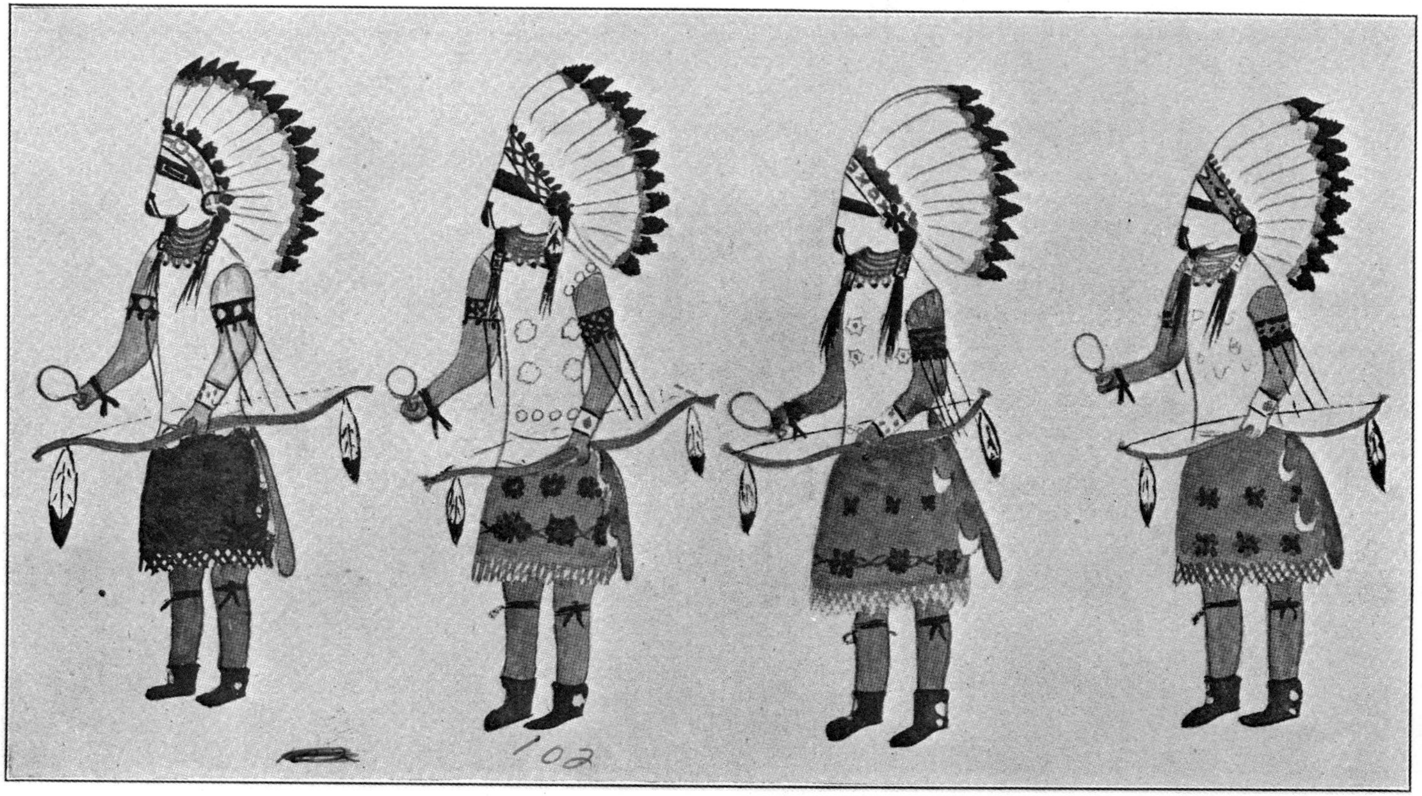

KUMANCE

THE "LITTLE DANCERS"

a, Hehe'a; *b*, Nahalico; *c*, Cula witsi Kohana; *d*, Itetsona.

THE "LITTLE DANCERS"

HEHE'A

(Plate 54, *a*)

Costume.—The face may be white or blue or black. He has tears running out of his eyes because he was hurt in the war with the Ḳänakwe. His mouth is crooked because he always makes faces at the Koyemci. On his head black hair and a bunch of red chili. He has an abalone shell in each ear. Rabbit skin around his neck.

The body is painted with red paint mixed with katcina clay from the Sacred Lake. The forearms and legs to the knees are painted yellow. Also yellow spots on the body and on the knees. The body from the navel to the knees is painted white with white clay from Acoma. He wears only a dark-blue breechcloth (piłaliana). He carries a fawn-skin bag filled with ashes or dirt of ground chili.

Ceremonies.—He can come in whenever there is a dance going on, but he comes mostly in the wintertime. Sometimes only one comes, sometimes three or four. He comes in late after everyone is in the plaza. Then while the Koyemci are playing he comes in to rat plaza. No one knows that he is coming, and he comes quietly and hides so that no one will see him or hear him, and he hides particularly from the Koyemci. While they are playing he shows himself. He runs in and makes donkey ears at them. He is full of mischief. Then the Koyemci say, "Who is coming?" Hehe'a runs up to them quickly and knocks them down with his bag full of pepper. The pepper makes them sneeze. Then he runs and hides in the crowd and runs off. Then when they begin to play he runs in again and knocks them down. Finally they see him and say, "Oh, its a nana (grandfather-grandchild). Let's catch him." Then they all hold hands and surround him, but he crawls out between their legs and hides in the crowd. Finally they catch him and ask him, "How did you come?" Then he starts to tell them all in sign language, "I woke up early." He makes the sign of a big sun with his hands, because the sun looks big when it first comes up. Then he tells them, "I met a rabbit and killed it with a stone, and it fell down, and then I roasted it." He tells it all in gesture. Then in the evening when the sun goes down the katcinas go back home, but he stays behind and plays.

He may come for any dance. During the winter dances this impersonation is very popular, especially among the boys who are too young to take part in the regular line dances.

(In the night of August 23–24, 1925, during the rain dance of uptsanawa kiva two Hehe'a and one Tcałaci came in and danced in the house of the Koyemci and in the kiva. They did not appear next day in the plaza. They just came to amuse the dancers because they could not go home to their wives that night.)

When he comes with Ololowicka he wears buckskin leggings and red moccasins and a fringed shawl as a kilt, with a silver belt. He carries their things. (See p. 1007, pl. 35.)

Comparative information on Hehe'a, p. 1017.

NAHALICO (CRAZY GRANDCHILD)

(Plate 54, *b*)

Costume.—On the head four turkey wing feathers tipped with downy feathers. The top of the head is covered with black hair. The face is painted blue with designs in red. The nose represents lightning, the painting on the cheeks is called lakwelanapa (hawk feather painting). There is more lightning on the back of the head. Spruce collar.

The body paint is red, with yellow arms and legs. The knees are red, the thighs white. Arm bands of blue buckskin with tabs and fringes of red for the clouds. He wears a dark blue breechcloth of native weave and an embroidered sash under it and a silver belt over it. He has yarn and dyed flannel on both legs and on the right wrist. Bow bracelet on left wrist. Yarn and beads around the neck. Blue moccasins, bells on right leg or in belt.

He comes in the winter. Sometimes one comes in the mixed dance or in the rain dance, especially at the beginning or end of the line. Sometimes a whole set all alike come to dance, and then they have societies to sing for them. Like Hehe'a, an impersonation of war among little boys.

Myth.—Nahalico lived at the Sacred Lake. He was a real Nahalico. When everyone was asleep he would go out to hunt. He went to the south where many tall trees were growing and where there were many turkeys. He hunted turkeys there, but he never brought them in when he came back. He just left them in the lake and came in without them. He never even brought their feathers. He just killed the birds to have a good time, and never considered that turkeys are valuable. He did that for three nights and no one at the Sacred Lake knew about it. But the fourth night he came in very late. Just before dawn when they felt the wind from the east he came in. Ya'ana saw him come in. He left his turkeys out in the lake and sneaked in as if he had been doing something wrong. Ya'ana saw him come in. When everyone got up Nahalico got up too. He did not feel tired or sleepy. Later in the morning Ya'ana said, "Where have you been? I saw you come in last night." None of the katcinas would believe that he had been up all night. He was afraid he had been doing something wrong and that was why he had hidden his turkeys and not brought them in.

Finally Pautiwa and Sayataca called him over and asked him, "Have you been out during the night?" At first he said, "No." Then they said again, "Please tell us. We do not want anyone to go and do anything wrong in the night. You must only go out in the daytime. Now are you sure you were not out at night?" Then he said, "Yes, I was out." Then they asked him, "What were you doing?" He said, "I was hunting." "How many nights have you gone?" He said, "I have gone out for four nights." "What did you hunt? Deer?" "No, I went to the south and I hunted turkeys." Then they asked him, "How many turkeys did you kill?" "I have killed four turkeys." "Now go out to where you left the turkeys and bring them right in. These turkeys are valuable and you have hurt them. Our fathers send their feathers here to us for our clothing. You have done wrong to kill them."

So the little Nahalico went out and brought in the turkeys he had caught. They were all torn up and their feathers were spoiled. There were four of them. He brought them in and laid them down in front of Pautiwa. Then they all talked about it, and Pautiwa said, "Oh, this is a wicked thing that you have done. These are our clothing, their wings, and their breasts." Then he said, "Now, my son, whenever the katcinas go to Itiwana you will wear these stiff feathers because you have done wrong. No one cares for these feathers and so you will always wear them because you have done this bad thing." So Pautiwa said and he pulled out the stiff wing feathers of the turkeys and tied little tiny feathers to their tips and put them on Nahalico. Before that he had worn pretty soft feathers like the other katcinas, but they took them away from him and gave him these because he had hurt the turkeys.

So that is how he comes. None of the other katcinas wear the stiff feathers, only he, because he did wrong. He hurt the turkeys. The people of Itiwana need the turkeys for their feathers, but he went and killed them in the night. And so he wears no feathers any place. And that is why his name is Nahalico, which means a foolish person.

Parallels.—Laguna, Ts'a·p' Nawish. Parsons, Notes on Ceremonialism at Laguna, Figure 11. San Felipe nawic (Bunzel, Note on San Felipe, J. A. F. L., 292).

CULAWITSI KOHANA

(Plate 54, *c*)

He dresses like Cula·witsi when he comes for initiation of boys— carries yucca, wears fringe of hair for a kilt. Body painted white with spots.

Itetsona (Double Face)

(Plate 54, d)

On the head, yellow parrot feathers with downy feathers. On the right side, two eagle-tail feathers; on the left side, a squash blossom with goat's hair hanging from it. One side of the face is painted red, the other blue, hence his name. On the back of the head is painted a frog. He has a protruding mouth. Spruce collar. His body is painted with clay from the Sacred Lake, mixed with red paint.

He is dressed like Sälimop̃iya with embroidered skirt, blue leather belt, anklets of porcupine quill embroidery, bare feet. He carries yucca in both hands, with little bells fastened to the bunch in the left hand. He has seeds of all kinds in the yucca in the left hand.

MISCELLANEOUS KATCINAS

Natcimomo (Grandfather Rattles All the Time)

(Plate 55, a)

Costume.—The mask is painted pink with pink clay from the Sacred Lake. The eyes are black. The painting on the back of the head is a frog, "because the frog always lives in the water." On the head, parrot feathers and downy feathers of the eagle. Sticking out in front and back, turkey feathers. The collar is of turkey feathers.

He wears a Sälimop̃iya skirt, blue leather belt, blue arm bands, blue moccasins, yarn on both legs, beads on both wrists (loo, hard things). Yarn on right wrist, wrist band on left. Rattle in right hand, spruce in left hand. Fox skin.

Ceremonies.—"He is the messenger. Formerly whenever the katcinas were coming they would send in a messenger to mark the road for them and tell the people they were coming. In the winter they still have a messenger come first, sometimes Koyemci, sometimes Kok̓okci, sometimes Natcimomo. They no longer send messengers in summer. The people know when they see the kiva director plant his feathers.

"He is very proud of his rattle and rattles all the time. That is how he got his name. He marks four lines and then the people know there will be a dance in four days."

Ne'paiyatamu

(Plate 55, b)

Costume.—The chin mask is painted yellow with corn pollen and honey to make fine days. There are two red stripes across the face to make him see well. He does his hair up in front (mitone) because he is wise. Sometimes the face is painted gray like ashes. (The

Ne'we·kwe face painting. That illustrated is the face painting of Bitsitsi.) The body paint is pink clay mixed with ashes.

"He does not always dress like a human person, the way he is shown in the picture, but he dresses like a society member, that is, barefooted and all naked except for a small blue kilt. But sometimes he dresses funny, he hangs onions in his ears and does other things like that to make people laugh. He always carries the Ne'we·kwe baton.

"He is the Ne'we·kwe of the katcinas. They have Ne'we·kwe in the Sacred Lake just as we have here."

Ceremonies.—"He comes after Ca'lako to bring in the Corn maids. In the story he is the one who finds the Corn maids and so he and Pautiwa bring them in. Then he comes unmasked and he must be a Ne'we·kwe man. When he comes with the Corn maids we call him Bitsitsi. When the earth was soft Bitsitsi himself used to come, but now a human man of the society of Ne'we·kwe brings them in.[22]

"He comes masked during the winter, sometimes in the mixed dance and sometimes by himself. Sometimes he comes to sing for Hilili. Sometimes a whole crowd will come and act like Ne'we·kwe.

"If any kiva wants to dance Ne'we·kwe, they will not dance real Ne'we·kwe, but they will dance Nehekało with masks. The headman calls the men together and asks who will be men and who women. Then they make up their songs and practice them. They make up funny songs. They say they have come from the Sacred Lake because their mothers were coming and they did not want them to come alone, and that they are afraid that their wives will be stolen. After they are ready they send in a messenger to announce that they will dance, and the next day they get their clothing ready. Then the headman goes to the headman of the Ne'we·kwe society and tells him that they are going to dance Ne'we·kwe and asks the Ne'we·kwe people to come and drum for them. Then the Ne'we·kwe man says, 'Very well. We are glad to have you do it, for our clothes are worn out.' Each man who is dancing makes himself a necklace of black yarn and a bracelet of yarn for the right wrist.

"Then the Ne'we·kwe man tells his assistant that the kiva has chosen them and they all go over there to be with them. Then they all dress in ceremonial costume and take their drum and go over to the kiva. Each man brings his Ne'we·kwe baton, for the men who are going to dance. They come in and then each one gives his baton to one of the dancers with a prayer. He prays for good weather and for luck in the dance. Then each of the dancers has one of the borrowed wands. Two real Ne'we·kwe men will lead the dance. They carry their children on their backs to make the people believe that they have really come from the Sacred Lake with their children.

---

[22] Two informants confused the masked personation Nepayatamu with the unmasked personation of Bitsitsi.

"When they have finished dancing the men return the wands and each man gives one of the Ne'we·kwe men the yarn necklace that he wore in the dance. He gives it to him and says, 'I am taking off this necklace. This is all my bad luck and I am giving it to you to get rid of it.' They always use backward speech."

Parallels.—Cochiti: The Cochiti equivalent of the Ne'we·kwe, the quirana, also have a masked dance. "The function of the quirana is to procure rain. They have their secret dances of shiwanna. The chief has a green mask with large black hands. There is a beard. The costume is the same stuff as the malinche's, with a dance belt. The other koetsame has a mask like those of Zuñi, no beard but a duck bill. He has a white shirt, a bandoleer called pani or manta of cotton, boots of (?), the queue beribboned, skunk skin at ankles. The chief says there is a heavy penalty for those who fail the day they dance at the ceremonies. When they take in a novice the malinche comes out, but the masked dance is always hidden." (Dumarest, p. 190–191.)

The masks illustrated, however (Pl. VI, 4, and fig. 26), do not agree with the foregoing description, but show striking resemblance (except in color) to Zuñi Koyemci.

NENEKÄ

(Plate 55, c)

Helmet mask with high crest edged with goat's hair, downy feather on peak. Crest and face painted turquoise with black line over eyes. Back white with dragon flies, wide mouth and long black beard, bunch of eagle and owl feathers at back. Wildcat skin over shoulders.

Fully clothed in white skirt, white kilt with blue stripe, buckskin fastened on right shoulder, fringed buckskin leggings, blue moccasins, fox skins. Hands painted white, beads on right, bow bracelet on left. Necklaces hidden. Yucca in both hands. Comes with Huponcilowa.

Neneǩä is mentioned in all accounts of Keresan katcinas (Dumarest, Goldfrank, White) and seems to be important in these villages. Neither mask nor character of the impersonation has been described.

His position in Zuñi is vague. Probably a recent importation there from the east.

PAKOKO AND YEBITCAI (NAVAHO KATCINA)

(Plates 56, 57)

Pakoko wears on his head eagle feathers tipped with yellow parrot feathers; ribbon streamers. Red hair around the face. Corn painted on the back of the mask, face painted blue with gum paint. Spruce collar. His body is painted white. He wears a great deal of silver, belt and bracelets, and wrist band with silver, and buttons like the Navaho wear. He wears a Navaho blanket instead of a kilt. Bright satin ribbons. Black knitted stockings, little red belts. Eagle feathers on the left leg. Fox skin behind.

MISCELLANEOUS KATCINAS

a, Natcimomo; *b*, Nepaiyatamu; *c*, Neneḵä.

PAKOKO ("NAVAHO" DANCE)

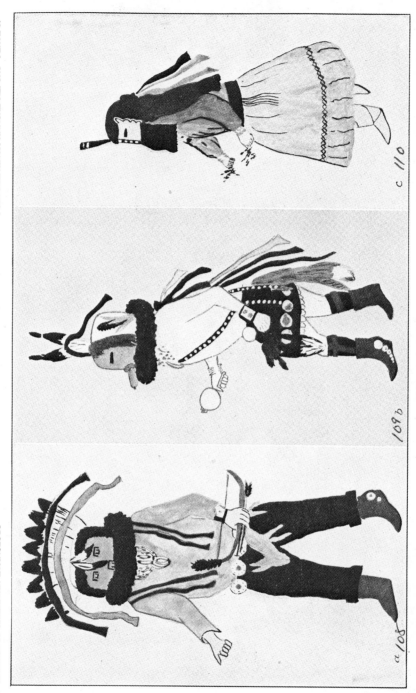

"NAVAHO" DANCE

a, "Yebitcai"; *b*, Pakoko; *c*, Pakok Oḳä.

SOCIETY MASKS

a, Cumaikoli (Cuma·kwe); *b*, Saiyap (Cuma·kwe); *c*, Kokokana (Newe·kwe); *d*, Mitotaca (Newe·kwe).

UNMASKED IMPERSONATIONS

a, Cula·witsi an tatcu; *b*, Ca'lako an'utona; *c*, Awek cuwahan'ona (Earth Purifier; Scalp dance); *d*, Sa te'tci e'lactoki (Santu dance).

UNMASKED IMPERSONATIONS

a, Bitsitsi; b, Łewekwe; c, Łewekwe Oḳä; d, Potsikic (Łewekwe).

DEER DANCE (OBSOLETE)

Yebitcai wears shirt and trousers, bright ribbons, silver belt, brown moccasins. He carries a young deer in his left hand, bow and arrow. Mask turquoise blue with border of black hair, eagle wing feathers standing up with ribbon streamers at their tips.

Ceremonies.—"They dance this in the fall before Ca'lako. This is not a kiva dance. The kiva chiefs have nothing to do with it. The young boys who want to dance get together and dance Pakoko without prayers. The song is very hard to sing, it is very high and only the young men with good voices can do it. They always have three groups and they take turns dancing, because the song is so hard to sing that they get tired quickly. Any young man who wants to and is a good singer will be the leader. Each group has its leader, and it is called by his ceremonial affiliation. The ne'we·kwe always come out for this dance. During the night the women bring food for the dancers and for the spectators. The Pakoko bring a whole sheep or a side of beef and give it to the ne'we·kwe to roast in the fire in the plaza. In the morning when the sun comes up they start their last song. They always go out to the north. Yebitcai leads and after him come the rest of the line, two by two, one man and one woman. Another dancer, dressed differently, comes at the end and waves his arms as if driving the others before him."

Folklore.—Long ago the people were suffering from a sickness of swellings.[23] At that time the Navaho had nothing to eat. They came here to buy corn and paper bread and other things to eat. The Navaho thought the Zuñi people were very kind because they gave them food in spite of the fact that they had just had a war and the Navaho had been cruel. While the Navaho were here the people were in great trouble on account of the sickness. There was one man who spoke Navaho very well and he told the Navaho what kind of sickness they were having. Then the Navaho said, "We have something to cure that kind of sickness. We have had trouble with that too, and we know all about it. We have a katcina who can cure swellings." So the Itiwana man and the Navaho decided that they should come and dance for the Itiwana people to cure the sickness of swellings.

Then the Itiwana man took the Navaho to the katcina chief. They came in and the man said, "My father, I have brought this man to you. We have had much sickness and all our people are unhappy because of it. This man says he feels sorry for us because we have been kind to his people. They have treated us badly and have made war on us, but now they have come here to buy paper bread and corn and we have been kind to them. So they want to help us to cure this sickness. That is why I have brought this man here to ask you if you want them to come and dance for us. They say their dance cures

---

[23] Probably mumps.

swellings. If this is true it will be a great help to us. So I have brought him here to see if you want his people to dance for us." Then the katcina chief said, "I am not the one to decide. I must see my bow priest. I do not want to decide this alone." So he sent for his bow priest and told him that the Navaho wanted to come and dance for the people to take the bad swelling away. He said, "Let us try it. The people are suffering terribly because of this sickness." So they decided and they told the Navaho, "Now you go and tell your people to get ready, and in four days you will come back with your people to dance, and all the people will wait for you and will give you paper bread and lots of good things to take back with you to pay for the dance."

So he went back and told his people that the Itiwana people wanted them to come and dance for them. He did not tell his people that they wanted them to cure the swelling. He just told the people, "The Zuñi people want us to come and visit and make up our quarrels and be good friends with them. And if we dance for them they will give us good things to eat when we come home." So he said, and all the people began to practice their songs and work on their masks and clothing.

At Itiwana the people were waiting for them. They came in in the night and they had a great fire in the plaza. They dressed out on the Gallup road and came in. The katcina chief had built a big fire in the plaza and they came and danced there all night and the Itiwana people took food to them in the night. The next day they went back. The Itiwana people thought they were taking away the sickness and they gave them lots of bread and good things to eat. They left in the morning and they went two by two around the village to cure the sickness of swellings. The man who had come before was the leader. He was Yebitcai and he led the dancers around the village. Then they went away to the north. As they left all the people spat and said, "Now you will take away with you this sickness," and they said to the sickness, "Now you will go with these people."

About five years after that the Itiwana people danced this dance themselves. A long time afterwards the Navaho wanted to come here and dance again, but the Itiwana people would not let them come. They had really taken away the sickness and the Itiwana people were afraid that they would bring it back with them if they came again. So now they just dance the Navaho dance with their own masks and it doesn't cost them anything.[24] (It was danced on the night of Ca'lako, 1929, just at sunrise. There were no Ne'we·kwe out.)

---

[24] The dance was introduced before the informant's father was born, probably about 75 years ago.

Pakok O′ka

(Plate 57, c)

Face mask painted red and blue, red beard. Hair flowing, turkey feather in forelock, ribbon streamers behind. Velveteen blouse, full calico skirt, red belt, white moccasins, carries spruce.

Comes with Pakoko.

Heppoko Musmo

Helmet mask black, round eyes of yellow, open mouth with teeth and small white beard, red feathers on head, red ears with turquoise earrings. Blue around neck is probably a blue woven breechcloth.

Body painted black. Probably belongs to Tcakwena set. (From drawing collected by Kroeber.)

Ahana

Helmet mask painted white, triangular figure over nose, at side colored terraces, colored yarn ribbons about head with several upright downy feathers. Blue horns tipped with feathers of many colors. Behind two eagle tail feathers with bunch of owl and turkey feathers, spruce collar. Body painted red with shoulder and forearms yellow. Spruce around wrist. No information except "he comes in winter."

Tsiᵗsikä

Helmet mask, face blue, top of head red, upright ears gray. Macaw feathers in head, at back lapaboawe. Spruce collar.

In right hand (held up) a branch of spruce and what looks like a mouse, adorned with strings of turquoise and feathers.

Pink body paint, arm bands, etc. (only upper part shown). From a drawing collected by Kroeber. This is not to be confused with the unmasked impersonation of the same name who comes with Kolowisi.

UNMASKED IMPERSONATIONS

Ca′lako An′uɫona (Ca′lako Impersonator)

Costume.—War chief's cap of buckskin with red ribbons and silver buttons, black or purple velveteen shirt with many colored ribbons on arms and shoulders, dark blue native woven breechcloth, fastened with embroidered belt. Bare legs painted yellow with red knees (drawing not accurate). Yarn around knees, with sleighbells, high red moccasins, many bracelets, long turquoise earrings, yarn, bow bracelet, basket of prayer sticks.

This is the costume before donning the mask with its body covering. There are two impersonators for each mask and they take turns in carrying it.

Cula·witsi Antatcu

(Plate 59, *a*)

Costume.—Yucca band and red feathers in hair, white cotton shirt and trousers, brown moccasins, woolen hose and red garters, a blanket robe (optional) and buckskin over shoulders. Carries a basket of prayer sticks for Cula·witsi to plant and corn meal. Many necklaces and bracelets. He comes with Cu'la·witsi at Ca'lako. (See p. 959 for his part in Ca'lako dances.)

INDEX

○